CIVILIZATION
IN EAST AND WEST

OXFORD UNIVERSITY PRESS
AMEN HOUSE, E.C. 4
London Edinburgh Glasgow New York
Toronto Melbourne Capetown Bombay
Calcutta Madras
HUMPHREY MILFORD
PUBLISHER TO THE UNIVERSITY

CIVILIZATION
IN EAST AND WEST

AN INTRODUCTION TO
THE STUDY OF
HUMAN PROGRESS

BY

H. N. SPALDING

OXFORD UNIVERSITY PRESS
LONDON : HUMPHREY MILFORD
1939

IN REMEMBRANCE OF
ELLEN REBE SPALDING
AND OF NINETY YEARS OF
COURAGE, FAITH
LOVE AND GAIETY

PREFACE

MAN is made for happiness, and everywhere he is unhappy. What is wrong with the world? And how can it be made right?

Our politics have broken down: nation is turned against nation and class against class. Our religions have broken down: we no longer know what to think about God and man's life in the Universe. And for the first time in history this bewilderment has fallen, not upon one civilization only, but upon all.

Yet, if men did but realize it, their resources far surpass their difficulties. Immense treasures of wisdom and imagination (together with much junk) have accumulated through the ages, both in East and West. Statesmen, poets, prophets, thinkers, seers, this civilization and that, have contributed things rich and strange that contain the clue to the problems that beset us. To appreciate the greatness of human achievement is to see a new dawn break over man, his society and his destiny. And as men grow more sensible and enlightened, science will cease from its menace and bring only its boon: will bring, not death, but life and opportunity to the whole population of the earth.

It is the business of this book to survey the marvellous progress towards happiness made by mankind during the last few thousand years, through the definition and development of a diversity of ideals, as well as to indicate the false ideals that fight against progress, and the fate that has lain in store for them. The past can show the present which road leads to ruin, and which to Renaissance and the goal of its desires.

If primitive man aims (like the social insects) at the survival of the society to which he belongs, the breakdown of these societies opens the way for the egoist on the one hand, and the statesman, prophet, and mystic on the other.

With the advent of the egoist arise Materialist States that grasp at wealth and power regardless of the needs of other nations or other classes. Hence arise wars and revolutions and the dissolution of society. Hence arise also inner discontents, for the principle of seeking only one's own is contrary to the nature of men, who are naturally friendly disposed to one another. Dictatorships have never endured.

Out of the confusion they create arise thinkers and statesmen who base society on this natural inclination of men to feel for and respect one another. Hence the civilization of the Chinese and of the Nordics, based on the moral ideal of self-discipline, good feeling, and good sense.

Moral conduct is strengthened by the sanction of a Moral God, the Righteous, Compassionate, Gracious Ruler of mankind. Hence arise the Hebrew, Moslem, and Catholic civilizations, whose ideal is a society carrying out the Will of God.

Yet even a morally ordered society and a Moral God do not satisfy the deepest cravings of man's spirit. In the midst of a world of change and death he needs Something That is Eternal to Which his soul may be reunited. This ideal—so strange to the this-worldly Nordic—is the basis of the civilizations of India and of Holy Russia.

Thus, some civilizations are primarily interested in Nature and human society, some in human society and God's relation to it, some in the soul and its relation to the Godhead. A part of reason looks on a part of Reality. But a fully developed reason would see Reality fully revealed. As each civilization enlarges its reason and its interest it will come nearer to the rest, until finally all are united in a common knowledge and love of Truth as a Whole. When they are so, mankind will have reached its goal; it will be free to know, love, and enjoy the Universe to the full.

So, standing at the gateway of our pilgrimage, we catch glimpses of the many lands through which we are to pass, and see at the end the dim but lovely country of the light.

A man needs no small measure of courage—nay, audacity —to stand up to such a theme: to survey the past and to surmise the future. He should be poet and lawyer and man of science in one: able to creep into the skin of each society and reveal the secrets of its desires, to define with nice precision, to marshal evidence and reason from it. He should

have the foresight of the statesman, the insight of the philosopher, the soul-sight of the saint. To cope with such a
subject is like wrestling with a python. Which will get the
better, the python or the man?

So ambitious an endeavour is bound to have many defects.
There may be mistakes of fact; worse still, mistakes of
interpretation. A man may wish to be fair, and yet be un-
fair; to portray, and yet caricature. This is pioneer work,
and to pioneer work much must be forgiven. It is a book
to pull to pieces and criticize and improve. It blazes the
trail, that others may tread the path and build the highway.

With so huge a theme compression has been difficult and
severe. Some passages may seem too fat with facts, others
scraggy with the protruding bones of principle. It has been
possible only to chart the main features, not to sail into every
creek and bay; to glance down avenues, not to explore them.
Pages (like publishers) are inexorable; brevity, like a pirate,
forces arguments and illustrations to walk the plank. Hence
the apparent dogmatism of a work that is not 'wedded to its
own opinion'.

In the crush some toes may have been trodden on; but
never with unkind intent. There is neither political nor
theological odium. A man's first loyalty is to Truth as God
gives him to see it.

Perhaps the pleasantest part of the galley-slavery of book-
writing—apart from the thrill of discovery—is the kindness
and wisdom of others—their forbearance, their conversation,
their inspiration, their criticism.

Gratitude, like charity, should begin at home: only a
ministering archangel can wive the troublesome author of
a troublesome book. The weeks spent at Medland, Devon,
when these chapters were pulled together are for ever un-
forgettable. Lively thanks are also due for the serene zeal
of the most loyal of secretaries, Miss Sheila Dalgliesh.

In Oxford men and women of many kinds and kindreds
come and all are welcome. The book is the child of talks
rather than of books. Bright-witted friends have made it.
The colour of their skins has differed, and so has the colour
of their thoughts. Men in the prime of life—nineteen and

twenty—have imparted dewy wisdom. A special debt is due
to Colonel P. N. Malevsky-Malévitch and other Russian
friends. Holy Russia, like India, bears witness that politics
and religion are inseparable, that society is in essence a
religious community. Many experts have been kind enough
to read the sections on which they are authorities: Professor
A. R. Radcliffe-Brown; Professor N. H. Baynes; Mr. Wang
Wei-cheng, Professor V. T. Harlow; Professor Norman Bent-
wich, the Imam of the Mosque at Woking, Dom Ralph
Russell, O.S.B., and Miss Barbara Ward; Professor Sir
Sarvepalli Radhakrishnan, Professor R. E. Hume, Mrs.
Rhys Davids, Dr. Nicholas Zernov. Many of these distinguished scholars have been good enough to say that the
outline submitted to them was 'fair and sympathetic'. The
merits are theirs, the mistakes are not. The Dictators have
been less kind: had they ceased from troubling, this book
would have been the better for further revision.

It might be supposed (by simpletons like the author) that
at least no howlers could pass through the meshes of so much
critical acumen. But this is not so. For doctors differ; and
the dogma of one doctor is the howler of another. In the
field of anthropology the upstarts of spade and speech challenge the arm-chair authority of great names. In spheres so
familiar as the Roman and the British Empires men of great
learning take opposing views. In that of Buddhism, the
conclusions of a ripe scholar that make intelligible what has
hitherto been unintelligible are still unacceptable to the
majority of her colleagues. Lies and libels about religion are
a special snare for the unwary. In this welter of opinion
reliance has been placed on quotations from the masterpieces
that enshrine the several ideals. But even here the ways are
treacherous, for the liberties of the translator are the perils
of the reader. Deep are the pitfalls that beset the path of the
humble student of civilization. Yet when all is said, the main
shape and outline which civilization has assumed stand un-
assailable, an impregnable rock in the sea of criticism.

To two distinguished men thanks are pre-eminently due
for having found time amid multifarious public services to
read and re-read the whole. This poor book and its readers
have every reason to be grateful to the Master of Balliol and

to Mr. Edward Thompson for all the unpleasant (as well as kind) things they have said about it.

But there is one debt so mountainous that it soars above all reckoning, unrepayable, unrepaid. To one lover of wisdom—critic, publicist, master of the philosophies of East and West, 'spectator of things Divine and human'—the book owes the central principle that organizes all and focuses all, the merciless criticism that has lifted its argument from the historical to the logical level, some illuminating passages unblushingly incorporated. Without him—brother in the flesh, father in the spirit—the book could not have been. The disciple gives thanks for his Master.

H. N. S.

OXFORD
26 *January* 1939

CONTENTS

CONTENTS

THE BIOLOGICAL STATE

MAN is a spirit inhabiting a body, an animal who has descended and ascended from the primal stuff of life that two thousand million years ago floated in archaean seas. But he differs from other animals in that the processes of his mind are set working independently of immediate sensations: for, whereas animals on the whole remember and imagine only when sensation stimulates their mental power, and apart from this stimulus tend to go to sleep, man can remember and imagine freely, and so can combine, draw inferences, reason. With other animals sensation is the penny that must be put into the slot to make the machine work; man is a machine that by some mystery sets itself working without the penny.

This strange creature appeared upon the earth about a million years ago, and for ninety-nine hundredths of that long period almost nothing is known about him. He knew the use of fire. He used stone tools; for thousands of years there was a steady growth in their development; quite recently, he learnt to grind and polish them. He made pots, though he had not yet discovered the potter's wheel. His weapons were spears, the spear-thrower, the boomerang, the bow—used primarily for hunting, sometimes for war. Spears were differentiated for these purposes, and some weapons, such as clubs, were for war only. With his early stone implements he carved wood, and thereby achieved a fairly elaborate house-building. He devised methods for catching fish, and invented rafts and canoes—it is not known when the sail came into use.

There were several species of man, near relatives of the apes, all of which perished save one, *homo sapiens*, so called in irony or in prophecy. During this long period *homo sapiens* spread over the earth. He developed an enormous number of languages: there are some dozens of families of languages now existing, and hundreds or even thousands of distinct languages. It is evident that he devised many forms

B

of society, as several thousand are known now to exist: those in Australia alone have been classified into fifty groups.

On this magnificent stalk civilization suddenly flowered, in a cluster that is still unfolding.

Somewhere between 7000 and 3500 B.C. man discovered how to domesticate animals and plants. Agriculture probably began in Mesopotamia or in Egypt, and appeared a little later in the Indus Valley; whether it began earlier or later in the Valley of the Yellow River is a secret the pre-Shang culture of China may presently reveal to the spade. Then came—of the utmost significance for farming—the discovery of the plough and of the wheel: man could now turn his furrow and transport his produce. In America, primitive man discovered how to grind his stone tools before he learnt how to domesticate plants; he never invented the wheel.

The domestication of animals was less important than that of plants, for the pastoral peoples have contributed less to man's progress than the agricultural. Once man could sow and reap, population could increase rapidly, as it did on the Yellow River and the Indus, in Mesopotamia and Egypt.

How human society began and how it branched into its many forms is hidden in obscurity. But it is evident that primitive man lived in societies with a language, a system of morality and ritual symbols. Further, the object of these societies, like the object of the societies of the social insects and herd animals, ants and bees, red deer and musk-ox, was survival—the survival, not of the individual, but of the group. Civilized man thinks of individual survival as important; primitive man thinks that what matters is to maintain the group or clan, in the same spot, with the same natural features, rocks or trees or wells, where it has been from the beginning of time, or where it has been placed by some supernatural being. The important thing is the perpetuation of this entity—land and plants and human beings—not of the individual. He, they think somewhat vaguely, may return to the same spot and be reincarnated in another individual, for the group cannot survive unless dead individuals are replaced. Soul is thus the social personality of the individual;

it consists in the social relations in which he stands to other people. This does not die, for the social relationships continue to exist. Among the Eskimos a man's name long survives because it embodies them.

Thus the differentia between uncivilized and civilized society is that uncivilized society is interpretable biologically: its end, like that of the animals, is survival, and, like that of social animals, the survival of a group. To ensure this survival it is necessary to observe a great variety of customs; and those who fail to observe them are strongly reprobated by normal respectable people, as among the Andaman Islanders the youth and girl who seek to avoid the unpleasant self-consciousness of the marriage ceremony are frowned upon by their elders and betters.[1] Custom expresses the activities of a tribe that make for its cohesion—its biological unity. To break a custom, therefore, is felt by its members to be detrimental to its social integrity, and is, therefore, called wrong. But this does not arise from any thought of a man sinning against his own nature as man, which would be the rational way of looking at it. A breach of custom is a biological wrong, not a moral wrong. In the same way, and on the same ground, as a tribe begins to deteriorate conscience begins to be felt, the feeling of a man that he is doing wrong; but this is based on the same biological, not moral, ground. So in the nursery a child feels that in disobeying his parents he is doing wrong, though he does not know the reason why. Were an uncivilized tribe to be found that definitely distinguished right from wrong by thinking, to that extent it would not be a primitive society.

The origin of religion goes back to completely primitive times. In order to survive, the tribe is obliged to a certain extent to control its natural environment. On the other hand, it sees that an enormous amount of that environment is not under human control at all. Man, in short, is himself a cause able to control many of the activities necessary to his life, but, as against this, he discovers that he is not the cause of the great majority of them. He feels around him the play of a causal activity, and so gains the feeling of the existence of an indefinable cause of all these uncontrollable

[1] A. R. Radcliffe-Brown, *The Andaman Islanders*, chapter v.

effects in Nature. It is this that the Polynesians call *mana*, the Huron Indians *orenda*, other tribes *tilo*, others *hasina*. It is in order to control this indefinable power that their religious rites arise and the vogue of so-called magic practices, sacrifices, and prayers: this mysterious power must be persuaded or forced to produce good effects rather than bad.

Naturally, each society tends to develop the religion it needs, the religion, that is, which will maintain the respect for its own social order. Hence the kind of religion it develops will depend on the kind of social order it has formed, or in other words the way that its individual members are spending their lives. The earlier cults centred round wild animals and wild plants used for food. Pastoral religion centres round cattle. Nothing is known of the religion of the early agricultural peoples, something of the religion of China in the Shang period, something more of that of Mesopotamia and Egypt. Early agricultural peoples were deeply concerned with the stars and the weather and also with the development of the religious calendar—all calendars are religious. Their deities were agricultural—Osiris, Adonis, Attis—lovers of Mother Earth, who died and rose again in spring, their worshippers taking part in their resurrection; the corn goddess of the Indians and Central Americans; the earth god and the earth goddess in China, still the most important spirits to the ordinary Chinese farmer—the Emperor was primarily a ploughman and calendar expert, who alone might observe the stars, while noblemen might observe the moon.

Primitive men, like civilized men, pray for material things: for rain, for good weather, for health, for children, and so on. The motive of this prayer may be merely materialistic, as it is when the peasant in South Europe prays God and the Saints that they will look after his agricultural or commercial interests. But this is only one side of the matter: crops, weather, health, and the like, affect not only the individual but the social structure.

This primitive religion, in Australia and elsewhere, aims at the survival of the social order. That is the function of primitive religion in all its forms—myth, magic, ceremony, and the like. What it provides for the individuals who take part is a sense of dependence on a universal power outside oneself. If one behaves properly, this power will support one; if not, not.

These primitive societies are biological, and their customs and religion are biological too. But what if custom is no longer followed, and religion no longer strong enough to sanction it?

There exist in New Guinea two neighbouring tribes, one of which (the Arapesh) is extraordinarily altruistic (in the biological sense of the term), while the other (the Mundugumor) is the opposite—almost all the members have reached a state of egoism, though a few still retain the memory of the old tribal virtue of obedience to custom, showing that at one time the tribe as a whole had a biological cohesion. Life among the Arapesh is relatively peaceful and happy; among the Mundugumor disorderly and difficult.[1] The reason for the deterioration may be that this tribe moved from a poor into a rich country, where there was no longer need to co-operate in order to live. The two tribes illustrate the general principle that men have by nature two contrary sets of impulses: one set co-operative or social, the other set non-co-operative and egoistic. Where co-operation is necessary for survival, there the co-operative instincts come into play; where co-operation is less necessary, there the non-co-operative instincts have their chance. But as biological societies get less coherent through the rise of egoistic individuality, they become much more conscious than hitherto of good and evil—of social behaviour and of egoistic behaviour. The consciousness of egoism gives rise to those theories that ultimately develop materialistic views of society and a materialist way of life. On the other hand, the great sages of mankind have sprung out of the apprehension by man of social virtue: the wise man has become conscious of it as a good in itself, not merely as a means to survival.

A society that has fallen into disorder has no ruler—no ruler in the shape of custom. There are two types of men who may take advantage of this situation: the tribal chief and the witch-doctor or medicine-man. If such a tribe then

[1] Margaret Mead, *Sex and Temperament*.

produces a chief or a witch-doctor who is a person of real
organizing power, he will attain a position in the eyes of his
fellows that will enable him to fulfil his own desires. He may
now for example begin by compelling order in the tribe, and
then further aggrandize himself by foreign conquest, as did
the Pharaohs and the Kings of Assyria. In this way he will
become an Autocrat in the State, reverenced by his people as
custom was formerly reverenced by them, and finally be
regarded as the very vehicle of power or *mana*—as the
Pharaoh of Egypt came to be known as the Son of Ra, and
the Emperor of China as the Son of Heaven. In other words,
a mighty individual has appeared out of primitive society,
and has consequently given the society a mobility and an
energy it did not possess before.

The other possibility is very different. Among the Mundugumor one man, Ombléan, an intelligent and thinking being,
is beginning to reflect on the disorder of his tribe; he may
be regarded as a sage in the making. In any society that
thus falls into disorder an abler mind may thus be spurred
to reflection, to the discovery that there exists in the mind of
man a reason that supports the co-operative instinct, while
it amends and improves it. Hence arise men's social philosophies. Thus in China the moral decline of the Shang
Dynasty led the conquering princes of Chou to formulate
theories condemning human licence and approving in man
contrary instincts 'given by Heaven': man has naturally a
fellow-feeling for his kind—is, in a word, a moral being.
With the new view old words acquired new meanings—*te*,
wonder-working power, came to mean virtue in the moral
sense—much as if in the West the 'virtue' of a poison or a
medicine had come to mean the 'virtue' of a man.

Or the disorder that gives rise to such thoughts may be
not social, but natural. A drought may parch the grass-lands,
as has happened periodically in Arabia; a river may change
its course, as has happened to the Yellow River. In such
cases a leader may step forth to play the part, not of a master,
but of a saviour of his people. He will resemble, not a
conquering Assyrian king, but such a potentate as the
sage Emperor Yü, who is said to have fought against the
floods. The difference between the sage reflecting on dis-

order and the moral statesman is that the sage has not the position of a ruler: he is a statesman, but not an executive statesman, though he may easily, like Confucius, be the spiritual father of executive statesmen and of his people.

As the powers of the mind develop, so do man's moral and spiritual interests. The mother may come to love her babe, not merely biologically, for the survival of the tribe, but morally, as a creature of interest and value in itself. The Autocrat may come to care for the State, not as the instrument of his ambition, but for its own sake. And so with Nature and God. The Egyptians took to measuring their fields for the utilitarian end of regulating the waters of the Nile; but this begat in a Greek observer of their methods an interest in geometry. Primitive men that thought of the unseen power as supporting their society came to conceive of a Divine Being to worship for Himself. Thus a rational interest arises in man in place of a biological, whether the object of that interest be Nature, or man, or God. The social saviour will always tend to be interested in God and Nature too, because of the connexion of both with man.

The passage from the biological to the rational thus occurs when the reason of the uncivilized sage discovers a rational morality in human nature; that is the most important moment in the history of the human race. But man's reason cannot go so far without discovering that the unseen power that controls the world is Moral too. That is the essence of the Yahweh announced by the great Prophets of Israel. Instead of the indefinable power of the Universe being capricious, and acting now in one way and now in another, like a person of whose activities no one can give an account, it becomes a Power Who always acts righteously, socially, and requires of His adherents that they, if they are to receive His Favour, should act righteously too. The rites of worship are now completely altered: for this God will demand of man the sacrifice of a broken heart, not of rams and sheep. In other words, the Prophet will make the distinction between God on the one hand and the idol on the other, and the distinction of the worship by man of God and the worship by man of an idol.

But there is a still higher view to which human society can ascend. If its confusion awakens in thinking men a conception of moral virtue, and moral virtue a conception of a Moral God, the suffering, death, and impermanence that are the conditions, not of a disorderly humanity, but of humanity itself, awaken in men a consciousness of the need for and of the Existence of a Being That is Unchangeable, Unbounded, Unsuffering—an Eternal Infinite Bliss. Such men arose in the little-known civilization of Vedic India. The Divine Self of the seers of the post-Vedic Upanishads is a conception even profounder than the God of the Prophets; though the Prophet himself does in his Monotheism conceive of God as more than Moral. 'I am That I am'; 'Holy, Holy, Holy'—Apart. This is the experience preliminary to that final and complete apprehension, man's mystical union with the Godhead. This union is more than any moral experience, and those who consider religion to have emanated from a Moral God find it hard to understand or appreciate; to those who have attained it, it is not morality that holds the chief place in religion, as in the case of the Prophet, but the sense of union with the Eternal and Infinite Being. It is this type of religion that is expressed in the Upanishads and generally in the religions that have originated in India.[1]

Such are the prodigious moral and spiritual developments that have originated in the last four, or even three, thousand years. They need far closer study, especially with a view to the indications they give of the further progress of man towards the goal where he would be.

[1] This chapter is largely indebted for its social anthropology to Professor A. R. Radcliffe-Brown and for its social philosophy to K. J. Spalding.

II

THE MATERIALIST STATE

AUTOCRACY in its two forms, secular and religious, arose because it was of service to the State: all human societies, civilized as well as primitive, are biological organisms, and, like other organisms, must change in adaptation to internal and external stresses, if they are to survive. This mutation was successful so long as autocracy served the good of the State. But just because autocrats are likely to be egoists, or to be incapable of their function of preserving their people, this particular mutation is dangerous, as is shown by the disturbed condition of history under autocracy, with its rise and fall of Empires. And so, with the need, a further mutation becomes possible in cases where the subjects are not only aware of the egoism or incompetence of the autocrat, but are prepared to remedy the resulting anarchy by their own action.

This phenomenon in history is as remarkable as that of the appearance of autocracy itself out of the primitive State: for it involves a realization now by the ordinary individual—not by the chief or priest or noble merely—of his own political individuality, and so lays the very foundation of popular government. As allegiance once shifted from custom to the autocrat, so now it shifts from the autocrat to the State itself, as the condition and guarantee of each man's individuality. At the same time, the individual gradually emerges from the family. Custom had been binding, not on individuals, but on families; but now status—the status of the son under the paternal power, of the woman under tutelage, of the slave without rights of his own—gives place to contract, the free agreement of individuals.[1] The farther this progress goes, the more custom tends to be criticized by the ordinary citizen as not good enough for him: the Chinese Sophists persuade the people to doubt established authority, the Greek Sophists oppose the old *nomos* or convention to what they call *physis* or nature.

---

[1] Maine, *Ancient Law*, pp. 167–9.

But individual thought and initiative are precisely what produce bad men on the one hand, and good men on the other, whatever view may be taken as to what is a bad man and what a good man. A primitive man is just an animal writ large, content with such satisfaction of his simple animal needs as enables his society to survive: maintenance, defence, generation. But when he becomes an individual, the restraints of custom are removed, and these old desires can swell out without measure. He will now want, not the continuance of the species, but the indulgence of his lust; not food and shelter, but wealth and luxury; not protection from foes and devils, but power over men and gods; and the more energetic his nature, the more exaggerated his wants will be. In short, as soon as man's desires are set loose by individuality, his life ceases to be merely biological, and he can become a materialist. His aim is no longer survival, but lust and wealth and fame, the three objects of the materialist's life. In order to attain them he tries to use as his tools or instruments or servants not only natural objects, but other living beings, seen and unseen, and even God. He himself is the centre of the Universe, round whom all else revolves.

But man has another side to his nature: he is a being endowed with reason, who cannot be happy unless his reason as well as his animal needs is satisfied. In so far therefore as individuality frees the moral and spiritual nature of man from the shackles of custom, he becomes, not self-seeking, but respectful or loving to his fellow-beings; he comes to love Nature (including his own body); he learns to find his supreme satisfaction in the adoration of God. To do any of these things, he finds he must discipline and control his animal impulses, or his passions will get the better of his spirit. He still needs material things, but he is not a materialist, because his desires for them fall into place among other and larger desires, and thereby themselves become moral, part of his love of Nature. Thus individuality also turns man to the three moral and spiritual objects, the objects which to know and love gives joy to a being endowed with reason— Nature and other living spirits and God; moral objects being those in the visible or sensible world, spiritual objects those in the unseen or intelligible world. Instead of trying to make these serve him, it is now his desire to serve and love them. Instead of the Universe centring upon himself, he finds that he centres upon the Universe. In it 'he is lost, and is found'.

It may be expected therefore that, during the centuries in which individuality is emerging or re-emerging after waves of barbarism, both materialism and morality will emerge too; and this in fact is what took place. As the earliest poems and chronicles show, the process is logical and more or less uniform. First, a moral or spiritual culture arises precariously among the individualized few. This civilization slowly disintegrates through war or schism or revolution into an anarchy of divided and jarring fragments, a break-down that stimulates sophists to justify materialism and philosophers to re-define morality. Finally, statesmen restore order by founding either a dictatorship on materialist principles or a strong government on moral principles. There are three kinds of civilization and of the anarchy into which it may fall, and (failing a moral solution) each kind of anarchy may be overcome by a corresponding dictatorship. A civilization may be political, like that founded by the Chou Dynasty; and the anarchy into which this falls may be suppressed by a National or State Dictatorship, like that of the First Emperor. Or the civilization may be religious, and be thrown into confusion by the rise of reforming sects, as Brahminism was by Buddhism and Catholicism by Protestantism; and then an ecclesiastical or hierarchical dictatorship may arise, like those that for a time perverted the ideals of the Brahmins, the Jesuits, and the Calvinists. Finally, a this-worldly civilization may be largely or predominantly economic, as are industrialized Europe and industrialized America: giving rise to strikes and syndicalism and revolution, and so to a Proletarian or Class Dictatorship such as Marx envisaged.

Where a civilization is disintegrating into an anarchy of State against State, Church against Church, class against class, or man against man, the first duty of the ruler is to restore security and order, and this can be done only by strong government. But strong government is of two kinds: materialist, when it relies upon force, and reduces reason to a minimum; and moral, when it relies upon reason, and reduces force to a minimum. The moral statesman aims, therefore, at securing internal unity and order, not by suppressing criticism and opposition, but by educating and conciliating it, through the removal of grievances, the explanation of policy and the promotion of high ideals. Similarly, while looking to his defences, he advances the interests of his country abroad by conciliation and co-operation with other Powers. Both at home and abroad he is never treacherous, and only uses force when he must. In this way he gradually builds up a free government in which individuals as they grow in discipline, intelligence, and good will can more and more take part, and a free society in which their whole personality can develop without constraint. Thus the Han Dynasty gave China a real and lasting unity by founding its government on the family virtues of the Confucians. Alexander the Great endeavoured to suppress the anarchy of antiquity, not by conquering Persia and India, but by taking them into partnership. The strong government of the Tudors in England, needed to cure the disorders left by the Wars of the Roses and to avert the menace of Catholic Spain, worked through Parliament and educated Parliament; and England resisted the attempts of the Stuarts to develop a strong government into a dictatorship. During the World War Great Britain resigned her freedom to her Government in order to save it; but not all the powers of the Defence of the Realm Act ever threatened to make that government a dictatorship. Sun Yat-sen and Chiang Kai-shek, while realizing the need for 'military operations', see them only as preliminary to 'political tutelage', that is itself a preparation for 'constitutional government'. Kemal Ataturk seems also to have been, not a dictator, but a strong ruler preparing for democracy. 'The master of this country (he said) is the Turkish peasant. In ten or fifteen years Turkey may be ready to govern herself.' Such rulers, while curing disorder and promoting unity, are simultaneously nursing freedom at home and peace abroad.

The materialist statesman or dictator likewise aims at overcoming anarchy at home and danger abroad, but his ideals and methods are very different. His highest end is the material supremacy and therefore the aggrandizement of his own State, or Church, or class (as the case may be); and to

achieve this he relies, not on education and argument, but
on compulsion and propaganda, caring as little for the free
self-development of his own subjects as he does for the welfare of any State, or Church, or class, other than his own.
At first indeed he seems to many of his people, and especially
to the young, to be, not a dictator, but the strong ruler that
anarchy needs, who will deliver them from poverty, defence-
lessness, despair, and give them work, a career, self-respect.
But the dictator does not stop there; his policy is aggression
and repression. He says: 'My country shall be as great as
I can make it. It shall extend its bounds and become an
Empire; it shall establish a hegemony over its neighbours.
It must therefore be armed to the teeth for war; though, if it
can gain the fruits of victory merely by the threat of war, so
much the better.' Similarly, ecclesiastical dictators wherever
possible seek to extend the power of their Society or Church
through war. The Jesuits, themselves an army, direct the
Thirty Years War; the Covenanters, invoking Jehovah,
invade England. In the economic dictatorships the 'class
war' is a real, not a metaphorical, war, to be carried on, not
in one, but in all countries; World Revolution is World War.

Thus, though dictators stop anarchy at home, they create
it abroad; for so long as none obtains supremacy and rival
units remain, each dictator is in fact an international anarchist
—humour is not his strong point. Anarchy and dictatorship
are in fact twin brothers masked to look as unlike each other
as possible; both use the weapons of treachery and violence.
Thus, while primitive society resembles that of the social
insects, patiently labouring, materialistic society is a jungle
in which nations prey upon nations like wild beasts, all teeth
and claws. Hobbes said that man is naturally a wolf to other
men; the old Beast Fables said that statesmen should be
jackals or foxes.[1]

Naturally economic activities are regulated in the interest
of the dictator's State or Church or class, with little regard
to the welfare of men as individuals and none to that of other
States. The sinews of war are arms and armies. The State
dictator therefore encourages the farmer who produces food
and families and the manufacturer who fabricates munitions

---

[1] H. H. Gowen, *The Indian Machiavelli*, p. 189.

of war, while as far as possible he discourages the import of food and raw materials, that his country may be independent of other countries. Many Jesuits and Calvinists have been similarly great traders; Communists passionately promote economic activity. In this way the people, 'the cow that gives the milk', may in some dictatorships be made prosperous for a time.

But the material strength of the State will be imperilled or impossible, if the nation is divided; and (in the view of the dictator) difference of opinion of any kind divides it. The second great characteristic of a dictatorship is therefore that all outward opposition or diversity is suppressed, in order that the State may become (in appearance at any rate) unified, consolidated, totalitarian. Every activity is under the control of the dictator himself, who may be a hereditary King like Louis the Fourteenth, a hereditary General like the Japanese Shogun, an elected Officer like the General of the Jesuits, or a self-made Leader like Lenin. He must be the unquestioned Head of the State, 'I who am alone';[1] 'l'État, c'est moi'. He generally obtains his power through an armed Party; all other Parties are suppressed. His word is law; the whole people must follow him blindly, for he knows what is good for the State, and they do not. Independent thought, discussion, argument, whether in meetings, newspapers, or books, are strictly forbidden; the one thinks for the many and a blare of propaganda proclaims his *ipse dixit*. Subversive news and views from abroad are carefully shut out; the Materialist State is an intellectual as well as an economic autarchy. Every one who speaks or acts contrary to the Leader's dictates must be punished or banished or killed. All differences are obliterated. A centralized bureaucracy regulates everything, assimilates minorities, wipes out all local, racial, cultural, and religious distinctions. The Inquisition extirpates heresy. Communism abolishes all classes except the proletariat. As the people cannot openly speak their minds, secret police and other spies are employed to report disaffection and to frustrate plots: a system that keeps the people in perpetual fear of every one they meet and the ruler very unreliably informed. Since plotters are still

---

[1] I. J. L. Duyvendak, *The Book of Lord Shang*, p. 27.

suspected, there are periodical 'trials' and executions—'the eradication of thorns'.[1] Thus the Materialist State seeks to secure unity and order by forcibly suppressing differences of all kinds and substituting the infallible opinion of the Leader; in contrast to the Moral State, which, not claiming infallibility, tolerates differences of opinion and seeks for willing reconciliation or compromise.

It follows that the Materialist State has a conception of morality, culture, and religion all its own, and that therefore the moral and spiritual ideals that are to non-materialists the most precious possessions of mankind are to the dictator and his Party mere moonshine, 'deception',[2] 'medieval rubbish'[3] —nay, worse, 'poison',[4] 'opiates of the people'[5]—to be suppressed at all costs. The individual who is at once a good citizen and a good man, the complete and all-round personality that can enjoy a many-sided Universe, is beyond their ken and horizon; pressed to its logical conclusion dictatorship leads, not to fullness of life, but to emptiness. The old morality—respect and love for one's neighbour, whoever he may be, as a human being—is deemed a failure of loyalty; outside one's own ring fence men are not human. In a dictatorship the only morality is subservience to the State or Church or class—in that sense alone the State is 'ethical',[6] the 'common interest' comes 'before self'.[7] Hence the materialist virtues are to 'believe, obey, fight'[8]—not to think, love, live at peace with all men.

It is true that in the subordination of self to the State much enthusiasm, discipline, courage, self-sacrifice is evoked in young and generous hearts that is moral in the true sense. But these and kindred virtues change their quality in so far as they are directed to hate and revenge and self-glory and aggression—they become materialist, not moral. Every virtue in the long run takes its character from the end at which it aims: virtues are materialist if their aim is materialist, moral if their aim is moral. 'War brings to those who take part in it tension of human energy, and puts the stamp of nobility on the people who have the courage to meet it.'[9]

[1] Kautilya, *Arthasāstra.*   [2] Lenin.   [3] Trotsky.
[4] Shang.   [5] Marx.   [6] Mussolini.
[7] Hitler.   [8] Fascism.   [9] Mussolini.

Yes, when Belgium resists an unprovoked invasion, for there war itself is moral; no, when a country treacherously launches aeroplanes and gas against an unarmed and unoffending neighbour. The mud of national egoism pollutes the pure stream of youthful generosity; when the core is rotten, the apple will go bad. Where discipline and courage are directed to violence and hate, they are only a façade; behind the fair mask of virtue leers the hideous visage of a deformed humanity.

Again, in dictatorships reason is dethroned and hysterical emotion takes its place. Hence culture consists, not in the creative work of the minds of the people, but in spectacles staged by the State. From the day when Peisistratus dressed up Phye as Athene to conduct him back into Athens, triumphs and circuses, grandiose buildings and grandiose Courts, ostentatious rallies and extravagant receptions have fed the nations on a diet of pickles and kept them in a state of unstable excitement. Finally, religion is either contemptuously tolerated if it does nothing, or if it tries to do something is either abolished altogether or given a materialist form. The Caesar or Leader becomes a god on earth, and a myth does duty for truth. The Divinity of the Emperor sanctifies the proceedings of the Japanese General Staff, and the claims of German blood find support in Nordic mythology.

Such is the outline of a typical dictatorship, though there will necessarily be some variation according as it is national, ecclesiastical, or economic. In some cases these features are not found in full. The ruler may seek to impose obedience to his commands, but not uniformity of Party or opinion: such States are authoritarian rather than totalitarian, despotisms rather than dictatorships. Some States may waver between dictatorship and strong government, uncertain on which side to come down.

Lastly, the principles of dictatorship are too irrational, too contrary to human nature, to be for long acceptable to the average man. Civilized men and women feel friendly towards other peoples, and do not want to go to war with them; nor do they want to see their comforts eaten up by needless armaments. When they are not allowed to leave their country, they feel as though they were shut up in barracks against their will;

and they find it highly irksome not to know what is really happening and what other people are thinking. It is horrible to be in jeopardy from Party men and spies, especially when they have old grudges to pay off. Nor will civilized men long be content to be deprived of a share in their own government, or to resign to the State the disposal of their lives.[1] Hence the Materialist State inconsistently contains many elements that are altogether superior to its principles, just as the Moral State inconsistently contains many materialist elements. The Leader and the Party men may be fanatics inaccessible to argument or self-seekers swayed by ambition; on the other hand they may have minds that can learn from experience. Dictatorship is often a façade concealing a moral people.

These facts go far to explain the impermanence of dictatorships throughout history. First, too much depends on one man. The Leader is the string that ties together a bunch of thorns and flowers; when death cuts the string, the bouquet falls to pieces. To succeed, therefore, dictators should be immortal; and they are men. The logic of the First Emperor was perfect when he sent an expedition to the Eastern Isles to bring back the Taoists' herb of immortality; but, empty-headed, it returned empty-handed. Other dictators have sought to circumvent death by a dynastic policy. The difficulty is particularly acute when the dictator is not heredi-tary but self-made. What happened when Lenin died? The State lapses into a new anarchy of jealous rivals, from which either a less competent dictator or the Moral State emerges.

But there are also inner and deeper causes of failure. The autocrat could rule in comparative security over a custom-bound community: the dictator is trying to narcotize a people whom individuality has awakened. The self-seekers and the vain-glorious may support him for a while, yet he has the deeper impulses of human nature to reckon with. Though men may be glad enough of a strong ruler to defend them from anarchy at home or aggression abroad, they do not wish for crises or wars, and see in an aggressive dictator only a danger. When therefore the country is once on its feet, a dictator is no longer needed, especially if foreign Powers adopt a friendly policy. Then freedom-loving citizens

[1] President Roosevelt, *The Times*, 5 January, 1938.

raise their heads again; and they are far more numerous
than was to be expected. For most people who are not in the
Party, and many who are, having reluctantly accepted dictatorship, not because they like it, but as at the moment the
only alternative to anarchy and humiliation, will insist upon
a share in their own government as soon as the danger is
past. Moreover, there are depths in human nature deeper
far than ever plummet of dictator sounded: yearnings to
understand and cherish, unlet of human hindrance, not
only Nature and man, but God Himself. Unless an outlet is
provided, these moral and spiritual forces will take advantage of every opportunity of circumstance (such as an unsuccessful war or prolonged poverty) to disrupt dictatorship,
just as steam in a boiler without a safety-valve will presently
cause an explosion.

Hence sooner or later the issue of the Materialist State
has throughout history almost without exception been the
Moral State. And this, even though the dictatorship is
thoroughly successful. The united China of the First
Emperor rapidly adopted the purely moral principles of the
Confucians. The horrors of the very war for which Chandragupta prepared so successfully converted his grandson to the
gentle service of the Buddha. The rigid dictatorship of
Rome and Byzantium passed into the spirituality of Catholicism and Orthodoxy. The dictators of the past have laid
their money on the wrong horse. Is it wise to back the same
animal again?

I. 1

Individuality first appears in the Far East in the cultural
achievements of the Shang or Yin dynasty. Like other over-
civilized cultures, the civilization of the Shangs lost in
morality as it gained in luxury. Its weakness led to its
conquest by the Princes of the House of Chou.[1] The Duke
of Chou is generally considered to have been the founder of
the culture characteristic of China. The duty of the worship
of ancestors developed under his influence into the duty of
filial piety, and the importance of the family as a State
institution became the leading principle of Chinese society.

[1] 1122 B.C.

Gradually, too, it was seen that the observance of social customs on which orderly society depended involved an inner order or harmony of the mind. A moral society began to shape itself among the few.

But in course of time this society disintegrated. Feudal chiefs rebelled; and other feudatories were commissioned by the Sovereign as Lords Protector to re-establish order on his behalf. More and more the feudatories fought each other, not for their overlord, but for themselves; until, abandoning pretence, some finally claimed the title of King. For the two centuries and a half called 'the Period of the War-ring States' What-is-under-Heaven was torn by their wars.[1]

As in the Greece of the Peloponnesian and Hellenistic Wars, a variety of doctors prescribed a remedy; it was indeed the classic age of Chinese philosophy. Confucians and Taoists, like Socrates and his followers, advocated a moral or spiritual solution. Cynics declared that material pleasures were the only good. 'Let us eat and drink; let us gratify the ears and eyes, get servants and maidens, beauty, music, wine. Each one for himself.' Others, pen in hand to explain their system, set up military dictatorships, enforcing order at home by the severity of their laws. These were the Legalists.

The first, Yang, an adventurer afterwards created Lord of Shang, deserted his own State of Wei for that of Ch'in (in South Kansu), where he became dictator for twenty years under Duke Hsiao.[2] The policy that he carried out in practice he or his followers expounded in a manual for dictators, *The Book of Lord Shang*. A Dutch scholar has summarized its doctrine as follows: 'By concentration on war and agriculture, by implicit obedience to the law, and by the prohibition of all cultural pursuits, the government is ab-solute master; it "unifies" and "consolidates"[3] the people, and the State will not only become powerful, but will attain supremacy, or, in other words, will establish its authority over the whole Empire.'[4] There can hardly be a more pregnant definition of a dictatorship.

The occupations of the people were to be war and agricul-ture. There was to be an army of able-bodied men, another

---

[1] 479–249 B.C.   [2] 359–338 B.C.
[3] I. J. L. Duyvendak, *The Book of Lord Shang*, ii. 5.   [4] Ibid., p. 88.

of able-bodied women, and a third of the old and weak—a
nation in arms indeed![1] The feudal privileges of birth were
to be swept away; military merit was to be the chief source of
promotion and reward; even members of the princely family
who had no military merit were no longer to be regarded as
belonging to the princely clan. The Duke 'cherished the
idea of rolling up the Empire like a mat, of lifting up the
whole world in his arms and of tying up the four seas in a
sack, moreover, he had the intention of swallowing up the
eight wild countries'.[2] Shang did in fact succeed in pushing the frontiers of Ch'in eastward at the expense of his
native State, setting an ambush for the enemy general.

The national economy was regulated for war. 'At home
(says an early Chinese biographer) Shang caused the people
to be active in the work of agriculture and weaving, so as to
enrich the State.'[3] Tilling and weaving are the 'fundamental
occupations'; all other pursuits are 'secondary'.[4] Hitherto
groups of eight families had cultivated squares of land in
common; Shang substituted individual ownership. Manu-
facture and trade were made as difficult as possible; they
encouraged luxury, and gave people time to think.[5] The
State was to pass from a money basis to a produce-basis, so
as to become self-sufficient: 'money kills grain, and grain
kills money'.[6] 'If the people (he writes) see comfort and
advantage accruing to artisans, merchants and scholars, then
they will indubitably shun agriculture; shunning agriculture,
they will care little for their homes; caring little for their
homes, they will certainly not fight and defend these for the
ruler's sake.'[7]

The government was a rigid bureaucracy, central and local.
At the head of the hierarchy of officials stood Shang as
Leader—'I who am alone.' Like other dictators, he found
it necessary to take precautions against attempts on his life.
Office and rank were awarded, at first only for military merit,
afterwards also for bringing in grain, the chief sinew of war.

[1] I. J. L. Duyvendak, *The Book of Lord Shang*, iii. 12.
[2] Ibid., p. 2.
[3] Liu Hsiang, 1st century B.C., *The Book of Lord Shang*, iii, pp. 3–4.
[4] Ibid., p. 49.   [5] Ibid., pp. 41, 44.   [6] Ibid., p. 49.
[7] Ibid., p. 48.

A later supporter of dictatorship, Han Fei-tze, has some caustic things to say on this point.

'Promotion in rank and office correspond to the merit acquired in cutting off heads. Now suppose there were a law that "those who cut off a head are ordered to become doctors or artisans", then houses would not be built and sickness would not be cured. For filling office knowledge and ability are necessary, and the cutting off of heads is the result of courage and strength; and if offices for which knowledge and ability are necessary are filled according to the results of courage and strength, it is exactly the same as if those who had merit in cutting off heads became doctors and artisans.'[1]

The most distinctive feature of the Chinese dictatorships was a replacement of moral principle by a legal system of punishments. In the view of the 'Legalists' the vast majority of mankind, rulers and people alike, are naturally bad, with no guiding motive but self-interest. 'The people's attitude towards profit (Shang writes) is like the tendency of water to flow downwards, without preference for any of the four sides. The people are only interested in obtaining profit, and it depends on what their superiors encourage what they will do.'[2] The proper course therefore is not, like the Confucians, to appeal to *li*, the rules of good behaviour, or to the moral example of the ruler, but to break up the cohesion between kinsman and kinsman, friend and friend, official and official, and enlist their private interests in support of the dictator. Hence the rewards of the law, and still more its punishments. 'The system of good government (he writes) is to neglect the virtuous and to abolish the wise'; the best results follow from taking an interest in the wicked.[3] Hence the law should be severe. 'If you govern by punishment the people will fear; being fearful, they will not commit villainies; there being no villainies, they will be happy in what they enjoy. If, however, you teach people by righteousness, they will be lax; if they are lax, there will be disorder; if there is disorder, the people will suffer from what they dislike.'[4] The reason for this severity is often repeated: 'If small offences do not arise, big crimes will not come, and thus people will commit no crimes and disorder will not arise.'[5]

[1] Ibid., p. 64.   [2] Ibid., p. 121.   [3] Ibid., p. 112.
[4] Ibid., p. 113.   [5] Ibid., p. 60.

Han Fei-tze rubs in the case for this severity with Chinese pith and point. 'In strictly managed households, fierce rebels will not appear, but a compassionate mother has spoilt sons; from this I know that by severity violence may be prevented, but that virtue and kindness are not effective in stopping disorder.'[1] Again: 'Take a boy who is a bad character. His parents may get angry with him, he does not change. His neighbours may reprove him, it has no effect on him. His masters may moralize to him, he does not reform; not a hair on his shins will change. But when the district official sends his soldiers and in the name of the law searches for wicked individuals, then he becomes afraid, changes his principles, and reforms his conduct. So the love of parents is not sufficient to teach a son morality, but the severe punishments of the officials are needed. People become naturally spoiled by love, but obedient to severity.'[2] Finally: 'The love of a mother for her son is twice as great as that of a father, but for getting orders obeyed by a son a father is worth ten mothers. The officials have no love for the people, but for getting their orders obeyed by the people they are worth ten thousand fathers and mothers. A father and mother accumulate their love and yet their orders are fruitless; officials apply severity and the people obey their orders.'[3]

This conception of a terrified obedience to the Leader of a warlike State was incompatible with the older conception of a moral Universe expressing itself in man as harmony and benevolence and giving rise to a corresponding culture. Hence to Shang virtues are 'lice', culture is 'poison'.[4] There are several lists of these offensive virtues, the virtues especially of the Confucians: care for old age, love of beauty, rites and music, benevolence and integrity, intelligence, filial piety, brotherly love, sincerity and faith, chastity, benevolence, right endeavour, criticism of the army, being ashamed to fight. And with the old ethical ideal the old education that produced it perished too. That education was based on the study of certain books, especially the Book of Songs and the Book of History; and these two were particularly offensive to the new school, for they inculcated the old virtues. Tradition says

[1] *The Book of Lord Shang*, iii, p. 113.   [2] Ibid., pp. 113–14.
[3] Ibid., p. 114.   [4] Ibid., pp. 85, 86.

that Shang taught the Duke Hsiao to burn them; Han Fei-tze advocated their abolition; the Duke's successor, the First Emperor, did burn them in 213 B.C. In a famous interview a Confucian scholar warns Shang of the superficiality of his reforms: 'Your Lordship takes improper measures and makes external alterations, but there is nothing that can lay claim to the name of instruction.'[1]

It was the successor of Duke Hsiao on the throne of Ch'in who in the following century, following Shang's principles, conquered the Middle Land and called it China after his own State.[2] But these principles did not survive their most successful exponent. Under the Han dynasty China reverted decisively to the Confucian morality that is the antithesis of Legalist dictatorship.

2

Some twenty years after Shang's death there arose in North India another king-maker and empire-builder whose principles and practice corresponded closely with those of Shang. This was a Brahman, Kautilya, whose patronymic was Chānakya. Like Shang Kautilya was a writer, and his *Arthasāstra* or 'Science of Ruling'[3] still glows like the City of Dis[4] across the sullen marsh of early Indian anarchy.

The Nanda dynasty was degenerate, and the invasion of Alexander had increased the confusion of Hindustan. But the Macedonian victories showed what a well-disciplined army could do. Kautilya attached himself as adviser to Chandragupta, a scion of the ruling house: and Chandragupta, collecting a formidable force on the North-West Frontier, conquered the Punjab, kept the Greeks at bay, deposed and killed the lawful king of Magadha, and extended his kingdom from the Sea of Arabia to the Bay of Bengal. But the people did not gain by the change of masters. Chandragupta 'after his victory, forfeited by his tyranny all title to the name of liberator, oppressing with servitude the very people whom he had emancipated from foreign thraldom.'[5] He ruled from 321 to 296 B.C.

---

[1] Ibid., p. 27.   [2] The First Emperor, 246–210 B.C.
[3] R. Shamasastry, *Kautilya's Arthasāstra.*
[4] Dante, *Inferno*, viii. 68, 74.
[5] Vincent A. Smith, *The Early History of India*, p. 124.

Kautilya's book sets out the principles of dictatorship as clearly as Shang's. There are four objects of government: to obtain a kingdom, by war and conquest; to keep it, by tyranny; to increase it, again by conquest; to enjoy it, when thus acquired. To obtain these four objects there are six kinds of policy: peace, war, neutrality, invasion, alliance, and double-dealing.[1] Neighbouring States are either stronger, equal, or weaker; and policy should seize advantage from each. The respective value of friends, gold, ability, the army, spies, and so on are cynically weighed.[2] There are four arms: elephants, cavalry, chariots, infantry.[3] Chandragupta himself increased his already huge army till it numbered 9,000 elephants, 30,000 cavalry, 600,000 infantry and a multitude of chariots. The *Arthasāstra* advocates the application of medicines, charms, and other 'wonderful and delusive contrivances' to injure an enemy;[4] the use of destructive gases, medicines and poisons to murder or maim opponents in war and peace.[5] 'Deceitful treaties' march with 'treacherous battles',[6] and a chapter is devoted to 'Making peace and breaking it': 'whoever is rising in power may break the agreement of peace'.[7] A deposed dynasty must be covered with as much obloquy as possible and the new order correspondingly glorified.[8]

Aggrandizement abroad involves despotism at home. The king's rule was absolute. 'Kings and gods are alike';[9] 'as all footsteps vanish in the footsteps of the elephant, so all other law or dharma disappears in the royal law (the raja dharma)'.[10] A king must accordingly be a strenuous person, not yielding to the 'enemies of a king'—lust, avarice, pride, drunkenness, insolence—and avoiding a king's special temptations— women, drink, hunting, gambling.[11]

If legal severity was the distinguishing note of Shang's system, that of Kautilya's was spying and treachery. 'An honest politician (says the *Arthasāstra*) is a no-thing.'[12]

---

[1] *Political Science Quarterly*, March 1929: H. H. Gowen, *The Indian Machiavelli*, p. 180.

[2] Ibid., p. 184.   [3] Ibid., p. 185.

[4] Kautilya, *Arthasāstra*, xiv, c. 2.   [5] Ibid., p. xix; Book xiv.

[6] Ibid., p. xix; Book vii. 17.   [7] Ibid., vii. 17.

[8] *Indian Machiavelli*, p. 185.   [9] Ibid., p. 179.

[10] Ibid.   [11] Ibid.   [12] Ibid., p. 187.

Government was to be vindicated by cleverness divorced from all morals. 'He who shoots an arrow kills even the babe within its mother's body.'[1] No one was to be trusted, not even wife or child: 'it is the nature of princes, as of crabs, to devour their parents.'[2] The spies of the Government were everywhere, disguised as ascetics, begging nuns, traders, foresters, peasants, prostitutes, cooks, bed-makers, jesters, dwarfs, tumblers. The ministers and officials were all spies.[3] Every public servant was to be tempted—by love, fear, greed, ambition, religion—to test his faithfulness to the Government; the harem was to be filled with spies and *agents provocateurs*. It was their business not only to discover the opponents of the Government, but to put an end to them— by bringing false charges, by poison, by the sword, by causing a wall to fall down on them, and so on.[4]

The system was to operate abroad as well as at home, in war as well as in peace. Ambassadors were an established form of spy. The evils of the passport system flourished. In war all was treachery; allies were to be separated by false witness, insurrections stirred up in the enemy's rear, his commanders won over by bribes. A tariff was laid down for assassinating enemies—with a maximum of 100,000 pieces of money for killing a king.

Notwithstanding, or because of, all these spies, there was need from time to time for a purge or 'eradication of thorns'.[5] People who were likely to prove troublesome were removed by whatever means, no matter how drastic or unscrupulous.

Even more than in China, the Government was a rigid bureaucracy. In agriculture nothing was left unregulated.[6] Everything that could be inspected was inspected: food, fabrics, slaughter-houses, courtesans, cattle-raising, sports, agriculture, water rights. State-owned drinking saloons were provided; 5 per cent. of the profits from gambling went to the Government. As in China, weights and measures were standardized, and the rates of interest regulated—at about 15 per cent.[7] Trade and most other things were taxed: benevolences were raised to replenish the empty treasury; the property of the rich was confiscated on false pleas of

[1] Ibid.   [2] Ibid., p. 188.   [3] Ibid.   [4] Ibid.
[5] Ibid., p. 181.   [6] Ibid., p. 183.   [7] Ibid., p. 182.

embezzlement or of profiting from a national calamity;
religious taxes were exacted and temple money robbed.[1]
There were four kinds of legal process; those dealing with
customs, contracts, sacred laws, royal enactments. The
people was 'the cow that gives the milk'.[2] If a cow is to give
milk, it needs looking after. Thus the village communities
were allowed a considerable extent of self-government.
Sanitation was provided; there were medical men in all the
chief centres. The Government allowed relief to widows,
orphans, the sick, and infirm. Cornering in trade and adul-
teration of foodstuffs were suppressed. The lot of the slave
was ameliorated, and 'no Arya could be a slave'.[3] Foreign
merchants enjoyed a kind of extra-territoriality: they had
'freedom from being tried in the common courts'.[4]

About the same time the Beast Fables that India loved
were turned to a new use.[5] They had originated in a fond-
ness for animal stories. The Buddha had used them to illustrate his moral precepts; the materialists prostituted them
to the new State morality. The ministers are jackals, easily
influencing their king, the lion, who is generally a foolish
personage. Like the fox, they have a reputation for low
cunning. The crocodile is the embodiment of wickedness.
The cat is a pious hypocrite. The spy crow is an example of
sagacity, held up to show that it is not only permissible, but
praiseworthy, to get the better of an enemy by treachery.
These Fables passed into Tibet, China, Persia, Greece,
Arabia, and along the highway of Muslim conquest to North
Africa, Spain, and Provence; the tales of Aesop, Boccaccio,
and La Fontaine are their echoes.

But the system of Kautilya and Chandragupta was no
more permanent than that of Shang and the First Emperor:
in India, as in China, morality proved stronger than materialism. Chandragupta's own grandson Asoka, shocked by the
horrors of the warfare for which his grandfather had so
zealously prepared, turned from the conquests of arms to the
conquests of love, to become the great Emperor of India
whose name is to this day revered by the Buddhist millions
of Asia.

---

[1] Kautilya, p. xix, c. v. 2.   [2] *Indian Machiavelli*, p. 180.
[3] Ibid., p. 187   [4] Ibid.   [5] Ibid., p. 189.

3

Individuality, as it emerged in the Mediterranean area, also gave rise to morality and to materialism. Graeco-Roman civilization is indeed difficult to place, on account of its great achievements. It might be supposed that the art and philosophy of Greece, the peace and the law of Rome, entitled it to rank among the civilizations with a predominantly spiritual or moral aim; but, though for a time this was true both of Athens and of Rome, yet on the whole Graeco-Roman history is a tale of anarchy followed by dictatorship. Dictatorship brought Mediterranean culture in its ancient form to an end. The moral achievements of Rome passed on into Catholicism, the spiritual achievements of Greece into Orthodoxy.

Whereas Indian history begins with philosophy and goes on to Epic poetry, Greek begins with the Epics and goes on to philosophy. The poems of Homer are the epics of the great man and hero, as Hesiod depicts the oppression of the poor. Yet already in Homer the ascendancy of the autocrat is questioned: Thersites is a radical anticipating the general revolt of individualism against mass-thinking. Then came the dark ages of the land invasion and the sea-migrations—individuality spread from kings and nobles to the people. All Hellas looked with disdain upon the unchanging 'laws of the Medes and Persians', the custom-bound autocracy that sought to enslave free men.

Thus it came about that democracies of the Greek city-states consisted of individuals who recognized themselves as such, but whose individuality expressed itself in one man as egoism, in another as altruism—one was an Alcibiades, another a Socrates: the egoists were more numerous than the altruists, and therefore the exponents of might wielded more influence than the exponents of right. As in the Warring States of China, so in the Warring States of Greece Sophists and philosophers went up and down teaching, and the Sophists prevailed. 'Justice is the interest of the stronger', said Thrasymachus[1]—might is right; and Polus argued that the successful wickedness of the tyrant is the surest road to happiness.[2]

[1] Plato, *Republic*, i. 338.   [2] Plato, *Gorgias* 472.

These opinions landed Hellas in anarchy. Faction clove her city-states. Every city was in a more or less chronic state of civil war, having become, as Plato said, 'not one city but two, one comprising the rich and the other the poor, who reside together on the same spot, and are always plotting against one another'.[1] Aristotle confirmed him. Rich and poor (he said) are the really antagonistic members of a State.[2] All existing polities are either oligarchies or democracies, according as the one or the other predominate.

This civil war was intensified by inter-city war, and especially by the Peloponnesian War, the forcing-house of every iniquity. Thucydides' brilliant mind, kindled at the ideal of Pericles, throws its mournful ray over the lawlessness and violence of Hellas, as the faction of class and class and the enmity of city and city revealed the greed of power and wealth instead of the love of beauty and wisdom.[3] 'The whole Hellenic world was in commotion. In every city the chiefs of the democracy and of the oligarchy were struggling, the one to bring in the Athenians, the other the Lacedaemonians' —as the Reds have their World Revolution and the Fascists their Axis to-day. In this anarchy of fighting factions 'the lover of violence was always trusted, and his opponent suspected'. 'Any agreements sworn to by either party, when they could do nothing else, were binding as long as both were powerless. But he who on a favourable opportunity first took courage and struck at an enemy when he saw him off his guard, had greater pleasure in a perfidious than he would have had in an open act of revenge.' As in Shang's and other systems, Party superseded family. 'The tie of Party was stronger than the tie of blood, because a partisan was more ready to dare without asking why. For Party associations are not based upon any established law, nor do they seek the public good; they are formed in defiance of the laws and from self-interest.'

The source of this world-war in microcosm was a materialist morality, and the intellectual confusion to which this gives rise. 'The cause of all these evils was the love of power originating in avarice and ambition, and the Party spirit

---

[1] *Republic*, viii. 551.   [2] *Politics*, v. 1303 B.
[3] Thucydides, iii. 82–4.

which is engendered by them.' As in the dictatorships of China and India, the old virtues were no longer of account. 'The simplicity which is so large an element in a noble nature was laughed to scorn and disappeared. Inferior intellects generally succeeded best.' At a time when Socrates, like Confucius and like the School of Terminology in the China of the Warring States, was insisting on the need for definition, the Peloponnesian War was illustrating the moral and mental confusion of those for whom words no longer corresponded with facts. 'The meaning of words had no longer the same relation to things, but was changed by them as they thought proper. Reckless daring was held to be loyal courage; prudent delay was the excuse of a coward; moderation was the disguise of unmanly weakness'—just as to-day wickedness is called realism and wars of aggression defence. 'Evil (says war) be thou my good.'

Even Athens, in Pericles' ideal 'the School of Hellas', betrayed her trust. She took advantage of her leadership of the Delian League, not to unite Hellas, but to aggrandize herself. Her envoys appealed openly to the philosophy of the Materialist State when they tried to coerce the Melians into their Confederacy: 'You know as well as we do that right, as the world goes, is only in question between equals in power, while the strong do what they can and the weak suffer what they must.'[1] The Melian massacre followed; justice was 'the interest of the stronger'.[2] When at length the Athenian fleet lay at the bottom of Syracuse harbour, her allies broke away from her; Sparta dismantled the walls of Athens to the music of the flutes.

Thus the faction of rich and poor, and the warfare of State and State, speedily ruined Hellas. In the anarchy of China a school of hedonists proclaimed the pleasures of the flesh the only refuge; in the anarchy of Greece the Cyrenaics, the hot blood of Africa within them, did the same. Plato and Aristotle, like Mencius and Hsun-tze, saw deeper. Surveying the ruins, they pointed to what had brought about the fall.

Neither of these two great minds perceived that the old political order was doomed. They still thought in terms of the

[1] Ibid., v, 89.   [2] Thrasymachus.

city-state, defended by soldiers against other city-states, not of a larger commonwealth that should include them all. A league of city-states remained an aspiration of Isocrates. It was Aristotle's great pupil who, anticipating Rome, saw the vision of a united East and West, bridging the gulf between Greek and barbarian. But Alexander died young; and his Generals and their successors, smothering the genius of free men under the rule of autocrats, claimed the divine right of the kings of Persia, and for three centuries of international anarchy collected taxes and conscribed men to support their armies and wage their wars. Then their sword descended to the Generals of Rome. Like a gangrene, disillusion and lassitude fastened upon the peoples. Poetry was replaced by learning and art by archaism; Stoicism, though it might sing the great hymn of Cleanthes, advocated endurance rather than delight.

The political solution for this disorder was to come from Rome.

The Roman genius differed from the Greek chiefly in this —that, whereas the Greek attained to a complete sense of individuality, the Roman attained merely a sense of political individuality. The Roman is neither an egoist like Alcibiades, nor yet a genius like Socrates; his one-sided individuality, without either self-interest or genius, concentrated upon the interests of the State. This condition of mind expresses itself, not, as in China, India, and Greece, in the cynicism of the Sophists and the speculations of the philosophers, but in a contempt for theory, and in leaving policy to the best heads in the State—the Senate. The elder Cato, the upholder of Roman power and tradition, is the typical figure. On the one hand, he would have Rome's chief political adversary razed to the ground—'Carthage must be destroyed.' On the other, he is the stern Censor of what he conceives to be the enemy of the Roman spirit, Greece with its free-thinking, luxury, and corruption. Both will imperil Rome's material success. He thus anticipates the 'ethical State', the 'common interest before self', of the modern dictator. Even Virgil thinks Rome fit, not for the arts and sciences of Greece, but only for war and government:

Do thou, O Rome, remember to bear Imperial sway.
Thy arts shall be to fashion the part that peace shall play,
To spare the subject peoples and war the proud away.[1]

Rome was from the first a military State, a State of soldier-farmers. In early days its unity was secured by referring the vital questions of war and peace to the 'centuries' or regiments of its well-organized army; and later, also to the men of property whose 'tribute' supported the army. As it expanded over Italy, its colonists, unlike Greek colonists, remained citizens of the parent State. To increase its man-power the neighbouring towns and tribes were granted citizenship. Rome thus represents, in its Republican stage, a highly disciplined Materialist State, and therefore one which avoids the general risks attendant on nascent indivi-duality, namely, incapacity and dissipation. Like any success-fully adapted organism, it accordingly got the better of less successfully adapted competitors—to spread, like any well-adapted creature, over the world.

The characteristic Roman virtues of *gravitas* and *dignitas*, appropriate to Empire-builders, were able to maintain them-selves so long as Rome was engaged in defending her exis-tence and expanding her power; but when in course of time this expansion brought her before the glittering luxury of the Greek East, her virtue, being directed merely to material ends, and having no deeper root in the nature of things, as Cato had foreseen promptly fell a victim. Virtue that was merely political, not moral, easily succumbed to the moral temptations that ruined the Roman's political excellence and thereby overthrew his Republic. Corruption of life and manners invaded the Roman world. The Roman Generals—the Sullas and Caesars and Antonys—like the Hellenistic kings whom they supplanted, fought one another for supre-macy. The end of the Republic was the end of its discipline, and marks the moment when the individual genius of the Roman developed more completely, and so assumed (like the Greek) forms subversive of the State when egoistic, as in the case of the Generals and Catiline, and superior to the State, when expressed as genius, as in the case of the poets. But on the whole the Roman world threatened to go

[1] *Aeneid*, vi. 851–3.

to pieces, as that of the Greek city-states had done. Then another Alexander arose, who did not die young. Augustus applied the principles that had made Italy strong and stable to the whole Graeco-Roman Empire, safeguarding it from war and giving it local freedom; the ideal of the citizen principate was *imperium et libertas*. Valour, justice, mercy, *pietas* or a sense of duty were, as the coins taught men, the virtues of the early Roman Emperors.[1]

Thus Imperial Rome was an autocracy only in appearance, and in the Emperors (who were never hereditary monarchs) and their administrators the political genius of Republican Rome still survived—though applied now to the government of a Commonwealth stretching from the Forth to the Euphrates. It is this genius that led to the age, so materially happy, of 'the immeasurable majesty of the Roman Peace'.[2] The principle of individuality emerged in a disciplined form. The rights of the individual were clearly recognized; an obscure citizen like Paul could not only claim but receive them. Cities and tribes within the whole vast Empire were free to manage their own affairs. This freedom was increased by the fact that they were not allowed to go to war with each other; for freedom to go to war, like freedom to murder, is a licence given to anarchy. The place of war was taken by justice. Disputes were settled by established law—no steam-rolling or standardizing Code, but, subject to the jurisdiction of the Provincial Governor, local laws springing from and varying with the genius of each city or tribe. The whole great structure of Empire was guarded within and without by a small police army, to support which light taxes were imposed. The roads of Rome, symbol of diversity in unity, spread trade and culture from end to end of the Empire.[3] Along them went the philosophies and religions of the East —Stoicism and Neoplatonism, Gnosticism, Mithraism, and Christianity. Such a State was by no means wholly materialist. Some Emperors at least regarded it as moral: Marcus Aurelius was the philosopher-king, founding himself on the teachings of the Stoics.

Had the Roman Empire, like the Chinese, developed its

[1] M. P. Charlesworth, Raleigh Lecture, p. 24.   [2] The Elder Pliny.
[3] Cp. Professor Hugh Last, *Listener*, 1932, p. 582*b*.

libertas rather than its *imperium*, and subordinated its material to its moral interests, it would have survived, as the Chinese did. It fell, because it tried to save itself materially—not, like China, morally—by gradually converting its government into a dictatorship. Augustus might call himself 'first among his peers', but when he entered the Gulf of Puteoli, the sailors chanted 'By him we live, by him we sail'.[1] Rome was the centre of everything: Trajan refused a fire brigade to a city of Asia Minor for fear of what it might do. The 'Providentia' of the Emperor later supplanted his more modest virtues. Marcian declared that it was his business 'to provide for the benefit of the human race'; Leo the Wise declared that 'all things have been made dependent solely on the Providence and government of the King'.[2] In the interest of efficiency in its resistance to the barbarians the centralized authority became more and more despotic, but the result was the reverse of what was intended: dictatorship drained the heterogeneous democratic communities of their natural political energies and left them incapable of resisting the attacks of external foes. 'The Central Government took charge; the resources of the Empire, human and inanimate alike, were ruthlessly organized in the interests of the Empire as a whole; the independence of the cities was destroyed, and the individual inhabitants lost their freedom.'[3] After the third century the Central Government had taken so many functions to itself that the peoples of the cities could no longer be called free. It interfered intimately with their daily life; men could not change their occupations and a son had to follow in the footsteps of his father. To maintain the Second Rome 'men must be held to their task by an obligation from which escape was impossible; one and all must be regimented into the State's service. A man's claim to mould his own life as he would—this was a luxury which the Empire could no longer grant to its citizens'.[4] Even thought was no longer free; one after another, Oecumenical Councils of ecclesiastics, summoned by the Emperors, defined for ever and a day, without possibility of

---

[1] Suetonius, *Augustus*, c. 98. [2] Charlesworth, p. 24.
[3] Last, *Listener*, 1932, p. 631*b*.
[4] Professor N. H. Baynes, *Listener*, 1932, p. 782*b*.

change, what all men must believe and all must say on the profoundest and least definable of all Objects, the Nature of the Divine Being.

In these circumstances 'the peoples of the Roman world lost their *joie de vivre*: they ceased to be masters of their own affairs and sank into a lethargic indifference to life which meant that the Empire had lost its vigour and was already in decay'.[1] Graeco-Roman civilization, in so far as it was materialist, could not sustain itself; in so far as it was moral and spiritual, it survives in Catholic and Orthodox civilization, and in the undying influence of Athens.

4

The invasions of Nordic and Avar barbarians plunged the Roman world into the darkness of anarchy for six centuries. Then arose a new Rome, sublimated now into a Holy Church and a Holy Empire, that struggled to make both men and society into a new moral and spiritual creation. But Church and Empire never succeeded in arresting the material appetites of their subjects or therefore the expression of these appetites in political forms, the aim of which was and is aggrandizement in this world.

Feudalism is the system by which common men were protected by a feudal lord in return for such services as they were able to render. The system seems to have recognized, even for the serfs, some at least of the rights of the individual—the descendants of Romans and Nordics would hardly have accepted any other. But it was a system which involved an almost total absence of social security—each feudal chief being a law to himself and ready at any moment to prey on another, like the chiefs in feudal China and the city-states of Greece. The Church endeavoured to drain off this egoism by the Truce of God, the Rules of Chivalry, the Crusades;[2] but the sufferers themselves, the common people, awaited any opportunity to improve their social condition.

They found their champion at the apex of the system—in the king; just as the people of the Greek city-states found their champion in the law-giver and the 'tyrant', and the

---

[1] Last, *Listener*, 1932, pp. 631–2.
[2] Dr. Eileen Power, *Listener*, 1932, p. 846a.

Roman people in the law-giving Decemviri. As John Ball put it under an ineffective king: 'We have no sovereign to whom we may complain, nor that will hear us or do us right.'[1] The kings were the peoples' friends, though sometimes rough and severe friends. Their claim to effective government was as much challenged by the feudal nobles as was the social security of the people; but between this hammer and anvil—king and commons—the feudal lords gradually lost their power.

It was out of this alliance between kings and peoples that the modern nation-states were born. But while kings slowly rose to power as the representatives of the peoples under them, the moral restraints of the Holy Empire and the spiritual restraints of the Holy Church became steadily weaker. Wars and civil wars undertaken in the name of religion were in reality more and more inspired by selfish nationalism, until with the death of Gustavus Adolphus, the rise of Richelieu, and the Treaties of Westphalia, even the pretence of right was flung aside. Absolutism at home was perfected in the interest of aggression abroad, and materialism set its triumphant foot on the neck of morality, alike in internal and in international affairs.

The whole development bears some resemblance to that of China under the Chou dynasty. There the early 'Sons of Heaven' tried, like the Church, to infuse a new-found morality among their feudatories and people. As these restraints grew weaker, wars arose between the feudal States, whose chiefs, at first commissioned as Lords Protector to restore order on behalf of the King of Chou, presently dropped all pretence and usurped the title of king themselves. Finally, to overcome this anarchy the peoples for a time submitted to the severe rule of dictators. In both cases the whole process lasted some nine hundred years. In China it ended, as it may end to-day, in a society founded on moral principles.

The prophet of the new Europe was Machiavelli, as Dante had been that of the Middle Ages. *The Prince*[2] is the antithesis of the *De Monarchia*. Its teaching follows the familiar

---

[1] Quoted by Dr. Eileen Power, *Listener*, 1932, p. 905a.
[2] Machiavelli, *The Prince* (Everyman's Library).

lines. The object of the State is war. 'A prince ought to
have no other aim or thought, nor select anything else for his
study, than war and its rules and discipline; for this is the
sole art that belongs to him who rules. It is not reasonable
that he who is armed should yield obedience willingly to
him who is unarmed, or that the unarmed man should be
secure among armed servants.'[1] Justice is still 'the interest
of the stronger'.[2] 'There are two ways of contesting, the one
by the law, the other by force. The first method is proper to
men, the second to beasts; but because the first is frequently
not sufficient, it is necessary to have recourse to the second.
A prince, then, should know how to employ the nature of
man and that of the beast as well.' The principles of the
Beast Fables have migrated from India. But force should
be supplemented by fraud; Kautilya might have written the
chapter on 'the way Princes should keep faith'.[3]

'A Prince should be a fox, to know the traps and snares, and a lion,
to frighten the wolves; for those who simply hold to the nature of the
lion do not understand their business. Therefore a wise lord cannot,
nor ought he to, keep faith when such observance may be turned against
him, and when the reasons that caused him to pledge it exist no longer.
Nor will there ever be wanting to a prince legitimate reasons to excuse
this non-observance. But it is necessary to know well how to disguise this characteristic, and to be a great pretender and dissembler.
A sagacious prince, then, cannot and should not fulfil his pledges when
their observance is contrary to his interest, and when the causes that
induced him to pledge his faith no longer exist.'

That is the doctrine of 'necessity of State', the 'scrap of
paper'.[4]

Thus the morality of tradition is cast aside—and for
Shang's reason, that men are by nature bad. Virtues are
'imaginary things', vices 'those which are real'.[5]

'Hence it is necessary for a Prince wishing to hold his own to know
how to do wrong, and to make use of it or not according to necessity.'[6]

'It is unnecessary for a prince to have all the good qualities I have
enumerated, but it is very necessary to appear to have them. And I

[1] Chapter 14, p. 115.   [2] Thrasymachus.
[3] Chapter 18, pp. 141–3.   [4] Bethmann-Hollweg, Aug. 1914.
[5] *The Prince*, Chapter 15, p. 129.   [6] Ibid., p. 122,

shall dare to say this also, that to have them and always to observe them is injurious, and to appear to have them is useful; to appear merciful, faithful, humane, religious, upright, and to be so, but with a mind so framed that should you require not to be so, you may be able and know how to change to the opposite.'[1]

Hobbes took a similar view. The State, the great Leviathan, is absolute, and its object is to show its power, moral or immoral. 'It does not alter the case of Honour, whether an action (so it be great and difficult, and consequently a signe of much power) be just or unjust; for Honour consisteth onely in the opinion of Power.'[2]

These theories were soon to be embodied in practice.

'Richelieu stands out upon the canvas of history as the first of that long line of statesmen who were actuated by purely selfish national interests. Unaffected by moral ideals, uninfluenced by religious motives, the rulers of the latter half of the seventeenth and of the eighteenth centuries made war upon each other purely in the interests of their crowns and of themselves. Personal glory, territorial aggrandizement, commercial advantage were the motives which led to the great wars of Europe from the Peace of Westphalia to the Congress of Vienna. Before the fierceness of these appetites the rights of nations, of races, even of humanity itself weighed not a feather in the balance. Germans must lose their speech and their fatherland, that France may push her boundaries to the Rhine. Poland must be wiped out of the map of Europe, that Prussia and Russia may be bigger and greater. Even African negroes must be torn from their homes, and sold as chattels in the market-places of the West, that the pockets of Englishmen and of English colonists might swell with gold. And if amid the dark scene of selfishness and rapacity there shines at times the nobler light which hallows the wars of liberty against the oppression of Louis the Fourteenth and Napoleon, yet the shadows deepen as they gather round the career of Frederick the Great, and the closing acts of the Napoleonic drama at Vienna, and the historian has sadly to acknowledge that in them are to be found the characteristic scenes of eighteenth-century diplomacy and war. It is the triumph of Machiavellianism on the large scale in international politics. It is the adaptation to the affairs of nations of Hobbes's description of the natural man. *Homo homini lupus.* Everything is permissible to a sovereign that tends to the security and greatness of his power, and nations are to one another as wild beasts. Nation stands out against nation in open and barbarous hostility on the principle of the old

[1] Ibid., p. 143.   [2] *Leviathan,* Chapter x, pp. 44-5.

moss-trooper's rule, that they shall win who have the power and they shall keep who can.'[1]

Justice once more is the interest of the stronger.

'Absolute power and territorial aggrandizement become the main objects of European kings. The nation is identified with the king; the larger and the richer the territory he rules, the greater his glory and circumstance. Before that all things give way. Differences of speech, differences of race, differences of religion, differences of government, count for nothing, and whole peoples are tossed about from one ruler to another like counters at the table of the diplomatists, not in cynicism but in sheer unconcern.'[2]

As a Spanish statesman put it: 'Ministers cut and pare states and kingdoms as though they were Dutch cheeses.'[3]

'To establish beyond all question the authority of the crown, to maintain a powerful and powerfully equipped army, to astonish the world by the splendour of the court, to push ever further and further away the frontiers of the nation, to extend a lordly protection, little short of vassalage, to weaker countries—such were the objects of a patriot king, such the rewards of a successful statesmanship. The nation was focused and crystallized into the person of the king.'[4]

This aggressive absolutism was best represented in France and Prussia. Richelieu perceived that by military and diplomatic conquest he could secure the national unity and monarchial centralization of France; and therefore launched France on a career of aggrandizement that acted as a spur to criminal ambition. Just as Shang converted Ch'in 'from a loose conglomerate of small feudal territories into a highly centralized administrative unit'[5] and Kautilya established in India a bureaucracy that regulated everything, so Richelieu drew the claws of the French nobility and destroyed the traditional local administration by establishing a permanent civil service of professional men of the middle class, wholly dependent on the royal favour, and placing in their hands the whole financial, judicial, and police machinery of the State. Louis the Fourteenth continued his system, waging further

---

[1] H. O. Wakeman, *The Ascendancy of France*, pp. 107–8 (shortened).
[2] Ibid., p. 187.
[3] Alberoni, quoted A. Hassall, *The Balance of Power*, p. 2.
[4] Wakeman, p. 188. [5] *The Book of Lord Shang*, pp. 39–40.

wars of aggression, but reducing his ministers from statesmen to clerks. Napoleon carried the system of despotism
at home and war abroad to its highest pinnacle.

Brandenburg was built by the Great Elector on the same
foundation; and ever since 'centralization of the government,
military rule and constant territorial aggrandizement have
been the characteristics of the Prussian monarchy'.[1] 'Germany was cradled in the horrors of the Thirty Years War,
nourished by the falsehood and the tyranny of the Great
Elector, and ushered into manhood by the cynical ambition
of Frederick the Great.'[2] The Great Elector

'grovelled upon the earth, and cherished its mire and its dirt if only
he could possess himself of one acre the more of it. A true Hohen-
zollern in his absolute identification of his country with his own crown,
he never rose above the pure selfishness of patriotism. Not one spark
of generosity illuminated his policy, not one grain of idealism coloured
his ambition, no sentiment of moral right ever interfered with his
judgement, no fear of future retribution arrested his action. Mean-
minded, false, unscrupulous, he was the first sovereign to display the
principles of seventeenth-century Machiavellianism, stripped of their
cloak of Italian refinement, in all the hideous brutality of German
coarseness.'[3]

The bad faith and dissimulation of his diplomacy would have
satisfied even Kautilya or Machiavelli; with him, as with
them, success justified everything. He too established a
central bureaucracy, and himself appointed all the chief
administrative officers in his various dominions—unlike
Louis the Fourteenth attaching the nobles to him by a
system of social distinctions and privileges. His grandson
organized Prussia as a Police State, initiating the system of
spies which Kautilya had long ago advocated, and which
Metternich afterwards carried into Austria, and Alexander
and Nicholas into Russia. Frederick the Great used this
'unified' and 'consolidated' State[4] for the cynical seizure of
Silesia and the ruthless Partition of Poland. Bismarck was
not backward in learning these lessons of bureaucratic centralization and of war. William the Second boasted of his

---

[1] Wakeman, p. 178. [2] Ibid., p. 175.
[3] Ibid., p. 174. [4] *The Book of Lord Shang*, ii. 5.

shining armour and his mailed fist. To his Chancellor a
solemn Treaty was 'a scrap of paper'.

These absolute States were without organized Parties
and without freedom of opinion. Richelieu declared it a
capital offence to publish a work against religion or the
State. Only licensed presses might print books, only licensed
booksellers deal in them. Censorship was introduced into
Germany in 1529, and there too there were thenceforth
numerous restrictions on the liberty of the printing press.
Public opinion was drugged by the vainglorious ostenta-
tion of Versailles and of the Courts that imitated it. Government propaganda was superfluous where the free spirit was
in abeyance. Before the World War it hardly existed, except
in the Press Bureau of the German Foreign Office.

Nor were the theorists behindhand. Hegel gives a sympathetic account of Machiavelli and his policy of force.
Clausewitz repeatedly said that 'war is nothing but a con-
tinuation of political intercourse with a mixture of other
means.'[1] Treitschke carried on the tradition.

The World War left most of Europe in anarchy, while it
raised up a formidable menace in Communism. Two Great
Powers fell a prey to disorder at home and humiliation abroad.
The proud military dictatorship of Germany suffered the
disgrace of defeat in the field and a dictated Peace that
shrivelled her defences, raided her wealth, disarmed her
frontiers, and redistributed her colonies. Italy, undistin-
guished in battle and intemperate in diplomacy, believed
herself to have been cheated of the advantages for which she
had entered the War. Each threatened to go to pieces, like
a wooden ship in a storm; dictatorship seemed at first to be
the rope cast about the straining timbers to keep the ship
together.

The times called for strong government; but of which
type should it be? The Tudors conquered disorder at home
and aggression abroad by the political tutelage of their
people and a reasonable military preparedness; the Kuoming-
tang is doing the same. Fascists and Nazis on the other hand
have fallen back on armaments, autarchy, absolutism, the

[1] Quoted by J. H. Morgan, *The German War Book*, p. 12.

replacement of the morality and culture of the individual by a totalitarian devotion to the State. In both systems Shang's policy lives again; the object of the State is power or supremacy, and to this end it promotes agriculture and prepares armies; the government under an irresponsible Leader 'unifies and consolidates' the people, and crushes all culture and morality that conflict with the material interests of the State.[1]

The object of Fascism is the revival of the Roman Empire, with the Mediterranean as its centre. Hence the conquest of Ethiopia, the invasion of Spain, the threats to France, the incitement of the Arab world. Yet the new Rome would be the reverse of the old, for it mistakes the nature of an achievement that lay, not in arms, but in the majesty of peace; not in disregard of treaties, but in respect for laws—the grounds of the world's admiration. The Duce is openly of the school of Shang and Kautilya and Machiavelli as regards both the use of force and the keeping of faith. Once more the ruler 'ought never to have out of his thoughts the subject of war',[2] but should encourage 'military merit'.[3] Mussolini boasts that Fascism does not believe in 'the possibility or utility of perpetual peace':[4] that war is the function of men, as childbearing is the function of women. Italy has accordingly become 'a military, militaristic and warlike nation'.[5] And this is how 'princes should keep faith'.[6] Fascist Italy, a leading member of the League of Nations, a guarantor of European peace, a signatory of the Pact of Paris, trampling underfoot no fewer than seven Treaties, launched a great army to the conquest of a defenceless fellow-member of the League and annexed the whole of its territory. Pledged to non-intervention, she sent an army to Spain and boasted of winning a war.

The aim of National Socialism is more ambitious: the 'mastery of the earth' by the German race.[7] Race is the principle of the Nazi Party—the purity and superiority of German blood to all other: a discovery reserved for the Nazi

---

[1] *The Book of Lord Shang*, p. 88.   [2] *The Prince*, c. 14, p. 116.
[3] Lord Shang.   [4] *The Times*, 4 Oct. 1935.
[5] Ibid., 9 Nov. 1936.   [6] *The Prince*, c. 18.
[7] *Mein Kampf*, 782; quoted, R. W. Seton-Watson, *Britain and the Dictators*, 43.

genius, and outside Germany unknown to history and medical science, which indeed maintain that German blood has been largely intermixed with that of Wends, Prussians, and other Slav tribes, and that an admixture of blood improves both the physical and the mental qualities of a people. Accordingly creatures such as Jews and Negroes are mere filth, unworthy of a free and equal citizenship; the Jew 'never possessed a culture of his own', and is 'the real enemy':[1] while, on the other hand, the German Reich oversteps the frontiers of the German State, and includes within it all those of German blood, whatever their citizenship, whether Austrian or Czechoslovakian, Swiss or Rumanian, Dutch or Belgian, Chilean or Brazilian, Canadian or American. As far as possible Nazi practice corresponds with Nazi theory. In Germany, Jews are insulted, persecuted, driven into exile; in other countries, an incessant propaganda and secret agents undermine the allegiance of German-descended citizens and stir them to rebellion. Unprecedented armaments fill air, earth, and sea. Security and defence are indeed the right and the duty of strong governments; and Germany, situated in the heart of Europe, obsessed from of old by the fear of encirclement, stripped defenceless by the Dictate of Versailles, invaded by France from the West and menaced by the Red Army from the East, might well build up her armaments and conscribe her citizens, as the safeguard of her frontiers against a ring of bayonets and as the bulwark of Europe against the Communist International. Far other is the doctrine of *Mein Kampf*. 'The stronger has to rule'— justice is again his interest.[2] 'Our mission is in the industrious work of the German plough, to which the sword only has to give the soil.'[3] Although 'we can in the first instance think only of Russia and the Border States subject to her',[4] yet 'anyone who desired the victory of the pacifist ideal in this world must aim at the conquest of the world by the Germans'.[5] The Leader advocates 'a peace resting, not on the palm-branches of tearful pacifist women, but on the victorious sword of a master-nation (*Herrenvolk*) which takes the world into the service of the higher culture'.[6] A State

---

[1] *Mein Kampf*, 330, 628.   [2] Ibid., 312.   [3] Ibid., 743.
[4] Ibid.   [5] Ibid., 315.   [6] Ibid., 438.

which in an era of race-poisoning cultivates its best elements 'must one day become master of the earth'.[1]

Not that war is used as the instrument of policy, when the threat of war will suffice. As Kautilya would have spies undermine the integrity of foreign States, so Nazi diplomatists, traders, educationalists, secret agents of every kind, working subterraneously, stir up disloyalty and disaffection and hold out hopes of personal gain, in order that when the time comes minorities can be represented as 'tortured creatures' and German troops march in to seize the spoils without bloodshed. The Nazi Party does not desire war, if intrigue alone can secure the fruits of victory.

Tilling the soil and land-reform, coupled with a distrust of foreign trade, characterize the Fascist and Nazi dictatorships, as they did those of the Legalists. There are three virtues in the peasant or small farmer: he is physically strong and has a large family; he produces the food and raw materials necessary for war; he is supposed to be stupid enough to swallow what he is told. Hence Mussolini drains the marshes, and Hitler breaks up the large estates. '*Italia fara da se*'; the German economic ideal is 'autarchy'. Shang said that the statesman should understand 'how to make the poor rich and the rich poor', so as to make the State strong;[2] to-day too the dictator tries to break down class barriers, because a class consciousness interferes with a State consciousness.

The modern dictator, like his predecessors, is an absolute ruler, 'I who am alone.' He is the Leader who cannot err, and his people are children who cannot reason; the motto of the dictatorships is the motto of the nursery: 'What Nursie says is always right, even when it is wrong.' He obtains his power through an armed Party, and afterwards tries to rest it on the army. Thanks to modern invention, this Party can keep in power for a time with little popular support: one man with a pike was as good as another, a man with a machine-gun is better than a hundred. A centralized bureaucracy regulates everything, as everything was regulated under Shang and Kautilya, Louis the Fourteenth and Frederick the Great. Like Kautilya and Metternich and Lenin, the dictators, unlet and unsupported by Diet or

[1] Ibid., 782.   [2] *The Book of Lord Shang*, p. 201.

Parliament, 'unable to know their peoples' wants, and unable to help them to know their own',[1] employ an army of spies and secret police to ascertain what their critics are thinking and to frustrate them, and themselves rely upon reports that ill-will or servility may distort.

Shang banished those who discussed his mandates to the frontiers—'thereupon none dared to discuss the mandates'.[2] Fascists and Nazis banish the 'carpers and grumblers' to the Lipari Islands and the concentration camps. There is an 'eradication of thorns'[3]—the massacre of 30 June, the murder of Dolfuss; just as in Soviet Russia there are continuous trials and executions of 'wreckers and Trotskyites'; just as in Japan ministers are murdered by army officers who disapprove their policy.

When the glorification of the State is the be-all and the end-all of the lives of its citizens, morality is identified with service to the State, religion with devotion to the State. Just as Shang regarded the Confucian virtues as 'lice' and the Confucian culture as 'poison',[4] just as Kautilya declared that 'an honest politician is a no-thing' and [5]Machiavelli despised Christian morals as 'imaginary things' and recommended vices as 'real',[6] just as Lenin and Trotsky hold that morality consists solely in loyalty to the Communist Party and that all other virtues are only 'deception',[7] so Mussolini's 'ethical State' is the State whose citizens live only for the Fascist Empire,[8] Hitler's maxim 'the common interest before self' means *Deutschland über alles*—everything for the German Reich. In dictatorships the good man is the good Party man—the good Nazi, the good Fascist, the good Communist—good servants of the State and especially good soldiers: anything further is superfluous or mischievous.

With a view to the making of such citizens education is militarized. In the Italy of Mussolini it is pre-military, military, and post-military; 'believe, obey, fight' are the

---

[1] Wakeman, p. 5.   [2] *The Book of Lord Shang*, p. 17.
[3] *The Indian Machiavelli*, p. 181.
[4] *The Book of Lord Shang*, pp. 85, 86.
[5] *The Indian Machiavelli*, p. 187.
[6] *The Prince*, c. 15, p. 122.   [7] Lenin (*infra*).
[8] Mussolini, 'The Political and Social Doctrine of Fascism', *Enciclopedia Italiana*, xiv (1931).

'three words of the Fascist creed', words stencilled large on the walls of every village in Italy.[1] In Germany 'the doctrine of force and revenge is inculcated in Hitler's own book and in the school-books of his country'.[2] Shows and rallies take the place of argument and discussion. Freedom of opinion is suppressed, and the means of forming it are withheld: popular assemblies are retained to applaud, the Press reflects the views of the Government, free speech is forbidden, foreign news, views, and books are shut out, foreign travel is made difficult for young and old, lest they become contaminated with liberal heresies or awkward facts. Hence the people have no adequate means of forming an opinion on questions either of peace or war, even if they had the power of voicing that opinion. In the Nazi ideal, emotion takes the place of thought, blind obedience sterilizes reason. Across the ages comes the voice of the Confucian scholar: 'Your Lordship takes improper measures and makes external alterations, but there is nothing that can lay claim to the name of instruction.'[3]

A Youth Movement encourages athletics and comradeship for the young, and a Strength through Joy Movement travel and recreation for the workers; Labour Camps bring men and women of all classes together in the common service of the community. In themselves these are fine things, that make a special appeal to the young, and reconcile many older persons to the régime. But they are coupled with an aggressive Party propaganda that inspires an overweening pride in Germany and an overweening contempt for other nations, and are too dearly purchased if they lead to the distortion of the mind through falsehood, or the disablement and death of the body through war. The turkey may revel in the rich feed that precedes Christmas, but the fate reserved for it is not happy.

Since the individual exists to make the State formidable, not the State to enable the individual to live a fuller life, religion is either contemptuously tolerated when it does nothing, or diverted to the service of the State, or cast into

---

[1] Mussolini, *The Times*, 27 Mar. 1939.
[2] Arthur Asquith, *The Times*, 31 Mar. 1936.
[3] *The Book of Lord Shang*, p. 27.

the limbo of evil things. The State is not on the side of God; God is on the side of the State. Some Nazis dream of a single German Church which shall include those strange bed-fellows Catholicism and Protestantism. The 'German Christians' dilute Christianity with Nordic legend. For the first time since Julian the Apostate, Christian States throw off their Christianity. The German Faith Movement tries to revive the heathen violence of Thor and Odin. Bolshevism seeks to destroy religion altogether.

Thus kings and other rulers of nations arose out of the feudal system as an expression of the popular spirit—as an organ helpful for the freeing of the people's will from the burden of oppression and anarchy, much as Peisistratus attained power in Athens by aiding the commoners to rid themselves of a burdensome oligarchy. But, like the Greek tyrants, the descendants of these kings mistook their position and imagined themselves to be the masters of the peoples they were raised to serve. They imagined themselves to have the position in the State which was really occupied by a Rameses or a Cyrus, among peoples who had not yet attained any sense of political individuality and therefore of political liberty. The liberty, in short, of the State was in their opinion confined wholly to the liberty of their own divine persons—to do their own pleasure at home and to enlarge their power by conquest abroad. This doctrine received its most complete expression in Louis the Fourteenth and the Great Elector.

But the French Revolution and its repercussions show that autocracy in modern Europe is an anachronism, and that it rests on the error of supposing that the modern European is the ancient Asiatic revived—the descendant of the primitive nature not yet individualized, rather than the descendant of the freedom-loving Nordic and Roman. In short, these sovereigns ceased to perform the function for which they were evolved, and suffered in consequence the fate of the sons of Peisistratus. The English, American, and French Revolutions were the Harmodius and Aristogeiton of modern times; and they have been followed by similar Revolutions in Latin America, Italy, Germany, and Spain. The Period of the Warring States (as the years from Westphalia to Vienna may be called) left Europe, not strong and powerful, but exhausted and weak; its peoples sick of oppression and aggression, disillusioned alike with Church and State, resolved on a new life of 'liberty, equality and fraternity'. New ideals arose, derived from the example of England, which, resisting absolutism at home, founded a constitutional monarchy upon the principle of 'civil and religious liberty'; and, resisting absolutism abroad, led those wars of liberty in the common interest that prevented any Power or potentate—Philip or Louis or Napoleon—from establishing a hegemony over Europe. Rousseau and other French thinkers inspired first France and then Europe and Asia with the desire to copy English political liberty.

But freedom is a flower that springs, not from constitutions, but from character; freedom could not prevail without a self-disciplined respect for others, which few nations possess. Consequently a struggle ensued between the ideals of absolutism and liberty, national aggression and a world order: a struggle which is still in the waging. Amid the confusion in which the Great War left the nations, dictators were acclaimed because strong government was needed to restore order, to secure equality, and to complete the spirit of nationhood. But these dictators would be profoundly in error if they supposed that they were masters and not ministers, beneficiaries and not trustees. Hitler, in saying 'I was the Supreme Court',[1] was as much in error as Louis in saying 'I am the State'; and Mussolini is wronging the intelligence of Italians when he lays down the principle 'Mussolini is always right'.[2] Nazis and Fascists were enthusiastic slaves because they are at heart enthusiastic freemen; beneath the surface numbers of Germans and Italians resent the loss of their liberties. The present dictatorships are thus temporary flurries on the stream of democracy, deceiving the eye only of those who look at the flurries and not at the stream. If the teaching of history is to be trusted, they will have no more permanence than the governments of Shang and Kautilya; self-discipline, good sense, and good will—in a word, human

[1] R. W. Seton-Watson, *Britain and the Dictators*, p. 227.
[2] *The Times*, 4 Feb. 1938.

reason—will again prove stronger than brutish violence and lawlessness in securing national unity and prosperity and in winning the respect and admiration of the world.

5

The development of Japan[1] has been retarded not by one but by two periods of anarchy, each issuing in dictatorship. She owes her culture largely to India and China—having studied the Confucian Classics in the sixth century A.D. with a view to reading the Buddhist scriptures in their Chinese translations. Nara and Kioto saw a flowering of the genius of a beauty-loving people, in literature, architecture, and art, under Chinese and Buddhist influence. But administration gradually passed from the Mikado to the family of Fujiwara, from whose daughters the Empresses were chosen. Meanwhile the frontiers were threatened by 'barbarians', to check whom expeditions were organized under a 'shogun' or general; gradually a 'military class' formed itself in distinction from the agricultural. Warlike clans grew in power, and turned their arms against each other. The tenth, eleventh, and twelfth centuries were a period of anarchy. Japanese civilization disintegrated. Buddhism, adapting itself to the times, proclaimed to the suffering people the joys of the Pure Land (Jodo), the Western Paradise awaiting those who have faith in Amida amid the miseries of this life.

The political solution was found in the military dictatorship of the Minamoto family, whose head, Yoritomo, was appointed shogun by the Mikado. When his heirs failed, his work of pacification was carried on by the Hojo family; the thirteenth century was a century of peace. This was broken by the rise in 1336 of rival Mikados, whose struggles for fifty-six years demoralized authority, ruined the peasantry, and gave over the country to lawlessness and brigandage. At the same time the shogunate passed to the incompetent Ashikaga family, and Japan was rent by the civil war of rival clans for three centuries. Buddhist monks and monasteries, abnegating the gentleness of the Buddha, joined furiously in the fray.

[1] See A. L. Sadler, *The Maker of Modern Japan: the Life of Tokugawa Ieyasu* (1937).

Once more the land took refuge in a hereditary military dictatorship, secured by Ieyasu for his family, the Tokugawa. As the Testament he left for the guidance of his House shows, he himself was not a little influenced by the teaching of Confucius, and it is the tragedy of Japan that the Tokugawa Shogunate, unlike the Han dynasty, did not succeed in making the principles of the Sage the foundation of their government. Iyemitsu, the third Shogun of the line, deprived the daimios or heads of the clans of all independence; they became feudal vassals, and many stringent regulations were laid down for their guidance. Each feudal noble in his turn had his own strict code for the regulation of the samurai or bushi, the hereditary soldiers of his fief. Bushido, 'the way of the warrior', exacted the military or materialist virtues of discipline, devotion to the chief, loyalty even to a horrible self-inflicted death if military honour were so much as breathed upon; but tended to drain the samurai dry of individual intelligence, benevolence towards men other than samurai, joy in life. They prided themselves on despising money; but nevertheless took from the tillers of the soil half the produce of the land. The art they encouraged was the decoration of arms and armour, and especially of the sword; 'the sword is the soul of the samurai', says Ieyasu's Testament. Religion was pressed into the service: the Zen or Contemplative School of Buddhism, which exerted a great influence over the samurai, stressed the transience of all visible things, and the warrior was thus induced the more readily to yield himself body and soul to the commands of his code and his overlord.

Thus the samurai exemplified on the whole the moral and spiritual emptiness and barrenness of all those whose rule is blind obedience to any kind of dictatorship. There is no little resemblance between them and the Jesuits in their less noble phase. They too scooped out their personalities in submission to their superiors, and would die a death of torture with the same heroism as the Jesuit missionaries in a better cause. The Shogun occupied a position at the head of a hierarchy comparable to that of the Jesuit General; and by a coincidence it was in both cases the third General of the series—Iyemitsu and Acquaviva—who squeezed from the system the more moral elements imparted to it by its founder. The Tokugawa dictatorship did, however, give Japan two centuries and a half of peace, during which the craftsmen and the merchant classes increasingly flourished, calling into being a wonderful popular art.

When, debilitated by time, the shogunate fell and the Mikado nominally resumed authority, a more liberal régime came partially into being, as it did in France in 1789. Shogun, daimios, and samurai all resigned their privileges. But they retained, in effect if not in law, control over the Army and Navy; and the military party, overriding all civilian elements and the Mikado himself, has seized Korea, Manchuria, and Inner Mongolia, invaded China proper, and dreamed of controlling Asia and the Pacific. The Mikado, descendant of the Sun-Goddess, is the myth of this dictatorship, as the Norse gods are of the Nazis. Every school-child is taught that in this divine sovereign all the powers of the State reside —though they are exercised only through the General Staff.

II

But patriotism is not the only virtue that may be perverted to materialist ends; religion may also become the instrument of aggression and repression. Just as in primitive society the leader may be a medicine-man instead of a chief, in autocratic society a priest instead of a king, so in civilized society a Church or an Order may degenerate into a dictatorship, no less than a State or a class.

The three types of dictatorship contain the same essential features, but differ in technique. In national dictatorship the State is seized and directed to materialist purposes. In economic dictatorships the State is 'smashed',[1] and a rival State, 'the Dictatorship of the Proletariat', created to replace it. In ecclesiastical dictatorships the State is converted into an instrument of the dictators, who use it, either secretly, like the Jesuits, from the court or the confessional, or openly, like the Calvinists, as the executive of the Church.

Ecclesiastical, like other dictatorships, are bred amid anarchy—ecclesiastical anarchy or schism. Especially was this the case when Western Christendom, already corrupted

---

[1] Marx, supported by Lenin, *The State and Revolution, passim.*

and weakened by the Captivity at Avignon, the Papal Schism and the Graeco-Roman Renaissance, was torn asunder by Protestantism. Then two movements, aiming respectively at Reformation and Counter-Reformation, and each prompted by a lofty ideal, were both perverted by the temporary emergence of dictatorship.

The aim of Ignatius Loyola, himself a soldier, was to forge the sword of the spirit for the conversion of the infidel and the conquest of the heretic. The blade was to be formed of the true steel needed for the purpose—spiritual men of perfect obedience; and the instrument was to be wielded by men of great spiritual power, a General and his consultative Council. That this ideal is the reverse of materialist is illustrated by the fact that in the Founder's 'Constitutions' the word 'love' occurs much more often than the word 'obey'.[1]

It was thus an ideal, not of a materialist, but of a spiritual authoritarianism: it envisaged the willing following of the nobler spirits by the less. In that it resembled the ideal of Plato, whose philosopher-kings ruled his Republic, not by force, but by the spirit. It resembled the ideal of Christ himself, the Anointed Ruler who died upon the cross to show that his Kingdom was spiritual, not material. But this particular type of polity is liable to a particular disease: a spiritual authoritarianism degenerates into a materialist authoritarianism when, without losing its spiritual trappings, its soul becomes materialistic—when, in other words, it turns from spiritual to materialist ends. That is what at one period of its career happened in large measure to the Society of Jesus.

The Jesuits were the army of the Catholic Church. 'Ignatius Loyola was a soldier before he was a priest, and his Society was a military organisation for religious purposes, the conquest of heresy and infidelity.'[2] Soon, however, the armour of God was exchanged for the armour of earth. The Fifth General Congregation 'severely and strictly forbade all members of the Society to interfere in any manner whatever in public affairs, even though they be thereto invited';[3]

---

[1] Archbishop Alban Goodier, S.J., *The Jesuits*, p. 35.
[2] Wakeman, p. 42.
[3] 1593–4. *Encyclopaedia Britannica*, 11th edition, *Jesuits*, p. 344.

yet many Jesuits became the shadow-rulers in courts and society. The end was stifled in the means. 'Ambition and intemperate zeal' led some of them, 'aggressive and self-assertive', continually to meddle in politics: to concoct conspiracies, to embroil States, to kindle wars. In England they intrigued against Elizabeth in favour of Spain; in France they perhaps originated, and certainly joined, the League against Henry of Navarre; in Bavaria and the hereditary dominions of Austria they backed the Thirty Years War. Here was only too tempting a field for men who in forwarding the political interests of the Society gratified their personal ambition. 'As confessors of kings, as instructors of the young, as the conquerors of Empires and the founders of colonies, the Jesuits thought the world belonged to them and that their supremacy would last for ever.'[1]

Their dictatorship not being territorial, they found the sinews of war, not in agriculture, but in trade. Ignatius had forbidden the accumulation of wealth, and the Sixth General Congregation all pursuits of a commercial nature. Nevertheless their missionaries established trading stations in Asia and America, from which they drew vast wealth. The Society developed into a rich, active, and important commercial firm, with branch houses in many parts of the world.

Thirdly, in proportion as the Society thus degenerated, it became essentially totalitarian. The ideal of the soldier-Founder was easy to pervert. He had willed the obedience of spiritual men; in so far as the members ceased to be spiritual, the ideal became blind, not intelligent, obedience; not unity, but uniformity. Ignatius's perilous 'Letter on Obedience' (which Rome itself was within an ace of condemning) distinguishes three grades: outward submission to command, the identification of the inferior's will with that of the superior, and the third and highest stage, 'the sacrifice of the intellect'. The inferior is not only to will what the superior wills, but to think what he thinks. 'Let us all think the same way, let us all speak in the same manner if it is possible', he said, in words that lent themselves to the policy of the dictator; 'no novelties', he was fond of repeating.[2] Just

---

[1] Hassall, *The Balance of Power*, p. 296.
[2] Quoted *Encyclopaedia Britannica*, 11th edition, Loyola, p. 836.

in so far as obedience ousted the love on which the Founder so constantly insisted, the whole hierarchy, from the novice whose will was to be replaced by that of the superior, to the General 'standing in the place of God' and therefore commanding implicit obedience, with its spying and its revelation of the most secret thoughts, came to bear a fatal resemblance to the hierarchies of national and of Communist dictatorship.

On the whole, too, it was obedience, not intelligence, that the Society, thus decayed, required of the world. Ignatius lays it down as the rule of orthodoxy that a man should be ready to say black is white if the Church declares it to be so. The Jesuits taught the Greek and Roman classics, but frowned upon their spirit of free inquiry, as all dictatorships frown upon it. Hence their ablest pupils—Pascal, Descartes, Voltaire—were apt to leave them. They made no permanent impression on the cultivated peoples of China, Japan, and India. Noble as was much of their work in preventing the oppression of native peoples by the secular Power, their mission stations in Central and South America trained their converts to will-less obedience to the Fathers, with no vices but little life, with the consequence that when challenged by secularism and atheistical freemasonry their pupils lacked power to withstand the assault.

Morality, too, as in all dictatorships, was pressed into the service of Party. Just as Lenin was later to say that 'Communist morality is identical with the fight for strengthening the Dictatorship of the Proletariat', so Jesuit morality tended to become a casuistry that justified whatever served the interests of the Society. That the end justifies the means might be in itself an innocent proposition. As interpreted in materialist interests, it might justify any crime that was found convenient—just as, interpreted by the Nazi conscience, it makes the murder of Dolfuss a heroic act.

Kings, statesmen and peoples, churchmen and thinkers, alike revolted from such a system. In 1741 the wise and able Pope Benedict the Fourteenth issued a Bull in which he disowned the Society as consisting of 'disobedient, contumacious, captious and reprobate persons'; thirty years later Clement the Fourteenth suppressed them.[1]

[1] 1773.

If Loyola was a soldier, Calvin was a lawyer; and if Loyola tried to forge the sword of the spirit, Calvin aimed at defining the spiritual law. He envisaged a world in which all men should live obedient to the Law of God as administered by a Consistory or Kirk of which the State should be the instrument. Exactly as in the ideal of Loyola, the men of greater spiritual power were to direct the less great, the men of lesser spiritual power to obey the greater. Here again was the noble ideal of the philosopher-king and of the Anointed King himself.

But here again was precisely the same danger of degeneration, as men, not of spiritual but of materialist outlook, gained the direction of affairs. Just in so far as this was the case, the Consistory in Geneva, the Kirk in Scotland, the Congregational Churches in New England, became an ecclesiastical dictatorship, regimenting the lives of those within the fold and vigorously opposing religious freedom.

Thus in Geneva, the model city, every citizen was legally compelled to attend public worship and to partake of the Lord's Supper. It was an offence punishable at law to wear clothes of a forbidden stuff, to dance at a wedding, to laugh at Calvin's sermons. Banishment, imprisonment, sometimes death, were the penalties inflicted on unchastity, and a child was beheaded for striking his parents. Heretics were beheaded or burned. It was the duty of the civil authority to enforce the decisions of the ecclesiastical Consistory set up to regulate morals and Church affairs, and every sin thus became a crime. Such a system was a remorseless tyranny, destroying all individual liberty, persecuting all who opposed.

Like other dictatorships, Calvinism tried to expand through war. It nearly conquered France, fought in Germany, established itself in Hungary, invaded England. Nor did it neglect the power of wealth. In the rising commercial city of Geneva Calvin sought in the business virtues of industry and thrift a substitute for the monastic austerities of Catholicism, with the result that worldly prosperity presently came to be regarded as the special mark of the Grace of God, and mercy and charity as inappropriate to the poverty that signified His disfavour. As the Society of Jesus became a great trading firm, so capitalism flourished in the strongholds of Calvinism.

Neither Loyola nor Calvin, sincere and zealous as they were, sufficiently realized that the Kingdom of God 'cometh not with observation', but is 'within us'; both believed that unquestioning obedience to the commands of external authority—General or Superior, Consistory or Kirk—would suffice to promote the Purpose of God on earth. Hence a movement that began 'to the Greater Glory of God' continued largely to the greater glory of the Society; the saints predestined to do the Will of God soon found themselves predestined to do the will of Calvin.

Yet Jesuitism and Calvinism as a whole are no more to be identified with ecclesiastical dictatorship than are German and Italian civilization with national dictatorship: one lapse no more makes a dictatorship than one swallow makes a summer. Jesuitism is a noteworthy chapter in the noble volume of Catholicism, and Calvinism one not less noteworthy in that of Nordic civilization. In spite of its lapse, each stands out as a manful attempt to uphold Christian teaching in a secular age.

III

Throughout recorded history the greater part of mankind has lacked economic opportunity for the development of individuality, the fuller expression of personality. Slaves supported the ancient world, serfs the medieval, proletarians the modern; slave-owners, feudal barons, bourgeois capitalists have battened at their expense. In the march of civilization multitudes have fallen by the way, weighed down by poverty and oppression. In the early centuries of the Chou dynasty a Chinese peasant sang:

> In the days of the second month we all go out,
> Keeping up the skill of war;
> The one-year boars we keep,
> The full-grown ones are for the lord.
>
> The maidens gather piles of southernwood,
> Their hearts are sad;
> There is the fear of their having
> To go to the young lords.[1]

[1] *Book of Songs* (*c.* 900–600 B.C.). A. Waley, *Book of Songs*, p. 165. The version given represents the view of Ko Mai-jo and E. R. Hughes.

Early conquerors treated the conquered as slaves, as did the Christian conquerors of Africa. Serfdom tied the peasant to the soil, and left him to the mercy or the caprice of the landowner. But the evil reached its climax when the Industrial Revolution took men, women, and children from their homes in the villages and exploited them without pity or protection in mines and factories. The balance between country and town life was upset. The beauty of the old handicrafts perished. Capital and labour were divided into two camps. A slum-dwelling wage-earning proletariat arose. In the tropics 'labouring hands' were mercilessly exploited.

If the poor were hindered from self-expression, so to a great extent were women, for they too were economically dependent on others. In Islam and India the purdah and the veil excluded women from society; in Europe woman's place was the home, and 'children, cookery, Church' her tasks. Men rationalized this subjection. Women have no souls, said the Arab; women have sinful souls, said the Hindu; women come next to lunatics and criminals, said the law-books of the West. It has recently been suspected that these views overstate the case.

Meanwhile the possessive classes did little to mend matters. Aristotle defended slavery on the ground that some men are 'by nature slaves', and for them 'slavery is alike expedient and just'.[1] The Church did something to lighten the lot of the serf. Many of the best friends of the wage-earners—Wilberforce, Shaftesbury, Elizabeth Fry—have been persons of wealth and standing, inspired to love their neighbour by the teaching of the Bible. But on the whole wealth has shown an easy or a greedy indifference. In Athens Nikias, in Rome Brutus cared nothing for the sufferings of his slaves in the mines. In eighteenth-century England an irate Duchess, refusing an invitation to hear some Methodist preachers, wrote: 'Their doctrines are most repulsive, and strongly tinctured with impertinence and disrespect towards their superiors, in perpetually endeavouring to level all ranks and do away with all distinctions. It is monstrous to be told you have a heart as sinful as the common wretches

---

[1] Politics, i. 4, 5.

that crawl on the earth.'[1] *Laissez-faire* was licensed anarchy. In the United States Big Business, like an octopus, grasped in its tentacles labour, government, law, the very Churches: it became a group of warring dictatorships.

'The great captains of industry controlled the fabrication of profits with a military discipline: they waged campaigns against their competitors which needed only the actual instruments of warfare to equal that art in ruthlessness; they erected palisades around their works; they employed private condottieri to police their establishments; they planted spies among their workers; and they viewed, doubtless with satisfaction, the building of armories in the big cities where the State Militia would be housed in times of stress to preserve "law and order". Herbert Spencer looked to industry itself to supplant militarism; he had not reckoned that industry itself might be militarized, any more than he had seen that warfare might eventually be mechanized; but between 1890 and 1920 all these things came to pass.'[2]

'Political freedom', says the Final Report of the United States Commission on Industrial Relations, which was presented in 1916, 'can exist only where there is industrial freedom. There are now within the body of our Republic industrial communities which are virtually Principalities, oppressive to those dependent upon them for a livelihood and a dreadful menace to the peace and welfare of the nation.'[3]

The doctrine, illegitimate descendant of Calvinism, that riches signify the Grace of God sanctified capitalist dictatorship.

This economic disorder, half anarchy, half absolutism, paved the way to proletarian dictatorship. It was obvious that the oppression, poverty, overwork and unemployment of the many were largely due to the selfishness of the few who owned the means of production. Hence from time to time the remedy has appeared to be, not to convert or control this selfishness, but to transfer the ownership of land and capital to the commons. This process has involved, in theory, the Dictatorship of the Proletariat; in fact, the Dictatorship of a Leader and his Party.

[1] The Duchess of Buckingham: G. W. E. Russell, *Collections and Recollections*, pp. 74–5.
[2] Lewis Mumford, *The Golden Day*, p. 235.
[3] Quoted by R. H. Tawney, *The Acquisitive Society*, pp. 162–3.

Aristophanes anticipated Marx, though only to laugh at him.

'I am going to introduce Communism and universal equality (he gibes in *The Women in Parliament*). First of all, everybody's money and land and anything else he may possess will be made common property. Then we shall maintain you all out of the common stock with due regard to economy and thrift. Money won't be the least use to anyone, because nobody will be poor. When everything will be in common, what will be the good of keeping anything back?'

In feudal England Communism was not laughed at, but seriously proposed.

'Ah, ye good people (cried John Ball), the matters goeth not well to pass in England, nor shall do till everything be common and there be no serfs nor gentlemen, but that we may all be united together and that our lords be no greater masters than we. What have we deserved or why should we be kept in servage? We be all come from one father and mother, Adam and Eve; whereby can they say or show that they be greater lords than we, saving that by that they cause us to win and labour for what they dispend?'

There followed a great, but fruitless, peasant revolt.

The practical Chinese once, though only once, went so far as to give the plan a trial. In the eleventh century[1] Wang Anshih, the Prime Minister, wrote:

'The first and most essential duty of a government is to love the people and to procure them the real advantages of life, which are plenty and pleasure. In order to prevent the oppression of man by man the State should take possession of all the resources of the Empire and become the sole master and employer. The State should take the entire management of commerce, industry, and agriculture into its own hands, with a view to succouring the working classes and preventing their being ground to the dust by the rich.'[2]

Accordingly the State became the sole owner of the soil, and regulated agriculture. Tribunals were established throughout the Empire to fix the price of provisions and merchandise. Taxes were confined to the rich, and the burden of military service laid upon every family. The Classics were reinterpreted in this sense and education was made more

---

[1] A.D. 1021–86.

[2] Père Huc, quoted by F. R. Martin, *Communism in China in the XIth Century, Introduction.*

practical. The experiment failed, and China reverted to the morality and government of the Confucians.

The great Communist experiment has been reserved for recent times. Marx stands to Economic Dictatorship as Machiavelli stands to Political; he would win supremacy, not for the Prince, but for the Proletariat. His ideal society is one in which all property is held in common throughout the world, and wealth flows 'from every man according to his ability, to every man according to his need'.[1] As there will be no exploiting class—slave-owner or land-owner or capitalist—'all the forces of social wealth will be pouring an uninterrupted torrent', for no sense of injustice will limit men's efforts to produce it.[2] In such a society a State of any kind would be a superfluity, and there will be none.

But how to reach that society? Not very difficult: all that is necessary is to 'concentrate against the executive power all the forces of destruction'[3] and establish a new State, the Dictatorship of the Proletariat, in order to break up, 'shatter, annihilate the power of the State'[4] and all the bourgeois beliefs and institutions that belong to it—private property, class culture, country and nationality, marriage (in favour of community of women), family, education, justice, morality, religion.[5] 'Communism abolishes eternal truths, it abolishes all religion and all morality.'[6] This done, the Proletarian State will 'wither away',[7] and mankind be left in the 'highest phase of Communist Society' to enjoy the earth and its plenty.[8]

Meanwhile the Marxian resembled other dictatorships. His 'class war' was no metaphor, but real war, a war for the 'smashing' of the *bourgeoisie*. And it was to be world-wide, a World Revolution; World Revolution is an integral doctrine of Communism. The means was to be a combination of treachery and violence. The Paris Commune was the model, the First International the spear-head.

[1] Marx, quoted by Lenin, *The State and Revolution*, 2nd edition, 1925, p. 124.　　　　[2] Marx quoted ibid., p. 123.

[3] Marx quoted ibid., p. 36.　　　　[4] Marx quoted ibid., pp. 49, 71.

[5] Marx and Engels, *Manifesto of the Communist Party* (1848), 5th edition, 1888, pp. 17–21.　　　　[6] Ibid., p. 21.

[7] Engels, quoted by Lenin, *The State and Revolution*, p. 21.

[8] Ibid., p. 123.

Once more the old religion and morality disappear in favour of the new. More than most devisers of dictatorships Marx, a student of Hegel, is a philosopher. Hegel had said that the Absolute is spiritual, and the world of men and things its appearance or manifestation; Marx, inverting the idealism of his master, maintained that the Absolute is material, and that it manifests itself, not only in things, but in beings that appear to have a will of their own. Because the Universe is matter, it is mechanical; and earth, beasts, men, and society are therefore mechanical too—cogs in a machine and nothing more. Matter is all that matters—all that is; to-morrow we die.

It follows (this philosophy deduces) that the old morality and religion are so much hypocrisy, invented by the rich to bamboozle the poor. All that civilized man holds dearest—love of family, love of country, immortality, God Himself—are 'mediaeval rubbish'.[1] Religion especially is 'the opiate of the people'.[2] As in every other dictatorship—Legalist, Fascist, Jesuit—morality is the service of the interests of the Party. With characteristic lucidity Lenin told the Young Communists:

'We do not believe in eternal principles of morality, and we will expose this deception. Communist morality is identical with the fight for the strengthening of the Dictatorship of the Proletariat. It is entirely subordinate to the interests of the class war; everything is moral which is necessary for the annihilation of the old exploiting social order and for the uniting of the proletariat. Our morality thus consists solely in close discipline and in conscious war against the exploiters.'[3]

Two attempts have been made by the Bolsheviks or 'full' Communists to realize this ideal. In Russia 'Militant Communism' saw the greatest and most ruthless massacres the world has ever seen. The Inquisition, Judge Jeffreys, the Terror of the French Revolution pale before them: one million and three quarters are reckoned to have perished, but 'God alone knows the numbers of the slain'. Abroad, Lenin, emulating Kautilya and anticipating Hitler, invented

[1] Communist Manifesto 1848; Leon Trotsky, *Encyclopaedia Britannica*, 1926, Lenin, p. 698a. [2] Marx.
[3] Quoted by R. Fülöp-Miller, *The Mind and Face of Bolshevism*, p. 278.

a new technique of revolution that married subterranean cunning to ruthless violence. 'Germ cells' of Communism were to be secretly formed everywhere—in fields and factories and especially in the armed forces—to destroy the strength of the body politic; when the Communist bacillus had infected capitalist society, the moment would be ripe for 'class war': the Dictatorship of the Proletariat would then be set up, and the revolver of revolution shoot down the exploiters. The failure of Militant Communism showed that the economic paradise could not be reached without systematic planning. The Five Years Plan accordingly electrified industry, collectivized agriculture, and mechanized a vast Red Army. The virtual enslavement of political and other convicts made possible a dumping of timber and wheat in foreign markets below cost price, an 'economic offensive' intended to throw multitudes of foreign workers into the misery of unemployment; when the Communist seed had taken root in this favourable soil, it could be represented to the peasants of the Red Army that their comrades were calling them to march in and complete the Revolution. 'The soundest strategy in war (said Lenin) is to postpone operations until the moral disintegration of the enemy renders the delivery of the mortal blow both possible and easy.'

This aggressive policy involved a totalitarian dictatorship: the so-called Dictatorship of the Proletariat was as much the rule of a Leader and his Party, as little that of proletarians, as any Fascist dictatorship. In the Soviet Union political and economic freedom—of assembly, of speech, of the Press, of Trade Unions—is rejected in favour of government by Secret Police, whose organization might astonish Kautilya. Spies are in every factory, every regiment, every family—the son fears the mother and the mother the son. In the very Cheka and its successors spy spies upon spy. There are awful 'eradications of thorns',[1] in which the most notorious of the Old Guard Bolsheviks, after tortures that emulate those of the Inquisition, confess impossible crimes. Education was remodelled to train comrades who should know nothing save the pure materialism of Communist principles

[1] Kautilya.

and practice. The newspaper and the wireless, controlled by the Dictatorship, poured forth a ceaseless propaganda. All facts and opinions that might contaminate the purity of Marxism were excluded from the Soviet Union.

Everything possible was done to uproot the old morality and the old religion. Marriage was no longer sacred, and children belonged, not to the parents, but to the State. The Orthodox Church—dear to the Russian heart—was persecuted, her property confiscated, her churches destroyed, her priests dispersed, her monasteries closed, her teachings blasphemously parodied, her unity rent by artificial schism. Other religions were similarly treated. Atheism, ruthlessly promoted by an anti-God campaign, is the established creed of the Soviet Union.

Hitherto, however, the Dictatorship of the Proletariat has obstinately refused to 'wither away' into that classless, Stateless society in which Marx predicted that each would contribute according to his ability and receive according to his need. On the contrary, it is Communism that has withered and the Dictatorship that has grown more and more capitalist or even Fascist. Bolshevism has failed twice over. Lenin himself confessed the bankruptcy of Militant Communism after a three years' trial; his 'New Economic Policy' diluted Communism with capitalist individualism. After the first two years the Five-Year Plan was steadily nibbled into by capitalist principles—payment by results, private ownership on the farms, classical education, military ranks, and the like. By 1935 the Government of the Soviet Union was no longer Communist, but opportunist. Nor did the World Revolution expected by Lenin at the end of the World War establish itself. Hungary expelled a Communist Government, China a Communist Army; Italy, Germany, and Japan countered with a military dictatorship. The Soviet Union, disowning but directing the Communist International, joined the League of Nations. How far these changes indicate a change of heart, and how far they are a screen for Lenin's principle of crouching back to spring the better, none knows outside, and perhaps inside, the Kremlin.

In the Russian heart idealism reasserts itself. The vision

that inspires the nobler natures to carry out the Plans with so much energy is not the economic paradise promised by Marxists, but the moral Paradise of the service of man to man. If religion has not yet openly re-shaped itself, this devotion to God's image may well anticipate the re-birth of devotion to God Himself.

IV

The present impact of the West on the East is the last and greatest of a series of contacts. For some centuries before Christ not only silk and gold but (it would seem) arts and ideas travelled along the Silk Route between China, Persia, Antioch, and Rome. The invasion of Alexander brought in its wake Greek science, philosophy, and art; their influence permeated Central Asia, and reached as far as China. Later they inspired the Renaissance of Islam; and Islam returned the compliment by restoring Greek science and philosophy to Europe. For a thousand years Nestorian Christianity pervaded Asia; Marco Polo passed through many of their bishoprics on his way to China; Mahayana Buddhism seems to retain a strong Christian impress. Along the steppes and tributaries of the North, Mongols, Persians, and Russians have brought each other gifts.

Since the age of the Discoveries the impact of the West upon the East has steadily increased. They not only opened up new routes to Asia, but new Continents—Africa and America. To-day steamship and train, motor-car and aeroplane, radio and moving picture are bringing all places of the earth into ever closer contact. For evil or for good, the advance of technical science is making the most distant nations next-door neighbours.

Europe has not, on the whole, shown to its fellow Continents its nobler or wiser side. It has brought both its anarchies and its dictatorships, national, religious, and economic. Spaniards, Englishmen, and Frenchmen have fought each other in America and in India; they have exploited territories overseas in defiance of the rights of the inhabitants. The national dictatorships of Europe encouraged dictatorship in Japan. The Jesuits antagonized Japan and emasculated South America. The rivalries of contending missions

have rent the seamless garment of Christ. In an era of
unregulated capitalism Chartered Companies and private
traders have appropriated tropic lands, exploited coloured
labour, carried on iniquitous traffics in black slaves and white
slaves, fire-water and fire-arms. Communist Dictatorship has
troubled China and Mongolia and Sinkiang, vexed Mexico
and other States of the New World, and everywhere created
unrest or civil war. Such enterprises have made strange
bedfellows. Livingstone described the 'blessings of civilisation' as 'commerce and Christianity'. The Treaty of Tientsin
opened China to Christianity and the opium trade.

Even the most disinterested efforts have often been
blighted by the unconscious pride and egoism that characterize the materialist mind. Europeans have been so certain
that they themselves are right, the benighted heathen wrong
—that theirs is the only civilization, and Asia and Africa
merely backward and undeveloped Europe! Hence even
their benevolence has been blind. How little have the British,
faithfully serving the body of India, seen of her soul—that
great mountain of spirituality that rises to Heaven under the
glittering life of her bazaars and the stricken poverty of her
villages? Himself ignorant of India and misled by Indian as
well as British opinion, Macaulay wrote, in his Minute on
Education: 'The question before us is simply whether, when
it is in our power to teach this language—English—we shall
teach languages in which, by universal confession, there are
no books on any subject which deserve to be compared with
our own.' He is speaking of the languages of the Upanishads
and the Gita, Sankara and the Buddha, Kabir and the
Quran! 'What we spend on the Arabic and Sanskrit Colleges
is not merely a dead loss to the cause of truth; it is bounty
money paid to raise up champions of error.' For a century
the soul of India has been cramped through speaking an
alien tongue—English instead of the vernaculars.

Christian missionaries—Dominican, Jesuit, Protestant—
have often been as well-intentioned and as ill-advised as
officials. In ill-informed self-complacency they have striven,
not to learn from other revelations of God to men, but to
impress Christian doctrines on minds they did not understand.

The heathen in his blindness
Bows down to wood and stone.[1]

Hence, destroying but not constructing, they have often, in place of the old spirituality, created a void into which science has introduced secularism, or Marxism inserted materialism.

The non-European civilizations have been little able to withstand this onslaught. Alike on the material and the moral sides they were at the moment of impact weak. The Aztec and the Inca social systems were unstable, Russian Orthodoxy was indifferent to government, Japan in decay under an effete Shogunate, India in anarchy, China rebellious under a foreign dynasty, Arabia divided by blood feuds, Turkey a sick man, Africa primitive. The ancient doctrines of Tao and of Karma had degenerated in weaker minds into fatalism, and increased the difficulty of action. The East was as little able to resist the glittering toys of the West— its guns, its factories, its materialism—as Rome was to resist the fascination and temptation of the Greek East. Turmoil resulted in the one case as in the other.

The Westernization of every country advanced by well-marked stages. At first the saner and more balanced minds desired a marriage between the old learning and the new. Peter the Great called in Western technicians, not to supplant, but to instruct his Russians. Chang Chih-tung, the great Chinese Viceroy, desired to add the science of Europe to the ethics of Confucius, on the ground that 'Western knowledge is practical, Chinese learning is moral'.[2] Ram Mohan Roy, who played a somewhat similar part in India, dreamed of 'the union of Asia and Europe', in which neither should sacrifice its individuality, but both come together in the 'Church of Brahma', where all might worship the One God.[3] Then came a stage of indiscriminate admiration for everything Western, good or bad, suitable or unsuitable, in which young men, Westernizing 'intelligentsias', neglect-

---

[1] Bishop Reginald Heber.
[2] Gascoigne Cecil, *Changing China*, p. 267.
[3] Hans Kohn, *A History of Nationalism in the East*, quoted by J. F. C. Fuller, *India in Revolt* (1931), p. 67.

ing or despising their country's traditional interests and beliefs, greedily and without understanding swallowed the enticing novelties of the West. Finally the pupil turned against his master: the seizure of territory, a ruthless commerce, the arrogance of white towards coloured peoples, set the East in revolt against the West. The spectacle of the World War hastened the process. It destroyed the belief of the East in the vaunted civilization of Christian nations: it carried round the world the doctrine of 'self-determination' that President Wilson intended for Central Europe.

Hence the reaction of the East to the influence of the West has been on the whole of a materialist, not of a moral character.

The genius of Xavier gave the Jesuits a foothold in India, China, and Japan. But they disappeared from India, they were valued in China for their science rather than for their religion, they were driven from Japan as political rivals. Their mission stations in South and Central America disappeared into the wild, leaving behind, not a flourishing Catholicism, but too often a contempt for Christ and his Church. The Calvinists in North America did no better; their Red Indian subjects were exterminated, not converted. Both failed to awaken the spirit of Christ.

Nor did Russia, attentive to religion but neglectful of government, find the system she needed in Europe. German Empresses and German statesmen Lutheranized the Government of the Church and Prussianized that of the State. The Decembrists sought to introduce the inapplicable principles of the French Revolution; the Nihilists, an anarchy governed only by the laws of Nature; the Constitutional Democrats, Parliamentary institutions they did not understand and could not work. Marxism, that won the day, imposed an economic materialism directly opposed to the genius of Holy Russia.

National dictatorship has taken its worst form in Japan, where the militarists, rising from the ashes of the old military dictatorship, are now armed with the guns and battleships and aeroplanes of the West, to pursue a policy of naked aggression in Manchuria, Mongolia, China, and the Pacific. The 'unequal treaties' imposed by Great Britain and other Powers as the result of wars, partly of misunderstanding but partly also of greed, have provoked deep and natural resentment in China; India ultimately resented a rule that, well-intentioned though it was, ignored or insulted her magnificent culture. Contact with the West has largely destroyed the tribal systems of Africa, and replaced their primitive religion and morality with the scepticism and vices of the invaders.

Thus Europe has become the teacher of the world, as Buddhism once became the teacher of the East and Catholicism of the West. But there are two great differences. The Sangha and the Church could influence men only within strict geographical limits; science enables the modern Master to exercise his influence over the whole earth. Again, while Buddhist and Catholic taught an essentially moral and spiritual Gospel, the general tendency of modern Europe has been to teach a materialist gospel—an outlook upon life that causes rather the warfare of the animal than the peace of the man. Hence the general unrest—the faction and war —which this teaching everywhere produces; men are as ready to receive a new doctrine as they were in the past, but with results very different from those of salvation.

V

The danger in which the European civilizations and the civilizations that imitate them find themselves at present does not come from any principle opposed to popular government, such as autocracy. Although there has been for a time 'a surface trend away from the democratic representative form of government',[1] because of the need for security from anarchy at home or attack abroad, civilized men will not permanently be content to renounce all share in their own government. The danger comes rather from the materialist form of that government: whether from the nationalist form that arms State against State, or from the Marxian form that arms the poor against the rich. Each of these forms of society, being materialist, not moral or spiritual, struggles for wealth or power against the threats or attacks of similar organisms; the poor struggling against the rich and the rich against the poor, nation-States struggling against other

[1] President Roosevelt, *The Times*, 4 Jan. 1938.

States, the moral being forced in such circumstances against their will to follow the lines of biology in order to survive against the threats of their neighbours.

These anti-social forces of a civilization, warring with its Good, are the cause of its instability. The national pride or fear that refuses to co-operate with other States in the building up of its wealth is self-destructive, for it implies the existence of economic units which have, in fact, no reality; the laws of economics are at war with the spirit of aggressive rivalry that political and economic egoisms provoke. Hence the means that nations take to raise themselves are the means that bring them down; and in endeavouring to secure their societies men are, in fact, destroying them. The love of wealth and power has in the past enfeebled or destroyed many civilizations. The egoism that produced the Peloponnesian War ruined the Greek city-states, the vainglory that modelled itself on the Court of Versailles left Europe spiritless and exhausted, the temptations of the world impaired the religious strength of the Jews, the Caliphate, and the Catholic Church. To-day the same selfishnesses are threatening civilization itself. It is not only the voice of religion that in all these civilizations has announced the fatal issue of these passions. It is evident to common sense that to 'seek one's own' at the expense of others without consideration of justice or mercy, first isolates the selfish nation from other nations, and next—within the nation—isolates class from class and citizen from citizen, until in the end that solidarity which characterized and made possible the original communities of men disappears altogether.

It follows that the present unit of society—the self-centred nation or Sovereign State—is as little adapted to serve either the material or the spiritual needs of men as were the Materialist States of the past. The Peloponnesian War, for instance, and the civil factions of which it was the forcing-house, enervated the Greeks and left them disillusioned about the State and the Commonwealth—just as the victory over the Persians gave them confidence. There was no longer a feeling of strength and freedom and *joie-de-vivre*: they became (as Demosthenes said) talkers, not actors. Then came Philip and Alexander: the environment of the city-state was no longer suited to the development of their spirit, but they could imagine no other political form. It was not till Rome realized the peaceful unity which was the dream of Alexander that the human spirit was re-born in the cradle of security, and Catholic civilization began its life.

In much the same way the buoyant optimism of the nineteenth century has also disappeared. The World War, like the Peloponnesian, has brought dejection, disillusion, pessimism. In their perplexity the nations fall back upon dictatorships, throw-backs to discredited theories and institutions that both history and reason have disproved. War, whether of nations or of classes, threatens the nation-states with disruption; and rival armaments and rival tariffs are as useless against the one, as selfish capitalism and Communist materialism against the other. As their internecine wars enfeebled the ancients, so the wars and threats of war of the moderns are enfeebling them in their turn. Temporary successes may here and there cause a heady elation; but, in general, fear of life takes the place of faith in life, and the energies of men are bent on staving off destruction rather than on reviving the spirit of civilization. The Sovereign Nation State is to-day as out of date as the City State was once, and mankind is finding it as difficult as did the Greeks to think out a more appropriate political form for the spirit of man to dwell in.

The pursuit by modern civilization of selfish economic and political advantage is already bearing its fruits. Some states, by making territorial conquests, impoverish their own and other peoples. Others struggle no longer for pride and luxury, but for the bare means of life—not to attain power and wealth, but only security and a living. If this condition of affairs rests on the anti-social forces in civilized man, it also involves a further development of them; for hungry men form mobs, not States, and, like animals in the jungle, rather devour one another than build up social communities.

Such is the threat to civilization involved in the materialism of the present day. But it goes deeper; for, unless materialism is resisted, it makes the Good of a civilization a branch that ceases to bear fruit. The dictatorships try to standardize the nation and would like to standardize the world. But to standardize men is to distort their spirit into a shape it was not meant to bear. The loss of freedom robs men of their vigour; the denial of orderly liberty prevents the recovery of man. For man is a political animal; and if his egoism has destroyed the environment in which alone he can flourish, he has not the energy required to conceive any form of the Good, or, if it be conceived for him, the energy to understand and attain it. To deprive men of their right to think and meet and speak is to choke up the fountain of wisdom.

The various dictatorships are 'unified and consolidated', 'totalitarian', but on the wrong principle of synthesis. The unity imposed by a Leader and his Party from without defies man's social and religious intelligence and the culture in which this expresses itself. The only healthy and enduring unity is based upon a quite different principle, that has its being within men. Democracy unites the people in a liberty in which each man disciplines himself and respects his fellows. Theocracy holds them together by a more spiritual and still stronger bond—their love for God and therefore for man.

Here, then, is one alternative before the world. The competitive scramble for wealth and power between man and man, class and class, nation and nation, Church and Church, East and West, may be allowed to develop. In that case war or revolution will become uncontrollable, civilization will crash, and (as after the fall of Rome) it may be centuries before it rises again.

Nevertheless the very threat to the Good of a civilization stimulates it to oppose that threat. Virtue unopposed tends to ossification, but virtue opposed to new life and energy. The Materialist State (unless in Japan) has never been able to maintain itself in the past; it has always, sooner or later, issued in morality. The confusion of feudal China stimulated philosophic thinking and led to the establishment of a moral order under the Han; the very wars for which Kautilya and Chandragupta made such mighty preparation converted Asoka to the gentleness of the Buddha. The Peloponnesian War and the Sophists' attack led to the revivification of philosophy in the minds of Socrates and Plato, the breakdown of Imperial Rome to Augustine and Medieval Catholicism. To-day the selfish materialism of Machiavelli and Louis and Frederic, though still strongly entrenched, is challenged by a moral conception of the relations between State and State, class and class, individual and Government; by forces in favour of world unity, of economic co-operation, of democratic government, resting on self-discipline, good sense, and respect for one's neighbour. Sound philosophies and the actions that spring from them push through the materialist morals taught by dictatorships like snowdrops pushing through the frozen earth, like crocuses that displace paving-stones. If evil attacks, Good counter-attacks. And success gives new impetus: the plant grows the quicker as soon as it reaches the light. The great days of Athens followed the defeat of the Persian, the great days of Elizabeth the defeat of the Spaniard; if confusion stimulates thought, so does liberty. Evil must sooner or later succumb to the unquenchable need and desire of reason for Good.

There is then before mankind a second alternative, at the opposite pole from the first. Instead of drifting ruinward on the current of materialism, the present spirit of dissatisfaction may develop an energy of desire that will discover, not the material, but the moral and spiritual principle: the knowledge, love, and enjoyment of other men and of God. Other nations will then be regarded, not at all with a view to aggression, not primarily with a view to trade, but as objects of understanding, admiration, and good will; other classes as organic parts of the society to which we ourselves belong; other religions as sharers in the one revelation. The alternative to World-Ruin is World-Renaissance.

The Chou dynasty in China, the Roman Republic and Empire, Europe from the Middle Ages to the present day, all lasted some nine hundred years. Rome, as a political State, succumbed because she never permanently succeeded in substituting moral for material principles, but fell back upon materialism in her testing hour. China has maintained a lofty civilization because, abandoning Shang for Confucius, she adopted moral principles in place of material, and of them built a stable social structure. At the present moment the choice has come for Europe and the World. Which will they follow—the example of Rome, or the example of China?

III

THE MORAL STATE

ALL societies, whether primitive or civilized, are bio-logical organisms in the sense that they need material things, and that the material things one has another cannot have—both cannot eat the same loaf; though a civilized differs from a primitive society as a better adapted species differs from a worse. As developed into materialism with its struggle for existence this principle was very well evidenced in the history of Greece—each independent community struggling for survival or mastery against the rest; and is equally well illustrated in our own day—one nation now struggling against others for its own existence or power. This biological principle of society leads, as history shows, to the war of 'Nature red in tooth and claw', and is the inevitable result of the merely animal side of man's nature.

But there is in man a totally different principle from that which causes him, as a political animal, to maintain or extend his own political organism at the expense of other organisms. This principle is reason—the moral and spiritual principle—which, in direct opposition to the materialist, constrains man to throw down the walls separating class from class and State from State and no longer to bear arms, but to link them. In other words, there is in man a principle which enables him to surpass the principle of the Materialist State, with its end of power, and to attain to the principle of the Moral or Spiritual State, with its end of mutual service, springing from respect or love for man or God. If these two kinds of State be contrasted, it will be found that the one which makes success its end, yet fails to succeed; the other, which does not, yet achieves it. 'Seek ye first the Kingdom of God and His Righteousness, and all these things shall be added unto you' is therefore a truism; for the principle of the rational State is one which of its own nature results in peace instead of in war, in mutual aid instead of in mutual destruction: symbiosis replaces the struggle for existence. The essence of this principle, politically viewed, is in effect this:

there is in men a possibility of a more than animal kind—of a supernatural kind—which has only to express itself in society to produce at once and of itself a more than animal form of civilization—a supernatural civilization, a 'Kingdom of God' in men. In other words, there is something much more than the possibility of a 'mutation' in the history of society; there is here a new principle that can revolutionize the basis of society and ultimately perfect it. Men are to become men instead of animals: to die therefore that they may live. 'Unless a corn of wheat die, it abideth alone: but if it die, it bringeth forth much fruit.'

A society composed only of moral and spiritual individuals, and embracing therefore the whole race of men, would be neither primitive nor autocratic nor materialist, but beyond all these—though nearest to the Materialist State in so far as it involved in all men a sense of their individuality and therefore of their freedom, not now as egoists, but as sons of God and brethren one of another.

If history provides examples of Biological and Materialist States, surviving and taking new forms to-day, it is also full of examples of this opposite kind of society—superbiological States, moral and spiritual civilizations. And here a much greater range and variety is to be found. For, whereas the Materialist State seeks in the last analysis only the good of the body—lust and wealth and power—having in origin only that end, and treats all else, whether Nature or man or God, only as instruments to be pressed into the service of the body: the Moral and the Spiritual State pursues in every case a far vaster object—one or another aspect of Nature, or of man, or of God, objects that alone satisfy the spirit or reason of man as such—and subordinates the interests of the body to these rational ends. Unless it so disciplines itself, it cannot pursue them, any more than an individual can pursue them. If a nation looks upon Nature only with a view to manufacturing armaments or luxuries, it will clearly be blind to its beauty and its law; if it exploits its workers or the peoples of other countries in order to grow rich, it manifestly cannot love them; and if it thinks of God as a Patron or an Ally, it can have no real knowledge of the Divine

Nature: just as for an individual to make getting drunk or getting rich or getting on his chief aim will inevitably prevent him from the knowledge and love of men or things or God that are the joy of the reasonable spirit. In a word, egoism involves stupidity. Self-discipline therefore is the root of all true greatness in a State, the source of those contributions to human welfare that awaken the gratitude and admiration of mankind. For only in so far as it frees itself from these passions is it clear-sighted enough to perceive its true Good: whether this be men, or Nature, or God. This does not mean that it should annihilate the desires that have their origin in the body, but rather that it should make them the servants of the desires of the spirit; and just in so far as this is done all things are seen in due proportion, and the society itself becomes harmonious. When it is achieved altogether—when the desires no longer even feel rebellious—then the society is perfectly temperate. Thus bodily enjoyment and wealth and power are excellent things when they serve man's higher interests, but foolish things when they blind him to them. The good things of this world are really good only when they take their place in a larger world.

It follows therefore that, in a civilization as in a man, outward acts are merely symptoms, and that care is needed to ascertain the underlying motive. Are power and wealth sought for selfish or unselfish ends—to undo other nations, or to promote the general welfare? If they are used as the means of aggression in the jungle-struggle, they degrade a society to the level of the beasts; if in the service of man or God, they exalt it to the heights of the angels.

Thus, as civilizations free themselves from the blinding tyranny of the animal passions, they become clear-sighted enough to pursue the objects proper to man; and it is in accordance with the object they seek, the ideal at which they aim, as well as the degree of discipline they have attained, that civilizations differ, as it is that men also differ. The man of science seeks to discover the laws of Nature, the statesman to serve man, the saint to be one with God; and his object gives to each his own distinctive quality or character. In like manner civilizations differ according to the nature of their chief aim. The Chinese and the Nordics seek to reconcile individual freedom with social solidarity: Israel-Islam and Catholicism to bring the individual and society into accord with the Righteousness or the Grace of God; Hinduism and Orthodoxy to attain some understanding of the Godhead as He is in Himself, and of the relation of the soul to Him. In the first group interest centres upon the seen or sensible world, in the second upon the interplay of the Seen and the Unseen Worlds, in the third, upon the Unseen World. There are thus this-worldly civilizations, both-worldly civilizations, and other-worldly civilizations, predominantly practical, practical-contemplative, and contemplative respectively. Where the principal stress is upon man, States or societies may be called Moral: where upon God, Spiritual; where upon both, Moral-Spiritual. In addition, there are certain marginal civilizations in which these main cultures mix: Japan is largely compounded of Chinese and Indian culture, Iran of Indian and Muslim, Poland of Slav and Catholic, France of Catholic and Nordic. What these lose in originality they gain in diversity. The six fundamental civilizations, together with their derivative civilizations and with Athens, include between them the moral and spiritual development mankind has yet attained. All with dimmer or keener insight are gazing toward the same Object—the One Ultimate Reality. But each sees a different side, or the same side from a different point of view: and this difference makes each as distinct from the others as one plant or animal species is from another.

It is surprising that these distinctions should be so clear and sharp; they seem originally to be due to environment. In the temperate zone Chinese and Nordics must win a sturdy livelihood from land and sea; this activity, leading them to control Nature and to organize society, leaves little room for contemplation. In the sub-tropical regions about the Mediterranean Hebrews, Muslims, and Catholics, though far from inactive, yet have greater leisure for contemplation. Where climate runs to extremes—in the tropic heats of India, in the boreal snows of Russia—work is less necessary or for long periods less possible, and the mind turns inward to the things of the spirit. Thus man's place upon earth and sea determined (it would seem) the development of his spirit.

But what societies achieve, like what men achieve, always falls short of their aims and ideals, and that in varying degrees. At their very summit stand those rare visitants to earth, the God-inspired seers, whose vision fixes the ideals of the peoples and determines the character of their civilization: Confucius, Paul, the forest sages, Jesus. The great leaders of mankind absorb and develop their teaching in word and deed: statesmen and men of science in the this-worldly civilizations, prophets and priests in the both-worldly, saints and mystics in the other-worldly. Then come the lesser minds, honest but second-rate, who desire to preserve these ideals, but in their measure dilute, distort, deaden them in the process: politicians who think that laws and institutions will suffice without character, priests who substitute a code for prophecy and a creed for philosophy, disciples who revere the Teacher more than the Teaching. Below these are the masses of the people, men and women with still less spiritual power, but often permeated to a surprising extent by the ideal of the civilization they belong to; though this varies as the ideal is within the grasp of the ordinary mind, or only to be touched on tiptoe—the Chinese farmer is steeped in Confucianism, the Muslim finds it harder to surrender to the Will of God, the Indian peasant will catch only a glimpse of the meaning of the Vedanta. As a Chinese philosopher puts it, there are, besides the Master himself, Complete Confucians, Correct Confucians, Common Confucians.[1]

At the base of the mountain, often hidden in a subterranean darkness, much that is primitive and materialist survives in the Moral and Spiritual States, still undisciplined and intemperate; just as in the Materialist States much that is moral and spiritual struggles into light. The egoistic individual—the materialist—with all his undisciplined appetites is still active in every type of civilized society, moral, moral-spiritual, and spiritual. Lust has often corrupted the Chinese and greed the Nordics, worldliness and intolerance taint the Moral-Spiritual States, social vices have disgraced India and Holy Russia. Much of the irrational mass-thinking

---

[1] *The Works of Hsun-tze*, viii, translated by Homer H. Dubs (1928).

of primitive peoples survives in civilized society, and primitive beliefs corrupt Taoism and Buddhism, Judaism and Islam, Hinduism and Christianity.

Again, when circumstances become specially favourable to man's materialist impulses, States are likely at first to succumb to temptation. For instance, the discovery of the New World and of the sea-route to Asia set hitherto undreamed-of wealth within reach of Nordics and Latins, and the strain thus put upon the Nordic and the Catholic ideal was very imperfectly resisted. The new lands were looked upon mainly or largely as sources of raw materials, markets for products, plantations for settlement; the natives were cruelly exploited and Christian Powers did not scruple to import slave labour. But all this was a falling away from the true Nordic and the true Catholic ideal, with the result that conscience presently awoke, the economic advantages of Empire receded into the background, the rule of native peoples was seen to be a trusteeship, and colonial administration and development were lifted to an ethical level. From the first, Jesuit and Dominican missionaries nobly resisted the cruelties of the Conquistadors; Protestant Churches later awoke to the duties of practical service. Where Chartered Companies once reigned with little sense of moral responsibility, Indirect Rule or self-government now often reflects the true ideal, whether in British, Dutch, Belgian, or French territories.

The same is true of the moral-spiritual civilizations: in the face of temptation the Kingdom of God is apt to become the kingdom of this world. The Chosen People have too often abused the opportunities of wealth; the Caliphs became the head, not of a spiritual, but of a military Empire; the Catholic Church, victorious over the Holy Roman Empire, fell for a time into schism, corruption, and greed.

This predominance, sometimes of the materialist and sometimes of the moral strain in the rational civilizations, gives them a plasticity which is apt to obscure the permanent and essential ideal of each. But that ideal remains constant, the law that regulates change itself. Nay, more, it develops. Thus the graph of civilization, despite its innumerable ups and downs, shows as a whole during the last few thousand years a prodigious and rapid ascent.

It is, however, one thing to be untrue to one's ideal, as
from time to time all civilizations may be: quite another to
depose that ideal and to set up a materialist ideal in its place.
That is the case when a Materialist State for a time displaces
a rational civilization. Moral and spiritual progress can be
violently interrupted, just as the cooling of the earth's surface can be interrupted: from time to time the forces of
egoism burst forth with volcanic intensity. The anarchy and
dictatorship of materialist society rush fiercely up in the
midst of a moral or spiritual civilization, overflowing to-day
the high attainments of Japan and Germany, Italy and Russia,
as they once overflowed those of China and India. Only
gradually are the Hell-fires that underlie civilization cooled
and quenched; anarchy and tyranny flare up, to be once
more overcome by righteousness and right. Some day these
volcanoes will be extinct, and harmony and freedom of every
kind will flourish in the rich soil. Slowly the pearl is cleansed
of the mud; slowly moral and spiritual society emerges from
the materialist and the biological, as the biological once
emerged from the society of the apes.

Thus civilization is like a palimpsest, with the worse
written below and gradually fading out, though now and
again showing through in big patches; and the better above,
gradually being rewritten more clearly and permanently.

If therefore all societies, moral as well as materialist, are
to be interpreted by their aims and ideals and the measure in
which these are being achieved, rather than by the opposite
principle struggling within them, it follows that it is the
ideals aimed at, the achievements reached, and the developments that have taken place, in the moral and spiritual
societies that show their true character, rather than the
primitive and materialist elements that still hold them back.
Nations, like men, are to be understood and judged, not by
the chiaroscuro of their history, but by the dream that is in
their heart.

I. 1

When individuality first broke down custom in a people,
the predominance of materialist over moral individuals led
as a rule to social collapse—for instance, to the fall of Greece

and then to that of Rome. But China recovered from her collapse: her leaders and teachers set their faces against the vices of egoism and the disorder they generate, and converted their country from a materialist into a moral society. To conceive of individuality and order as consistent—of one as the instrument of the other—is the very root of the Chinese way of thinking. To universalize this reconciliation—to reconcile men, not only with one another, but with Nature and God—that was the work of her philosophers. The result has been the stablest, and on the whole the happiest, of human societies.

The Chinese have always been farmers, and it is natural that society and religion should have been largely influenced by husbandry and the seasons. The social unit was the family, whose members worked daily together in the endless labour of the fields. The father, the experienced farmer who directed them, was accepted as the natural head; and this recognition of his rightful authority was continued after his death in reverence for his spirit. Families spread into clans; and the clans were held together by a king. This incessant preoccupation and struggle with Nature is the root of the practical outlook of the Chinese people. Their family life is the foundation of their social organization.

Farming depends on Father Sun and Mother Earth, on rain and the passage of the seasons. Sun and Earth were living spirits, adored for the fertility they bestow. Cloud and thunder were roaring dragons; dangerous, yet also fructifying. The New Year or Spring Festival saw fecundity rites; seed-time and harvest became the great religious festivals. Over all was Heaven—Shang-Ti, the Spirit who protected the dynasty and the country.

The Shang dynasty,[1] which tradition said succeeded that of Hsia, like the Roman Republic grew more corrupt as it grew more complex. The primitive virtues of the State decayed, and with its virtues its customs, ceremonies, and laws. Then from the North-West came the conquering Chous, a simpler and more manly people. The worshippers of a 'vast, somewhat Impersonal, Over-ruling Deity' termed T'ien or Heaven, they drew from its sovereign 'Decree' the

[1] 1766–1122 B.C.

Prophet-like doctrine that 'rulers are appointed by "Heaven" for the purpose of ruling the world so as to bring about the welfare of men'.[1] King Wu and his brother, the Duke of Chou, were model rulers—transmitting the simple virtues of Chou, as Augustus fostered the Stoicism of Rome to resist the luxuries of the East. The Duke in particular seems to have laid stress on the importance of filial piety, and to have practised it himself in all its particulars. As the ages passed, the Chou kingdom expanded; but it became weakened by internal disorders, till in 771 B.C. a barbarian invasion threw it into confusion. Loyalty degenerated: the feudal chiefs warred against each other, and taxed and oppressed their peoples to fill their war chests and support their armies. It was this confusion that led to the emergence in the sixth century before Christ of Confucius, and (later) of Lao-tze, the two reformers who more than any other men have made China what she is.

What, Confucius asked, was the way out of the disorder, especially for the suffering commons? He answered: society can never be harmonious unless the people who compose it are themselves harmonious; or, conversely, when men and women are virtuous, their virtue will show itself in their social relations. The foundation of all reform is therefore education, but the right kind of education—education in virtue.

But what is virtue?

Confucius[2] was probably the Head of the Knights, learned in the *li* or rites of the 'ancients', the honouring of ancestors, the ceremony of Courts, the rules of family life. In his mind therefore *li* stood for any kind of outward behaviour that makes for the order and stability of the State. It was because these traditional customs were not faithfully observed that society was falling to pieces. But why were they not observed? Even before Confucius' day some Chinese thinkers were beginning (it would seem) to point out that their value lies, not in the outward act, but in the state of mind of which they are the outcome; somewhat as Catholic thinkers, while still regarding outward and visible signs as essential to the validity of the sacraments, came to emphasize that they do

---

[1] H. G. Creel, *The Birth of China*, p. 343.   [2] 551–479 B.C.

not bring the Divine Grace unless the will of the recipient is in a condition to receive it. Confucius insisted on the importance of this state of mind: 'True goodness (he said) springs from a man's own heart; it cannot be got from others.'[1] His great contribution was to point out that the only thing that made these observances profitable was *jen*, fellow-feeling, and that this feeling resulted in harmony or temperance both in the individual and in the State.

Jen is the identification of self with others—fellow-feeling, benevolence, humanity—'my heart as your heart' is its written character. 'What you would not wish done to yourself, do not do to others.' This benevolence is warmer than justice, since it includes, besides justice, a sense of equity and family love. This, in Confucius' view, is the essence of virtue. Virtue is natural to man. 'Is goodness indeed so far away? If we really wanted goodness, we should find that it was at our very side.'[2] This imaginative power to realize that others are human as well as oneself will make a man righteous in his dealings with them: 'the princely man knows the importance of righteousness, while the mean man knows the importance of gain.'[3] It will make him eager to learn and so sagacious: 'Love of goodness without the will to learn casts the shadow called foolishness.'[4] It will make him love sincerity or reality: 'I do not see how a man without sincerity can be good for anything.'[5]

On its negative side this fellow-feeling involves also 'obedience to an inner law of self-control';[6] for if a man feels for his neighbours, he will subdue the impulse of the natural man to indulge or enrich or exalt himself at their expense. 'He who seeks only coarse food to eat, water to drink and a bent arm for a pillow, will without looking for it find happiness to boot,' says Confucius. 'Any thought of accepting wealth and rank by means that I know to be wrong is as remote from me as the clouds that float above.'[7] Nor can a good man be a prig, proud of his own goodness: 'Your

---

[1] Lionel Giles, *The Sayings of Confucius* (1920), p. 62.
[2] Arthur Waley, *The Analects of Confucius* (1938), vii. 29.
[3] Quoted by Chiang Yee, *The Chinese Eye*, p. 85.
[4] Giles, p. 107.   [5] Ibid., p. 95.
[6] Ibid., pp. 39, 62.   [7] Waley, vii. 15.

goody-goody people are the thieves of virtue.'[1] Thus *li*, the outward behaviour that makes for the order of a State, springs from good feeling for others and the temperance in heart and act with which this is inseparably associated.

Humanity and harmony are thus the tonic and dominant of the Chinese character. From the days of Confucius onward the five cardinal virtues of China have been fellow-feeling or benevolence, manifesting itself as righteousness, practical wisdom and sincerity or a sense of reality, and based upon the self-control or harmony without which the more positive virtues cannot exist. He who attains them is the *chun-tze* or princely man. Their implications have been constantly developed, especially by Mencius.

All five are moral virtues, virtues that manifest themselves in social relations. Of these there are also five, all based more or less directly upon the life of the family. Foremost stands filial piety—the respectful affection of the child for the father. The wife is also to be loyal to her husband, the younger brother to the elder. Similarly the people are to be loyal to their King, as their Father; he is the Son of Heaven, the intermediary between Earth and Heaven, and the loyalty felt towards him is therefore specially sacred. Thus loyalty to the head of the house and loyalty to the head of the State are the two pillars of Confucian politics. In all four relations duty is reciprocal: the rule is to be in righteousness and benevolence, the submission in righteousness and sincerity: a ruler must rule in the interest of his people, a father must consider his son—'we ought to have a wholesome respect for our juniors'.[2] The fifth relationship is that between friends; and here the guiding principle is mutual encouragement in virtue.

Confucius was a realistic idealist, perhaps surrounded by young men who thought themselves budding statesmen. His practical mind therefore was not content with abstract principles; in the sacred dead of earlier ages he found his ideal of good men and good government. The great kings of old—especially the founders of the reigning dynasty, King Wan and the Duke of Chou—were themselves magnificent examples of what a ruler should be. Therefore Con-

[1] Giles, p. 108.   [2] Ibid., p. 101.

fucius preserved and would have his rulers study the records
of this Golden Age. There was (or so later men believed)
the Book of Changes or Divination written by King Wan.
There was the Book of Songs, much of it probably written
by the people themselves, a record of the joys and sorrows
of ordinary human life—young love, parting, love of the
land, oppression: it is the common people and their lives
that government ought always to consider. Practical peoples
have a care for history, and the Chinese had from very early
times recorded their history and preserved it in State archives.
Confucius would have this history studied too; and under
his influence the dim lives of very early rulers were later
embellished into those of 'Model Emperors', the 'sage kings'
of old. He preserved too the Book of those Rites and Ceremonies that maintain social order and harmony (later burnt
by the First Emperor). By way of contrast he himself made
a bald record of bad government—the feudal confusion of
the two and a half centuries that preceded him—the 'Spring
and Autumn Period'.[1] Apart from that he wrote nothing:
he was (he said) a transmitter, not an innovator. His teaching
is thus essentially conservative, though the tradition he
preserved continually received fresh development.

The secret of good government is personality—the example shown by the good ruler, the *chun-tze*. 'If the ruler is
good, the people will be good; not more surely does the
grass bend before the wind than the masses yield to the will
of those above them.'[2] The model ruler produces the model
people. 'A virtuous ruler is like the Pole-star, which keeps
its place, while all the other stars do homage to it.'[3] He
anticipates dictatorship only to repudiate it. Moral leadership is more important than laws and punishments: 'People
despotically governed and kept in order by punishments
may avoid breaking the law, but they will lose their moral
sense. People virtuously governed and kept in order by the
inner law of self-control will retain their moral sense, and
moreover become good.'[4] He understands too—what the
dictator does not—that to fight for moral ends is a virtue,

---

[1] 722–481 B.C.
[2] Quoted by K. Saunders, *Ideals of East and West*, p. 49
[3] Giles, p. 39.   [4] Ibid., p. 39.

for materialist ends a vice. 'The man of perfect goodness is sure to possess courage, but the courageous man is not necessarily good.'[1] 'Good government consists in providing the people with food to eat and keeping soldiers to guard the State', but more important than these material things is the moral element: 'without the confidence of the people no government can stand at all.'[2]

One requirement of government is notable. Confucius or his followers, like Thucydides and Socrates in a similar age of disorder, insist on the need for definition, 'a rectification of names'. The art of government involves clear acting and therefore clear thinking: 'Let the sovereign do his duty as a sovereign, the subject his duty as a subject, the father his duty as a father, and the son his duty as a son.'[3] The Confucian doctrine resembles the Platonic: each class has its own duty to perform. Hence the need for clarity of thought.

'If terms are not correctly defined, words will not harmonise with things. If words do not harmonise with things, public business will remain undone. If public business remains undone, order and harmony will not flourish. If order and harmony do not flourish, law and justice will not attain their ends, the people will be unable to move hand or foot. The wise man, therefore, frames his definitions to regulate his speech, and his speech to regulate his actions. He is never reckless in his words.'[4]

Thus Confucius' solution for the problem of his age—the social confusion caused by unsocial individualism—is the harmony of society that springs out of harmony in the souls of men and the mutual service that results from their fellow-feeling for one another. 'Our Master's teaching amounts simply to this: truth to oneself and charity to one's neighbour.'

With the spiritual as opposed to the moral virtues Confucius concerned himself but little. He knew indeed that the knowledge which is innate is higher than the knowledge that is acquired by study—which is all (he maintained) that he himself possessed; accordingly he would never talk about supernatural beings, holding that wisdom consists in attending to the needs of the living rather than to those of the spirits.

---

[1] Giles, p. 66.   [2] Ibid., p. 40.
[3] Ibid., p. 41.   [4] Ibid., pp. 43-4.

'Till you have learnt to serve men, how can you serve spirits?'[1] He believed in Heaven: 'At fifty I knew what were the biddings of Heaven. At sixty I heard them with docile ears.'[2] 'Does Heaven speak? The four seasons hold on their course, and all things continue to live and grow. Yet tell me, does Heaven speak?'[3] But the development of the idea of the harmony of the soul with the Universe itself he left to others.

Later Confucians (tradition said the Sage's grandson Tze-sze) took up the task, perhaps under the influence of the Taoists. The Classic called The Central Law[4] ascribes to the Sage an account of the Moral Law of the Universe, alike in itself and as it affects men and society. 'Tze-sze' philosophizes and universalizes the Chinese Good. It is Infinite, at once intimate and mysterious.

'The Moral Law is to be found everywhere, and yet it is a secret. The simple intelligence of ordinary men and women of the people may understand and carry out something of the Moral Law; but in its utmost reaches there is something which even the wisest and holiest of men can neither understand nor carry out. Great as the Universe is, man with the infinite moral nature in him is never satisfied. For there is nothing so great but the mind of moral man can conceive of something still greater which nothing in the world can hold. There is no place in the highest heavens above nor in the deepest waters below where the Moral Law does not reign. The Moral Law takes its rise in the relation between man and woman; but in its utmost reaches it reigns supreme over Heaven and Earth.'[5]

It is irresistible, governing both man and Nature. 'The Power of Spiritual Forces in the Universe—how active it is everywhere! Invisible to the eyes, impalpable to the senses, it is inherent in all things, and nothing can escape its operation. Such is the evidence of things invisible that it is impossible to doubt the spiritual nature of man.'[6] Truth and the moral laws established by China's ancient rulers 'harmonize with the Divine Order which governs the revolutions of the

[1] Waley, xi. 11.   [2] Ibid., ii. 4.
[3] Giles, p. 108 (translating 'God').
[4] J. Legge, *The Doctrine of the Mean*; Ku Hung-ming, *The Conduct of Life*.
[5] Ku, p. 23.   [6] Ibid., p. 43 (shortened).

seasons in the Heaven above, and fit in with the moral design which is to be seen in physical nature upon the Earth below. These moral laws form one system with the laws by which Heaven and Earth support and contain, overshadow and canopy, all things; by which the seasons succeed each other and the sun and moon appear with the alternations of day and night.'[1] This Law produces individuality, but at the same time harmonizes individuals. 'It is this same system of Laws by which all created things are produced and develop themselves, each in its order and place without injuring one another; by which the operations of Nature take their course without conflict or confusion. It is this—One System running through all—that makes the Universe so impressively great.'[2]

Thus if social harmony depends on harmony in the individual soul, that in turn, together with the harmony of natural phenomena, embodies the Harmony of the Universe itself. The opening passage in the Classic called The Great Learning[3] expresses magnificently this great inter-locking conception. This book, which strikes the keynote of Chinese education, begins: 'The Great Learning teaches to illustrate illustrious virtue'—that is, to show the goodness that is natural to man; 'to renovate the people'—by the example of goodness; and so, when both these aims have been achieved—'to rest in the highest excellence'. Then with Chinese clarity the whole process is stated first from without inward, and then conversely from the centre to the circumference.

'The ancients who wished to illustrate illustrious virtue throughout the Kingdom (that is, the known world) first ordered well their own States Wishing to order well their States, they first regulated their families. Wishing to regulate their families, they first cultivated their personalities. Wishing to cultivate their personalities, they first rectified their hearts. Wishing to rectify their hearts, they first sought to be sincere in their thoughts (to see things as they really are). Wishing to be sincere in their thoughts, they first extended to the utmost their knowledge. Such extension of knowledge lay in the investigation of things'—

meaning apparently the investigation of the Universe. Then

---

[1] Ku, pp. 54–5.　　[2] Ibid., p. 55.　　[3] Translated by James Legge.

step by step he repeats the idea from within outwards, beginning with the investigation of things and ending with a world of virtue. And he sums up: 'From the Son of Heaven down to the mass of the people all must consider the cultivation of the personality'—moral and spiritual education— 'the root of all else.'

The great edifice of Chinese civilization is founded upon these ideas. The Confucians especially developed the relation between man and society; Mo Ti, the Taoists, and the Buddhists the relation between man and the Universe. But it is this-worldliness that is fundamentally congenial to the Chinese character; down the ages the Chinese feel about Confucius, as the English feel about Shakespeare,

> Others abide our question, thou art free.

Mencius[1] develops the idea of the Moral Law as it shows itself in action—in good government. Man, he insists, is by nature good, because his nature forms part of the Goodness or Moral Order of the Universe.

'Water will flow indifferently East or West; but will it flow indifferently up or down? The tendency of man's nature to goodness is like the tendency of water to flow downwards. By striking water you may make it leap over your forehead; by damming and leading it you may make it go uphill. But such movements are not according to the nature of water; it is the force applied which causes them. When men do what is not good, their nature has been dealt with in this way.'

As Chu Hsi, the great Neo-Confucian of the Sung dynasty, put it, they do evil because there is 'a beclouding by creaturely desire'. In the saints and sages human nature is like a pearl lying in clear water; in the foolish and degenerate it is like a pearl lying in muddy water. 'To make manifest illustrious virtue' is to cleanse the pearl from the mud.

This view is wholly characteristic of the Chinese. Virtue and therefore social order do not seem to them adventitious to man, but his essence—just as political liberty and the virtues on which it rests do not seem to the Nordics adventitious, but essential. On the other hand the other-worldliness of the Buddhist and the Catholic are to these peoples ad-

[1] Fourth or third century B.C.

ventitious, because neither the Chinese nor the Nordic has on the whole a natural genius for religion.

Mencius may be called the founder of monarchical democracy in China. The conditions of a true democracy (as he saw it) are twofold; first, the rule of wise men with a philosophy of the Universe; secondly, a people ready to follow them—not with a blind obedience, but with a critical will of their own. His view is anticipated by the old Chinese saying in which he delighted: 'Heaven sees as the people sees, Heaven hears as the people hears.' The true characteristics of the great man are, 'when he obtains his desire for office, to practise his principles for the good of the people; and (he seems to be thinking of Confucius) when that desire is disappointed, to practise them alone'. A good government must be animated by a spirit of benevolence, and always pursue a policy of righteousness. Its aim must be, first, to make the people prosperous, and, secondly, to educate them. No one was fit to rule who could be happy while the people were miserable, or who delighted in war. Livelihood must be secured for all, and agriculture and commerce encouraged accordingly—by irrigation, free trade, light taxation. Next, schools of four kinds were to be established, in the villages and in the towns, for the poor as well as for the rich, that none might be ignorant of his duties in the various relations of society. A virtuous, prosperous, contented people, well-fed, well-clothed and well-principled, sitting under the shade of their mulberry trees, responding to the example of the 'Minister of Heaven, and flocking to him as to their parents' —that was the ideal of Mencius, as it has been the Chinese ideal of government and society down the ages.

Hsun-tze[1] on the other hand, learning from the Legalists, added some practical touches to this idyllic society, and so prepared the Confucian teaching for acceptance and application by the Han dynasty. Living in the last dreadful days of feudal depravity, as Augustine lived in the welter of the fall of Rome, Hsun-tze, like Augustine, maintained that human nature is originally bad—a heresy that has cost him his place in the Confucian canon, as Gotama's rejection of

---

[1] Born 340 B.C. See H. H. Dubs, *The Works of Hsun-tze*; *Hsun-tze the Moulder of Ancient Confucianism*.

the Brahmins cost him his place in Hinduism. But just as Augustine held that man could rise through the Grace of God within him, so Hsun-tze held that he could rise by the virtue latent in human nature.[1] The 'original man' becomes in turn the 'Common', the 'Correct', and the 'Complete Confucian', corresponding respectively to the profligate, the incontinent, and the continent man of Aristotle, and finally to his temperate man or *phronimos*.

Owing to this original badness Hsun-tze saw too, like the Legalists, that law was necessary; but unlike them he saw that law in itself was not enough—what mattered was the equity of the Law and the personality of the officials who administered it. Law, supplementing the unorganized 'virtue' of Confucius, derives its sanction from three sources: the Moral Law of the Universe itself, its formulation by the ancient sage-kings, and its promulgation by living 'princes and teachers'—the powers that be. Under the Han the Classic called The Book of Rites, hardly recoverable after the burning of the books by the First Emperor, was re-edited by the Confucians in the spirit of Hsun-tze, and Chinese law was thus placed on an ethical basis. But the Chinese have always laid greater stress on morals than on law, on the good ruler than on Habeas Corpus.

'Princes and teachers': the education of the ruler (Hsun-tze means) is indispensable to good government. 'The rule of civilized conduct and ritual and justice are the beginnings of good government; the man of honour is the beginning of the rules of ritual and justice. To carry them out, to practise them, to study them, to love them greatly, this is the beginning of the man of honour.'

It was the adoption of these principles by the scholar-rulers of the Han dynasty and their continual development in later ages that has made the history of China so great. For they were at the same time lofty yet within the reach of ordinary humanity.

Mo Ti[2] is the prophet of China, as the Confucians are its statesmen and Lao-tze and Chuang-tze its mystics. If for

---

[1] K. J. Spalding in *The Individual in East and West*, p. 71.
[2] 470–391 B.C. See Y. P. Mei, *Works of Motse*; *Motse, Rival of Confucius*.

Confucius love of mankind grew from love of the family, for Mo Ti love of the family grew from love of mankind. On a 'universal' love that issued in righteousness Mo Ti laid the foundations of his ideal society. Like the Nordics he found the bond of the State in the relation between men as men, though the relation he advocated was of a more spiritual and therefore of a closer kind. Only when men love one another can there be righteousness among them, and to him, as to the Hebrew Prophets, this righteousness was itself a realization on earth of the Divine Righteousness, the Will of Heaven. He anticipated Jesus again in seeing that righteousness would result in peace and prosperity: 'Seek ye first the Kingdom of God and His Righteousness, and all these things shall be added unto you.'[1] Love is the means to righteousness, and righteousness the means to prosperity; Mo Ti therefore is no more a utilitarian than Jesus, for what both aim at is love and righteousness; love and righteousness are the end of their doctrine, material good the consequence of it. 'When there is universal love in the world, it will be orderly; when there is mutual hate, it will be disorderly.'

The Chinese were families of farmers; and if the family was the root of Confucianism, farming favoured the spread of Taoism. For the farmer continually observes the face of the sky, and particularly the constant round of the seasons; and it was this larger and loftier interest that helped the development of the doctrine of the Tao.

To earlier Chinese thinkers Tao had seemed the orderly 'Way' in which Nature and human nature when true to themselves proceed. But Lao-tze, like Spinoza, perceived a further and deeper truth: though the procession moves, the Way remains. Beneath the changes of Heaven and Earth and of the things and men that spring from them, is Something That changes not, That knows no bounds and no conditions, That is the Source and Significance of all else.

> We can but call it the Mystery,
> Or rather the 'Darker than any Mystery',
> The Doorway whence issued all Secret Essences.[2]

---

[1] Matthew vi. 33.
[2] Arthur Waley, *The Way and Its Power* (1934), chapter i.

The Way is like an empty vessel
That yet may be drawn from
Without ever needing to be filled.
It is bottomless; the very progenitor of all things in the world.[1]

     Formless yet complete
It existed before Heaven and Earth;
Without sound, without substance,
Dependent on nothing, unchanging,
All-pervading, unfailing.
One may think of it as the Mother of all things under Heaven.[2]

Lao-tze, again like Spinoza, derives his ethics and his politics from this Infinite Substance.

     It is there within us all the while.[3]

First, Tao is Infinite, and therefore man should have an all-embracing love.

The ten thousand creatures owe their existence to Tao and it does not disown them.

Tao, though It covers the ten thousand things like a garment,
Makes no claim to be master over them.[4]

Man's love, like Tao, should embrace good and bad alike. The sage

     Uses the heart of the people as his heart.
     Of the good man he approves,
     But of the bad he also approves,
     And thus he gets goodness.[5]

Secondly, Tao has unity, and man should have a corresponding simplicity:

     'Give men simplicity to look at,
     Give them selflessness and fewness of desires.[6]

Lastly, and chiefly, Tao is Eternal, Unchanging, and man should likewise be tranquil, calm, unmoved. Lao-tze says with Isaiah, and for the same reason: 'In quietness and in confidence shall be your strength.'[7] He would not have sympathized with any motionless posturing: the good man, like Tao, is vigorous in action, but undisturbed within, for

[1] Ibid. iv.   [2] Ibid. xxv.   [3] Ibid. vi.   [4] Ibid. xxxiv.
[5] Ibid. xlix.   [6] Ibid. xix.   [7] Isaiah xxx. 15.

his mind itself is part of the Changeless Tao. Only he who knows this inward peace—who has within him the Peace of the Eternal Itself—can act vigorously and wisely in outward things; and there too he will not interfere unnecessarily, but will trust largely to the force of example and the awakening of calm by calm.

> The Sage relies on motionless activity,
> Carries on wordless teaching,
> But the myriad creatures are worked upon by him.[1]
> By this very inactivity
> Everything can be made active.[2]

This is especially the case in government:

> The more prohibitions there are,
> The poorer the people will be.
> The more laws are promulgated,
> The more thieves and bandits there will be.[3]

'Ruling a large kingdom is like cooking a small fish',[4] he says wittily; act, but without fuss. The worst form of action is war:

> If Tao prevails upon earth,
> War-horses will be used for agriculture.
> If Tao does not prevail,
> War horses will be bred even on the sacred mounds.[5]

Like Jesus, Lao-tze holds that greatness lies, not in self-assertion, but in humility.

> How did the great rivers and seas get their kingship over the hundred lesser streams?
> Through the merit of being lower than they.
> Therefore the Sage
> In order to be above the people
> Must speak as though he were lower than the people.
> In order to guide them
> He must put himself behind them.[6]

> The man of highest power does not reveal himself as a possessor of power;
> Therefore he keeps his power.[7]

---

[1] Waley, *The Way and Its Power*, ii.   [2] Ibid. xlviii.
[3] Ibid. lvi.   [4] Ibid. lx.
[5] Ibid. xlvi. Cp. Giles, *Sayings of Lao-tze*, p. 26.
[6] Ibid. lxvi.   [7] Ibid. xxxviii.

This is true, not only of individuals, but of States. 'If a great kingdom humbles itself before a small kingdom then it will win over that small kingdom; and if a small kingdom humbles itself before a great kingdom, it will win over that great kingdom.'[1] In fact, 'the highest good is like that of water. The goodness of water is that it benefits the ten thousand creatures; yet itself does not scramble, but is content with the places that all men disdain. It is this that makes water so near to the Way.'[2] The lowest place is the ocean; but the ocean is Infinity.

On the other hand, when rulers and people are ignorant of Tao, then they are unlike it. This ignorance is due to the disproportionate demands of the body—its lusts, its avarice, above all, its pride in force and power—in a word, to materialism. 'Men feed life too grossly.'

They wear patterns and embroideries,
Carry sharp swords, glut themselves with drink and food, have more
    possessions than they can use.
These are the riotous ways of brigandage; they are not Tao.[3]

Fame or one's own self, which matters to one most?
One's own self or things bought, which should count most?
Be content with what you have and are, and no one can despoil you.[4]

To be content with what one has is to be rich.[5]

Heaven is eternal, the Earth everlasting.
How come they to be so? It is because they do not foster their own
    lives;
That is why they live so long.
Therefore the Sage
Puts himself in the background; but is always to the fore.[6]

Lao-tze says with Jesus: 'If any man desire to be first, the same shall be last of all, and the servant of all.'[7]

Thus Lao-tze, like other Chinese sages, was concerned for the evils of his day; but he measured them, not merely by the principles of social morality, but in themselves as sins of the soul, sins against the Supreme Principle. Like Plato, he develops the philosophical side of the ruler—to such an

---

[1] Ibid. lxi. Cp. Giles, *Sayings*, p. 34.
[2] Ibid. viii.   [3] Ibid. liii.   [4] Ibid. xliv.
[5] Ibid. xxxiii.   [6] Ibid. vii.   [7] Mark ix. 35.

extent that the ruler's interests pass beyond the bounds of
the State into the Universe as a whole, portending the appearance in philosophy of individuals who are not citizens
of a State only, but of the Universe. The end of man is to
live in harmony with Tao, the Ultimate Principle; social
harmony is but an incidental result. If Confucius is the
Paul of the Chinese spirit, the founder of a society on earth,
Lao-tze is its John. The world in its perfection is the Logos;
but behind the Logos is the One, Infinite and Eternal, the
Ineffable, That has no name. The mystical summit of Taoist
thought was climbed by another Taoist mystic, Chuang-
tze[1]; the soul that is at one with Tao is an 'I that has lost
its me'.

It is often supposed in the West that China has always
lived in isolation; but nothing could be further from the
truth. Along the Silk Route that crossed Asia came the
wealth and art and thought of Persia, Greece, and Rome;
the Han dynasty extended the knowledge and the Tang the
frontier of the Empire as far west as the Caspian. In the
seventh century Japanese and Koreans, Zarathustrians and
Manichaeans, Muslims and Nestorians gathered in the
brilliant capital of the Tang. The Pekin of Kublai Khan saw
the meeting of Mongols and Muslims, Armenians and
Italians—merchants like the Polos, missionaries like Monte
Corvino. Under the Mings came the Jesuits, welcomed by
the scholar officials for their knowledge of mathematics and
astronomy; under the Chings the British East India Com-
pany settled outside Canton, and presently came a representative of the British Crown. China the creative has learnt from
many lands.

But of all the foreign influences that have touched her in
the past that of the Buddhists has been the greatest. As
the Han rule broke down and Confucian morals weakened,
Indian missionaries came in numbers, and monarchs, ministers, and people welcomed them with Chinese tolerance and
comprehension. The world of the senses (they told the
practical Chinese) is only apparent; the realities are personal
merit and the Buddha's compassion. Yet there were points

[1] 335–275 B.C.

of contact. If Taoism had its Islands of the Blest, Buddhism had its Western Paradise: if the heart of Taoist philosophy was tranquillity, the Buddha's Path of Perfection ended in a mystical concentration. Of all the Schools of Buddhism two made the deepest appeal: Ching-tu, the Pure Land, where dwelt Amitabha the All-Father, and Chan or Contemplative Buddhism, rooted in the Dharma as Taoism is rooted in the Tao.

Thus while Confucianism developed the ethics and politics in which the genius of the Chinese naturally expresses itself, Taoism and Buddhism sought to apprehend that unseen world without which reason feels itself incomplete and therefore restless. The three together form the established religion of China. A noble and comprehensive philosophy is her first and central contribution to mankind.

I. 2

As Quesnay pointed out, China was the first civilization to discover that the true foundation of government is education.[1] The purpose of education, as The Great Learning proclaims, is moral: and for upwards of two thousand years—from the rise of the Han to the collapse of the Ching—the rulers of China have been chosen by examination for their knowledge of individual, family, and public virtues, of the view of the Universe on which these rest, of the good government and happiness that issued from them under the sage kings of old, and of their break-down in the disorders of the Spring and Autumn Period: in a word, for their knowledge of the Confucian Classics. The Tang dynasty further required that they should be able to write poetry, and to this the Sung Emperor Hui Tsung, himself a painter, added painting: candidates were expected to illustrate a phrase or line from the Classics or some well-known poem.

Thus the Government of China became an aristocracy of character and culture. The choice of rulers for their knowledge of ethics, personal and political, expressed in terms of the arts as well as of administration, became the chief means of holding the vast Empire together, and proved one of the most successful devices ever invented by man. Not in vain

[1] Chang Peng-chun, *China at the Crossroads*, p. 151.

did Confucius and Lao-tze both rely on the force of example. The Chinese have always been more eager to obey a governor who was a good poet or a good painter; Britons and Americans do not often seek these qualifications in their public men.

But virtuous and cultured rulers could have done nothing without a people in a measure virtuous and cultured too. If Chinese administrators have since the days of the Han been chosen for their knowledge of the ethics of Confucius, his polished sayings have become household words in the mouths of the common people—the 'sons of Han'. 'Hundreds of thousands of scrolls and tablets in every corner of the Empire' repeat his moral maxims.[1] The Chinese peasant and his family may have been illiterate through the ages; but uneducated they were not, for they have been brought up to believe in the essential goodness of human nature, which is naturally orderly and kind and only unnaturally selfish and anti-social; to see that this inner harmony expresses itself in a harmonious and happy family life and in the larger society that is founded on the family. Confucius' Sayings, The Central Law, The Great Learning and Mencius are learnt by heart. To this day the pupils in many a Chinese School may be heard chanting: 'What the Great Learning teaches is to illustrate illustrious virtue, to renovate the people, and to rest in the highest excellence'—words that, graven on their hearts from childhood, will unfold their meaning as life itself unfolds. Until recently the many branches of a swiftly multiplying family have lived together in a house of many courts; and just as in a dictatorship the common life of the camp and the army is the school of discipline, so in China the common life of the large family has been the training-ground of the Confucian virtues of harmony and humanity—with this difference, that army life is directed towards war, and family life towards peace. In the crowded home the Chinese learnt from early childhood respect for his superior, tolerance for his neighbour, kindness for all. 'Peaceableness brings good luck', 'the hundred patiences', 'help thou thy brother's boat across, and lo! thine own hath reached the shore', are familiar proverbs.

[1] Giles, *Sayings of Confucius*, p. 19.

Families of the same name form a single clan, the unit of local administration, for which the Confucian teaching, no less than the remoteness of the Central Government, have made the Chinese singularly apt. Each clan had its funds, to be used for roads and bridges, payment of the local tutor and the like. After the Revolution these purposes were extended to cover hospitals and private schools. And as the people looked to the heads of their clan in family affairs, they looked to the Elders in the affairs of villages and towns. The public-spirited man, the shrewd man, and always the scholar (unless he were a fool) were chosen as Elders.

The Confucian virtues created the best elements in the national life. The Chinese farmer is famous for his industry, the Chinese merchant for his honesty. The courtesy of the Chinese is of the tissue of their minds. And a people who are so temperate and kindly are naturally gay, light-hearted, laughter-loving. They love a party and a cup of wine; they have a keen sense of humour, very much like an Englishman's.

Because the Chinese are civilized and intelligent, they love peace and hate war. 'Within the four seas all are brothers', said a disciple of Confucius; 'the greatest conquerors are those who overcome their enemies without strife', said Lao-tze. Until Japan became a menace, a Chinese father would no more think of making his son a soldier than a Western father would make his a scavenger; fighting was the lowest of all callings, and soldiers were classed with criminals and prostitutes. As the proverb puts it: 'Good iron is not used for nails, and good men are not used for soldiers.'

On the other hand, Taoism and Buddhism, great and beneficent as their influence has been, have proved on the whole above the reach of the matter-of-fact Chinese. Lao-tze is the Spinoza of the East, and Spinozas have not many to understand them. Ethically, the Confucians criticized him as unpractical: if we are to requite injury with kindness (Confucius was reputed to have said) with what shall we requite benefits?[1] Taoists themselves have seldom risen to the heights of Lao-tze and Chuang-tze. If Confucianism is the guide of prosperity, Taoism is the refuge of failure—of

[1] Giles, p. 67.

personal misfortune, of national disaster. It has given the unlucky, not merely endurance in suffering, but the capacity to pluck happiness out of hardship. Like their Master, who (legend said) rode forth on an ox into the wilds of the West, they take refuge among the streams and the mountains, and there, communing with Nature, find a tranquillity that the world can neither give nor take away: a serenity, a mellow calm, that, far though it be below the bliss of the soul at one with Tao, uplifts them above the heart-ache of the world. In lower minds Taoism degenerates into an easy acquiescence and care for creature comforts, while on the lowest level of all it early admitted a flood of primitive superstition. What was meant symbolically was taken literally, as Jesus' 'gnashing of teeth' was taken to refer to real teeth.[1] Thus the saying: 'If a man is possessed of Tao, he endures for ever: though his body perish, yet he suffers no harm,'[2] was interpreted by the animal mind as meaning 'a deathless man' in flesh and blood, endowed with supernatural powers; and herbalism, alchemy, geomancy, and other magic arts speedily corrupted Lao-tze's teaching. Fairy tales set the herb of immortality in the Islands of the Blest.

If Taoism failed partly, Mo Ti failed almost wholly; his ideal was too high for the China of his time, and his Church endured only for a century. The Confucians preached a lower doctrine—the moralized clan—a doctrine that the Chinese masses could grasp and hold. Of late Western influences have lapped over China, but they have not changed the Chinese spirit. Her rulers have realized that scientific education must supplement, not replace, moral education. Sun Yat-sen foresaw that reconstruction must be gradual: that 'military operations' must first restore order at home and defend 'the People's Sovereignty' abroad; that a period of 'political tutelage' must prepare for the goal of 'the People's Government'; and that meanwhile 'the People's Livelihood' must be restored. With these three principles, given spiritual and moral energy by the New Life Movement, General and Madame Chiang Kai-shek and their colleagues have carried out a noble and singularly successful reconstruction, inspired by the profoundest of all principles.

[1] Matthew viii. 12.   [2] Giles, *Sayings of Lao-tze*, p. 24.

'These rebels (wrote the kidnapped Generalissimo when in hourly expectation of death) are very dangerous people. I am determined to fight them with moral character and spiritual strength and with the principles of righteousness.'[1]

I. 3

Nothing so well illustrates how deeply the three faiths have entered into the soul of China as the passion for beauty of every kind that pervades her people. The Chinese dearly love and honour the things of Nature, both because natural objects inspire harmony and tranquillity, and because they reveal a deeper and mysterious Reality. They love them, not with a vague yearning, but with an every-day allegiance[2] —a love that is an ever-flowing stream, not a gush of water turned on at a tap. Students will linger at evening on the banks of a river, and the loveliness of the sunset will move them to tears; sometimes they will harken to the silence, sometimes embroider it with the flute. Flowers are a necessity for this people; chrysanthemums beautify even the prisons.

Art—from the humblest utensils to the highest master-pieces—is a great mirror reflecting Chinese civilization in all its aspects. Jades, bronzes, fabrics, porcelain, reveal a loveliness not diminished but enhanced by the sobriety that tempers their magnificence. How different from the un-thinking or vain-glorious art of Versailles! The scrolls and rolls that carry Chinese pictures are silken miracles of har-monious contrast; the placing of the vermilion seals is a matter of the nicest care. The stately beauty of rites and ceremonies fosters a corresponding order and beauty in the soul, as the religious songs and dances of India foster the spirit of religion. Confucius, himself a musician, anticipated Plato in saying that music was necessary to the making of a harmonious character. The twin sisters, painting and poetry, show even more clearly how Chinese art is rooted in philo-sophy. Scenes from daily life, dainty idyls of Confucian kindness and contentment, recall the Book of Songs: children playing in a courtyard, women gathering flowers, court

[1] General Chiang Kai-shek in *China at the Crossroads*, p. 176.
[2] Ann Bridge, *Peking Picnic*, p. 216.

ladies receiving admonition. Chinese poetry is full of such
scenes:

> Little girls ought to be daintily fed:
> Mrs. Tsao, please see to this!
> That is why I have packed and sent a silver spoon;
> You will think of me and eat up your food nicely.[1]

The portraits of illustrious persons—poets, philanthropists,
heroes, scholars—do not flatter the sitters, but 'transmit
spirit'—generally as memorial pictures, commissioned for
edification or for ancestral 'worship'.[2] The force of example
must not perish with death.

The loftiest extant works are the paintings inspired by
Taoism. The great Sung landscapes to the seeing eye
express the Infinite and Mysterious Source of the stream of
life, the Reality that underlies and is embodied in Heaven
and earth and all finite things. Hence the unique emphasis
laid on empty space, the absence of any other background,
the minute details of the foreground. Hence, too, the first
canon of Chinese painting, 'rhythmic vitality': the whole
picture and its every detail should display the harmonious
life that flows from the Infinite Source of all life. And
because all things proceed out of Tao the Chinese like them
better as Tao made them than as man 'improves' them: a
twisted tree is to them more significant than a park specimen,
a plain lady more attractive than a palace beauty.[3] All things
are sanctified by their Origin.

To the Taoist, unlike the Greek, man is not 'the measure
of all things', but one among countless orders of beings
through which the Tao-born life continually streams. Hence,
notwithstanding Confucian figure-painting, the human body
is little emphasized, and never in the nude; sculpture, its
natural medium, is not an art, but a craft. When a Chinese
wants to paint a Sage he will show a tiny figure in the midst
of a great landscape; it is not the man's body he is painting,
but the contents of his mind. What the Taoist loved above
all else were those 'mountains and streams' (as the Chinese
call landscape), often mysteriously scarved in mist, hushed

---

[1] Po-chui A.D. 772–846; Waley, *A Hundred and Seventy Chinese Poems*,
'The Silver Spoon', p. 156.

[2] Chiang Yee, *The Chinese Eye*, p. 68.   [3] Ibid., pp. 11–13.

in snow, bathed in moonlight, amid whose solitude, escaping from the world, he was wont to find his soul and his tranquillity. They are looked at from above—as they proceed out of the Tao. From landscape the Taoist painter developed those 'bird and flower paintings' which uniquely reveal the majesty of simple things. Western 'still life' shows a dead bird, cut flowers in a vase, a medley of objects, with a background confining them within the space of a yard or a foot. To the Taoist painter flowers and trees, insects and fish, birds and animals, significant upon their background of space, are all alive, all part of the rhythm of the Universe.

But the greatest of all Chinese paintings were the vast frescoes on the walls of Buddhist temples, three hundred of which were by Wu Tao-tze, by common consent the greatest of Chinese painters. They have perished, like the Buddhist Renaissance that gave them birth. Yet there remain many pictures and statues of Heavenly Presences, Powers of serenity and compassion, assisting the human soul in its effort after self-enlightenment—the Buddha himself, his Apostles or Lohan, the Bodhisattvas who have earned the bliss of Nirvana, but renounced it till the salvation of all living beings be accomplished—especially Kwan-yin, the supreme Bodhisattva of Compassionate Love. The spirit that produced them is still alive in the soul of China.

Thus China has solved, as no other country has ever succeeded in solving, the problem of combining the personal originality of the higher civilizations with the social solidarity of the primitive world. This she did by showing that both are rooted in the nature of things: that the Universe is a Moral Order in which individual men participate; that the virtue or love which is their essence makes them, not the tyrants, but the servants of society. Hence the social bond becomes, not instinctive, but reasonable; not self-interest, but harmony—the harmony of the soul with the Universe, expressing itself in a social harmony. That is China's contribution to humanity, embodied in her philosophy, her government, and her art. This great achievement accounts for the stability of Chinese civilization. While great personalities have destroyed other civilizations—that of Greece, for example—in China they have tended to make the State more moral and therefore more secure.

This is not of course wholly the case. The leaders' doctrine could not be expected to be, and actually was not, received in its entirety by the people or by their rulers. Its essence was in different measures diluted by the primitive mentality or by the egoism or incapacity of those who received it—as wine is diluted by water; and it was the more diluted in proportion as the doctrine was more remote from the average mind. The corruption of Taoist doctrine is easy to understand; but even the Confucian was sometimes pressed into the service of lustful or greedy rulers. Other men, though few, remained uninfluenced by either doctrine, and found for their spokesmen philosophers of a very different temper: the individualist, Yang Chu, the legalist, Lord Shang.

The Chinese ideal of a clan or family society had thus to wage its war with opposite ideals, exhibiting themselves in practice in social disorder and alarms—alarms which, giving rise to a Chinese 'problem of civilization', may serve to prove that only as men follow a Way similar to that of Confucius or Lao-tze can man and society attain to harmony and tranquillity.

No country of Central Asia or the Far East—Tibet or Turkestan, Mongolia or Manchuria, Korea or Japan—has shown the same creative originality as China; and their civilizations are therefore more imitative and derivative, borrowing both from China and India, and climbing the heights only with the help of Confucius and the Buddha. But while they adopt, they adapt; they, too, make each a special contribution to humanity.

Fujiyama, so dear to Japan, is typical of her; for the mountain is at once dangerous and beautiful. While the countrymen of Yoritomo, even the monks, have from age to age been fierce and ruthless fighters, and have twice purchased peace only at the price of a life-sapping military dictatorship, the soul of the people has persevered through all discouragement, gay in a unique enjoyment of the beauty of natural things. The minute observation and appreciation of common things is perhaps the greatest glory of Japan, and her chief contribution to the welfare of humanity.

The land itself is loveliness—a mountain-island of cherry blossom, of fields of flowers, of exquisite miniature gardens. Her very people are artists. The young child will look long at the movements of a fish in a bowl, then run to record in a few sure strokes as much as he can remember.[1] The Japanese observe minutely, but draw from memory, for it is life they love, not the weary pose, the essential, not the inessential; the swift flight of the bird, the gliding sinuosities of the fish. They relish symmetry, but not repetition; hence the orchid is a favourite flower. Most of them are farmers, working in the rice-fields and among the mulberry-trees, temperate and frugal, a kindly people. With these happy virtues they go light-hearted, gay and gaily clad. Small wonder that such a people have produced great craftsmen and artists!

From across the seas came the enriching influences of China and India. In the eighth century A.D. Universities were founded in Nara and Kioto. Confucianism appealed to the rulers. Ieyasu and several of his successors encouraged learning, even among the samurai; a group of 'Chinese scholars' (Kangakusha) addressed a new audience of wealthy merchants and mechanics. In a dozen Schools Buddhism adapted itself to a variety of needs. In the Fujiwara epoch it begot from the native love of beauty a marvellous civilization, whose exquisite temples exquisitely adorned still give to Nara and Kioto a dreamlike beauty. Then came the long centuries of anarchy and dictatorship, darkening letters, and degrading the skill of the craftsman to the decoration of arms. In the miseries of the times multitudes cried to Kwannon, Goddess of Mercy, who turned back from the gates of Paradise at the sound of a child's crying, and whose thousand mystic hands for ever reach out to console human sorrow. Like Luther, Honen and Shinran cast away the 'trashy doctrine' of merit and proclaimed faith in Amida as the only way of salvation; while they looked forward after the troubles of this life to the Western Paradise of Bliss, the 'Pure Land' that gives these Schools their name of Jodo.

But it was Zen, the 'Contemplative' or mystic Buddhism,

[1] Mortimer Mempes, *Japan. A Record in Colour* (1901).

that united with the national love of Nature's beauty to produce the loveliest creations of art. Zen is almost indefinable. It is neither a religion nor a philosophy, it defies logic; yet it pervades Japanese culture. That which the eye can see suggests truth revealed only to the spirit. Ask a painter to show you flowers, and he will paint you a tiny patch of green grass amid the snows: were flowers there already, they would be about to die. Japan's tiny poems of a few syllables favour this suggestiveness:

> Two butterflies:
> Ah, my dear love is dead!

The tragedy of two lovers in two lines! And deeper:

> The bamboo shadows sweep across the steps,
> But the dust is not stir'd;
> The moon shines from the bottom of the stream,
> But there is no hole in the water.

Behind the appearance that passes is the Reality that passes not. The Substance is within the heart, the shadow without. Zen is the subtlety of contemplation that catches the Abiding and the Whole from the delicate insinuations of the transient and the part.

II

When an Englishman climbs to the temperate altitudes of the Himalaya, he feels a sense at once of familiarity and unfamiliarity; the flowers he finds there are like and yet unlike those he knows in his own temperate islands—not brothers, but first cousins. Similarly when a Chinese goes to England or an Englishman to China, he finds that most things are unlike those at home, and yet akin to them. If at a dinner-party in China you can come and go as you please, you can do the same at a tea-party in England. If Chinese ladies squeezed their feet, English ladies squeezed their waists. Chinese and Englishmen both like gadgets—the Chinese light, the Englishman heavy; papier mâché against metal. The landscape, even many of the buildings, share this likeness in unlikeness. (Chinese music may, like the olive, perhaps be an acquired taste.) And so with greater things. The ethical ideals of the two countries, the *chun-tze* and the

gentleman, have much in common, and so have the systems of education devised to train *chun-tze* and gentlemen;
the respect for the father, the friend, and the sovereign that
govern Chinese society resemble the respect for authority,
for friends, and for opponents, that govern the Nordics. These
principles translate themselves into local and other institutions that have not a little in common; and if in China they
embody themselves in the arts, among the Nordics also they
undergo a higher development. The two civilizations are
variations on a common theme, species of the same genus.
Each reflects the view of the world, of a people at once
practical and moral.

The first pictures of Nordic civilization are those painted
by Caesar and Tacitus.[1] The 'Germans' Tacitus knew lived
in the lands beyond Rhine and Danube and across the Baltic
in southern Scandinavia. The latter were 'powerful in ships',
and 'honoured wealth'[2]—they were traders. As the hold of
Rome on Britain weakened, Saxons, Angles, and Jutes left
their North German homes for the milder and more fertile
ploughlands overseas; later on they were followed by Vikings
from Scandinavia. Canute even joined Scandinavia and
Britain in a single kingdom. From Great Britain descendants
of Celts and Anglo-Saxons, Northmen and Normans presently spread out to people North America, South Africa,
Australia, and New Zealand.

Of all the Nordics the Germans are the least typical,
partly because many of them were originally Slavs, partly
because Germany's exposed position in the centre of Europe
has denied her the security in which to develop a political
freedom, and turned her to the mysticism and music that are
the freehold of the spirit. Her civilization therefore, though
on the whole Nordic, requires separate consideration. On the
other hand the United States and the British Dominions are
still young, and some of them include alien elements; their
ripe fruits belong to the future. But upon Scandinavia (as
Tacitus pointed out long ago) the ocean forbids the sudden
inroad of enemies; and this is even more true of Great
Britain, behind its 'moat defensive',[3] 'the sure shield' of the

---

[1] *The Agricola and Germany of Tacitus*, Church and Brodribb.
[2] Ibid., c. 44. [3] Shakespeare, *Richard the Second*, ii. i.

Navy.[1] Scandinavia therefore, and still more Britain, between which a close affinity exists, are the norm of Nordic civilization.

If Chinese civilization owes its character to the family life of a community of farmers, Nordic civilization springs from the self-disciplined independence of a people that loves the country and the sea; and from the first, as harmony in society has been the ideal of the Chinese, so freedom in society has been the ideal of the Nordics. 'They live apart each by himself (Tacitus wrote) as woodside, plain or fresh stream attracts him.'[2] They were 'free-necked men', 'weaponed men' who could defend their freedom.[3] At the same time they saw that more was needed than weapons to secure freedom. They must respect each other; the freemen must agree among themselves or they would be overwhelmed from without or fight each other at home. Hence they adopted the custom of holding gemots or meetings—*consilia* or Councils—there to lay their minds alongside and freely reach agreement. 'About minor matters the chiefs deliberate, about the more important the whole tribe. The king or chief is here, more because he has influence to persuade than because he has power to command.[4] The kings have not unlimited or arbitrary power, and the generals do more by example than by authority'—a Confucian touch. 'If they are energetic or conspicuous or fight in front, they lead because they are admired.' The Germans were law-abiding, and in the Councils magistrates were elected to administer law in the cantons and the townships, supported by the advice and influence of a hundred associates chosen from the people. Yet character was at least as important. 'Good habits are here more effectual than good laws elsewhere.'

The Englishman's custom of lingering over the wine to discuss politics before joining the ladies was already anticipated by his Teutonic ancestors, who were fond of assembling round the 'ale-board'. 'It is at their feasts they generally consult on the reconciliation of enemies, on the

---

[1] King George the Fifth.   [2] Tacitus, c. 16.

[3] J. R. Green, *A Short History of the English People*, p. 2.

[4] Tacitus, c. 11 (shortened). The quotations of the next two paragraphs are from the same source, c. 7–24.

forming of matrimonial alliances, on the choice of chiefs, even on peace and war'; though they do not come to a conclusion till the following day. As among Britons and Americans, 'their marriage code is strict. No one in Germany laughs at vice.' Already they respect women. 'They do not despise their counsels or make light of their answers.'

The family ties of the Chinese are replaced by personal ties, for as soon as a youth is able to bear arms he is invested with shield and spear: 'up to this time he is regarded as a member of a household, but afterwards as a member of the Commonwealth.' After this the young are attached to a chief, and 'vie keenly with each other as to who shall rank first with him'. They are full of warlike ardour, and 'inaction is odious to their race'; but they are without natural or acquired cunning. Already the young Nordics were devoted to dangerous games, in which 'experience gives them skill, and skill gives them grace'.

These qualities were intensified when they took to the sea. The sea increased alike their love of liberty, their sense of discipline and their respect for one another; for while the members of a crew must show individual initiative, they must also act together. The roaming habit also confirmed their tendency to break up the family; kinship gave way to comradeship. The naval and military organization of a group of migratory Anglo-Saxons was based on the discipline of a ship's crew, and on the personal attachment of professional fighters to the chief who had organized the expedition.

Thus the green woods and the blue seas bred a different civilization from that of the yellow loess. The free-necked men in meeting were the root of the one, as the families of farmers of the other. The Chinese were settled, the Nordics rovers; the Chinese therefore based their political theory on the ethical character of the family, the Nordics' political theory has an origin independent of the family in the council and the crew. With the Chinese ethics are the source of politics; with the Nordics politics determine the form of their ethics. The Nordic relation between man and man is higher than the Chinese relation in so far as respect for a man as such is more rational than respect for a man merely as a kinsman—a respect that has a biological as well as a moral element. But just because it is higher, it is more difficult to attain. For this reason the restless Nordic needs more government, and therefore his freedom is more likely to be attacked by kings and ministers. For this reason also, while the cement of society in China is virtue, among the Nordics it is virtue embodied in law.

III

The ethical ideal of these amphibians was one of fighting men and laymen, 'not overburdened with brains or troubled about their own souls'—much like the ideal of English schoolboys and young men to-day.[1] They had a high sense of honour and much kindly good nature: hating cowardice, desertion, lies, dishonourableness of any kind, and admiring manliness, courage, generosity, loyalty in service and in friendship, good cheer. They followed their leader, worked with their friends, and learnt to get on even with men they didn't like. All were comrades. While therefore the self-discipline of the stationary Chinese sprang from ceremony, that of the young Nordics sprang from common enterprise by land and sea. While the kindness of the Chinese was the kindness of the family, the kindness of the Nordics was the kindness of companions in arms. At the same time there existed in them the pensiveness, the sadness, of men of the sea: a sense of their finitude and—as in the Greeks of Homer, who were also men of the sea—a sense of their ultimate powerlessness. The shadow of the unseen broods over them; all things are in the hands of Fate, and in the end shall come the twilight of the gods. 'The present life of man upon earth is like the swift flight of a sparrow through the house where the king sits at supper in winter with his thegns before the fire; the sparrow passes from winter into winter again. So this life of man appears for a little while, but of what is to follow, or of what went before, we know nothing at all.' This sense of other-worldliness has survived most strongly in the Germans.

This Nordic ideal of heroic manhood was corrected by the Christian ideal of gentleness: 'Blessed are the meek.' For soon strange voices were heard speaking a new language—

[1] G. M. Trevelyan, *History of England*, p. 50.

of the superiority of the soul to the body, of sin and an uneasy
conscience, of humility, of love for one's neighbour and for
God, of the fires of Hell and the hope of everlasting blessedness. The Nordics modified these ideas to suit their own,
as the Chinese modified Buddhist ideas; and thus modified
they reinforced the existing tendencies to chastity, to loyalty,
to consideration for friend and enemy. Thus manhood was
completed by gentleness, and the two ideals were welded
into the name and ideal of 'gentleman'. If 'gentleman', like
chun-tze, meant at first no more than 'of good family', the
Church saw to it that it should soon connote what a man of
good family ought to be—at once gentle and manly. The
gentleman as so defined is essentially the ethical ideal of
Nordic civilization.

What is a gentleman? Unfortunately the Nordics, to
whom 'inaction is odious', have never, like the Chinese,
produced philosophers to formulate their virtues. They have
put them, as it were, straight into their institutions, and from
their institutions learned them again. Hence it is from the
working of these institutions and from the sayings of statesmen and people that their ideal of virtue must be distilled
drop by drop.

The gentleman bears a strong resemblance to the *chun-tze*,
because the virtues of both are moral, directed to the good of
society. Confucius says: 'The princely man has three virtues. He is truly benevolent and free from care; truly wise
and free from delusion; truly brave and free from fear.'[1]
'He makes the sense of duty the ground of his character,
blends with it in action a sense of harmony, manifests it
in a spirit of unselfishness, and perfects it by the addition of
sincerity and truth.'[2] The gentleman may be defined as a
man with a high sense of duty towards his neighbour. It is
because the Englishman's 'sense of duty is the ground of his
character' that Nelson is his national hero, and that 'England
expects that every man will do his duty' strikes a responsive
chord in every Englishman's heart. In typical Nordics (the
Germans are not typical) this duty involves three things;
self-discipline, practical clear-sightedness, respect for others.
The good Nordic, unlike the Latin and the Slav and most

[1] Giles, pp. 66–7.   [2] Ibid., p. 68.

other peoples, does not let his passions get the better of him. He controls his appetites, his greed, his ambitions; he is not cowardly, or lustful, or disorderly, or violent, or excitable, or grossly selfish. Nor is this discipline imposed from without; his policeman is in his own breast. Secondly, because his passions are not his masters, blinding his eyes, he sees things as they are; he is not carried away by 'delusions', baseless theories or grandiose schemes, but is a realist in the true sense of the word. Consequently he lacks cunning and hates lies; he is mistakenly thought to be hypocritical only because political genius implies adaptability and therefore changes of policy, and because his character and institutions are anomalous and therefore hard for others to understand. Thirdly, because his eyes are clear of passion, he sees that other men are indeed men, men like himself, and that their point of view and their interests are as worthy of respect as his own; he is ready to discuss, to agree, to compromise. A gentleman has indeed been defined as a man who shows consideration for others.

If the five principal Chinese virtues show themselves in five relationships, these three Nordic virtues show themselves in three relationships: there is respect between ruler and ruled, between colleagues or friends, and between opponents.

First, the good Nordic with his free-necked love of liberty respects duly constituted authority, as the good Chinese shows piety to his father and loyalty to the Emperor and the scholar-rulers. From the first the followers respected their chief, the crew their captain. The Nordic sees that freedom depends on self-disciplined obedience to the chosen leader and the chosen law, or else disorder will overwhelm his freedom. It must be a leader and a law that derive authority from the governed: the schoolboy will punctiliously obey his own captain and his own customs, but defy the master and the master's rules. It does not matter how thin or fleeting the authority may be: let a steward at a concert ask people not to sit in the gangway, and they will continue to obey him when his back is turned: the doorkeeper of Almack's tells the Duke of Wellington that the rules require that he wear knee-breeches, and the victor of Waterloo goes obe-

diently away. The British policeman is the officer, not of
the Government, but of the people, the friend of order and
therefore of freedom, loved and laughed at in his blue uniform and big boots, controlling crowds, not with bludgeons
or revolvers, but with good humour and jokes. A British
Government is elected by the people, respected by the
people, rejected by the people. The idea of revolution never
enters their heads. Above all, the King is the embodiment
of his people, without responsibility for the mistakes of his
Ministers, standing above criticism, concentrating the love
and loyalty of a world-wide Commonwealth.

But, as in China, this duty is reciprocal. If a Chinese
father must consider his sons, and a sovereign his subjects,
a Nordic ruler must do more: his rule must be not merely
'in righteousness and benevolence', but also acceptable to
the people. Good government is not enough for the Nordics; they must have self-government. Reform must not
run ahead of public opinion, but lead it along by the hand.
This oneness between ruler and ruled runs through Nordic history. Simon de Montfort perceived that government
could be strengthened 'by calling representatives of all the
communities together and talking to them'.[1] Edward the
First saw that the Royal power would be more efficient if it
were in constant touch with the life of the governed. The
secret of Tudor greatness was a 'curious instinct of oneness
with the English people'.[2] Louis the Fourteenth might say:
'I am the State', but Henry the Eighth, who knew the value
of genuine advice and criticism, told the Commons that in
Parliament: 'We as head and you as members are conjoined
and knit together in one body politic.' His imperious
daughter thanked the Commons as she yielded to them, and
at the close of a long reign declared the secret of its splendour:
'Though God hath raised me high, yet this I count the glory
of my Crown, that I have reigned with your loves!'

It was because her successors failed to understand this
need for unity with their peoples that one lost his head and
another his crown. 'Liberty and freedom (said Charles on
the scaffold) consists in having government, those laws by
which the subjects' lives and goods may be most their own.

[1] Trevelyan, p. 178.   [2] Ibid., p. 297.

It is not their having a share in the government, that is nothing pertaining to them. A subject and a sovereign are clean different things.' His son James would dispense with the laws; and his people dispensed with him. But the lesson taught by the Tudor kings was well learnt by the English people. The genius of Pym, the father of Parliamentary liberty, made the Royal executive amenable to Parliament. Henceforward government and public opinion went hand in hand. Walpole refused to press his Excise Bill in the teeth of popular opposition—'I will not be the Minister to enforce taxes at the expense of blood'—though he foresaw that it would make London a free port and double English trade. Conversely, Wellington and Peel allowed the great Reform Bill to become law in spite of their hearty disapproval, because popular opinion loudly demanded it. Wellington's maxim was: 'His Majesty's Government must be carried on', however much Ministers might disagree with Parliament or people. Lesser authorities are just as reasonable: railway guards in dealing with tickets, majorities in considering minorities.

In the second place, the Nordics have a gift for spontaneous co-operation such as exists nowhere else but in China; and this is to be found in all departments of their life. English men and women club together in Trade Unions, Co-operative Societies, Leagues and Boards, Commissions and Committees for every conceivable purpose of philanthropy or culture —'the preservation of Washington's Manor, the study of Browning, the purification of the English language'. Services that are undertaken by the State in Latin countries are in China and Britain largely or wholly promoted by the people: education, hospitals, the care of the sick in their homes, the protection of children and of animals, the preservation of the countryside, the improvement of the theatre. A European Commission visiting China finds private enterprise promoting schools; the English member welcomes this, the other members are horrified. When wrongs are to be righted, private individuals devise remedies and stir opinion, until (if necessary) the Legislature acts: thus Wilberforce attacked slavery, Elizabeth Fry reformed prison life, Shaftesbury protected the factory workers. Social measures like the Children's Bill, the Town-Planning Act, the Sweated Industries Act, the Small Holdings Acts are supported by voluntary or municipal effort through Care Committees, Play Centres, Boy Scouts, the Workers' Educational Association, and the like.

Most significant of all, this love of freedom for oneself and others involves respect for opponents. They, too, are well-disposed men; they, too, love their country, and like ourselves wish to serve. Though our differences are important, our likenesses are more important still. 'Good relations with his fellow-men are more important to the Briton than anything else: he accepts as a matter of course that his opponent too belongs to the community.'[1] Hence the sayings: 'Live and let live', 'agree to differ', 'we agree perfectly in everything but opinion.'[2] Opponents are not enemies, but friends; not factions, but servants of the common good. In the Universities young men of every class discuss every subject; in the smoking-room of the House of Commons duke's son and cook's son meet in complete equality. Never a drop of blood is shed; a thing that, surprising to other nations, the Nordics take for granted. In frank and friendly discussion views are put forward, terms defined, misunderstandings cleared up, opinions exchanged and changed, compromises and agreements reached. Hence an absence of bitterness in the social struggle. Keen political opponents dine together once a week, or sit *tête-à-tête* in a smoking-room for a comfortable chat. The Parties out of office are not enemies of the State: responsible and constructive criticism is a healthy tonic for a Government; with the turn of the tide His Majesty's Opposition will become His Majesty's Government. Mr. Landon telegraphs to Mr. Roosevelt, who has just beaten him in a Presidential Election: 'The nation has spoken. Every American will accept the verdict and will work for the common cause of the good of the country. That is the spirit of democracy. You have my sincere congratulations.' Mr. Roosevelt replies: 'All of us Americans will now pull together for the common good.'[3] The Nordics respect each other, have open minds, do not think themselves infallible, believe

---

[1] Count Keyserling, *Europe*, p. 30.   [2] Thomas Carlyle.
[3] *The Times*, 5 Nov. 1936.

that others may know something too. They have taken to heart Cromwell's injunction to 'think it possible they may be mistaken'.

At one great moment of history this triple principle of respect for authority, for friends and for opponents found a splendid embodiment. The Nordics on the American Continent 'brought forth a new nation, conceived in liberty and dedicated to the proposition that all men are created equal'. Fourscore and seven years later that nation, at Gettysburg, 'highly resolved that, under God, it should have a new birth of freedom; and that government of the people, by the people, for the people, should not perish from the earth'.[1]

Many consequences follow. Moderation: Nordic freedom rejects instinctively 'the falsehood of extremes'.[2] The Nordics are ruled by central opinion, not by extremists— Die-hards or Revolutionaries, Right or Left. Their cross-bench minds, not easily brigaded with sect or party, sway to this side or that, as circumstances persuade; a massive middle opinion is, like Cromwell, 'joined to no Party, but for the liberty of all'.[3] The two or three Parties are led by moderate men; France pays the penalty of too many Parties in too many crises.

Hence, too, a Chinese tolerance. Cromwell writes: 'The State, in choosing men to serve them, takes no notice of their opinions; if they be willing faithfully to serve them, that satisfies.' The root of this tolerance is not indifference, but love of truth. 'A little generous prudence (Milton argues), a little forbearance of one another, and some grain of charity might win all these diligences to join and unite in one general and brotherly search after truth, could we but forego this prelatical tradition of crowding free consciences and Christian liberties into canons and precepts of men.'[4] The settlement in State and Church for which Cromwell struggled and Milton reasoned was summarized as 'civil and religious liberty'. Men may meet, speak, write what they like, worship as they will, provided they respect the 'rights and liberties' of others; intolerance is futile, for compulsion does not

---

[1] President Lincoln's Gettysburg Speech.
[2] Tennyson, 'Of old sat Freedom on the heights'.
[3] Richard Baxter. Cp. Buchan, *Cromwell*, p. 226.   [4] *Areopagitica*.

bring conviction. This apotheosis of tolerance is one of the greatest achievements of the Nordics. More anticipated it, Hooker advocated it, Cromwell fought for it, William the Third secured it, Locke defended it.

Hence the Nordics, however much at loggerheads, when challenged instantly close their ranks. To the amazement of foreigners the victory of Blenheim harmonized the rancours of Whig and Tory into a chorus of rejoicing.[1] The invasion of Belgium instantly united Liberal and Conservative, Orange and Green, a few hours before on the verge of civil war. The General Strike opened with a football match between the police and the strikers; the Prince of Wales made a personal contribution to the strikers' funds; workers went on strike out of loyalty to their Unions, and took national work out of loyalty to their country. Not a soldier was needed, not a life was lost. The World Depression produced National Governments in Great Britain, New Zealand, Australia, pledged to make cuts in pay; and drastic privations were willingly endured.

This respect for opponents means too that the victory of one Party is accepted by the other. Peel wrote: 'We are making the Reform Bill work, and we are falsifying our own predictions, which could be realized but for our active interference. We are protecting the authors of the evil from the work of their own hands.' The future Lord Salisbury said, after the fierce controversy over the Reform Bill of 1867:

'It is the duty of every Englishman and of every English party to accept a political defeat cordially and to lend their best endeavours to secure the success, or to neutralise the evil, of the principles to which they have been forced to succumb. England has committed many mistakes as a nation in the course of her history, but the mischief has been more than corrected by the heartiness with which, after each great struggle, victors and vanquished have forgotten their former battles and have combined together to lead the new policy to its best results. As far as our Liberal adversaries are concerned, we shall dismiss the long controversy with the expression of an earnest hope that their sanguine confidence may prove in the results to have been wiser than our fears.'[2]

[1] Winston Churchill, *Marlborough*, vol. ii, p. 517.
[2] Quoted by Winston Churchill, *The Times*, 26 Sept. 1935.

Winston Churchill accepted the India Act of 1935 in the same spirit and in the same words.

Hence the continuity of British public life, its combination of tradition and progress; the past is never swept away, but glides on into the future. The French pull down their Constitutions and their Cathedrals to build a new and logical whole; the English Constitution and English Cathedrals grow from age to age in harmonious illogicality. Versailles is built in a single style, Windsor Castle is the patchwork of centuries. The Nordics, like the Chinese, are conservative liberals. They prize tradition, but keep it up to date: they cherish institutions, but maintain them in repair. They have learnt 'how to graft the revolutionary slips upon the former stock, and preserve that continuity without which a human society descends into chaos'.[1] Confucius declared that he was a transmittor, not an innovator; the Nordics innovate as they transmit.

> May freedom's oak for ever thrive
>   With stronger life from day to day;
> That man's the best Conservative
>   Who lops the moulder'd branch away.[2]

Pym said: 'These commonwealths have been ever the most durable and perpetual which have often reformed and recomposed themselves according to their first institution and ordinance. By this means they repair the breaches, and counterwork the ordinary and natural effects of time.' That, too, was the doctrine of Burke. Hence a Chinese reverence for the ceremonial of the past; the British memory is a Book of Rites. The public schools are aggressively tenacious of school customs; Oxford and Cambridge carry on medieval forms; Parliament retains Plantagenet usages; the monarchy is dignified with the ceremonial of centuries. On the Continent a war sweeps away the past every century; in his sea-girt security tradition roots the Briton in the past at the moment when he is shaping the future.

This respect for opponents and for the past makes revolution rare among the Nordics, especially among those that are shielded by the sea: they cannot 'smash' men they respect,

---

[1] Buchan, *Cromwell*, p. 229.   [2] Tennyson, *Hands All Round*.

or start again with the year 1. They conduct their revolutions on conservative lines, with a nice regard for law, when necessary bidding legal fiction lend its artful aid. A Cambridge College desires to elect a Master who will not be parted from his dog; but the Master's Lodging is in the middle of the buildings, and the Statutes forbid the presence of a dog. So the Fellows 'deem' the dog to be a cat. The British people desires that Parliament should elect William and Mary as King and Queen; but Parliament cannot lawfully be summoned without the sign manual of the King, and James the Second has fled the country. They therefore deem that he has 'abdicated the government', and that 'the throne is thereby vacant'.[1] The English have conquered the fierce beast of revolution and domesticated him: a General Election is as much a legalized revolution as a rugger scrum a 'conveniently civil' battle.[2] The vote of the electorate is more 'convenient' than the axe of the headsman in overthrowing an unpopular ruler, for (beside being less unpleasant for the fallen man) the superseded statesman can if required pop up again, while the beheaded statesman is down for ever. The French (said Napoleon the Third) do everything by revolution, nothing by reform: even the Chinese could not dethrone the Son of Heaven without great disorder.

II. 2

The chief expression of the Nordic character is the Nordic Commonwealth.

Nordic education has always resembled the Chinese in being essentially moral: it aims by practice and precept at teaching men how to live—and how to die. Just as Chinese education trains them in the give-and-take of family intercourse, and in the principles and achievements of the sage kings and peoples of old, so Nordic education trains the character in the tumble of life, and widens the mind by the teaching and example of Romans, Greeks, and Hebrews.

From the first it has been an education in responsibility. The young German of Tacitus followed a chief, medieval lads became pages in castles or apprentices in shops; modern boys and young men play their parts in the common life of

[1] Bill of Rights, 1689.   [2] Davenant.

the Schools and the Universities. They are trained both in following and in leading—the page becomes the squire, the fag the prefect, the undergraduate the secretary or captain of a club; self-government is an integral part of British education, as it is of Nordic civilization.

The ancestral vigour lives in their games, now disciplined, intelligent, respectful, civilized by the rule of law. In boat-racing the Vikings once more put to sea: a bumping-race is a disciplined sea-fight, accompanied by 'savage cries'.[1] Football, that used to be 'nothyng but beastely fury and extreme violence, a develishe pastime not very conveniently civil in the streets',[2] is now, under Rugby and Association rules, a reasonably civil battle. Cricket is essentially the Englishman's game, both because it so well combines individual with team work, and because the love of the game counts much more than victory. Played in the Nordic spirit games teach the Nordic virtues. A famous athlete has said: 'Men are taught the importance of duty and discipline; they bring out the best that is in a man.'[3] The player must train, endure, dare. The team spirit leaves no place for selfish individualism, for personal glory; it teaches to win without boasting and to lose without ill feeling. Games clear the mind: Rugger combinations need careful working out; rowing coaches differ as acidly as Doctors of Divinity. Those responsible must think of everything and of every one. Games teach respect for others: lawful authority must be obeyed, authority itself must learn to know men and to manage men —as presently it must know them and manage them in a larger world. There must be a perfect fairness to opponents, no foul play; a rough justice ducks or 'debags' the transgressor of the unwritten law. As Confucius said, the *chun-tze* behaves like a *chun-tze*, even when competing in a shooting-match.[4] 'To play the game', and in particular 'to play cricket', sums up the duty of the Englishman.

But the Nordics also value a liberal education—the humanities that direct their vigour. Greek and Roman culture have profoundly impressed their vocabulary. Roman poetry and

---

[1] Ear-witness of a young French lady.
[2] Sir Thomas Elyot, *Boke named the Governour* (1531), Davenant (*c.* 1634).
[3] Lord Burghley, *The Times*, 1 Oct. 1929.   [4] Giles, *Sayings*, p. 56.

oratory appeal to a people engaged in Imperial government
and in Parliamentary debate; Greek poetry opens the mind
to beauty, Greek philosophy to reason. Reading and study
(wrote Cromwell) 'fit for public services, for which a man is
born'. The Cecils and the Bacons fitted themselves by their
academic studies to govern the country. For centuries the
wise and urbane words of Horace were quoted in the House
of Commons. The younger Pitt steeped himself in Thucydides while yet a schoolboy: Derby, thrice Prime Minister,
translated the *Iliad* and quoted it at length on his death-bed.
The pity is that, unlike the political leaders, the leaders of
industry have as a rule lacked a humanist education.

Still deeper has been the influence of the Hebrews. What
the Classics were to the Chinese, the Quran to Islam, Paul's
letters to Catholicism, the Upanishads to Hinduism, the
Fourth Gospel to Orthodoxy, the Bible has been to the
Nordics. The Authorized Version is the canon of English
prose, and its words have entered as deeply into English
speech as the sayings of Confucius into Chinese. Its precepts have softened their manners; its doctrines, interpreted
in the light of Rome, of Wittenburg, or of Geneva, and
received with piety rather than with understanding, have
given them background in life and hope in death.

All through life the Englishman remains at school. When
he goes into a Regiment, or into the Cabinet, he is a new boy
again. The House of Commons is very like a public school:
bumptiousness is hated, courage is admired, a man is valued
for himself. To the end of his days the Briton may go to the
wicket with high hopes—and trail back to the pavilion with
a duck's egg.

The Nordic is a freedom-loving creature, and his instinct
is therefore to have as little law and government, both for
himself and others, as is consistent with the preservation of
freedom. When things are going well, his policy is *laissez-
faire*; when freedom is threatened from any quarter, government is strengthened just in so far as may be necessary to
maintain freedom. Thus free government means both freedom from government and government for freedom.

'In normal times Whiggism, *laissez-faire*, is the temper of

England',[1] the United States and the 'free-necked' Nordics generally. Macaulay, the Whig historian, said that England looks for success, not to the 'intermeddling of an omniscient and omnipotent State' (such as a dictatorship), 'but to the prudence and energy of her people'.[2] 'Inaction' is still 'odious to the race';[3] the old Viking vigour is unabated. In the century and a half of 'civil and religious liberty' that followed what the English call their Revolution 'the nation marched forward to undreamed-of wealth, to a humaner and freer social life, to triumphant heights in letters and science and thought', thanks to 'the untrammelled vigour of the individual', little helped or hindered by State action.[4] It was an age of great individuals—of Marlborough and Chatham, Nelson and Wellington, Clive and Warren Hastings, Arkwright and Stevenson, Reynolds and Burke, Scott and Wordsworth, Shelley and Keats.[5] It was an age of scientific discovery and of poetic creation, of industrial expansion at home and of imperial expansion overseas. The wars of liberty against the France of Louis and Napoleon were fought and won. The Nordic spirit moved vigorously and freely.

But freedom is not always so fortunate. It may be attacked by a variety of foes—foreign Powers, Churches, armies, kings, Provinces, the Mother Country. Engelbrekt delivered Sweden from the alien rule of Denmark. Henry the Eighth's legislation freed England from Papal domination, Laud's execution from an attempt of the Church of England to dictate uniformity of creed and worship, Cromwell's victory at Dunbar from the dictation of the Kirk. The English Parliament after its experience of the New Model kept the purse that paid the army; the doctrine of the Nordics is the doctrine of Blake, soldier and sailor too: 'It is not the business of a seaman to mind State affairs, but to hinder foreigners from fooling us.' England freed herself from would-be dictator kings by transferring the last word in policy from the king to Parliament. 'Civil and religious liberty' was the outcome of her struggle: civil liberty from kings and captains, religious liberty from popes and kirks.

---

[1] Buchan, *Cromwell*, p. 521.   [2] Quoted ibid.
[3] Tacitus, c. 14.   [4] Buchan, *Cromwell*, p. 521.
[5] Cp. Trevelyan, p. 506.

Or one region may threaten another: Cromwell subdued
Scotland because of its menace to England. (Spain in the
twentieth century is confronted with all these dangers, as
England was in the seventeenth.) Or the Mother Country
may meddle in colonial self-government; hence the revolt
of the Colonies of North America from Great Britain and
of South America from Spain. The Declaration of Independence, drafted by Jefferson, denies hereditary privilege,
asserts the rights of the individual, and proclaims that no
people should ever abandon its fate to any authority it cannot
control. Freedom has two further enemies still only partly
tamed: poverty and war.

How are these enemies overcome? Only in the last resort,
when reason seems altogether to have failed, do the Nordics
use force: they see that a settlement—agreement and compromise—cannot be reached without meeting to discuss,
though in words they sometimes battle mightily. That is a
solution possible only to self-disciplined men who respect
authority and one another. Such meetings are all in essence
'parliaments', assemblies where men parley or talk. One
form of 'talking-shop'[1] is developed after another: the village
concilium or gemot, the Witenagemot, the King's Court,
Parliament, Riksdag, Congress, Trade Unions, the Trade
Union Congress, Imperial Conferences, the League of
Nations: sometimes the work of great men, but in the main
the creation of a conference-minded people. The German
Chief parleyed with the people; afterwards the King with the
Wise Men, then with the Bishops and Barons. But this was
not enough. When Sweden was to be delivered from the
yoke of Denmark, Engelbrekt called into council with the
Bishops and Barons representatives of the citizens and
peasants—the sturdy miners of Dalecarlia—and the Riksdag came into being. Simon de Montfort (or a myth of the
same name) 'called representatives of all the communities
or "Commons" together and talked to them';[2] knights of the
shire and representative burgesses now have their say besides
the big men; Parliament has begun. This public parleying

---

[1] Thomas Carlyle.
[2] Trevelyan, p. 178. The iconoclasm of recent scholars disputes this.

serves three purposes: the people tell the Government what they want; the Government explain to the people what they are doing; the different classes of the people listen to each other. The English kings would sometimes assemble the Commons to hear their grievances, 'so as to be able to govern in accordance with real local needs, and to keep a check upon the misdeeds of local officials'.[1] The 'bills' or petitions of the Commons as a body led to the right of their House to initiate legislation; the redress of grievances conditions the grant of supplies. Secondly, government is a tricky business and Parliaments need education; the Tudor monarchs educated theirs. Their able Privy Councillors, University men educated in the humanities of Greece and Rome and further trained by foreign travel and the study of law, explained to the Commons the policy of the government, and if necessary modified it to meet their criticisms. 'This leadership was the chief process of education by which the House of Commons was trained to face the real problems of government and to deal with high affairs of State.'[2] So successful was this education that in the following century Parliament not only resisted the attempt of a Stuart king to take away its share in government, but transferred the final word in that government from the Crown to Parliament. Hence the give-and-take of explanation and criticism between Ministers and Members of Parliament to-day. In the third place Parliament enabled different classes of the community to meet and hear one another. As long as the villeins were left out, they had no way of presenting their grievances but the 'direct action' of revolt. The enfranchisement of the working classes and then of women made Britain a democracy.

The same principle has been at work as new problems arise. Need for discussion, agreement, and compromise led Alexander Hamilton and his colleagues to make Congress the central feature of the Constitution of the United States, Lord Durham to initiate colonial self-government in the British Commonwealth, Joseph Chamberlain to call into being its Imperial Conferences, and Wilson, Smuts, and Cecil to devise the Council and Assembly of the League of Nations.

[1] Trevelyan, p. 193.   [2] Ibid. p. 276.

Generally speaking, the characteristic of Nordic constitutions is their flexibility. Even Alexander Hamilton relied, not so much upon the document he drew up so ably, as upon his countrymen's 'general genius for government'; 'particular provisions (he said), though not altogether useless, have far less virtue and efficacy than is commonly ascribed to them.' The comparative inflexibility of written constitutions produces great inconvenience in a world of changing and unforeseeable circumstances, as the Constitution of the United States and the Covenant of the League of Nations have recently shown. The British are more fortunate. Their Constitution is the fruit of a long, uncodified experience of Parliamentary government.[1] It is as amorphous as a jellyfish, but it has the vitality of a jelly-fish.[2] It is not a paper structure but a thing of life and growth, springing from age to age from a people that love liberty for themselves and others; illogical, gnarled as an oak, but deep-rooted in the past, and spreading its branches far and wide. There is in it 'a want of logic, an indifference to formalism, a great respect for the lessons of the past, a deep sense of the realities, and, above all, such great moderation that no one ever claims the strict application of his constitutional rights in every detail, if this is contrary to good sense.'[3] It is the worst in the world, if judged by its opportunities for mischief; yet the best in the world, if judged by the character that created it and makes it work better than any other. What sane man drafting a constitution would make the head of the Judicature a Member of the Cabinet? Yet, though the Lord Chancellor always sits in the Cabinet, the British Government never interferes with the administration of justice. Who would give the Second Chamber a legal right to block whatever bills it likes? Yet the House of Lords respects the will of the people as expressed through the House of Commons. What constitution-maker would leave the selection of bishops to a Prime Minister who may be a Unitarian, a Jew, or an agnostic? Yet the Church of England is as well bishoped as the qualifications of her Ministers permit. 'To change this Constitution requires no special procedure; an ordinary law

---

[1] Sir John Simon, quoted in *The Times*, 1 March 1935.
[2] Susan Buchan, *The Sword of State*, p. 92.   [3] Sir J. Simon.

will do. The British Parliamentary system has been gradually
formed in keeping with the daily needs of the people. It
may be compared to an old garment that has gradually
worked itself into a perfect fit on its owner's shoulders—
though it may not fit another man so well.'[1]

If in the interests of freedom the Nordics love to 'agree
with their adversary while they are in the way with him',
they are also sedulous to observe what they have agreed upon.
If the Chinese rely upon virtue rather than upon law, the
Nordics embody their virtue—their respect for one another
—in law; good law to them is the embodiment of good feeling
and good sense. They eschew indeed all grandiose promises
of rights that have no legal remedies. The Declaration of
the Rights of Man was followed by terror and tyranny;
constitutions that declare man's rights—freedom of person,
property, and the Press, free speech, free assembly, free worship—provide that the 'constitutional guarantees' for them
can be 'suspended', and they generally are just when they
are most needed. The Nordic method is to look at what is
wrong and set it right; where the shoe pinches, there it is
eased. Henry the Second sends his judges on circuit to suppress the arbitrary jurisdiction of the feudal barons and to
establish a 'Common Law'; the barons in their turn secure
in the Great Charter the right that men shall be tried only by
juries of their peers. Has the king been illegally imprison-
ing the subject? Parliament devises the Writ of Habeas
Corpus. Has he been packing juries with 'partiall, corrupt
and unqualifyed persons', requiring excessive bail, imposing
excessive fines? The Act that changes the succession to the
throne enacts that juries shall not be packed, excessive bail
required, unreasonable fines imposed.[2] Where individual
members of the House of Commons complain that the Common Law is too rigid, the tenderer conscience of the Church
is called in to remedy the injustice of the law by equity. The
intelligence of the Judges interprets and develops the Common Law in accordance with the changing requirements of
the time. Thus the insight of Lord Mansfield adjusted the
Common Law to the needs of a country commercialized by
the Industrial Revolution, and in so doing transformed it;

[1] Sir J. Simon.   [2] Bill of Rights.

while the doctrine of negligence has given the law of tort a corresponding flexibility in our own day. Much of the law of England turns on what a jury considers that a 'reasonable' man would do—a man who respects the rights of others as well as his own.

Not only is the law thus kept in harmony with the facts, but the Nordics follow it in the spirit rather than in the letter —as a means rather than as an end. Law is their servant, not their master: if a notice says 'Keep to the left', they go to the left if the way is crowded, to the right if it is not and that is the shortest cut. As a law becomes obsolete, it is less and less observed, until it lapses into desuetude; or if there is opposition to the change, it is revised by compromise and consent, though often only after a sharp struggle.

If the genius of the Nordics for self-government is due not a little to the tutelage received by Parliament from the Privy Councillors of the Tudors, the respect in which they hold the law is largely due to the legal tutelage of four centuries received by the countryside from Justices of the Peace.[1] The worthy squire who expounded and enforced the law for ordinary folk in ordinary things 'may not have known much law, but he knew his neighbours and was known of them'.[2] Thus the law saturated the people, not as a code imposed from above, but as the embodiment, rough though it might be, of what their moral nature felt to be right. Hence their devotion to it. As the Venetian envoy observed in the days of the first Tudor: 'If the King should propose to change any old established rule, it would seem to every Englishman as if his life were taken from him.'[3] His land is still

> A land of settled government,
>   A land of just and old renown,
>   Where freedom slowly broadens down
> From precedent to precedent.[4]

A practical people must inevitably try to control Nature, and the Nordics have set about it from the first. There were the clearings in the forest, the ships that crossed the seas—

[1] Edward the Third to George the Third.
[2] Trevelyan, p. 199.   [3] Quoted ibid., p. 275.
[4] Tennyson, 'You ask me, why, tho' ill at ease'.

while slaves urged the galleys of the Mediterranean, freemen navigated the sailing ships of the North. The bowmen and the broadsides (invented by Henry the Eighth, the founder of the Royal Navy) won England's battles by land and sea. The weaving of fine cloth, learnt from Flemish and Huguenot refugees, spread wealth through the English countryside, as presently the spinning-jenny, the spinning-machine, the power-loom spread it through the towns. When the oak woods of the Sussex Weald gave out, coal and then oil supplied new power to the steam engine, the dynamo, and the internal combustion engine. Machinery multiplied production and promised fantastical wealth. Communication was transfigured by land, sea, and air.

Meanwhile the Discoveries opened a new East and a new West, and the Nordics settled in North America, South Africa, the Indies, Australasia. The Nordic character and Nordic institutions were carried round the world.

Yet not without creating new problems. The new wealth multiplied population, and so aggravated poverty. The new settlements awakened jealousies, and so imperilled peace. The Nordic love of freedom for all, victorious over kings and Churches, faced new enemies, poverty and war.

Accordingly 'the nineteenth century rivalled the Middle Ages in its power to create fresh forms of corporate and institutional life, while yielding little to the eighteenth century in the spirit of self-help and personal initiative'.[1] In Great Britain the State runs great enterprises, protects the unfortunate, provides social services, taxes more equitably. Characteristically, its motive has been moral; characteristically, too, it has tackled its problems piecemeal, without grandiose theories, not overturning the old to gamble with the new. The British Parliament and Lincoln restricted and then abolished slavery. The right of the workers to bargain collectively was restored. Shaftesbury secured for factory workers legal protection under Government Inspectors. Disraeli inspired the young Tories with a desire to redress the inequalities between 'the two nations', the rich and the poor. Gladstone provided education for the children, Balfour for older boys and girls. Lloyd George won medical attendance

[1] Trevelyan, p. 617.

for the sick, pay for the unemployed, pensions for the old. One-third of the national wealth of Great Britain is now paid in rates and taxes to finance the public services. Here is Fabian Socialism. This slow Revolution has come to the back door, and entered without ringing the bell. In Sweden similarly, a well-disciplined Socialism has done much to meet the needs of the people.

The Industrial Revolution reached America later, and its remedy later too. The author of the New Deal also bases his reforms upon ethics.

'The money changers having fled from their high seats in the temple of our civilisation, we may now restore that temple to the ancient truths. The measure of the restoration lies in the extent to which we apply social values more noble than mere monetary profit. Happiness lies not in the mere possession of money; it lies in the joy of achievement, the thrill of creative effort. Our true destiny is not to be ministered unto, but to minister to ourselves and our fellow-men. Recognition of the falsity of material wealth as the standard of success goes hand in hand with the abandonment of the false belief that public office and high political position are to be valued only by standards of pride of place and personal profit; and there must be an end to a conduct in banking and business that too often has given to a sacred trust the likeness of callous and selfish wrong-doing.'[1]

President Cleveland said (without joking) that 'public office is a public trust'; President Roosevelt adds that 'private office is a public trust'; those who rule over others, privately as well as publicly, must base their conduct on 'good ethics and good morals'.[2] Justice in business must spring from 'opinion and conscience', only in the case of the blackleg from the compulsion of the law. The New Deal rests on the principle 'humanity first, profits after'. In a land emerging from the abuses of *laissez-faire*, it sought to protect the needy from the greedy, to regulate competition by codes embodying fair play for the public, the workers, and the owners of capital, and to supply the services required by the less fortunate members of society.

Where different nations live together, freedom requires, on the one hand a recognition of their diversity, on the other,

---

[1] Inaugural Address, 4 March 1933.
[2] President Roosevelt, *On Our Way*, pp. 262–4.

its subordination to the common good. The condition of freedom is here again a fellowship of men who respect each other, whether this fellowship take the form of an Entente, a League, a Commonwealth, a Federal Union, or a Unitary State.

Thus England, Wales, and Scotland, supposed for centuries to be natural enemies, have become a United Kingdom —not by superiority of conquest, but by equality of regard. Wales gives the heir to the throne his title. Scotland sprinkles England and the Empire with Prime Ministers, Archbishops, Cabinet Ministers, merchants, and shopkeepers. Ireland (at long last) has become a Free State, and the Free State has developed into Eire.

The Viking spirit has carried Britain, with her character and her institutions, over all the seas. Her Empire grew by accident, not by design. The process was spontaneous, the work of traders and settlers; not political, the work of Governments. Freedom and trade were its inspiration, not the desire to found an Empire. Seeking freedom of worship she founded the New England colonies. Fighting the hegemony of Spain, she won for all the freedom of the seas; fighting the hegemony of France, she rescued India from anarchy, and was able ultimately to plant the flag of freedom in Canada. There have been, and to a lesser extent still are, selfishnesses that war with her ideal. But on the whole her Empire is an Empire without Imperialism, from which she draws no tribute, which serves no strategic purpose, in which she tries to put native above national rights, and to share with other peoples the benefits she derives herself.

Like Imperial Rome Britain has applied throughout this earth-wide Commonwealth the principles that have made her great in her own island. The freedom that she loves for herself she loves for others; and liberty spells variety. Under the indirect rule of a disinterested trusteeship the institutions of primitive peoples become schools of education in self-government, the basis of societies that shall presently become partners in a British or more than British League or Union of Nations. The Dutch are similarly training the peoples of the East Indies. At a moment when dictatorship is in the ascendant in Europe and Asia, India is the scene of the

biggest experiment in self-government the world has ever
known: tentative and gradual, like all successful political
developments, but having as its goal the full self-government
of a free Federation within a free Commonwealth. The
peoples of each of the British Dominions have become,
like the mother kingdom, self-governing and (generally
speaking) united—French and English in the Dominion of
Canada, Boer and British in the Union of South Africa,
Labour and non-Labour in the Commonwealth of Australia.
If within these Federations there are sometimes tiffs, they
are after all only family quarrels. At Versailles the mother
led her daughters to the Council-table of the nations; in the
Statute of Westminster she acknowledged that they had
come of age, and were henceforth free to direct their own
destinies. Rejecting a Federation that might have cramped
the growth of nationhood, she declared that 'they are autono-
mous Communities within the British Empire, equal in
status, in no way subordinate one to another in any aspect
of their domestic or external affairs, though united by a
common allegiance to the Crown and freely associated as
members of the British Commonwealth of Nations'. King
George the Fifth in a Christmas broadcast to his peoples
referred to this Commonwealth as a 'great family' and to
himself as its head—once more illustrating the kinship of
spirit between the Chinese and British Empires.

In one great case the political, though not the moral, bond
has been broken. Britons and Americans are not foreigners;
they may have their quarrels, but these, too, are family
quarrels. Criticism of the English is an American preserve;
and woe to the rash Frenchman who trespasses upon it![1]
The War of Independence was the work of Englishmen;
Washington was a typical English gentleman, fighting for
English ideals, supported by English statesmen. For a century and a quarter these kinsmen have waged no war; the
three thousand miles where their territories run together is
the best-defended frontier in the world, without a gun and
without a man on either side, but secure beyond a peradventure through the good will and good sense that go to make
'good neighbours'.[2]

[1] André Siegfried.   [2] President Roosevelt.

Americans have changed their name, but not their nature. The Viking spirit has sent pioneers, not in ships across oceans, but in wagons across prairies. If the remoteness of the wilds has disposed some of them to take the law into their own hands—to emphasize individuality at the expense of discipline—they still retain the love of freedom and respect for others that is the Nordic heritage. They expelled slavery, and are now struggling to expel economic servitude. If in the passage of the Atlantic the old culture has to some extent been broken at the roots, it has at least been replanted in virgin soil. In the vast spaces is a new sense of youth; the ideal, if not yet the actuality, of free opportunity for every man. A great variety of peoples contribute their traditions, as Celts, Romans, Germans, Scandinavians, Normans, Frenchmen, and Flemings have contributed to British civilization. A new species of Nordic civilization is in the making.

The same principle of freedom for each and all governs the foreign policy of the Nordics. As Scandinavians, British, and Americans alike perceive, a civilized society involves a legal and political order, not at home only, but abroad; the nations must therefore themselves form some sort of community or commonwealth. Hence, with the break-up of Catholic Christendom, the rise of international law, formulated by a Dutchman;[1] and the scrupulous regard paid by these nations to the sanctity of treaties. Hence, broad and large, foreign policies that seek not only the good of their own country, but also that of others. Sweden let Norway go, and reaped her reward in friendship. Great Britain fought four great wars against Powers and potentates that sought hegemony at the expense of liberty: Philip of Spain, Louis the Fourteenth, Napoleon, William the Second. They were waged, in Marlborough's words, 'for the good of the Common Cause'.[2] But British foreign policy not only resists tyranny, it assists freedom. The Napoleonic wars left Britain the arbiter of war and peace, free to seek her own if so she would—mistress of the seas, controller of raw material, supreme in industry and finance; and for half a century[3] she used this power, not in her own interest only, but to secure

[1] Grotius, *De jure belli et pacis.*
[2] Winston Churchill, *Marlborough*, ii. 231.   [3] 1815–70.

for others the liberty she loves for herself. Canning 'called in the New World to redress the balance of the Old', and freed its Latin Republics. Palmerston was the irreconcilable enemy of slavery, injustice, and oppression, and used the power of Britain to oppose them. She did much to free Greece, Belgium, and Italy from foreign domination, and tried to secure more liberal government in Portugal, Spain, and Hungary. Gladstone, 'a great Christian statesman',[1] restored the Ionian Islands to Greece, averted war with the United States by arbitration, with burning words denounced Neapolitan prisons and Bulgarian atrocities, and declared in 1870 (in words adopted by Asquith in 1914) that 'the greatest triumph of our time will be the enthronement of the idea of public right as the governing idea of European politics'.[2] Under Monroe and Roosevelt the United States have sought the freedom of the American Republics; under Wilson and Roosevelt the freedom of the world.

It has been said that British policy is nothing but 'a sound and justifiable egoism', to which 'all other considerations, friendships as well as enmities, have always been subordinated'.[3] But this is a profound mistake, a reflection of the unsuccessful egoism of the critics. It is said that Britain already has all she wants; but she has it because her Empire, like the Roman in its best days, is on the whole run unselfishly, for the good of the component peoples and of the world. The nations acquiesced in her expansion, because they perceived that it was not aggressive, and appreciated a policy of free trade and opportunity for all. Lord John Russell in a confidential dispatch to Queen Victoria declared that the general principle that should guide British foreign policy was 'the grand rule of doing to others as we wish that they should do unto us'.[4] He added that 'the honour of England does not consist in defending every English officer or English subject, right or wrong, but in taking care that she does not infringe the rules of justice, and that they are not infringed against her'. The British have succeeded in

[1] Lord Salisbury on Gladstone's death.
[2] *The Times*, 26 September 1914.
[3] Prince Bernhard von Bülow, *Imperial Germany* (1914), p. 21.
[4] Monypenny and Buckle, *The Letters of Queen Victoria*, ii. 428.

building up and preserving a World Empire, not because of a healthy egoism, but because of a healthy altruism. The Nordic ideal of foreign policy is 'good neighbourliness'.

The end of the World War saw the Nordics take their stand upon the same principle of freedom for themselves and others: self-determination in a League of Nations. Like the Chinese, like India and Russia, the Nordics regard aggressive war, not merely as disastrous, but as morally wrong; and they aimed, in a solemn Covenant, at ending it by moral means— the turning of foes into friends.[1] The Pact of Paris outlawed war as an instrument of national policy.[2] The Declaration of Lima affirmed the solidarity of the American Republics.[3]

Thus the Nordic spirit is essentially that of a crew—and its end is the navigation of the ship of State. This political genius expresses itself—like that of a crew—in a spirit of willing self-discipline for the common good. It has for its basis, not the ethical harmony arising from family ties, but rather a respect for other men, of one's own and other communities, and for their rights as citizens of those communities. Hence the Nordic's sense of fair play and honour, and his abhorrence alike of the tyranny that destroys freedom and of the licence that ends in chaos.

This is the dominant spirit that has manifested itself throughout the course of Scandinavian, British, and American history. Its heroes and leaders have consequently been exponents of political and social liberty. But just because this spirit has been realized more than the ideals of most other nations in the ordinary citizen, its institutions—formed by the will of the common people—have been more remarkable than its philosophers: its schools, its Parliaments, its commercial enterprise, its free Federations and so on.

The States of the Nordic Commonwealth thus rest on the securest foundation on which earthly States can rest, the political intelligence and aptitude of their citizens: an intelligence that enables them to dispense with the logical formulae and codes that must guide other nations, and allows them to solve each problem of public life as and when it arises. The empirical logic of the Nordics is thus, in political

[1] 1919.   [2] 1928.   [3] 1938.

affairs, superior to the deductive logic of other nations: it is an unphilosophical sagacity comparable in its results to the sagacity of the Romans, and producing, like the Roman, an ability and genius for government superior to that of other peoples.

II. 3

The Nordic genius, however, though, like the Roman, expressing itself primarily through political life, and possessing therefore the characteristic virtues of the Roman—a sense of justice and a respect for the rights of other men— has, unlike the Roman but like the Chinese, other characteristics, which appear in their moments of leisure and at times of renaissance. These find expression more particularly in their scientific and literary works—exhibiting the Nordic mind in new and higher relations to Nature and God, as well as to man.

The Nordic's science and religion are indeed akin to his social philosophy. For science involves the discovery in Nature of order and law, and Nordic religion conceives of God rather as some one who is interested in behaviour than as a Remote and Mystical Holiness. But there branch from these roots other and less practical developments of the spirit of man. His poetry shows a love of natural beauty to which he gives a more than natural significance, as in Spenser, Shelley, and Wordsworth; his respect for man rises into a complete and profounder love for man, as in Chaucer, Scott, and Shakespeare; his respect for God is transformed into the mystical experience of Cromwell, George Fox, Walt Whitman. It is such poets and seers as these that give to Nordic culture a larger than political significance and, as in China, prove the possibility of the union of earthly with heavenly wisdom in the minds of a people. For if it is the loftier spirits of Scandinavia, Britain, and America who reveal the wonder of Nature, the excellence of man, the greatness of God, it is the common people who plant their gardens, build and support their hospitals, and worship God in secret.

All this is nowhere so well shown as in the great Renaissance of Elizabethan days, when the English character was perhaps most perfectly itself. As the English had advanced beyond other nations in political liberty, so in religion they were already freer than others, when the discipline of the Church was challenged by Luther and its authority shaken by the European nations generally. As in the case of these nations, so in that of the English, this discovery of their freedom—this sense of being let out of school—led to a great burst of energy. But whereas the Latin nations derived their inspiration largely from the Romans and Greeks, the English were mainly self-inspired. Tudor lyrics and Tudor music are like an English spring morning, and it is in the cities and meadows of England that Shakespeare found those men and women whom his imagination exalted into a Henry the Fifth and a Rosalind, a Falstaff and a Prospero. It was an age that discovered with the ecstasy of youth, not God, but Nature and man—'This goodly frame, the earth: ... this most excellent canopy, the air; ... this brave o'erhanging firmament, this majestical roof fretted with golden fire. .... What a piece of work is a man! how noble in reason! how infinite in faculty! in form and moving how express and admirable! in action how like an angel! in apprehension how like a god! the beauty of the world! the paragon of animals!'[1] Again the Vikings sailed the seas, for the Spanish Main and El Dorado, carrying the new England to the New World. Bacon, throwing away the syllogism, began to peer for himself into 'Nature's infinite book of secrecy',[2] to find out worlds greater still. A burst of drama, inspired by the greatest of playwrights, held up a mirror to the burst of energy in man. The ideal of the age was magnificence—great-doing; and Spenser wrote its epic, grouping his knights around the Faery Queen, Gloriana, the adored Elizabeth. Two centuries later an old beggar in Scotland was to talk like Hamlet of Nature and man: '*Me* no muckle to fight for! Isna there the country to fight for, and the burnsides that I gang daundering beside, and the hearths o' the gudewives that gie me my bit bread, and the bits o' weans that come toddling to play wi' me when I come about a landward toun?'[3] In America's 'Golden Day'[4] Walt Whitman was to show a

[1] *Hamlet*, II. ii. [2] *Antony and Cleopatra*, I. ii.
[3] Edie Ochiltree, Scott, *The Antiquary*, c. xliv.
[4] Lewis Mumford.

similar love for Blades of Grass and for the Children of
Adam. His voice too, stilled by the clamours of post-war
materialism, fell silent before it sang of the Eternal.

In its general character the Englishman's appreciation of
Nature, like that of the Chinese, is probably due to his feeling
that the world is a good place to live in—a home brightened
for him by common flowers and standing trees—the simple
things of earth rather than the artificialities of men's imaginations, however spiritual and heavenly. Englishmen love the
open air, not the office stool. Almost every Englishman
would like to live in the country; he leaves it when he must,
and returns to it when he can. He loves living and growing
things, as a Chinese enjoys their 'rhythmic vitality'. 'Spare
us a flower, lady' cries the urchin in the London slum, with
a Chinese love of beauty. The Englishman's garden is the
cottage garden, of mingled vegetables and flowers, usefulness
and beauty. The herbaceous borders of great houses are
founded upon these; gardens of ornate formality are due to
foreign influence.[1] He loves the great park, and has bounded
his very fields with hedges that shoot forth the living charm
of Nature. The country-side is the Englishman's most characteristic work of art.[2]

It is indeed the sphere where his spirit expresses itself in
his leisure hours—when he is not occupied in his perpetual
task of maintaining and improving the fabric of his State.
Here he indulges in the sport he loves. Isaac Walton
angling in the brook is perhaps the greatest expression of
the Englishman at ease. He loves to feel his foot upon the
heather, as his ancestors loved to tread the great spaces
before them. Gilbert White looking at the birds of Selborne
is again very English.

This genius of the Englishman at ease—so little understood abroad—is the source of much of his poetry and painting. Like the Chinese he excels in landscape; and English
poetry from Chaucer to Tennyson is full of love of the country
and of the spiritual meaning of natural things. The greatest
of the English poets of Nature, and the greatest of English
landscape painters, both look upon Nature as a Taoist might.

[1] Clutton Brock.
[2] Grant Allen, *The European Tour.*

Wordsworth, gazing at the mountains and streams above Tintern, feels

> A Presence that disturbs me with the joy
> Of elevated thoughts; a sense sublime
> Of Something far more deeply interfused,
> Whose dwelling is the light of setting suns,
> And the round ocean and the living air,
> And the blue sky, and in the mind of man:
> A Motion and a Spirit, that impels
> All thinking things, all objects of all thought,
> And rolls through all things.

Turner, brooding like the Vikings, similarly sees in mist and water and sunlight the symbols of the Infinite: 'the sun is God.'[1]

At the same time the Nordic is deeply interested in natural science, owing not only to his desire to control Nature but also to his interest in human law. Roger Bacon of Oxford was almost the first to perceive the value to the study of Nature of mathematics and experiment—'the lord of sciences, the door to knowledge, the criterion of truth'. Francis Bacon was led from his knowledge of the case law of Rome, France, Scotland, and England to his 'new instrument' of experiment and induction.[2] As the interest in religion waned, an increasing interest was felt in the exploration of Nature for its own sake, and the Royal Society was founded to foster it. Newton, regarding Nature, not as the Tao whence all things spring, but as a universal system of law, discovered both the law of gravitation and the principles of optics; and these prepared the way for the immensities of modern astronomy and for the minutiae of modern physics, which reveal a universe extended between the infinitely great and the infinitely small. Darwin showed that man and other species were evolved from a primal plastic stuff, a view that demanded adjustments both in philosophy and in theology.

The Nordic's understanding of man is due in large measure to the fact that a disciplined freedom involves a sympathetic consideration of the points of view of other men —a respect for men in themselves. Those who take council

---

[1] His last words.   [2] Mary Sturt, *Bacon: a Biography.*

must be at pains to understand each other—not treat each other as cogs in a machine. In the greater minds this respect for others flowers into love—love for one's neighbour in the full sense. In Shakespeare love reaches a sublime height; but it rises from the foot-hills of ordinary English friendliness.

This sense of respect and love, this liking for all and sundry, is closely akin to the sense of humour, and that again to a feeling of tolerance. Hence the motley crowd of every class and kind that jostles through the pages of English fiction. Chaucer rides with his pilgrims to Canterbury and records their tales. Scott drinks his whisky with the shepherds of the Border and draws tale and talk from the litigants of Selkirk and Edinburgh. Burns is the most human of poets. Dickens, laughing and loving, sees the common people like transfigured spirits. The creator of the Forsytes lingers over the middle classes. And what a keen eye Nordic women have! Selma Lagerlöf, Miss Austen, Charlotte and Emily Brontë, George Eliot, Mary Webb. Above all others towers Shakespeare, understanding and loving the whole range of men and women—kings and clowns, white and black, saints and sinners. He knew the worst: man's ingratitude and jealousy cast him in middle life deep into doubt as to the reality of good at all.

> How weary, stale, flat and unprofitable
> Seem to me all the uses of the world!
> Fie on't! O fie! 'Tis an unweeded garden
> That runs to seed; things rank and gross in nature
> Possess it merely.[1]

But a fresh energy of love conquered this scepticism, and with the insight that accompanies love he sees that man is in his true nature 'a thing Divine',[2] a Godlike being—as the Chinese see his natural goodness, his share in the Tao. Hence Shakespeare's pictures of the young lovers Florizel and Perdita, Ferdinand and Miranda, and the self-portrait of his mature wisdom, Prospero. And he who sees that man's nature and destiny is to be Godlike can do no other than forgive man's sin in all its beastlikeness:

> I do forgive
> Thy rankest fault; all of them.[3]

[1] *Hamlet,* I. ii.   [2] *The Tempest,* I. ii.   [3] Ibid. v. i.

If the Nordics resemble the Chinese in their love of Nature and of man—in 'making righteousness their aim in human affairs'—they resemble them also in having little genius for religion—they 'treat superhuman beings with respect',[1] but have as a rule scant insight into the Unseen. The essence of religion among the Scandinavians and Anglo-Saxons has been to give a Divine sanction to human liberty—to make that spirit religious:

> Lord God of Hosts, be with us yet,
> Lest we forget, lest we forget.

Political self-discipline involves an acute conscience—a sensitiveness to any act which contravenes its ideal; as a schoolboy's sense of honour has its obverse in his bad conscience. When this ideal becomes religious, it naturally assumes a Pauline form—social misdemeanour, such as lying, becomes sin, while good behaviour tends to be identified with religion itself.

Although, therefore, the Nordics early accepted Christianity from Rome, as the Chinese accepted Buddhism from India, to eke out the deficiencies of their own reason, their religious spirit has always been more ethical and practical than sacramental and liturgical. They have produced few saints, and only recognized those of the more active kind—Dunstan, Edmund of Abingdon, Bridget of Sweden; the few mystical saints—Rolle, Hilton, Julian of Norwich—have been lost in an uncongenial civilization. What England admires is the parish priest setting the example of good works and a good life—as the Chinese love the example of the scholar-ruler. Chaucer says of his poor parson:

> This noble ensample to his sheep he yaf,
> That first he wroghte, and afterward he taughte;
> He was a shepherde and no mercenarie.[2]

As Wycliffe taught in Oxford, the true title of the priest to 'dominion' over men's souls is not outward authority but inward righteousness. In Utopia, wrote Sir Thomas More, 'there be few priests, but they be exceeding holy'.

The decay of the Roman Church tended to destroy the

---

[1] *Analects*, vi. 20.   [2] *Prologue*, 496–7, 514.

more spiritual element in the religion of the Nordics, and the endeavour of the Counter-Reformation to re-conquer the North by means of the Spanish Armada and the Thirty Years War led to its religious spirit becoming fanatical in its opposition to Rome. While the Anglican Church settled down into compromise between Catholicism and Protestantism, and those who dissented from her won first toleration and then equality, the place of Rome as the ultimate authority was taken by the Bible, variously interpreted by the competing dogmas of the time. In Lutheran lands God was envisaged as the man Jesus Christ, the friend of sinners, and faith in His atoning sacrifice took the place of the sacraments as the chief channel of Grace. For the Calvinists the God of Wrath tended to obscure the God of Grace; Wrath was predestined for the many, Grace for the few. All pleasure in Nature and man was wrong, as holding the soul from God. The maypole went with the monks; bear-baiting was hated, 'not because it gave pain to the bear, but because it gave pleasure to the spectators'.[1] In Britain public opinion still frowns upon ethical unconventionality and innovation; in the United States a passion for 'uplift' takes the form of a profusion of prohibitions.

Nevertheless Puritanism at its highest presented an ideal for society and for the soul far surpassing that of the ordinary Nordic, though it is the goal to which all individualism must lead. 'The mind was the man', Oliver Cromwell told Parliament; 'with an impure mind man was no better than a beast, and a beast could not rule; the State must be controlled by the seeing eyes and the single hearts.' Government should be in the hands of the good and wise—the people of God. The best should govern, but—as the ultimate ideal—all would be the best; for every immortal soul, though dwelling in the humblest body, is of transcendent value. Hence Cromwell's zeal for education and the faithful preaching of the Word. On his deathbed he prayed: 'Lord, I may, I will, come to Thee for Thy people. Continue and go on to do good for them. Give them consistency of judgment, one heart, and mutual love, and go on to deliver them, and with the work of reformation, and make the name of Christ

[1] Macaulay, *History of England* (1849), i, c. ii, p. 161.

glorious in the world. Teach those who look too much on
Thy instruments to depend more upon Thyself. Pardon
such as desire to trample upon the dust of a poor worm, for
they are Thy people too.' Burke, the prophet of individualism, wrote of him and his fellows that 'their rising was to
illuminate and beautify the world. Their conquest over their
competitors was by outshining them. The hand that like a
destroying angel smote the country communicated to it the
force and energy under which it suffered.'[1] Under such
rulers, he said, society would become 'a partnership in every
virtue and in all perfection'.

Cromwell was at heart 'a mystic, and the core of his
religion was a mystical experience continually renewed'.[2]
Much of his life was spent in a communion outside the world
of sense and time. 'You cannot find nor behold the face of
God but in Christ,' he wrote to his son, 'therefore labour to
know God in Christ, which the Scriptures make to be the
sum of all, even life eternal. Because the true knowledge is
not literal or speculative but inward, transforming the mind
to it.' Here his unspeculative mind rises intuitively to the
heights of the *Vedanta* and other mystical philosophies: man
knows God, not with the outward eye of sense, not with the
arguments of the intellect, but by the Godlike soul's immediate experience of God.

Of the three greatest Britons—perhaps the three greatest
Nordics—Newton, like Lao-tze, has a deep, though not a
mystic, insight into Nature; Shakespeare, like Confucius, a
deep insight into man. The Nordic world reveres both.
Cromwell, like Mo Ti, centred upon God, stands apart from
and above his countrymen, often depreciated, seldom understood.

Like Taoism, Puritanism failed partly; like Moism,
mysticism failed altogether. And because it failed, the
modern man stands more and more bewildered. Natural
science, puzzled itself, looks upon man simply as a product
of Nature, while a Conscious God stands unexplained on the
fringe of the system, or vanishes altogether from the eye of
argument, possibly to reappear as a Mathematician. The

[1] *Reflections on the Revolution in France.*
[2] Buchan, *Cromwell*, p. 67.

Nordic in his heart refuses assent, but nevertheless is profoundly disquieted. He re-names Fate Entropy, and again a
twilight falls upon the gods; the unphilosophic descendant
of the Norsemen is slow to recognize in Infinite Nature the
symbol of the Infinity of the Divine.

Only in Germany, the least typical, the marginal Nordic
land, did freedom take, not a political, but a spiritual form.

Germany stands apart from the other Nordics, as Japan
does from the Chinese, and for the same reason: feudalism
has through the ages divided both countries into small
competing States, lacking the pacific local government of
China and the effective central government of Great Britain.
In addition, Germany, defenceless in the heart of Europe,
has time and again been invaded from without. Hence,
with less opportunity to develop a creative originality, both
peoples have been more open to foreign influences. The
minds of both are malleable, mutable, impressionable,
quickly responsive to example good and bad.

Nor have they been as well able to blend together the
more heroic and sometimes brutal native strain with the
gentler and more spiritual ideals imported by Buddhism and
by Christianity. Hence the militarism and the mysticism of
Japan. Hence in Germany a magnificent martial courage, but
also the swaggering and over-bearing ideal of Odin and Thor,
Siegfried and the Superman, Junker and Nazi, 'German
Christianity' and the German Faith Movement; and also
the marvellous spiritual strength and beauty of the German
mystics, musicians, and idealist philosophers. In the *chun-
tze* and the gentleman the two ideals are welded, as they
are in Plato's watch-dog, the guardian soldier whom education in 'music' and gymnastic has made both gentle and
manly. In Germany, as in Japan, the welding is less
complete.

Thus the Germans are inferior to the other Nordics in
political capacity, but superior to them in the higher regions
of the spirit. Because Germany has never attained a national
unity, and even tends to disintegrate into an anarchy of over-
impressionable individuals, her efforts to express her political soul have emphasized the need for the discipline rather

than for the individuality involved in liberty—the reverse of
what has happened in America, where individuality is emphasized at the expense of discipline, because individuality
was required in the backwoodsman. But if Germany has
contributed little to political freedom, she has, true to the
liberty-loving genius of the Nordics, contributed much to
that higher freedom, the inward energy of the spirit.

When Germany, like the other Nordics, grew up and
broke away from the schoolmastering of Catholicism, the
revolt against the Church was led by a man who combined
both the German strains. Luther's movement was at once
a vigorous, if sometimes brutal, assertion of independence
against authority—a claim for the German to think out his
own religion and to seek his own salvation without interference from Rome (so far, save for the brutality, it resembled
Wycliffe's)—and the unsealing of a mystical depth and tenderness belonging to another world. Luther thus became the
most beloved of Germans because he is the ideal of Germans
—the German who combines heroism with mysticism. But
on the whole the other-worldly strain has predominated over
moral vigour. Quietism, abandoning this hopeless world to
the Princes and the Prince thereof, inspired the German
Lutherans to trust in Jesus as the Supreme Friend in the
wretchedness of this life, and to look to Heaven as the place
of blessedness hereafter; just as in Japan the Pure Land
Schools inspired the common people to trust in the pitying
loving-kindness of Amida while waiting for the Paradise
of Bliss. Luther might have written some of Shinran's
hymns.[1]

As the higher spirits of Japan are touched with the
mystery of Zen, so are the higher spirits of Germany with
mysticism, idealism, and music. Eckhart maintained that all
things are One and That One is God; the end of the human
soul and of all else is union with God through 'an unknowing
knowing'. The Friends of God and their successors—Suso
and Tauler, Ruysbroeck and à Kempis, wandering up and
down the Rhineland or meditating in forest or monastery,
claimed 'spiritual freedom'. Nicholas of Cusa told of a
knowledge above knowledge, an 'incomprehensible com-

[1] Kenneth Saunders, *Epochs in Buddhist History*, p. 179.

prehension', a 'mystical Theology'.[1] Luther himself could say: 'I do not know it and I do not understand it, but, sounding from above and ringing in my ears, I hear what is beyond the thought of man.'[2] Later, the great idealist philosophers Fichte, Hegel, and Schelling were to conceive the Universe as an Infinite Absolute Ego; though even into this conception the other German element, the brutality of force and war, was liable to enter.

'Next to Divinity (said Luther) no art is comparable to music.' If it be not in mysticism, it is in music that the German spirit soars to its height. In it is a springtime vigour that recalls that of the Elizabethans. There is a Tudor beauty and romance in the music of Schubert and Schumann, a Shakespearian searching for the Infinite in the Symphonies of Beethoven. In Bach and Mozart the German spirit triumphs, reaching a sublimity that the Anglo-Saxon spirit has perhaps never attained. The Mass of the one, the Requiem of the other, are a revelation of God comparable only to the revelation of man in *Cymbeline*, *The Winter's Tale*, and *The Tempest*.

These high achievements of their leaders have been reflected in the lives of the German peoples. If a genius for central government has been conspicuously absent, a genius for local organization has made their Cities and States an appropriate setting for *Gemütlichkeit*, the sense of bodily and spiritual comfort. Cleanliness and order have reigned in their streets and in their homes. Theatres, books, concerts, opera have been good, plentiful, and within reach of light purses. A room may be but an attic, yet the tiled stove and polished floor have consented with a warmth of singing and of talk. Whole families would go of an evening to the beer-halls, where the good music went down so well with the good Schnitzel and the good beer; of a Sunday to the well-loved lakes and forests, there to eat and to sing part-songs upon the grass.

Thus Anglo-Saxons have sought for freedom in society,

---

[1] Evelyn Underhill, *Mysticism*; Rufus M. Jones, *Studies in Mystical Religion*.
[2] Quoted by Buchan, *Cromwell*, p. 528.

Germans for freedom in the spirit. Other civilizations have tried to combine something of both, to achieve the solidarity of society, not primarily through respect for man, but through respect for the Will of God, the Divine Ruler in Heaven. Judaism, Islam, and Catholicism are not merely moral but moral-spiritual civilizations—not democracies, but Theocracies.

IV

THE MORAL-SPIRITUAL STATE

MO TI would have men love one another, and so realize
on earth the Divine Righteousness, the Will of
Heaven; Cromwell would have a community with 'consistency of judgment, one heart and mutual love', who would
thus be 'the people of God'. If such an ideal was above the
reach of Chinese and Nordic, it took root in the minds of
Arab and Latin, and found expression in the two great
civilizations that aim at a Divine rule on earth.

The greater part of the Arab and Latin lands lies in the
sub-tropical zone, avoiding the sterner climates of the Chinese
and the Nordics, as well as the extremities of Indian heat
and Russian cold. The yellow fields, the Viking seas, the
factories, and the prairies give place to desert sands, an in-
land sea, white cities lazing in the sun. These lands have
been favourable both to action and to contemplation. The
Semites and the Romans have been great soldiers and traders;
but they need less food, less clothing and shelter than the
Chinese and the Nordics under their more rigorous skies,
and therefore have not been compelled to fight with and subdue Nature, and have had leisure to be alone and dream. It
is enough for the Arab to munch a handful of dates as he
walks away from his tent: 'haste is of the Devil, and delibera-
tion of the Merciful'. The Arab lying in the sun is a
lazy dog to the bustling Nordic; yet he may be 'heard as a
song of praise where God is'.[1] The two civilizations lie
adjacent, and each has overflowed into the lands of the other,
Rome into Arabia and Arabia into Rome. The Arabs have
always looked, not to the Indian Ocean, but to the Mediterranean for their enterprise, their expansion, and their
cultural sympathies:[2] the Phoenicians sailed the rocky Straits
to Tarshish and the Scillies, the followers of the Prophet
established themselves in North Africa, Sicily, and Spain.
The Romans for their part occupied the Arab lands as far

---

[1] Cp. Robert Hitchin, *The Garden of Allah.*
[2] T. E. Lawrence, *Seven Pillars of Wisdom*, p. 35.

U

as the Euphrates and the Tigris, and Crusader kings reigned in Jerusalem.

Both civilizations have a foundation of hard, successful, well-organized materialism. The Arabs were originally a pastoral people, tribesmen scouring deserts and grasslands on their beloved camels. In Babylonia, irrigating the waste with the waters of the Euphrates, they settled down to till. In Babylon, Tyre, and Carthage, Arab townsmen turned to trade by land and water; their Jewish kinsmen have since Solomon carried on this tradition of commerce and finance. The blood-feuds of the Bedouin, the conquests of Nineveh, the far-flung armies of Islam show that they are a warlike people. Similarly the foundation of Roman civilization was practical and material; it was the civilization of the farmer who was also soldier and senator.

Private morals were those of a materialist people. The Prophets denounced in the Hebrews the debauchery that Muhammad deplored in the Arabs. Paul's letters continually complain of the 'rioting and drunkenness, chambering and wantonness' of the Graeco-Romans, with the 'strife and envying' that sprang from them.[1]

The religion of both civilizations was materialist too. Each Arab tribe had its god—local Baals that were worshipped with human and animal sacrifices amid obscene orgies. The Romans deified Caesar, the 'universal Providence' of their Empire.

Judaism, Islam, and Catholicism originated in attempts to spiritualize these societies by penetrating them with a consciousness of the Power of God as the Ruler of the world, and of His Righteousness, Compassion, or Grace towards His people, provided they escaped from their materialism by obedience to His Will as expressed in His laws. God was not a Man, but a Being Ineffable, in whose Image man had been created. So intensely Real was He that men could hear His Voice speaking from the Desert or receive His message from the Heavens. 'Thus saith the Lord', wrote the Prophets of Israel; God's Uncreated Word was brought to Muhammad; the Catholic believes that God has

---

[1] Romans xiii. 13.

revealed certain Truths about His Inner Life and Dealings with men that unaided reason could not have discovered. Everything in the religion of Semites and Latins is as vivid, as sharply defined, as the objects around them, clear-cut in the light of the sub-tropical sun: God and Devil, Heaven and Hell, angels and demons, saints and damned.

The first to conceive this Moral God seems to have been Abraham, who went forth from Ur to obey His Command. Muhammad revealed Allah, not as a material, but as a Moral Deity, and he too set forth upon a mission. Paul taught Caesar-worshipping Rome of another Divine Ruler, the Man from Heaven, and journeyed to preach this crucified King. But the seed took some centuries to spring from the ground and bear fruit. Amos took up the task of Abraham and inaugurated the Prophetic age in Israel. The teachings of the Prophets were adopted and adapted by Muhammad. Augustine revived the doctrines of Paul, but the era of Catholic sanctity did not come to full flower till the Middle Ages.

A vast attempt was made by all to extirpate materialism, viewed as the sin that alienates men from God, and in its place to establish the righteousness that should reconcile them to His Righteousness. That is a fundamentally different view from the humanism of the Chinese and Nordics. Nevertheless, of the three civilizations Judaism stands nearest to the this-worldly societies, Islam holds an intermediate place, Catholicism approaches the other-worldly. In Jewish doctrine there is no antinomy between body and soul, any more than there is in Nordic: God created material things and 'saw that they were good'. Of the Arabs, on the other hand, Lawrence of Arabia writes: 'Body and spirit were forever and inevitably opposed.'[1] Paul laid down, in words that are among the foundation-stones of Catholicism: 'They that are in the flesh cannot please God. The body is dead because of sin; but the Spirit is life because of righteousness'. That is, the flesh is sinful until it is regenerated by Christ.[2] The finer spirits of Islam and Catholicism turned their back therefore on this too attractive world to seek in the solitude of desert, cave, or cell the God that hideth Himself;[3]

[1] Lawrence, *Pillars*, p. 42. [2] Romans viii. 8, 10. [3] Isaiah xlv. 15.

Muhammad, Paul, Benedict, Francis, Ignatius Loyola, all retreated to the eloquent silence of the wild or the monastery before beginning their mission to mankind. Jesus did the same. Then they returned to tell that the Almighty has Compassion on those who surrender to His Will, and Grace to perfect the 'natural', whether body or soul, by raising it to share the Supernatural, the God-Life.

Inevitably a religious society will tend to be led by religious leaders. But in this respect again the three civilizations differ as they are less or more other-worldly. Israel has dreamed of a Messiah, a King Anointed of God, but has never recognized this ideal as taking human form. Islam since the Prophet's death has been ruled by his Successor or Caliph, the Catholic world since Christ's death by Peter and his successors as Christ's Vicars. And so with the lesser leaders. Israel is guided by rabbis, the doctors or teachers of the Law, authorized to deal with questions of Law and ritual, and Islam by mullahs, doctors of Theology and the Law. The priests of Israel, growing in power, became after the Exile the only national functionaries among the Jewish subjects of the Persian or the Greek; but only in the atoning rites by which breaches of holiness were expiated did they mediate between God and man, for the essential idea was that Israel was a kingdom of priests. A similar idea obtains in Islam, which has never had a priestly class. In Catholicism, on the other hand, the Grace of God cannot as a rule descend upon the faithful in the sacraments without the mediation of ordained priests, who are generally also learned clerks.

All three civilizations formulated a conception of the Last Things, though again with characteristic differences. The Jewish ideal was of a righteous nation; under Persian influence the righteous dead were conceived as rising from the grave at the coming of the Messiah to establish His Kingdom on earth. Islam, on the contrary, promised the faithful Muslim the joys of Paradise, material and spiritual: houris and rivers of wine, and to see the Face of God. Catholicism has commonly held out the prospect of a material Hell and Purgatory, and of a spiritual Heaven.

Thus, if in the this-worldly civilizations the main interest is focused on Nature and man, in the both-worldly it slips

away from Nature, especially from the laws of Nature, and
centres upon the One Righteous God, the Ruler of the
world, and a society whose function is to do His Will.
From God's Unity springs the ideal of a single Commonwealth of mankind; from His Righteousness, the ideal of a
reign of righteousness upon earth. That Commonwealth will
tend to spread over the world; that righteousness to take the
form, not of a human, but of a Sacred Law, aiming especially
at correcting the old evils of idolatry and wickedness.

Society is thus conceived, not as a democracy, but as a
Theocracy. Theocracy is a loftier conception than democracy,
but less easily attainable by ordinary human nature; it is
easier for men to become good citizens than to become 'the
people of God'. What Theocracy gained in elevation it lost
in the political aptitude of its members and the organization
of their affairs. Nor could the higher side of its ideal always
maintain itself. Inspiration tended to harden into tradition,
revelation to conflict with freedom of thought, love to ossify
into law; God-hearing Prophets gave place to learned rabbis,
the knowledge of God became mere obedience, Apostles
were succeeded by priests. The lofty conception of a dedicated people under the Rule of God sometimes degenerated,
in fact, into a Kingdom of this world ruled by worldly
Sadducees, Caliphs, or Popes.

Yet the inherent strength of these civilizations has continually reasserted itself: Judaism, Islam, and Catholicism
have all had astonishing Renaissances. The vivid imagery
of the Mediterranean does not supersede philosophy, which
is, indeed, the artist's imagination analysing itself. The effort
is made to conceive God and man rationally: the Prophets
urge man to know God, Islam and Catholicism produce
famous scholastics. This attempt gives birth to great academies and universities, Jewish, Muslim, and Catholic, and
to an interest in the same objects of study: the Divine Nature
upon Which all centres, the Sacred Law that expresses His
Will, Medicine; other arts and sciences are considered subordinate. Each of the three civilizations has shown a wonderful power of absorbing what is best in other civilizations,
especially the philosophy of Aristotle and the mysticism of the
Neoplatonists, as well sometimes as Greek or Nordic science.

I

If China crowns its civilization with the noble idea of a universal harmony in which the meanest of mankind has his own part to play, and the Nordics with the kindred conception of an orderly freedom for all men, if the Hindu and the Russian spirit soars to a mighty conception of the Godhead and of the fundamental Divinity of man, there is a sense in which the civilization of Arabia unites elements of both. For there arose out of her primitive culture men who developed in a spiritual direction the materialist idea of god as the saviour or patron of their tribe—of his people—which exists in primitive society. To change this tribal notion of god into that of God the Lord and Ruler of all men, whose Nature is at once moral and Infinite—this was the first part of the work of the Prophets. To show what man must be for such a God to be seen of him—this was the second part. Through the first they approximate to the highest flights of the religious spirit; through the second, like the social reformers of the this-worldly civilizations, they mould man into a being who of his own free will cares for the widow and the orphan and for social good in general. God and His Kingdom on earth—that was their twofold revelation.

I. 1

Abraham[1] stood at the head of the movement, as two thousand years later Muhammad stood at the head of the movement that continued that of Abraham. In the midst of idolatry and human sacrifice he seems to have known One God, Almighty and All-Comprehending, throned in the Heaven, honoured without priest or temple, to Whom the faithful had personal access. He could hear the Eternal calling; and in obedience to the Divine Command led forth from Ur a band of kinsmen, not, like other Bedouin, for plunder or conquest, but on a religious crusade.

They settled first in Egypt, where presently a boy Pharaoh, inspired like Abraham, acclaimed One God of all the world Whose Goodness satisfies all His creatures.

[1] c. 1550 B.C.

How manifold are all Thy works!
They are hidden from before us,
O Thou Sole God, Whose Powers no other possesseth.
Thou didst create the earth according to Thy Desire,
While Thou wast Alone:
Men, all cattle large and small,
All that are upon the earth;
The countries of Syria and Nubia,
The land of Egypt.
Thou settest every man in his place,
Thou suppliest their necessities.
How excellent are Thy Designs, O Lord of Eternity![1]

Centuries later a herdsman of Tekoa brought a similar
message to another luxurious and idolatrous people. Amos[2]
denounced at once the false and formal worship of his countrymen and their immoral life, especially their hypocrisy and
avarice. God is a Moral God, desiring not material but moral
offerings. The very Words of the Divine Voice thunder in
the Prophet's ears.

I hate, I despise your feasts,
I will take no delight in your solemn assemblies.
Yea, though ye offer Me your burnt offerings and meal offerings, I
    will not accept them.
But let judgment roll down as waters
And righteousness as an ever-flowing stream.[3]

But how can righteousness prevail when men

swallow up the needy
And cause the poor of the land to fail;
Dealing falsely with balances of deceit,
That they may buy the poor for silver,
And the needy for a pair of shoes,[4]

when they lie luxuriously 'upon beds of ivory' and 'eat the
lambs out of the flock'?[5] Immoral men can have no knowledge of a Moral God! Nor are the neighbouring nations any
better; 'for three transgressions, yea, for four' they too shall
be punished equally with Israel and Judah.[6] The One God
is the God of all nations.

---

[1] Quoted Breasted, *History of Egypt*, pp. 373–4.   [2] Floruit *c.* 760 B.C.
[3] Amos v. 21–2, 24.   [4] Ibid. viii. 4, 5.   [5] Ibid. vi. 4.   [6] Ibid. i. 3.

The Prophets who followed developed this view, both of God and of human society. They insisted on the Unity of God; all other gods were idols. With biting irony God exclaims through the mouth of Hosea:

> My people ask counsel at their stock,
> And their staff declareth unto them![1]

while the Second Isaiah laughs:

> A man planteth a fir tree, and the rain doth nourish it,
> He kindleth it, and baketh bread,
> Yea, he maketh a god, and worshippeth it.
> He warmeth himself, and saith,
> Aha, I am warm, I have seen the fire—
> And the residue thereof he maketh a god![2]

It is because God is One and not many that the Book of the Law—Deuteronomy—lays stress on the Single Sanctuary: the people shall destroy the high places and the idols, the wooden posts and the stone pillars, and 'resort to the sacred spot that Yahweh your God shall choose amid all your clans as the seat of His Presence'.[3]

This One God is at once Infinite and therefore Incomprehensible to men, and the Ruler and Lover of His people.

The first or Impersonal Aspect of the Divine was to receive a fuller development in the minds of the Hindus, the Platonists, and the mystics generally; but the Hebrew Prophets were well aware of it. Thus in the vision during which Isaiah is called to prophesy God is revealed as 'Holy, Holy, Holy', that is, Apart, 'the fullness of the whole earth is His Glory';[4] while the Second Isaiah knows that 'there is no searching of His Understanding'.[5] Job lays still greater stress on this tremendous conception: the Infinity of the Divine Wisdom explains the inability of man's tiny understanding to fathom the problem of human suffering.

> Where wast thou when I laid the foundations of the earth?
> Declare, if thou understandest.
> Who measured out the earth, if thou knowest?
> Who stretched the builder's line?
> When all the morning stars sang together,
> And all the sons of God shouted for joy.[6]

---

[1] Hosea iv. 12.   [2] Isaiah xliv. 14–16.   [3] Deuteronomy xii. 5.
[4] Isaiah vi. 3.   [5] Ibid. xl. 28.   [6] Job xxxviii. 4.

On the other hand, the Prophets of Israel have expounded more vividly than any other men the Moral Qualities of God in His relation to mankind, His Righteousness, Goodness, Love. If Amos revealed the Divine Denunciation of impiety and egoism, Hosea realizes the Pity of God for the pain man must suffer in his passage from sin to the righteousness destined for him. As Hosea's own wife had proved unfaithful to him, yet he had pitifully forgiven and restored her, so Israel had been unfaithful to God, but the Divine Pity would forgive and restore likewise. In a metaphor of exquisite pathos God says:

> When Israel was a child, then I loved him,
> And called my son out of Egypt.
> I taught Ephraim to go,
> (as a mother teaches her little one to walk)
> I took them in My arms.
> How shall I give thee up, Ephraim?
> My heart is turn'd within Me.
> For I am God and not man,
> The Holy One in the midst of thee.'[1]

The Second Isaiah unites the Divine Grandeur of Job with the Divine Tenderness of Hosea:

> Behold, the Lord God will come as a Mighty One,
> And His Arm shall rule for Him:
> Behold, His reward is with Him,
> And his recompence before Him.
> He shall feed His flock like a shepherd,
> He shall gather the lambs with His Arm,
> And carry them in His Bosom,
> And shall gently lead them that are with young.[2]

From the Nature of God and His Love for men the Hebrew Prophets and Prophet-statesmen derive their conception of what individual men and human society should be. If a man is to know God he must forsake his old egoism and impiety, his lust, his covetousness, his pride, and the idolatry to which they give rise, and obey God's Law of Righteousness. This Law, as the Prophets conceive it, is not a code of formal enactments imposed from without; it is the Command of God spoken to the heart of the nation or the

---

[1] Hosea xi. 1, 3, 8, 9.   [2] Isaiah xl. 10, 11.

man: 'Thus saith the Lord.' It aims first, negatively, at the uprooting of materialism, 'sin'; the Decalogue is a series of prohibitions: 'Thou shalt not.' Sin is essentially the three lusts that constitute materialism: self-indulgent luxury and debauchery, often cloaked as the worship of Astarte; covetousness, and the economic injustice to which it leads; and pride—the lofty looks of man shall be brought low, and his haughtiness bowed down.

These vices are evil because they make men ignorant of what will really satisfy them—of other men and especially of God. As Hosea puts it: 'Harlotry, wine and new wine take away the intellect.'[1] Hence it comes about that

> There is no truth nor mercy,
> Nor knowledge of God in the land.
> My people perish for lack of knowledge.[2]

Men are more thoughtless and stupid than beasts, God tells Isaiah:

> The ox knoweth his owner,
> The ass his master's crib,
> But Israel doth not know,
> My people doth not consider.[3]

And again, in words sanctioned by Jesus, to whom also a 'change of mind'[4] was the first thing needed:

> You hear continually but never understand,
> You see continually but never perceive,
> The heart of this people is obtuse,
> Their ears are heavy of hearing,
> They have closed their eyes;
> Lest they should see and hear and understand
> And turn again to be healed.[5]

Thus the Prophets of Israel say with Socrates that 'vice is ignorance, virtue is knowledge'. 'The fear of the Lord, that is wisdom, and to depart from evil is understanding.'[6] It is only to the materialist that vice looks like wisdom, because he sees with the eyes of an animal and therefore understands only material things. Therefore what is needed to

---

[1] Hosea iv. 11.   [2] Ibid. iv. 1, 6.   [3] Isaiah i. 3.
[4] Mark i. 15.   [5] Isaiah vi. 9, 10.   [6] Job xxviii. 28.

rescue man is education, a knowledge of God and His Will:
'Come now, and let us reason together, saith the Lord.'[1]
When a man is set free from his vices, he can both see and
hear:

> He hath showed thee, O man, what is good:
> And what does the Lord require of thee,
>> But to do justly,
>> And to love mercy,
>> And to walk humbly with thy God?[2]

With his eyes opened he can now 'love his neighbour as
himself', the poor, the widow, the fatherless, the stranger,
even the beasts and birds; for all these the spirit of love
breathes strongly in the Prophets and in 'the Book of the
Law'.[3] Above all he can now hear the greatest of the Commandments: 'Hear, O Israel! The Lord our God is One
God; and thou shalt love the Lord thy God with all thy
mind, and with all thy soul, and with all thy strength.'[4] The
ethical ideal of Israel is the righteous man who knows the
Righteous God, and knowing Him does His Will.

But God is not merely the God of Goodness; being One,
He is also the God of the whole earth, the Supreme Ruler,
whose Plan and Purpose is not merely to educate His people
from the sin that alienates them to a knowledge of Himself,
but to make them the Servant that shall presently draw all
nations to Zion and enable them also to know Him. That
progress and the ideal State to which it leads are the magnificent vision of the two Isaiahs.

At the time this vision must have seemed incredible.
Israel and Judah were two tiny kingdoms squeezed in between Great Powers, Egypt on the one hand, Assyria and
Babylon on the other; they were certain to be destroyed in the
end, as indeed, materially, they were. Yet Isaiah,[5] a practical
statesman, the Foreign Minister of Hezekiah, sees God as the
Supreme Statesman governing mankind, working His Will
through a human statesman, the Anointed or Messiah, the
ideal ruler or king of Israel. At first his imagination pictures him as the magnificent leader of men, 'the Wonderful
Counsellor, the God-Hero, the Everlasting Father, the

---

[1] Isaiah i. 18.   [2] Micah vi. 8.   [3] Deuteronomy.
[4] Deuteronomy vi. 4, 5.   [5] *Floruit* 740–701 B.C.

Prince of Peace';[1] then as one on whom will rest the Spirit of God:

> The spirit of wisdom and understanding,
> The spirit of counsel and might,
> The spirit of knowledge and of the fear of the Lord,
> And his delight shall be in the fear of the Lord:
> With righteousness shall he judge the poor,
> And decide with equity for the meek of the earth.[2]

Finally he foresees him as a figure of supreme righteousness who, bodhisatlike, shall save men from the storm, the scorching heat of the world's tribulations:

> Behold, a king shall reign in righteousness,
> And princes shall rule in judgment,
> And a man shall be as an hiding place from the wind,
>   And a covert from the tempest;
> As rivers of water in a dry place,
> As the shadow of a great rock in a weary land.[3]

Two centuries later a second Isaiah[4] even more boldly envisages, not a glorious statesman, but a stricken people, as the instrument of God for the regeneration of the world. It is now fifty years[5] since Nebuchadnezzar took Jerusalem; and sitting by the waters of Babylon the captive people has learnt in tears that the healing of men is to come, not through any material triumph, not even through a reign of righteousness, but through the opening of the eyes of the spirit by suffering. This captive nation is personified as a man, much as Great Britain is personified as Britannia; only, whereas Britannia merely rules the waves and embellishes pennies, this suffering servant-nation is the agent through whom God will bring all other nations to an understanding of their wickedness and a knowledge of Himself. In that day the enlightened and penitent world will say of Israel:

> He hath borne our griefs and carried our sorrows;
> He was bruised for our iniquities;
> And with his stripes we are healed.
> All we like sheep have gone astray;
> We have turned every one to his own way;
> And the Lord hath laid upon him the punishment of us all.[6]

[1] Isaiah ix. 6.   [2] Ibid. xi. 2, 4.   [3] Ibid. xxxii. 1, 2.
[4] Time of Cyrus, 549–529 B.C.   [5] 587–537 B.C.
[6] Isaiah liii. 4–6, 10–12.

Thus through Israel God's Purpose of Mercy will be fulfilled: 'the Pleasure of the Lord shall prosper in his hand.' For he comes to enlighten all nations: 'by his knowledge shall my righteous servant Israel make many righteous.' In that day the nation, suffering no longer, will triumph like a conqueror dividing the spoil.

Through statesman and nation, then, God will lead mankind to the ideal State. This State will embrace the whole world; Israel's two greatest enemies shall unite with her in the midst of the people of God.

> In that day shall Israel be the third with Egypt and with Assyria,
>   A blessing in the midst of the earth:
> For that the Lord of hosts hath blessed them, saying,
>   Blessed be Egypt my people,
>   And Assyria the work of my hands,
>   And Israel mine inheritance.[1]

The knowledge of God shall overflow the earth, driving away all brute-like violence and harm and bringing peace and joy to Nature and man in their innocence:

> The wolf shall dwell with the lamb,
> And the leopard shall lie down with the kid;
> And the calf and the young lion and the fatling together,
> And a little child shall lead them.
> They shall not hurt nor destroy
> In all my holy mountain:
> For all the earth shall be full of the knowledge of the Lord
> As the waters cover the sea.[2]

I. 2

As a civilizing or spiritualizing influence the great ideal of the Hebrews was clearly less intelligible to the mass of men than those of China and the Northlands, and therefore attained a slighter hold over their minds. Not all could hear the Divine Voice; but all could obey the Divine Law. During the Prophetic period therefore, and still more when the great afflatus was over, many worthy men became echoes or imitations of the Prophets, following the letter rather than the spirit: the rabbis, unable to soar on the free wings of the

---

[1] Ibid. xix. 24, 25.   [2] Ibid. xi. 6, 9.

Prophets, walked uprightly on the earth. With no comparable knowledge of God, but with a sincere desire to do His Will, they contrived a ritual worship that competed with righteousness, and developed a legalism that rivalled love. Deuteronomy indeed caught the Prophetic sublimity: 'Hear, O Israel; the Lord our God is One Lord, and you must love the Lord your God with your whole heart, with your whole soul, with your whole mind, and with your whole strength.'[1] Leviticus, too, enjoined: 'You must love your neighbour as yourself.'[2] These Commands the Law contained—but how much else! Ezekiel elaborated a 'Law of Holiness' consisting largely of ceremonial obligations and of abstinences from the defilements of Babylonian superstition. On the return from the Exile the Prophetic righteousness hardened into a Priestly Code attributed to Moses as the law-giver of old. In this Code material sacrifices—burnt-offerings, meat-offerings, peace-offerings, trespass-offerings, part of the common ritual of unspiritual man—encroached upon those offerings of the heart which it is the special glory of Jewry to have vindicated. A ceremonial, not a spiritual, purity was prescribed. For a time, too, while the nation was under foreign rulers, came the supremacy of a priestly aristocracy that moved still further from the Prophetic spirit.

While the conception of righteousness thus degenerated, so did that of human society. The ideal State was to be, not a spiritual, but an earthly kingdom, brought about by the miraculous intervention of God. The Anointed became, no longer the ideal statesman, but a warrior king, slaughtering the enemies of Israel with his own hands. The Day of Judgement was regarded, not as a spiritual, but as a material climax to human history.

Yet the moral greatness of the Hebrews corrected this literalism. The rabbis—laymen and often artisans—perceived that to save the spirit of the Law it was necessary to modify the letter in accordance with the circumstances of a changing age and the social conditions of the Dispersion. The Pharisees adapted the Oral or Traditional Law accordingly; Jesus himself said that he came, not to destroy the Law, but to fulfil it. The piety of five centuries further

[1] Deuteronomy vi. 4.   [2] Leviticus xix. 18.

defined it. The Mishna supplemented the Mosaic Code with laws embodying the practices that had developed among the more civilized and ethical Jewish people after the Captivity; then the Gemara collected, beside a digest of the Law, much folk-lore, ethical teaching and story as 'words of blessing and consolation' to edify a people in distress.[1] These developments took place in Rabbinical Schools or Academies at Jamnia and Usha, Caesarea and Tiberias in Palestine, at Nehardea, Sura and Pumbeditha in Babylonia. Then for another five hundred years[2] the Presidents or 'Excellencies' of the Academies of Sura and Pumbeditha, the Geonim, continued to give Responses to questions concerning the Law from far and near, and so to form a central authority for the scattered congregations of Jewry. These centres perished in 1038, but the Law survived throughout the Dispersion.

It relates to every subject of life: to sex and hygiene, to dress and diet, to property and inheritance, to agriculture and business, and to many other matters. Judaism is not only a creed, but a way of life.

Not of course that it is always obeyed; in spite of Prophetic and legal denunciations of lust and avarice and oppression, the animal nature would take in days of prosperity like those of Solomon the common form of conquest, and in days of adversity like those of the Dispersion the common form of cupidity. The nation that could produce an Isaiah at one end could produce a 'Shylock' at the other. Yet Jewish usury is mainly the creation of Christian law, which on the one hand forbade Christians as a rule to lend money, and on the other excluded Jews from most callings and so virtually forced them to become money-lenders. If the power that this gave them over the fortunes of their fellows caused them sometimes to lapse from the high standards of the Prophets, the persecutions and pogroms with which Christians have retaliated are no less a lapse from the standards of Christ.

Sometimes obedience to the Law was formal, not moral:

> Woe to you Pharisees!
> You tithe mint and rue and every vegetable,
> But justice and the love of God you disregard.[3]

---

[1] The Mishna *c.* A.D. 10–220, the Gemara *c.* A.D. 220–500.
[2] *c.* A.D. 589–1038.   [3] Luke xi. 42.

Sometimes a ground of self-righteousness and pride:

> Woe to you Pharisees!
> You love the first bench in the synagogues
> And salutations in the market-places.[1]

Sometimes an adhesion to the letter in defiance of the spirit: unworthy Jews have even been known at sundown on a Friday to slip a bottle of water beneath them in a railway carriage to fulfil the law that forbids travelling on the Sabbath except upon water.

It is possible, too, to make the Law a burden to oneself and others.

> Woe unto you, jurists! you load men with irksome burdens.[2]

Yet as a rule the Jew has obeyed the Law because it has been his delight. 'O how love I Thy Law! It is my meditation all the day.'[3] No subject is more governed by the Law than the observance of the Sabbath rest; yet festival songs are written about it. Just because no penal sanction is attached to the Law, it commands a loving allegiance. The heavier the pecuniary sacrifices it entails, the more it is enjoyed by the generous-hearted Jew.

I. 3

But the higher energies of Judaism have not been confined to the development of the Law. Jewry has made noble contributions to art and to science, to philosophy and to mysticism.

It has been able and ready to absorb much from other civilizations, and has given back what it took enriched with its own genius. The practical saws of Egypt and Babylon influenced the so-called Wisdom literature. Persian imagery and Persian dualism showed Israel a world of angels and devils, the Last Judgement, Heaven and Hell. Greek philosophy has deeply influenced the Hebrew thought of many ages. Aristotle inspired Saadia, the greatest of the Geonim, in his *Book of Beliefs and Convictions* to base faith upon reason as complementary to revelation. Three centuries later another Jewish Aristotelian, Saladin's physician the Rabbi Moses Maimonides, wrote *The Guide of the Perplexed*, a

---

[1] Luke xi. 43. [2] Ibid. xi. 46. [3] Psalm cxix. 97.

powerful argument for reason in faith and toleration in Theology. Its influence has been incalculable, not only upon Judaism, but upon the Christian Church, as well as upon such philosophers as Aquinas and Spinoza. 'From Moses unto Moses there arose not one like unto Moses.'

Jewish philosophy has, too, its Platonic strain. Platonism inspired Philo to look upon God as the Supreme Perfection Who fills and encompasses all things with His Being, through the mediation of Logoi, the Operative Ideas that are part of the Operative Reason of God. Neoplatonism led the followers of the Kabbalah, the mystical 'doctrine received by tradition', to show how human life might become perfect through communion with the Infinite One that is Immanent in the soul of man. Spinoza, the Lao-tze of the West, held that all things are of God, Who manifests Himself in two modes, extension and thought—Nature and Spirit. To know God is to love Him; the 'intellectual love of God' is the supreme duty of man. Like Lao-tze, too, Spinoza derives his ethics and politics from his metaphysics, developing a philosophy of law and government, and reasoning eloquently in defence of liberty of thought and speech in speculative matters.

Nor has this impetus died away. In the eighteenth century Moses Mendelssohn, the 'German Socrates', put forth in his book *Jerusalem* a plea for freedom of conscience that Kant described as 'irrefutable'. A Liberal Judaism, drawing much of its inspiration from the life and teaching of Jesus, would, like him, loosen the rigidity of the Law and seek to make the worship of the One God world-wide. Music and its mate mathematics, physical and medical science, and international finance also owe much to the genius of the Hebrews.

II

In Islam the religion of Israel stooped to conquer. Two thousand years after Abraham the great mass of the Arabian peoples was still primitive. The Quran testifies to their vice and their avarice. The tribes were divided by blood-feuds: fights and forays, personal and tribal, were the disorder of the day. Each tribe had its own gods and idols (in Mecca the tribe of Kereish called the Supreme Being Allah), to whom human and other sacrifices were offered. Sun, moon, and stars were worshipped; stones, hills, and trees were the homes of deities. Some attempt was made to mitigate this confusion. The first three months of the so-called 'Spring' were sacred, and during them custom proclaimed peace throughout Arabia.[1] As the rains covered the land with grass and flowers and plenty, men rode their camels over the green downs, met and made friends. During one of these sacred months a pilgrimage was undertaken to Mecca, where a black stone, the Kaaba, was kissed and other sacred rites were performed.

But as loftier religions penetrated Arabia, the Arab became dissatisfied with his primitive ways. In Syria were Greek Christians from Byzantium, to the South-East Zarathustrians from Persia; Jews were scattered up and down the long trade routes. To which should he turn for refuge from social disorder and for a more satisfying religious faith?

II. 1

A young conductor of caravans, familiar in his journeyings with all these faiths, arose to answer the need. Rejecting Christianity on the ground that it taught the worship of three gods, he selected the religion of Abraham and, like Abraham, went out upon a mission. For some years Muhammad was virtually a Jew, and he and his followers turned in prayer, not to Mecca, but to Jerusalem; the Kaaba was afterwards substituted as the House rebuilt by Abraham. He permanently retained the Jewish Scriptures and acknowledged the authority of the Patriarchs and Prophets; while he accounted Jesus as the greatest of the Prophets save one: he himself was the Prophet of God who 'sealed' or completed the series.

His achievement was in fact an adaptation of Judaism to primitive Semitism. He taught a doctrine of God and human society founded on that of the Prophets, but lowered to meet the needs of a rude and warlike people. The God of Muhammad is One, Compassionate, All-Powerful. His Unity is the first article of the Creed: 'There is no god but Allah', to which, as his mission succeeded, he added: 'Muhammad is a

[1] C. J. Lyall, *Ancient Arabian Poetry*, pp. xxi–xxii.

Prophet of God.' Every chapter or sura of the Quran begins with the words, derived from Judaism: 'In the name of God, the Compassionate, the Merciful'; yet in an undisciplined world Muhammad laid more stress on the Divine Power. Allah is the Creator, the Sustainer, the Evolver of the destinies of the world. He sustains like a loving father, though unlike a human father he has control over human destiny, ordaining all in accordance with His Will, allotting good and evil now and hereafter.

Accordingly the whole duty of man is summed up in one word, Islam: the 'surrender' or 'resignation' of one's own will to the Will of the Almighty. It is a surrender far removed from that required in the Materialist State; for it is one thing to surrender to Mussolini, another to surrender to God. He who surrenders, the Muslim, has a twofold office, other-worldly and this-worldly, spiritual and moral; to know God's Will and to carry it out. Like the Templars and Hospitallers he was presently to encounter, the Muslim was at once a monk and a soldier, daily and yearly performing religious exercises, ever ready to fight the Holy War. It was a war primarily against evil; 'the biggest Jihad (said the Prophet) is against one's own self';[1] only when the sword is drawn against religion must the sword be drawn in reply. Five religious duties were laid on the believer. First, the recital of the Creed. Next, daily worship at dawn, noon, afternoon, eve, and nightfall. What is he silently repeating, as he stands, bows, prostrates himself with motions of military precision? A prayer perhaps modelled on that of Jesus, for besides containing the same number of lines, it too gives glory to God and beseeches His Goodness for those who obey Him.

> In the Name of God, the Compassionate, the Merciful.
> Praise be to God, Lord of the worlds!
> The Compassionate, the Merciful!
> Master of the day of reckoning!
> Thee only do we worship, and to Thee do we cry for help.
> Guide Thou us on the straight path,
> The path of those to whom Thou hast been Gracious—with whom Thou art not angry, and who go not astray. Amen.[2]

---

[1] Sayings of Muhammad.   [2] Quran, Sura I.

Further to reinforce the sense of unity among his Arab followers, Muhammad seized upon the ancient customs of fasting and pilgrimage. The sacred month of Ramadhan was to be observed by all with the severest austerity. Pilgrimage was to be made by all Muslims to the sacred House at Mecca, just as pilgrimage had been made by the Jews to the Single Sanctuary at Jerusalem; and during this pilgrimage the Truce of God was to be observed. Finally, the movement was financed by a religious tax or 'alms', a Muslim Peter's Pence.

Such were the religious duties. Nor were the moral duties neglected. Here again the Jewish Law served as a model. The sensual and selfish Arab was to be disciplined. He was not to drink wine. He was to set limits to his lust. Monogamy was the rule, and the Prophet himself was for the greater part of his life a monogamist, though the Quran allows polygamy in extraordinary circumstances, as when the male population has been decimated in battle. Married life was not thought inconsistent with the life of an ascetic. The Muslim was forbidden to gamble, to give false measure, to lend upon usury. Kindness to the widow, the orphan, and the poor was enjoined. The Prophet (Muslims claim) is the first man in history to legislate for the emancipation of slaves, and he himself bought slaves in order to set them free.

Alone of the great faiths Islam did not wait for the canonization of a Sacred Book. The Quran, Muhammad declared, was not his own work, but the Word of God, Uncreated, brought to him from God by the Archangel Gabriel.

But Muhammad was the founder, not only of a religion, but of a State, although it was from the first a religious State, a Theocracy, a combination of other-worldliness with this-worldliness. Islam was to be one people, obedient to the Word of God and the Prophet of God, and spreading the sacred truth over the whole earth.

He himself 'was accepted in Medina, not merely as the teacher of a creed, but as the founder of a State. He was the sole Head of the civil administration, the supreme Judge, the Commander-in-Chief of the army.'[1] He was the chief executive officer of the Will of God upon earth.

[1] Sir Thomas Arnold, *The Islamic Faith*, p. 38.

Like the Prophets whom he succeeded, he foresaw that mankind is destined to become a single religious community, one Kingdom under One God: 'The East and the West is God's; therefore, whichever way ye turn, there is the Face of God: truly God is Immense and knoweth all.'[1] The present world accordingly consisted of Muslims who obeyed the Word revealed by God to the Prophet; Jews and Christians, to whom God had vouchsafed a previous revelation of Himself—these were not to be forced to embrace Islam, but were to pay a poll tax; and idolaters, who were to be converted to the worship of the One God, and resisted only when they resisted. 'Fight for the cause of God against those who fight against you; but commit not the injustice of attacking them first; God loveth not such injustice.'[2]

The Muslim was encouraged to submit to God's Will, and especially to risk his life in battle, by the prospect of the joys that awaited the surrenderer after death. For Muhammad saw man's destiny not, like the Hebrew Prophets, primarily as an ideal State of the nations upon earth, but as a Paradise of Bliss for the good Muslim, or as a 'pit of raging fire' for the bad Muslim and the unbeliever.[3] His Paradise reflects his duality. It is a garden of pleasant fruits and streams, where the warrior saints, adorned with bracelets and brocades, drink flowing wine without headache, and love the large-eyed maids without exhaustion. But the joy of joys is to behold night and morning the Face of the Almighty as He walks in the garden. 'Grace from thy Lord—that is the grand bliss: Good Will from God—that is the mighty happiness.'[4] 'No soul (says the Quran) can comprehend what is reserved for it.'

II. 2

This grand and simple faith in One Almighty Compassionate God and man's unceasing worship and surrender went far to combine a sense of the supremacy of the other world with a moral ordering of this.

'While Islam has been throughout its history an ethical religion,

---

[1] Quran, Sura II, The Cow.   [2] Ibid.
[3] Sura CI, The Blow.
[4] Sura XLIV, Smoke; IX, Immunity.

and stress has been persistently laid upon due performance of moral duties, there has been in the Muslim consciousness an abiding realisation of the unceasing manifestation of God's Creative Activity in each and every one of the actions of His servants, and the thought that every righteous deed is an embodiment of the Will and Command of God Himself.'[1]

God is to the Arab (says Lawrence of Arabia)

'not natural or tangible, not anthropomorphic or moral, but a Being without colour, without form, not to be touched, Who alone is Great: a Comprehending Being, the Egg of all activity. There is a homeliness, an everydayness in this God of the Desert Who is their eating and their fighting and their lusting, the commonest of their thoughts, their familiar Resource and Companion—so unlike that God Who is wistfully veiled from the Christian by despair of his carnal unworthiness and by the decorum of familiar worship.'[2]

The effect of Muhammad's teaching, religious and practical, was rapid and immense. Christians and Persians lay at the moment enfeebled by a long and desperate strife; the spoils of Chosroes and of Caesar were for the taking. Egypt and North Africa, the Gothic kingdoms of Spain, were exhausted. In the century of the Prophet the Arabs conquered Syria and Persia, in the following Central Asia, North Africa, and Spain; later they overran India and Malaya.

In the lower minds these gains were dearly purchased. Most of the Caliphs or Successors of the Prophet cared more for empire than for the Will of the Almighty. Military despotism and religious scepticism marked the two centuries that followed his death. After the death of the Caliph Harun[3] the political unity of Islam was rent by the selfish ambition of its rulers, as the China of the Chous was rent by the Warring States, and Catholic Christendom by the rise of the modern nations. Later, leadership passed to a non-Arab people, the Turks: and when the Mongols took Bagdad[4] and the Castilians Cordova,[5] the great centuries of Islam were already ended. Slavery, polygamy, and the seclusion of women are to a large extent corruptions of the middle ages of Islam, the eleventh to the eighteenth centuries of the Christian era. The

---

[1] Arnold, pp. 23–4.   [2] *Seven Pillars of Wisdom*, pp. 40–1 (altered).
[3] 809.   [4] 1258.   [5] 1236.

best monarchs have, however, been monogamists: the Taj Mahal may serve as the monument of the faithful love, not only of Shah Jehan, but of Aurungzebe and others.

In the higher minds the Prophet's teaching inspired a marvellous Renaissance. If in Islam the spirit of the Semites stooped, it also triumphed. It taught the primitive Arab, it learnt from the philosophic Greek and the mystic Persian. As the movement was primarily religious, the seat of this education was the meeting-place of the community, the mosque; and the mosque developed into the University, the greatest glory of Islam. The Universities at Damascus and Bagdad, Nishapur and Bukhara, Cairo and Kairuan, Seville and Cordova for six centuries kept the lamp of knowledge burning. They founded scholarships, remunerated teachers, conferred degrees. Wandering scholars, using Arabic as a universal language, kept University in touch with University, from Samarcand to the Atlantic.

The object of education was twofold, as became a two-worldly civilization: first, to give knowledge of value for the life to come; and second, to produce Theologians and lawyers for the conduct of the affairs of this world.

All Muslim education revolved round Theology. At the head of the studies of the mosque inevitably stood the Quran, the Uncreated Word of God. From the Quran and the Tradition of the Prophet's life and sayings, the Islamic equivalent of the Gospels, Muslim theology was deduced. As the transference of the capital from Medina to Damascus and then to Bagdad brought the Muslims into contact with Christians and then with Persians, disputations and heresies arose. The rise of more than the seventy-three schools foretold by the Prophet may have shown a living energy of thought, but it caused bitter dissension. The questions that were to perplex Catholicism perplexed Islam. Predestination was questioned, the supremacy of reason affirmed. Eventually the great schoolmen, led by Ashari and Ghazali, the Albertus and Aquinas of Islam, reasoned these difficulties into harmonious solutions.

The foundation of the sacred Law was also the Quran and the Tradition. Later, as old-time thoughts and habits

reasserted themselves, the agreement or *ijma* of the people
of Medina or of the Muslim world generally also came to
be regarded as authoritative. In this way a vast quantity of
primitive custom and superstition crept back into the reformed religion, as through the Unwritten Law it had crept
back into Judaism. As Islam spread through India, Malay
and Java, Mongolia and Africa, its effect was often superficial: it laid a veneer upon primitive survivalism. Finally,
reasoning by analogy (*qiyas*) from the Quran, the Tradition
and agreement was admitted. The guardians of this Sacred
Law were the Ulama, the 'Learned'; and Four Schools of
Law arose, varying, though not greatly, as the Ulama
emphasized this, that, or the other of the four ingredients.

The 'Learned' came in course of time to rely upon worldly-
minded Caliphs, and thereby, though not priests, to arrogate
to themselves the authority of a worldly-minded priesthood.
The spirit of scientific research was silenced by such mullahs,
and the Law became in consequence too rigid and un-
adaptable.

But the unbelievers did more than compel Islam to discuss
and settle its Theological difficulties. If the States conquered
in the Holy War were materially weaker, they were culturally
stronger than Islam; and they did her the great service of
conquering her in turn with their science, their philosophy,
and their mysticism, just as Chinese culture conquered the
invading Mongols, and French culture eighteenth-century
England. Islam might have said with Pope:

> We felt our captive's charms;
> Her arts victorious triumph'd o'er our arms.

The mathematics, medicine, and philosophy of Greece
flooded into the universities of Asia, Africa, and Europe.
Hunain and his family translated the works of the Greeks
into Arabic. The whole world was ransacked to establish
or extend vast libraries. Mamum's House of Science
in Bagdad, the Fatimite Hall of Wisdom in Cairo were,
by way of exception, scientific rather than religious.
Normally, science and philosophy were combined into
encyclopaedias, as they had been by Aristotle, the Grecian
held in the highest repute. Muslim philosophers commented

upon Greek philosophy, and formulated systems of their own. In Spain especially, philosophy took an idealistic direction. Ibn Bajja (Avempace) declared that intellect, rising from animal to rational principles, can grasp the higher truths, and so become in a measure Divine. Ibn Rushd (Averroës) widened the scope of this doctrine by asserting the Unity of the Intellect: human intellect is a manifestation in the individual of the Universal and Eternal Intellect of God. Averroës was the bridge between Islam and Catholicism, as Paul had been between Israel and Catholicism.

Finally, there grew up, especially on Iranian soil, a Muslim mysticism. From the first there had been in Islam, simple and practical though it was, a mystical element: in the Quran God says: 'We are nearer to man than his neck-vein. Wherever ye turn, there is the Face of God.'[1] Amid the scepticism of the centuries that followed the Prophet's death, the more spiritual natures felt the need for a loftier type of religion. The new movement arose, said Junayd of Bagdad, 'not from disputation, but from hunger and taking leave of the world and breaking familiar ties and renouncing what men deem good'.[2] Men and women so minded became ascetics, sufis 'clothed in wool', wanderers from place to place, alone or in small parties. They lived by alms or by their own labour, and Christianity inspired them to constant prayer and to faith in God (*tawakkul*). Presently this quietism passed into mysticism, into the desire to die to self and to live to God. 'O God! (says Ibrahim) Thou knowest that the eight Paradises are little beside the honour that Thou hast done unto me, and beside Thy Love, and Thy giving me intimacy with the praise of Thy Name, and beside the peace of mind that Thou hast given me when I meditate on Thy Majesty.'[3] Five centuries after the Prophet's death mysticism became an accepted part of orthodox belief under the influence of Ghazali:[4] and 'since his time the revelation of the mystic has taken its place beside tradition and reason as a source and fundamental principle of the faith'.[5] Mysticism is indeed the soul of Islam: every Muslim must believe in revelation—that the soul speaks with God and listens to God.

[1] Sura L. Kaf, II, The Cow.   [2] R. A. Nicholson.
[3] Idem.   [4] 1058–1111.   [5] Arnold, *Islamic Faith*, p. 58.

Sufism was defined as 'the apprehension of the Divine Realities'.[1] Grounded upon the purest morality, the philosophies of Neoplatonism, Neo-Buddhism, and the Vedanta led the Sufis nearer and nearer to the passing away, the 'fana' or nirvana, of the individual consciousness into the Consciousness of God. 'I am the wine-drinker and the wine and the cup-bearer!' cried Abu Yazid (Bayezid):[2] 'I went from God to God, until they cried from me in me "O Thou I"!'[3] Thus arose a long line of poet-mystics who together with the poet-Prophets of Israel are perhaps the greatest lyric poets the world has seen. The greatest of them, 'the Splendour of the Faith', Jelal-ed-din Rumi, founded an Order of monks whose mystic dance recalls Francis of Assisi dancing before the Pope in the ecstasy of his love for God.

> With Thy Sweet Soul this soul of mine
> Hath mixt as water doth with wine.
>   Who can the Wine and water part,
> Or me and Thee when we combine?[4]

II. 3

The vitality of Islam has survived long tribulation. Modern times have seen fresh developments. The simplicity of the Desert, the science and morality of the West, the mysticism of the East, again bring forth fruits after their kind.

Early in the eighteenth century the Wahabis of Central Arabia went back to the Quran and the Tradition; to the Unity and Power of God, and submission to Him in all matters of daily life. Their stern Puritanism (they flog for wine-drinking and for smoking) is to-day the backbone of the new Arabian States.

Elsewhere the West has again deeply influenced Islamic thought. Sir Syed Ahmed Khan,[5] founder of the Muslim College at Aligarh, sought to harmonize the teachings of Islam with modern science. The younger men, like the Wahabis, follow the principle 'Back to the Quran'; while

---

[1] Maruf of Bagdad.   [2] d. 874.   [3] R. A. Nicholson.
[4] William Hastie, 'The Festival of Spring' from *The Divan of Jelaleddin* (1903), p. 10.   [5] 1817–1898.

decrying Christianity, they tend to paint the character of Muhammad in colours that are hardly inconsistent with the character of Christ, though they would have surprised an Arab of the decadent middle ages not a little. Modern Islam, however, does not go so far as the modern West: while it never justifies slavery, there is still some segregation of women and sometimes polygamy.

The Sufis also have their successors, aiming at universal religion and universal brotherhood. In Persia a young Prophet, the Bab (the Gate or Door)[1] proclaimed that the common foundation of all religions is the inspiration of the Holy Spirit, and that true religion manifests itself in a peaceful union of the peoples, wherein each man shall labour in the spirit of service and of his own will share his wealth with others. In India Ahmed,[2] declaring himself to be the Messiah alike of Islam, of Hinduism, of Buddhism, and of Christianity, 'the hope of all the nations of to-day', also preached universal peace and brotherhood as the fruits of universal religion.

Other modernists, striving to return to the simple faith of the first century, colour it with mystical thought. Such poets as Sir Muhammad Iqbal in India and Ziya Gok Alp in Turkey express with equal beauty the this-worldly and the other-worldly side of Islam.

> Where all men, high and low, have knowledge of the Will of God,
> O son of the Turks, that is thy Fatherland.[3]

III. 1

In Catholicism both-worldly civilization is seen even more clearly; for there the two worlds, spiritual and temporal, Supernatural and natural, are at once sharply distinguished and closely interlocked.

Just as the Prophets from Amos to Muhammad set about correcting the materialism of their day, the lusts and avarice and blood-feuds and idolatry of the Hebrews and Arabs, so the Catholic Church has throughout its long history set itself to correct the sins and errors of those whom it has tried

---

[1] Ministry 1844–1850 .   [2] 1839–1908.
[3] Arnold, *Islamic Faith*, p. 75.

to save. It arose at a moment when the Graeco-Roman world had broken down, and was searching everywhere for salvation. Excessive individualism had been the ruin of the self-governed city-states, and so had led to the loss of the political environment in which the Greek genius had flourished, and destroyed their faith in life. The public spirit on which the political genius of Rome depended had also disappeared; so that to the 'loss of nerve'[1] of the Greek was added the disillusion of the Roman. Disillusion bred degeneracy; the lusts of the flesh knew no bounds. Paul drew the picture of a rudderless world adrift upon an ocean of depravity.[2]

Later, to the disillusion of pagan Rome was added the barbarity of Nordic invaders, and still later the lawlessness of feudal kings and nobles. The Church, in spite of a vast endeavour, failed in the main to subdue these passions, with the result that at the Renaissance they again broke loose in the form of sovereign independent States, and have led to the uncontrolled rivalries, military and economic, of the dictator governments of modern times.

Pagan Rome sought a solution of these troubles in two directions, political and spiritual. Augustus and the Antonines organized the Empire, Virgil and Horace beatified it, Seneca and Marcus Aurelius ruled it with Stoic virtue, the worship of the Caesars gave it sanction. Later, when Constantine migrated to his New Rome on the Bosphorus and left the old Rome derelict, its Bishops took over the government of the Latins and their invaders. Four centuries later the Papacy had itself fallen into deep abasement; then Caesar found in Charlemagne[3] another successor, this time not merely a Roman Emperor, but a Holy Roman Emperor. Thus the dual office, other-worldly and this-worldly, filled in Islam by the Caliph, came in Catholic Christendom by a historical accident to be divided between Pope and Emperor.

On the spiritual side the disillusioned Graeco-Romans sought for an issue out of their afflictions in philosophies and in religions. They became imperturbable with the Sceptics, pleasure-loving with the Epicureans, enduring with the Stoics. Colonies of Jews sought salvation in their Law.

[1] J. B. Bury.   [2] Romans xiii. 13.   [3] Crowned Emperor A.D. 800.

Other men looked to the Mysteries of the East, to escape from death to life, from darkness to light. Reverence transformed the old magical acts into sacraments. A sacred baptism purified, a sacred meal bestowed the Divine life, a sacred marriage united to God, a sacred drama enabled the initiate to share the death and resurrection of some lover-god of Mother Earth, Serapis or Attis or Sabazius. Or from the Heaven of Light above the planets, the Seven world-creating Powers, some Divine Being, 'Faith' or 'Wisdom' or 'Primal Man', mercifully descended to rescue miserable man.

To this medley of administrators, philosophers, Jews, and initiates (he pressed the ideas of all into contribution) Paul came with a message that shook the winter of the world like a spring breeze: the doctrine of the healing of the sin of man by the Grace of God through faith in Christ Jesus. As Abraham originated the solution of man's problem given by Israel and Islam, so Paul formulated that given by Catholicism (albeit many Catholics, especially the mystics, find their chief inspiration elsewhere). At once a 'Hebrew of the Hebrews' and a Roman citizen, he is the link between the Semitic and the Latin civilizations. Like other Arab Prophets, before beginning his mission he 'went off to Arabia';[1] where (it seems) he 'was caught up to the Third Heaven', a 'Paradise' in which he 'heard sacred secrets which no human lips can repeat'.[2] Accordingly his God is not so much the God of the Desert as the God of the Heavens; he gave the message of his Master the character of a Mystery: indeed, he himself said it was one, a 'mysterion'.[3] But how different a Mystery! For whereas 'Faith' and 'Wisdom' and 'Primal Man' were cold and colourless abstractions, Paul showed a Being—Christ, the 'man from Heaven'[4]—who was at once Superhuman and human too—as much a man as the Caesar whom men worshipped, yet how far removed from him in Godlikeness! a Divine man whose purpose it was to bring joy to his believers, saved from their sin here and hereafter. God and the Prophet of God

---

[1] Galatians i. 17.   [2] 2 Corinthians xii. 2, 4.
[3] 1 Corinthians ii. 7.   [4] Ibid. xv. 47 (Moffat's translation).

were the strength of Islam. God in Christ Jesus come down
to earth for man's salvation—'the Power of God and the
Wisdom of God',[1] yet born of a woman—was the strength
of Catholic Christianity.

The idea of sin and Grace dominated Paul's mind: sin in
the flesh through Adam's fall, not to be overcome by any
moral struggle to fulfil the Law, but only by the Grace of
God in Christ, the second Adam.[2] This Grace (said Paul)
must be received by faith; faith in God, hope in God, and love
for God and His creation, 'these three' are the 'abiding
things'.[3] But Paul the Roman citizen was a statesman as
well as a writer; and with a statesman's eye he founded his
Churches in the chief provincial capitals of the Roman
Empire, Antioch and Corinth and Ephesus, besides following Peter to Rome itself. In these Churches, as in Stoicism
and the Mysteries, 'there was no room for Greek and Jew,
circumcised and uncircumcised, barbarian, Scythian, slave or
free man'; 'Christ was everything and everywhere'.[4] These
Churches (he said) were colonies of Heaven. The Church was
the body of which Christ was the Head;[5] the Church therefore was both of earth and of Heaven. And since Infinite
Wisdom is also Infinite Love, it cannot consign 'the creation
groaning and travailing in pain'[6] to permanent torment or
destruction; Heaven must in the end be attained by all,
God's purpose is universal salvation.

God has consigned all men to disobedience
    that He may have mercy upon all.
All comes from Him, all lives by Him, all ends in Him. Glory to Him
    for ever, Amen![7]

At the moment when Rome was falling to the barbarians
Paul's work was taken up by Augustine.[8] Augustine's conversion was like Paul's, a Supernatural or psychical experience that led him from the sinful flesh to salvation through
the Grace of God. Beyond all others he is the 'Doctor of
Grace'. But, again like Paul, he is also a statesman. As the
Roman Empire crashed, he recreated it by fusing the spirit

---

[1] 1 Corinthians i. 24.　　　　[2] Romans vii, viii.
[3] 1 Corinthians xiii. 13.　　　[4] Colossians iii. 11.
[5] Philippians iii. 20.　　　　　[6] Romans viii. 22.
[7] Ibid. xi. 32, 36.　　　　　　[8] 354–430.

of Augustus and Paul in a single institution, the Catholic Church. Amid the despair of the times he saw arise the mighty vision of a new world-order, 'one Commonwealth of all Christian men'; the Grace of God was to unite mankind. Yet not all mankind; for the horrors of the barbarian inrush into degenerate Rome more and more burnt into Augustine's soul an awful sense of the predominance of sin. He read Paul's great passage proclaiming the ultimate salvation of all ('all ends in Him') in what seems exactly the opposite sense from Paul's: if the Grace of God predestined some to salvation in the City of God, His Wrath predestined many more to damnation in the City of Destruction. The fear of Hell fire was to play at least as great a part in the disciplining of the barbarians as the hope of the spiritual joys of Heaven.

Thus Paul and Augustine clearly laid down the distinction between the Spiritual or Supernatural world of Grace, and the temporal or natural world which, though created good by the Creator, has fallen into sin; the Divine Grace descends to re-unite man to God. This is the central doctrine of Catholic Theology. To restore men to the Supernatural Life through Jesus Christ is the task of the Catholic Church.

First, then, just as God is to the Hebrew a God of Righteousness, and to the Muslim a God of Greatness, so to the Catholic He is pre-eminently a God of Grace. But if of Grace, also of Wrath. The extent to which men's final destiny depends, on the one hand on Divine Predestination, on the other on human free will, Catholicism has never exactly determined; but she has determined that those who are saved owe their salvation to God, with Whom they must freely co-operate, and that those who are lost are not predestined by God to Hell, but suffer punishment only by reason of their own personal sin. Owing to Adam's fall man is born in original sin—that is, alienated from God, deprived of Supernatural Life; but, further, he has fallen into actual sin, the lusts of the flesh. Grace descends into this fallen world to redeem it—to cleanse the soul from the stain of sin and to make it participant of the Divine Nature or Life.

But how? First and foremost through the Incarnation of God in His Son Jesus Christ, the Second Person of the Trinity, and His Death on the cross as a Sacrifice for the redemption of man's sin. But Christ ascended into Heaven; not, however (says St. Matthew[1]), before he had given St. Peter the keys of Heaven to bind and loose, and on that 'rock' had built His Church. Thus Christ left behind Him (the Church holds) a Vicar or Representative, who should be Supreme Head of the Church on earth, as Muhammad left behind him a Caliph or Successor to rule Islam. The Apostles, too, left behind their successors, the priests and Bishops of the Church. These are strictly separated from the lay members of the Church by their power to administer the sacraments; and it is pre-eminently through the sacraments that the Grace of God continues to descend to man and to lift him from the moral to the Supernatural plane of life with the Divine.

Their number was in the Middle Ages recognized as seven. Sacramental Grace sanctifies the three great moments of earthly life, birth, marriage, and death. It confirms the faith of the baptized who come to years of discretion, it absolves from sin those who confess, repent, and do penance. It ordains a man as one of the successors of the Apostles, and thereby makes him a priest, capable of offering the Sacrifice of the Mass. For in the Sacrament of the Eucharist Grace descends with Christ Himself again, Who is thereby offered anew a Sacrifice for sin; bread and wine change their substance and become His Body and Blood, bringing the Divine Life to the faithful communicant. But though there are seven channels, the same Grace comes through them all, as the same light enters a building through differently coloured windows.

Yet, where God wills, He grants Grace without priest or sacrament; and not only to the Catholic, but to the non-Catholic and even to the non-Christian. 'There is no salvation outside the Church', says an old maxim, that is, no salvation where sin causes a man deliberately to refuse the Church and her ministrations; but, 'To him who doth what in him lies God does not deny Grace.' There is a 'baptism of desire', desire for the Supernatural life in God, and those who are so baptized—though 'invincible ignorance' may keep them from the Church, or they may never even have heard

[1] xvi. 18.

the name of Christ—are yet saved by the Infinite Mercy of
God.

Only those who are thus sanctified by Grace are capable of
rising from the moral to the Supernatural or 'Theological'
virtues of Paul:[1] faith in God, as He has revealed Himself
to man, hope in Him, and especially in a blessed immortality with Him, and love for Him, a share in His Own
Knowledge and Love of Himself and of His worlds, 'so far
as good is borne from Him to them'.[2]

If the Incarnation of the Second Person of the Godhead
brought down the Divine Grace and His Crucifixion re-
deemed faithful men from sin, it is the office of the Third
Person, the Holy Spirit, to reveal those new and Supernatural
Truths, contained in Scripture and Tradition, that (the
Church finally decided) can neither be discovered nor de-
monstrated by human reason; and further, to safeguard from
error the final definitions of these Truths given in Creed and
dogma by Oecumenical Councils and by the Pope speaking
ex cathedra. Thomas Aquinas seeks to show that reason can
go far, but that these Mysteries are beyond its reach. Foremost among them stand the Holy Trinity and the Incarnation.

III. 2

But if the task of Grace is to lift the soul to the Supernatural plane where it may share the Divine Life, it is first
necessary to restore the world to the moral goodness which
it retained even on the plane of Nature until the sin of Adam
and his descendants corrupted it. This was (in theory at
least) the task of the Holy Roman Empire, the State. 'On
this threshing-floor of mortality' (wrote Dante), this earth
where the chaff is separated from the grain, 'life should be
lived in freedom and peace'[3]: the memory of the Pax Romana
haunted the Middle Ages like a heartache.[4] For a thousand
years[5] Western Christendom had two leaders who, though
in fact in constant strife, were in theory complementary to
each other. As Head of the Church the Pope was to lead men
to eternal life in accordance with revelation; as Head of the

---

[1] I Corinthians xiii. 13.　　　　　[2] Dante, *Paradiso*, 26. 66.
[3] *De Monarchia*.　　　　[4] Eileen Power, *Listener*, 1932, p. 845*b*.
[5] 800–1803.

State the Emperor was to lead them to temporal felicity in accordance with philosophy. The function of the Church was to enable them, by the exercise of the Theological virtues of faith, hope, and love towards God, to share the Divine Life here and hereafter. The function of the Empire was 'to assuage the waves of greed',[1] to purge the sins of man's animal nature, the 'flesh', by the four moral virtues (already known to Greek and Roman paganism), temperance, courage, justice, and practical wisdom. If the Theological virtues unseal the joys of the unseen world, it is the moral virtues that 'leave the human race free to rest in the tranquillity of peace'. Thus Pope and Emperor bore the two swords of God's authority. Church and Empire were the two halves of a single perfect sphere, a united Christendom, the 'one Commonwealth of all Christian men'.[2]

But in practice it was the Church who sought to curb and discipline those sins of mankind that were leading them, not to felicity, but to misery, here and hereafter. The scope was great. Feudal society, a compound of Latin and barbarian, was lustful, greedy and violent; even at the end of the Catholic Renaissance Marco Polo[3] could compare the wars and disorders of Christendom very unfavourably with the civility and tranquillity of Kublai's China. The Church indeed set about her task as the Chinese had done: just as Confucius gave to fellow-feeling, harmony and the other virtues a social application in the five relationships, so the Church gave to the four virtues that turn men's energies from animal to moral ends tangible expression in the remedy of evils and the building up of good. Temperance, courage, justice, and practical wisdom were nothing unless they found social embodiment.

First, she strove to discipline men's bodily appetites and lusts. They lead (as Paul pointed out) to bickering and strife. Like all other vices, they stunt the growth of the soul and blind its eyes to the vision of the Good. Temperance therefore was the ideal. The excess of barbarian passions was counteracted by the excessive value placed upon asceticism; as to straighten a crooked stick it must be bent too far the other way. Even marriage, advocated for the saints of Islam,

---

[1] *De Monarchia.*   [2] Augustine.   [3] *c.* 1254–1324.

was, though a Christian sacrament, forbidden to the priests and monks of the West.

Next, the Church did what she could to discipline men's fighting instincts. She could not abolish war between Christians. But she proclaimed a Truce of God, like that of early Arabia and of Islam; she tamed the ferocity of the fighting men with Rules of Chivalry that helped to make the fierce barbarian the gentle perfect knight. Then she turned the wars of Christendom into Crusades against the infidel. They were a Christian Jihad; when Crusader encountered Saracen, like was encountering like. Courage for selfish ends was brutal, courage for Christian ends a virtue.

Further, like the Prophets and the Prophet, the Church strove to regulate the acquisitive instincts, the avarice, the injustice of mankind. She lightened the lot of the serfs. She laid down codes of conduct for workers and employers. Interest on loans, for instance, was limited to cases where there had been delay or serious risk; prices were regulated on the principle that the producer should receive a return suited to the station in life in which he could give his best service to society. In the application of such principles a large body of case law was built up. But justice did not consist only in avoiding injustice; it was also positive. In the Catholic view, society was essentially functional: each class had its own duty to do, and in return for this service was entitled to receive what was due to it. In this division of labour it was the duty of the workers and merchants to provide material goods, of the fighting men to defend and order Christendom, of the priests and monks to study Truth and to guide the souls of men. Medieval society thus conceived of the social order much as Indian society conceived of the caste system, or Plato conceived of the four classes in his *Republic*. Every class had its own law or duty, its sva-dharma; justice was not 'the interest of the stronger', but the 'doing of one's own duty' to society as a whole by each class and by each man.[1]

While these four classes extended over Catholic Christendom, there were within it innumerable little local groups —manors, guilds, towns, monasteries, and so on—which

[1] *Republic*, iv. 433.

were also functional and had each its duty to society. Medieval organization was thus corporative, the individual found his life in a fellowship of function devised in the interest of justice from all to all.

What the Brahmins and the sannyasis were to Hindu society, what the philosopher-kings to Plato's *Republic*, that the clergy and monks were to the Catholic world: the 'head' of the body politic, its thinkers or wise men. They were its leaders. Indeed, they were too much and too long its leaders, and therein lay the chief defect of Catholic civilization: it directed too much, it educated too little. It was this cause more than any other that presently brought the great endeavour low.

III. 3

But meanwhile they led nobly, and taught nobly. Vowed to poverty, chastity, and obedience, the monks showed the way from darkness to light. In the chaos of the Gothic invasions Benedict established an Order with a Rule that has perhaps had a profounder influence over Europe than any other writing save the Bible. It inculcated hard work in the fields, scholarly labours in the cloister, and, at the heart of all, the worship or 'work of God' in the Oratory. His monasteries spread from Italy till they stretched over northern Europe from Ireland to Prussia: islands of peaceful labour, learning, and adoration amid the tumult, ignorance and profanity of the Dark Ages. From the Benedictines came the movement that was to originate and inspire the Catholic Renaissance of the Middle Ages. For in the tenth century the monastery of Cluny made an innovation; its daughter houses, instead of separating from the Mother House, remained her faithful subjects. Union, they found, was strength; and if in the Order of Saint Benedict, why not in the Catholic Church? Hence from Cluny emanated the idea that the Papacy, rescued from its degradation, should reform the wrongs of the world and lead it to salvation; a Clunyite monk, Hildebrand (afterwards Pope Gregory the Seventh), was the protagonist of the movement. In the spirit of Confucius when he insisted on the power of example to renovate the people, the reformers began by setting an example of holiness. The spirit of the Benedictines flowed into new Orders. Camaldoli and Vallombrosa rose above the stripling Arno; Carthusians and Cistercians spread from France over Europe. Each Order had its saints, Romualdo and Gualberto, Stephen and Robert, Bruno and, greatest of them all, Bernard, mystic and statesman, more potent than Popes. These were no monks of the Desert, engaged only in a mystic communion; true to the genius of a moral-spiritual civilization, they sought while worshipping God to redeem man. A lax clergy took the vows as Austin or Regular Canons—Canons with a Rule—thenceforward to live like monks and work like clerks. Lax Crusaders did the same, in Soldier Orders that followed the Rule, some of the Austin Canons, others of the Cistercians.

Later, the command of Jesus to his disciples to go forth penniless to preach that the Kingdom of Heaven is at hand and to heal the sick,[1] heard by young Francis of Assisi in the Chapel of St. Mary of the Angels, sent men out into the world as brothers—friars.[2] Making Lady Poverty their bride, Francis and his 'little brothers' in a springtime of love and joy preached and practised among the poor and the afflicted; Dominic and his Preaching Friars, kindled at that sacred flame, lit up the Gospel with a reasoned Theology. Even this, Francis saw, was not enough: the ordinary man and woman, earning a living and bringing up a family, unable therefore to preach or to heal, still had often as deep a desire for holiness, for the life with God, as any monk or friar; there should be room for them too, as tertiaries of his Order, friars in daily life.

So, reforming themselves, the reformers went forth to reform mankind. No bishop or abbot should be a vicious hireling selected and 'invested' by king or noble: all should be faithful pastors of the flock approved by the Church itself. Then the reformers sought to pass beyond the Roman Communion, and to heal the schism with the Orthodox. Still farther afield they aimed, first by the Crusades and then by the missions of the Friars, to restrain the infidel and gather him into the fold of Christ.

[1] Matt. x. 7–10.
[2] 1209 A.D. Paul Sabatier, *Life of St. Francis of Assisi*, c. iv.

Hand in hand with this vast attempt at righteousness went an equally great attempt at enlightenment. This too sprang from the Benedictines, who in their cloisters copied and studied both secular and spiritual works of learning. Monastery 'schools' bred scholars and thinkers, and presently produced a 'scholasticism' that tried to establish a harmony between philosophy and Theology, reason and revelation. 'True philosophy is true religion', said Erigena, 'and conversely, true religion is true philosophy.'[1] 'A doctrine is believed', said Abelard, 'not because God has said it, but because we are convinced by reason that it is so. Doubt is the road to inquiry, and by inquiry we perceive the Truth.' Albert the Great and Thomas of Aquino laboured to establish this harmony, though they were compelled to regard as above the sphere of reason and philosophy the crowning 'Mysteries' of the Trinity and the Incarnation.

The conquest of Islam in Spain brought the philosophy of Aristotle and his Muslim commentators within the orbit of Christendom; and after half a century's hesitation Catholicism baptized Aristotle into Christ. His propositions on morals and religion were compared with those of the Christian Fathers, recently summarized in Books of Sentences by Bishop Peter of Lombardy and others: and then generally incorporated as they stood, more rarely modified to accord with Christian principles. The result was an enrichment of Christianity comparable only to that effected by Paul when he baptized elements of Judaism, Stoicism, Roman Law, and the Mystery Religions into the Mystery of Christ. Thus Scholasticism grew vast in bulk (the critics of Alexander of Hales said that his works weighed as much as a horse), but vaster still in its vision of a Universe centred upon God.

These interests gave rise to Universities no less magnificent than those which similar interests had originated for Jewry in Palestine and Babylonia, and for Islam from Samarkand to Cordova. At Salerno there had long been a School of Medicine, devoted to the study of Hippocrates. At Bologna the partisans of the Empire eagerly studied the law of Rome, sanctioned by and sanctioning the power of the Emperors.

---

[1] *De Divina Predestinatione*, Proem.

To offset this, the monk Gratian codified the Canon Law, derived from the works of the Fathers, the Canons of Councils, and the decisions of Popes and other jurists in the Courts of the Church. The teaching of Abelard, heretic though he was, made Paris the centre of the study of scholastic philosophy and Theology. The lawyers studying at Bologna, the Theologians teaching in Paris, formed themselves into guilds: Universities had come into being.

Paris, learning from her sisters at Salerno and Bologna, became the model University, and the mother of many others. The Arts, descended from the schools of ancient Rome, formed but a preparatory and therefore 'inferior' faculty. The quadrivium or 'four-way', the scientific arts of arithmetic, geometry, music, and astronomy, dealt with the phenomena of the physical world; the trivium or 'three-way', the liberal arts of grammar, dialectic, rhetoric, trained the mind to reason, that it might proceed to moral philosophy and Theology. The studies of the three 'superior' Faculties sought to perfect on all sides the life of man. Medicine would preserve in him a healthy body. Law held up before him an ethical ideal in the life of Church and State. These two Faculties led up to the crown and culmination of all education, the highest Faculty, Theology—the study of God's revelation concerning His Own Nature and His Dealings with the Universe, which unaided reason could not have discovered, but which reason, by it raised into a Higher Life and thus illumined, can sometimes prove in a rational philosophy, and sometimes show, though incapable of proof, to be nevertheless consistent with reason. Oxford chose as her exulting motto:

'*Dominus Illuminatio mea*—God is my Light.'

Universities so organized had a far-reaching and irresistible power. From one to another, as in Islam, went the wandering scholar, uniting the Catholic world in a common culture. Paris organized her Arts students into 'Four Nations', and other Universities followed her example. At Oxford and elsewhere, groups of teachers and scholars, living together in one building, presently formed themselves into Colleges, each with its Statutes and Governing Body, the better to train men for service in Church and State.

The thirteenth century was the climax of Catholic civilization, that vast attempt to fit men to live a moral life in a peaceful society, and a Supernatural life through the Divine Grace. Men thought of human life as a transition from birth to Heaven or Hell, and of human history as a transition from the creation of the world to the Last Judgement. The monuments of the age, secular and religious, especially the Cathedrals, embody its wealth of ideas, in statues, in glass, in pictures. Look at the fountain of Perugia—the City's new waterworks of 1280. The sculptured figures round its lower and its upper basins illustrate respectively the ideal life for the individual and the ideal life for society. Walk round the Cathedral of Chartres. Here is the creation of the world and the fall of man; the Old Dispensation, with special glorification of the Virgin; the greatest event in history, the Incarnation of God and man's redemption; the New Dispensation, with Apostles, confessors and martyrs; the Last Judgement, Heaven and Hell. It is the pilgrimage described in Augustine's *City of God*, illumined with other formulations—the trivium and quadrivium, the labours and pleasures of the seasons, the moral and the Theological virtues, the nine choirs of angels. Dante's Comedy, the poem of Catholic Scholasticism, shows the end of that pilgrimage: the damnation of the unrepentant; the purging of sin and restoration to moral purity; the Paradise where 'His Will is our peace',[1] and 'the scattered leaves of all the Universe' reveal their meaning when bound together in the Divine.[2]

The Comedy is the work of a mystic in an age of mystics; for at the moment when Catholicism began to decline, it also rose above itself to supreme heights. From the days of Augustine the influence of Neoplatonism had always been strong. Erigena, developing it, declared that 'there are as many unveilings of God—Theophanies—as there are saintly souls';[3] and among the Spiritual Franciscans and the Beghards and Beguines of Germany was a widespread belief in man as an incarnation of the Holy Spirit. The Friends of God—most of them laymen—distinguished between 'knowledge about' God and 'knowledge of experience' of Him:

---

[1] *Paradiso*, 3, 85.   [2] Ibid., 33, 85–7.
[3] Rufus M. Jones, *Studies in Mystical Religion*, p. 113.

'God has a few to whom He whispers in the ear.'[1] Temporal things are the 'outer court of the Eternal', 'a guide and a path to God and Eternity', Which can be reached by a spiritual ladder of three stages—purification, enlightenment, and union.[2]

The boldest of all Christian mystics is Eckhart. 'That person who has renounced all visible creatures and in whom God performs His Will completely—that person is both God and man. His body is so completely penetrated with Divine Light and with the Soul Essence Which is of God that he can properly be called a Divine man.'[3] 'The perfect spirit cannot will anything except what God wills, and that is not slavery but true freedom.'[4] 'We are transformed totally into God.'[5] Jesus himself is a symbol of the Divine humanity to which men's souls should rise: 'when the soul brings forth the Son, it is happier than Mary.'[6] Thus transfigured, men see that 'all things are One Thing'; 'when I attain this blessedness of union, then all things are in me and in God, and where I am there God is, and where God is there am I.'[7] Yet all the fullness of created things can as little express the Godhead as a drop of water can express the sea. Behind God manifest to His creatures is the unmanifest Godhead. 'God works, so doth not the Godhead. The End of all things is the hidden Darkness of the Eternal Godhead, unknown and never to be known.'[8]

If the Nordic peoples were in one sense, like healthy schoolboys, ready and able to learn, they also continued to possess those other interests—of more earthly but yet manly virtue—which had brought their armies into the Roman world. Accordingly, though the Church might invent for these interests the pious game of the Crusades, like a schoolmaster superintending the out-of-lessons hours of his pupils, yet it never succeeded in swaying completely to its ends the spirit of the peoples, whatever might be the dreams of a Hildebrand or an Innocent. The temporal spirit of the barbarians maintained itself against the religious ideal of

---

[1] Ibid., p. 259.   [2] Ibid., p. 297.   [3] Ibid., p. 223.
[4] Ibid., p. 223.   [5] Ibid., p. 241.   [6] Ibid., p. 237.
[7] Ibid., p. 233.   [8] Ibid., p. 225.

the Church; and this spirit gradually freed itself from the Church and ended the Catholic Renaissance.

The Latin world revolted too. In them this earthly or secular spirit developed, concurrently with the religious spirit inspired by Rome, a political system opposed by and opposing the Church, a system in which the interest of the Latin peoples in the world about them might succeed increasingly in expressing itself, and to which the natural genius of the invading Franks and Lombards contributed. Accordingly, like schoolboys whose growth makes them less amenable to the dictation of their masters, the Latin peoples proceeded to educate themselves in accordance with the more secular spirit natural to them. The schoolroom of the Church became more and more irksome to them, at the very time when its lessons became less inspired. Accordingly, turning away from the Church, remaining away from school, their leaders began to secularize their pursuits. Aided at this moment by the accident of the fall of Byzantium and the discovery of the humanistic art and literature of the Greeks and Romans, they began to conceive of man, and then, aided by the discoveries of Columbus and Copernicus, of Nature as objects of study on their own account, independently of their relation to God. Painting especially, in Italy and elsewhere, came down from Heaven and looked at earth, though it was long before she forgot her origin. The Latin nations consequently, though they never abandoned the Church, yet proceeded to develop their politics and their humanism apart from her, while turning with zest to an inquiry untouched until this time by any civilization save the Greek, and at rare moments the Hindu—the empirical study of Nature. The discovery of Copernicus was typical of the time; earth seemed to be no longer the 'threshing-floor of mortality', but to be 'itself in Heaven'.[1] The liberation of these this-worldly interests, which the Church failed to absorb, led, first to the further confusion of the Church, and then to her increasing rigidity.

For while the laity thus found a new interest in men and things, the Church became at once more worldly and less inspired. The division of authority between Pope and Em-

[1] Dowden, *Shakespere, His Mind and Art*, p. 12.

peror proved unworkable; and as the Church of the great
Popes sought to do the work of the State, and therefore to
subordinate the State, it became itself too much a kingdom
of this world,[1] too little a Kingdom of Heaven. The lust
and luxury of the hierarchy scandalized the laity; their love
of money wounded them in the pocket. The Pope claimed
both suzerainty over this world and power to remit the
punishment of those in Purgatory, till the sale of Indulgences
gave the signal for revolt. In the second place, as the intelligence of the laity grew, the weak spots in the Church's
teaching became more manifest. As soon as Constantine
had established Christianity as the State religion, a flood of
primitive beliefs and customs swept in—as they had swept
into Israel in the Priestly Code and the Oral Law, and were
to sweep into Islam in the guise of 'agreement'. Many of
the local godlings of southern Europe still masquerade as
Christian saints, from whom material favours may be coaxed
by presents or prayers. The 'baptism of repentance' enjoined by the Gospel became by the time of Cyprian the
baptism of infants incapable of repentance. The sacraments
generally, when administered to the unrepentant, ceased to
be true sacraments and became merely magical acts, though
none the less powerful instruments in the hands of worldly-
minded priests. And then, as thought became freer, Theology stiffened, as in Israel and in Islam the knowledge of
God had stiffened into Law. The temper of Rome was
legalistic; and the Roman Church attempted to define too
closely spiritual experience that words cannot define. The
doctrine of the inspiration of the Holy Spirit, as conceived
by the Church, muffled the Divine reason in man, and
the inflexibility resulting from the supposed infallibility of
the Bible and the Creeds hampered a free inquiry into the
Nature of God and His worlds. The great attempt of the
Schoolmen to rationalize dogma was abandoned by Duns
Scotus and William of Occam, in the pious hope of exalt-
ing revelation above reason, but with the disastrous result
of turning reason against revelation. When the chasm
thus opened was widened by the inquisitive spirit of the

---

[1] Matt. iv. 8. Cp. Dostoievsky, *The Brothers Karamazov*, p. 271 (The
Grand Inquisitor): translation by Constance Garnett.

Renaissance, the Council of Trent, in a noble attempt to re-state Christianity, failed nevertheless to allow sufficient scope for the new energy of thought. Ignatius Loyola, the greatest of the Counter-Reformers, advocated obedience even to the 'sacrifice of the intellect' at the very moment when the intellect required a greater freedom.

Thus the Church, after teaching men, played the school-master too long, with the result that her pupils mutinied. But the error here lay, not so much in the fact that the Church still continued to play the Master, as in the fact that the Master did not change his system of tuition and adapt his lessons to the new needs of his pupils. In the new era the old lessons became out of date, as the fairy stories of the nursery grow out of date in the school. This was the par-ticular error which overtook the Church and which led to the desertion of the most active of her children. In other words, the Church was not wrong in maintaining a principle of authority, but in maintaining it in a useless form. A principle of authority was still needed. For, in deserting her, her children deserted the Moral-Spiritual State and returned by degrees to the Materialist, as is all too evident in the secularism and militarism of succeeding centuries. Most people, in fact, were not yet capable, as political beings, of exercising their freedom in other than a materialist way. At the Renaissance they no doubt attained a freedom. But it was the wrong kind of freedom—the freedom of the City of Babylon and not the freedom of the City of God, the freedom of the Prince of this World and not the freedom of the Anointed King. In conquering their freedom men con-quered the Church. It is only in restoring the Church that they will conquer themselves.

Thus a cleavage opened in the midst of the Catholic world—a chasm between the spiritual and the secular—to which no other civilization has shown a parallel. The Nor-dics broke away from the Church in fierce hostility, and proceeded to develop their natural genius for the investiga-tion of Nature and for the foundation of States in which civil and religious liberty could give free scope to an adven-turous but this-worldly individualism. France, in Gallican detachment, laic indifference, or anti-clerical hostility, turned to the military and artistic vulgarities of Louis the Fourteenth and Versailles, presently to seek salvation, not in a Theology of Grace and the 'one Commonwealth of all Christian men', but in a scientific scepticism and a 'liberty, equality, and fraternity' derived from Nordic sources and too narrowly regardful of Paris. Italy and Spain, ruled largely by Jesuits, sank into political and intellectual torpor. The life of the Latins no longer centred upon God, and lost thereby its chief inspiration.

Yet in spite of its partial failure Catholicism remains a mighty achievement and a lofty ideal. In the Counter-Reformation the Church set her house in better moral order, and in Theresa and John of the Cross again touched the heights of mysticism. From that time onward her high aims and widespread organization, if impaired by the rigidity of her dogmas and sometimes by the worldliness of her methods, nevertheless uphold in a secular age the ideal of a Kingdom of God in which man may share the Divine Life here and hereafter.

THE SPIRITUAL STATE

THE remaining pair of civilizations—Hinduism with Buddhism and Orthodoxy—is at the opposite pole from China and the Nordics, as the other world is at the opposite pole from this. The Chinese and Nordic ideal, being social, did not admit of anything in the nature of a flight from ordinary human experience: as Confucius said, 'absorption in the study of the supernatural is most harmful'.[1] In India and Russia, however, precisely such a flight from experience did take place; and with it came a certain neglect of experience and of interest in the world of things and men.

If the Chinese and the Nordics are the Marthas among the nations, India and Russia are the Marys; not busy and practical, but on the whole meditative and mystic. Perhaps the climate and character of the two countries, both as large as continents, lie at the root of the difference. India is in summer a land of extreme heat, Russia in winter of extreme cold; the rains of the one, the snows of the other, are less favourable to work than to meditation. India and Russia resemble each other, too, in being lands of plains and forests, endless and mysterious, traversed by great rivers and crowned with huge domes of sky—lands whose boundless breadth and height suggest Unity, Mystery, Infinity. Thus environment gives the leisure for contemplation, and suggests the Cosmos as its Object. Moreover, just as Arabia lay contiguous to the Mediterranean, and helped to determine the form of Catholicism, so the Indo-Platonic spirit of the Fourth Gospel and of Plotinus, wedded with its near kinsman the Slav temperament, is the parent of Orthodoxy in Russia.

Again, the nature of the evil with which they feel they have to cope, and consequently their solution of it, are likewise at the opposite pole from those of the Nordics and Chinese, and half way from those of the Semites and Latins. The Sino-Nordic problem was how to overcome social con-

[1] Giles, *Sayings*, p. 94.

fusion, and they answered that a harmonious society was to
be won by men with harmonious souls, and a free society
by self-disciplined men who respected one another. The
problem of the two-worldly civilizations was how to overcome idolatry and sin and the social confusion that resulted
from them, and their solution was knowledge of the One
God and obedience to His Righteous Will and faith in
His Grace. The problem that perplexed the Indian and
the Russian was fundamentally different—perhaps because
their vast and fertile lands left them more leisure to reflect.
What struck the sages of early India was the evil incident to
humanity as such, however orderly and however righteous:
the transience of this world, and especially death. The soul
could find 'freedom' (*moksha*) from this unreal world of
changing things and changing moods only in the One Eternal Self That changes not: for humanity to become perfect
it must realize that it is Divine. The founder of Buddhism,
the greatest of the many reformers of Hinduism, was confronted by the same problem—change and death, the most
striking example of the impermanence of life and of everything that seems to be. He found 'emancipation' from the
animal desires or 'cravings' that cause the continual round
of births and deaths in the strenuous following of the Inner
Law or Monitor that leads to 'the height of the Immortal'.[1]
Finally, what troubles the Slav spirit is also this unsub-
stantiality, this incompleteness of the world of sense, and in
particular death—death physical and spiritual. He accordingly finds his solution in the soul's 'resurrection' to the
eternal life in God that he calls Theosis, Deification, and in
the final transfiguration of the world. The intimate and
profound connexion between these civilizations is illustrated
by the early prayer that is still daily recited by the Hindu,
of which the first line is specially applicable to Hinduism,
the second to Buddhism, the third to Orthodoxy:

> From the unreal lead me to the Real,
> From darkness lead me to Light,
> From death lead me to the Immortal.[2]

[1] Mrs. Rhys Davids, *What was the Original Gospel in 'Buddhism'?* c. 7.
[2] *Brihad-aranyaka Upanishad*, i. 3. 28.

This view involves a new and still loftier conception both of human nature and of the Divine Nature, and of their relation to each other. In the both-worldly civilizations God is thought of as far Greater than or far Above man—the God of the Desert, the God of the Heavens—however often and familiarly He may walk with man or descend to him; but in the other-worldly civilizations the Godhead is to the mystic at once the Object That is sought and the subject that seeks—the Transcendent is also the Immanent. As the soul of man grows more moral and more intelligent, the gulf between it and God is seen to grow narrower, until the one perceives that it is united with the Other or realizes that it is That Other. 'That art thou'; man reaches the Eternal, is Deified. The Godhead is the Eternal, Unchanging Reality, Knowing and Loving Itself and therefore Blissful; but This Mystery finite mind cannot fathom, it only knows that the Godhead is the Source and the End of all lesser being and wisdom and love and bliss—is the wisdom that knows, the love that loves, the joy that rejoices, as well as What is known, loved, enjoyed; in a word, He is the Reason in the Universe and therefore the reason in man. Hence in Hinduism man's true self is the Supreme Self; in Buddhism the moral Way leads to the perfection that is an intuitive realization of the Eternal;[1] in Orthodoxy man rises to Theosis—the Deification of the human soul. As soon as the mystic has perceived this, he perceives also that not only his self but all selves, all things, are one with the Godhead and therefore with one another; and this union forms the Cosmos, which, because it is Divine, is also Bliss, in which all its parts may participate. In distinction from democracies and Theocracies, the civilizations that are governed by this idea may be called Cosmocracies.

Thus the ideal of the other-worldly civilizations is a Cosmos That is an Unchanging Boundless Reality of Living Light, Love and Bliss; but, since evil has to be accounted for, they see Nature and man as descending from the Godhead—the Divine Source of all truth and good and joy—and destined to ascend to It again. We are like sparks (says the Hindu) that fly forth from and back into the Fire of

[1] As in the *prajna-paramita* (intuitive perfection) literature.

Brahma. We forsake the Divine on the Way of Pursuit or Power, and seek It on the Way of Return or Self-realization. The Buddha's Way, illumined by the Law, is essentially this Way of Return, leading through right views and loving deeds to an acute awareness and 'the height of the Immortal'. Origen similarly sees all human life as having fallen from God and as destined to be restored to Him; while to the Russian it is a pilgrimage through time to the Heavenly or Eternal City. With this view of the Divine Origin and nature of the soul all three civilizations tend to believe that this escape from evil is for all—salvation is universal. Moreover, the love in the perfect soul cannot be fully satisfied until all shall enter into Bliss. Hence the bodhisat will not himself enter until all living beings do so too; and the Orthodox is conscious of vicarious responsibility and the duty of vicarious suffering. When the soul knows its oneness with God, 'That art thou', it knows 'that art thou' of man also.

It follows, too, from this vision of the Universe, that those kinds of Good which appeal primarily to the this-worldly civilizations, and in a subordinate degree to the both-worldly civilizations—Nature and men—have in themselves a still less important place in the regard of the other-worldly civilizations. In the system most characteristic of Hinduism —the *advaita*, the One without a Second—Nature and men are not real. They are appearances, unreality, *maya*; the Godhead is All in all, the Reality behind these semblances. To the Buddhist, men and things are likewise impermanent, and so lacking in reality; salvation lies in escaping from them. To the Orthodox, Nature and man are real; but he sees them, not in the this-worldly manner, as separate and detached worlds unconnected with each other, still less as a Universe in which man springs out of Nature—he sees Nature and man as alike destined to transfiguration under the Rays of the Divine Light.

This general view of the Cosmos has naturally determined the ethical, cultural, and social ideals of these civilizations. Their ideal man could never have been conceived as the *chun-tze* or the gentleman, or even as the righteous man or the 'Muslim'. In India he is the *sadhu* or holy man—the forest recluse, the *yogi* who 'concentrates' on Brahma, the *mahatma* or 'great soul', the *sannyasin* or wandering saint and teacher. With the Buddhist he is the *arahat*, the man made worthy, or the *bodhisat*, whose infinite pity helps suffering humanity. In Holy Russia he is the holy man, whether layman or monk, and especially the hermit and Teaching Elder—he who serves God in contemplation, rather than he who serves his fellow men materially. Thus in all three cases the ideal man is God-loving first, then man-loving because God-loving. All set value, not (as do the this-worldly peoples) on a utilitarian virtue, but on a spiritual—a virtue that helps men to God rather than to social prosperity. They suffer much, because they have neglected the ordering of society; but they see that suffering drives the soul back to its Source in the Eternal. Hence they do not try, like the active peoples, first and foremost to abolish it.

This religious ideal determines the character of the education of these civilizations. Just as the education of the Chinese and the Nordics is the common life of the family or the school, with its emphasis on social training and on ability to read and write, so the education of the Hindu, the Buddhist and the Russian lies, not in literacy, but in a training that the this-worldly peoples hardly think of as education at all: in religious stories, poetry and works of art, in worship, in pilgrimages, in the teaching of the disciple by the Master, in the contemplative life of the monastery or of the hermitage, sometimes in the philosophical studies of the monastery-university. As in Plato's *Republic*, the highest life is divided into four periods: preliminary education, life in the world, contemplation on that life, and—in rare cases—the mystic life that is bliss within and power without.

So with the culture of these civilizations. Because of their subordination of man and Nature to the Divine, little attention has been paid to natural science; and when, as in India, they have produced men of science, it is characteristic that what interests them most is the endeavour to discover in Nature the ultimate Unity of the Universe—'Oneness amid the manifold'.[1] Art, again, is not an imitation or impression

---

[1] Sir J. Bose, quoted Lord Ronaldshay, *Heart of Aryavarta*, p. 248.

of Nature, but an expression of a spiritual ideal; the dancing
Siva expresses the Energy of God, the seated Buddha the
peace of enlightenment, the ikons of the Orthodox the joys
of Heaven. Indian and Orthodox music is pre-eminently
religious—'music is the language of the soul'. Even the
décor of Hindu dancing and the Russian ballet—their cos-
tumes and accoutrements—is as other-worldly as the statues
and the ikons; all are informed by a spirit that seems to the
West to savour of fantasy.

In precisely similar fashion these civilizations regard
history, not (like the Chinese and the Nordics) as a record
of events, but as a spiritual interpretation of them. Hence
the epics of India, with the exaggerations that seem so per-
versely unmeaning to the this-worldly minded peoples—the
seas of treacle and butter and the kings thirty feet high—
and the epic songs and legends of the Slavs into which a
mystic symbolism enters so largely—'that was no damsel
weeping, but the city-wall lamenting, because she hath
foreseen ill fortune for Kiev'.[1]

The social ideal of these civilizations also comes from
their view of the Universe: they are first and foremost
not political but religious communities. Indian society is
divided into classes or castes, each soul being reborn into
its own caste, low or high, according to its baseness or excellence in its preceding life; and each caste performing its
own work as a religious duty—as 'worship of Him That is
the Source of all that lives'. Buddhism tends to make every
man a monk, at least for part of his life, that he may the
better practise the virtues of the Way that leads through
the worlds. Russian society is primarily conceived, not as
a State, but as a Church, or rather, as part of the Cosmic
Church. 'I am Orthodox,' a Russian used to say; not 'I am
a Russian'.

Such a view of the Universe is loftier than any other; but
it pays the price. For it is—and must remain, until the
powers of the human spirit are far more developed—largely
out of reach of the mass even of the peoples who have
originated it. In order to attain social harmony and liberty
the Chinese and the Nordics have fostered and practised the

[1] Isabel Florence Hapgood, *The Epic Songs of Russia*, p. xi.

social virtues; compared to other peoples they are disciplined, they speak the truth, they are honest, they have cultivated social morality generally; they normally touch neither the heights nor the depths, but occupy the intermediate levels. Islam and Catholicism stress the moral virtues too, emphasizing that those who neglect them will be punished everlastingly in Hell. All these peoples are, in a greater or less degree, political and practical. But all these virtues the other-worldly civilizations tend to neglect; between their spiritual virtues and their unsocial vices a great gulf yawns. The Hindus and the Russians are undisciplined and the Russians prone to violence. Notwithstanding their gentleness, they lack social morality: the Indian is apt to be litigious, untruthful, a nepotist with a feeble sense of virtue; the Russian to be feckless, ineffective, lacking in practical wisdom. Concentrated on thoughts remote from everyday experience, India and Russia have the same verbal exuberance, the same undisciplined flights of fancy; they are apt to be too comprehensive, too hospitable to views that are incompatible. They fail to see that Truth combines reason with experience, theory with fact.

I. 1

Birth—the fleeting world—man's fleeting life—death! The evil that struck the early Indian thinker, meditating in his forests during the rains, was the transitory character of man's mortal state, its unsteadfastness (*anityam*), its change (*vikara*). Men go from life to life, from death to death; nothing abides. Yet there is Something Abiding, Deathless, Eternal, That the soul desires, That alone can satisfy it. Man, like Nachiketas in the *Upanishad*,

> Knowing there That Which does not die nor grow old
> Finds himself here growing old, dying.[1]

Another ancient sage, Yajnavalkya, gives up house and home in order to find eternal life in this Eternal Something, leaving his possessions to his two wives. But one of them, Maitreyi, refuses these and all the riches of the world: 'If

[1] *Katha Upanishad*, quoted Rudolf Otto, *Mysticism East and West*, p. 19.

I am not thereby free from death, what are these to me?'[1]
And, indeed, it was perceived that what kept men from this
One of their desire was the goods of this world, or what
appeared to them to be the goods of this world. These
desires for finite things can never be satisfied, for when one
has been won another is wanted: the materialist is for ever
cheated. 'Whatever he reaches, he wishes to go beyond. If
he reaches the sky, he wishes to go beyond.'[2] Especially,
'no man can be made happy by wealth'.[3] 'The hereafter
never rises before the eyes of the careless youth, befooled by
the delusion of wealth. "This is the world", he thinks,
"there is no other." Thus he falls again and again into the
power of death.'[4] But 'wise men, knowing the Nature of
What is Immortal, do not look for anything stable here
among things unstable'.[5] This animal desire for the things
of this world and the action to which it gave rise was early
called *karma*; it carried the soul in a ceaseless round from
life to death and from death to life; and the doctrine served,
not only as an explanation of evil, but as a deterrent. This
coming forth from the Eternal in the pursuit of the lower
self and its interests was the Way of Pursuit, the Way of
Power; both terms well describe egoistic individuality conceived as a force antagonistic, not to society, as the Chinese
and Nordics conceive it, but to religion—the salvation of the
soul through its union with the Everlasting.

But if fleeting and illusory things cheat the soul, what
is the Eternal Reality That will satisfy it? The steps of
Indian thought led to a stupendous answer. The Vedas show
the primitive Aryans worshipping anthropomorphic powers,
natural and other deities, which dispose of the material world
and of the destinies of men. But the distinction is often
made between 'that which moves and That Which moves
not';[6] and the early parts of the Vedas already know a 'One
and Only Reality' (Ekam Sat), 'One Being—sages call it by

---

[1] *Brihad-aranyaka Upanishad*, ii. 4. 3, and iv. 5. 4.
[2] *Aitareya Aranyaka*, ii. 3. 3. 1.
[3] *Katha Upanishad*, i. 27.
[4] Ibid., ii. 6.
[5] Ibid., iv. 2.
[6] Edward J. Thomas, *Vedic Hymns*, p. 15.

many names', Prajapati, the Lord of Creatures.[1] He is the
Origin and Essence of all things visible:

> Who is the One God over the gods—
>> What God shall we serve with our offering?
>
> May He not harm us, Who is the Begetter of Earth,
>> True of law, Who begot Heaven,
> Yea, Who begot the bright mighty waters—
>> What God shall we serve with our offering?
>
> Lord of Creatures, none other save Thee
>> Containeth all these born beings.[2]

This 'One' was from eternity

>> Self-Dependent;
> Beyond This there was naught whatsoever.[3]

A corresponding change took place in the view of man,
and of his relation to this Being. There are five selves in
man, the first four enfolding the innermost self like sheaths.[4]
The two outermost are the inanimate or material and the
animate or breathing body. Within that is the 'self formed
of perception and will', the animal man, who sees only the
things of space and time and accounts for them by anthropomorphic gods, whom he worships for worldly ends with
priestly ritual, including brahma-spells that exercise a magical power. Within that is the 'self formed of understanding',
where ritual gives way to thought; the priest's 'measuring'
(*manas*) at the altar has become the 'mind' that conceives,
and brahma is no longer a spell but a function of the mind,
a spiritual prayer or contemplation. But the Reality, the
One, is still separate from mind, which can only argue and
reason about It. In the fifth and innermost self—the 'self
formed of bliss'—this separation is overcome: mind and its
Object are One. Brahma the thought in the mind is now
Brahma the Conscious Reality; the true self of man is the
Self That is the Universe. There is here no longer argument, inference, philosophy, but a mystical knowledge, a
direct experience, because this innermost self realizes that

---

[1] *Rig-Veda*, i. 164. 46, (L. D. Barnett, *The Heart of India*, p. 20).
[2] *Rig-Veda*, x. 121, 8–10 (translated by Barnett, p. 22).
[3] *Rig-Veda*, x. 129, 2.
[4] *Taittiriya Upanishad*, ii. 1–5 (L. D. Barnett, *Brahma-Knowledge*, p. 26).

itself *is* Reality. 'All is One—Universal Thought without object—and that is my Self.'[1]

At this point, therefore, the Hindu makes his tremendous affirmation: '*Tat tvam asi*—That art thou': the 'One Being', now identified with Brahman, and my self or *atman* are the same.[2] The outer selves of sense and of argument that separate me from the Divine fall away, and I realize that my innermost self is indeed the One Self that is the Universe. The knowledge, therefore, which is salvation is no mere intellectual knowledge—it is an intuitive realization of the Divine, a mystical experience felt by man's whole being. If the pleasures of this world by themselves darken man, the belief that merely intellectual knowledge suffices to enlighten him produces a still greater darkness. As one of the early Upanishads puts it, in words that might have been written by Lao-tze: 'Into blind darkness pass they who worship ignorance; into still greater darkness they that are content with knowledge'—that is, with mere argument.[3] Sense and inference are but the wrappings of the inner or true self, that 'seizes hold of and animates the body', and that 'sees with the mind';[4] and this self—or soul or spirit—of which body and mind are the instruments can recognize Brahma, for it is part of Brahma, the One All-Embracing Reality. Man is Divine; as the old sages put it in the Upanishads: 'We are born from the Immortal.' Those who have this highest experience cannot tell it—for words were invented to express the experience of another realm than this, the realm of the sense, not of the spirit. 'From Him come back baffled both words and mind.'[5] Yet about this consciousness of the Reality Who is the Supreme Self and our own soul there is nothing vague: it is as real as the consciousness of an amalaka fruit held in the palm of the hand.

This is the fullness of all experience: for 'He Who is the Brahma in man and He Who is That in the sun, these are One'.[6] When one can say, with one of the sages in the

---

[1] L. D. Barnett, *Heart of India*, p. 12.
[2] *Chandogya Upanishad*, vi. 8. 7.
[3] *Brihad-aranyaka Upanishad*, iv. 4. 10.   [4] Ibid. i. 5. 3.
[5] *Taittiriya Upanishad*, ii. 4.
[6] Ibid. ii. 8. and iii. 10. 4 See also *Isa Upanishad*, 16.

Upanishads: 'I have known Him Who is the Supreme Person,' one can also say: 'He Who sees all creatures in Himself and Himself in all creatures, no longer remains concealed.'[1] 'The Brahman, the Power Which presents Itself to us materialized in all existing things, Which creates, sustains, preserves, and receives back into Itself again all worlds, this Eternal Infinite Divine Power is identical with the *atman*, with that which, after stripping off everything external, we discover in ourselves as our real most essential being, our individual self, the soul. This identity of the Brahma and the *atman*, of God and the soul, is the fundamental thought of the entire teaching of the Upanishads.'[2] As a modern Indian philosopher puts it: 'God's dwelling-place is in the heart of man. The inner immortal self and the Infinite Cosmic Power are One and the Same. Brahman is the *atman*, and the *atman* is Brahman. The One Supreme Power through Which all things have been brought into being is one with the inmost self in each man's heart.'[3] As an Archbishop of Canterbury has said: 'Since God is Himself the Truth of the whole Universe, the quest of that Truth is a quest of God. Nay more, God is the Spirit Who, moving in and through the minds of men, inspires and guides them in this quest. God is both the Truth which is sought and the Spirit which moves men to seek it.'[4]

This 'One without a Second' (*Ekam Advaitam*) is Undivided and Indivisible; for (says Sankara, the foremost of India's religious thinkers) 'were there division, That Which is Eternal would become mortal; but Perfection is Eternal, Undying, Fearless, Unchanging, Unmoving and Constant';[5] it is 'Omniscient, Omnipresent, Eternally Satisfied, Eternally Pure, Intelligent and Free of Nature, Understanding and Bliss'.[6] This Being, since it includes everything, includes both Consciousness and the Object of Conscious-

---

[1] *Brihad-aranyaka Upanishad*, iii. 9. 10. *Isa Upanishad*, 6.

[2] Deussen, *Philosophy of the Upanishads*.

[3] *Chandogya Upanishad*, vii. 3. 1. Sir S. Radhakrishnan, *Philosophy of the Upanishads*, p. 4.

[4] *London University Centenary Commemorative Volume*, 1936, sermon in St. Paul's Cathedral.

[5] Commentary on *Mandukya Upanishad*, iii. 19 and ii. 21.

[6] Sankara on *Brahma-sutra*, i. 1. 4.

ness: it is Consciousness of Self, Thought and Being in One. And, since the innermost self is the 'self formed of bliss', this Self-Consciousness is Bliss, Rapture (*ananda*). 'Brahma is Bliss', says the *Taittiriya Upanishad*: 'Out of Bliss these creatures spring, by Bliss they live after their birth, and into Bliss they return when they depart hence.'[1]

For the Hindu therefore the Divine Perfection is at once Reality (*Sat*), Soul or Consciousness (*Chit*), and Bliss (*Ananda*)—in a word *Sat-Chit-Ananda*,[2] Being-Thought-Bliss, the All-Embracing Reality Conscious of Itself and exulting in that Consciousness. Men, until the barriers of appearance are broken down and they know that they are God, ascribe to Him Virtues like, though surpassing, their own; the Hebrew, the Muslim, and the Catholic, thinking of God as a separate Being, try to see Him in relation to this world, and therefore attribute to Him an Infinite Righteousness, Compassion, or Grace. But the Hindu, carrying thought and experience a stage farther and higher, realizes that these quasi-human Qualities or Gunas are appearances, symbols of What the Divine Reality must be. Brahma as He really is has no such Qualities: all that man can say of Him is negative—'*Neti, neti*—Not so, not so':[3] He is not changing, but Eternal; not bounded, but Infinite. The Nature of this Infinite Being could not be known to a finite mind; and the bliss of the experience of oneness with Him words were powerless to explain.

But this reasoning was for the wise, this experience for the saint. They did nothing to solve the problem of social organization, except for those who needed no solution; and they gave the ordinary man little he could understand about God or about the way to God. The laymen, less philosophic, took the matter in hand: Krishna, Gotama, Mahavira, two of them Princes. In the *Bhagavad-gita*, the 'Song of the Lord', Krishna deals with both problems. It shows the religion of the Supreme Self as it may enter into the life of the ordinary man, consecrating the daily duties of his station and inspiring him with the love of a Personal God.

---

[1] *Taittiriya Upanishad*, iii. 6.　　　　[2] The later *Vedanta*.
[3] Ascribed to Yajnavalkya, *Brihad-aranyaka Upanishad*, iv. 2. 4.

When the Aryans penetrated into India they probably found village communities consisting, partly of agricultural families with roots in the soil, partly of workers without rights. They themselves settled down as landowners, with a class of labourers and craftsmen, the Sudras, below them, and, still lower, outcastes doing scavenging and other necessary work that was ceremonially unclean. In course of time the landowners apparently became differentiated as Brahmins, the priestly class, Kshatriyas, the fighting and ruling class (perhaps originally the medicine men and the chiefs respectively) and Vaisyas, the merchant class. Already the *Rig-Veda* recognized the four castes: Brahmins, Kshatriyas, Vaisyas, and Sudras, which sprang respectively from the head, arms, thighs, and feet of the Creative Spirit. Similarly Medieval Catholicism regarded the priests as the head, the nobles as the arms, and the peasants and workers as the feet of society. Plato in the *Republic* knew the same four castes —philosophers, soldiers, landowners and merchants, workers and craftsmen. These four classes are indeed more or less necessary to every organized society: thinkers, rulers, organizers, manual workers; though machines may be destined largely to replace the last. The metaphor of the body brings out the organic nature of society, of which each part has its own function.

The facts of Indian history were, however, like those of Catholic Europe, rationalized to conform with religious belief. The caste into which men are born (said the *Vedanta*) depends upon *karma*: sin or righteousness in his previous life determines a man's place in society here and now, as sin or righteousness here and now determines his place in the next life. Plato held the same view. Nevertheless it is manifest that men and women of whatever caste can and sometimes do reach a life of supreme holiness. In rare cases, Plato said, men rise from one class to another; men rise above caste altogether, says the *Gita*, when they become *sannyasins* or saints.

> Who refuge take in Me,
> Though they be born from the very womb of sin,
> Woman or man; sprung of the Vaisya caste
> Or lowly disregarded Sudra—all

Plant foot upon the highest course; how then
The Holy Brahmans and My royal saints?[1]

Here the Indian ideal, moving away from caste, approaches
that of the Hebrews.

In the *Gita* Krishna describes to Arjuna the virtues which
by nature characterize the four castes:

> A Brahman's virtues, Prince,
> Born of his nature, are serenity,
> Self-mastery, religion, purity,
> Patience, uprightness, learning, and to know
> The Truth of things which be. A Kshatriya's pride,
> Born of his nature, lives in valour, fire,
> Constancy, skilfulness, spirit in fight,
> And open-handedness and noble mien,
> As of a lord of men. A Vaisya's task,
> Born of his nature, is to till the ground,
> Tend cattle, venture trade. A Sudra's state,
> Suiting his nature, is to minister.[2]

Plato defined justice or righteousness in the State as the
doing by each class of its own duty—not the duty of others:
a good soldier was a man who did his duty as a soldier, not
as a merchant or philosopher. The *Gita* takes the same
view: each caste has its *sva-dharma*, its 'own law' or duty:

> Better thine own work is, though done with fault,
> Than doing others' work, even excellently.
> He shall not fall in sin who fronts the task
> Set him by nature's hand! Let no man leave
> His natural duty, Prince!
> Whoso performeth—diligent, content—
> The work allotted him, whate'er it be,
> Lays hold of perfectness.[3]

The virtues of caste have social results. Indeed, the performance of certain duties is necessary if society is to hold
together at all; and India has not of course wholly neglected
social organization. The body requires health and a suffi-
ciency of wealth (*artha*). In providing them the natural
desires and emotions (*kama*) must be satisfied too. Still more

---

[1] *Bhagavad-gita*, ix. 32–3 (Sir Edwin Arnold, *The Song Celestial*, p. 53) (altered).
[2] Ibid. xviii. 42–4 (p. 106).   [3] Ibid. xviii. 47–8, 45 (p. 107).

important is the discipline of the body and of the desires
and emotions—they must obey the law (*dharma*) which
brings them into proportion. But (says the *Gita*)—and here
the Indian mind differs radically from the Chinese and the
Nordic—these caste duties have to be undertaken, this caste
law has to be obeyed, not primarily with a social end in view,
but as a service to God, that shall enable the soul eventually
to attain *moksha*—the spiritual freedom of those who realize
that the human self is truly the Supreme Self. To the Hindu
therefore it is the spiritual motive, not the material consequences or 'fruit', of an action that matters; characteristically
of an other-worldly civilization he thinks, not of the seen,
but of the unseen results—of the effect on the soul rather
than on the body. When performed in this spirit these duties
are themselves worship—sacraments, outward and visible
signs with an inward and spiritual meaning. A man finds
perfection (says the *Gita*)

> through worship, wrought by work,
> Of Him That is the Source of all that lives.

Duties performed in this spirit are therefore the first stage
of the way to God—the *karma marga* or way of works.

To these simpler souls the Supreme Principle is revealed,
not as the Self without Qualities of the philosopher, but as
a Personal God, Isvara, Who manifests Himself as a Three-
fold Being, the Trimurti—Brahma the Creator, Vishnu the
Maintainer, Siva the Destroyer and Restorer. Vishnu in
turn reveals Himself in incarnations or avatars, of Whom the
principal are Krishna and Rama, the heroes of the two great
Epics. Thus the Supreme Brahma makes Himself known,
to men still labouring under the imperfect apprehension of
Reality to which the limits of mere body and mere mind
give rise, as a separate Being with Love and other Qualities.
Ordinary men have a God Whom they can love and Who
loves them.

The Krishna of history seems to have been a chief of the
sixth century before Christ ruling in the Middle Land between Jumna and Ganges, who was later interpreted as the
chief incarnation of the Eternal, just as (about the same time)
Gotama and Jesus came to be interpreted as incarnations of

the Eternal. This Eternal Krishna is Himself both the
Origin and the End of the Universe, its Father and Mother,
the Life of All creatures, the Wisdom of the Wise and the
Strength of the Strong; the Friend, the Refuge, and the
Goal. As the Eternal He reveals Himself in all His Fullness, not to the physical, but to the spiritual sight of his
cousin:

> Behold! This is the Universe! Look! What is live and dead
> I gather all in One—in Me! Gaze, as thy lips have said,
> On God Eternal, Very God! See Me! see What thou prayest!
> Thou canst not! nor, with human eyes, Arjuna! ever mayest.
> Therefore I give thee sense Divine. Have other eyes, new light
> And look! This is My Glory, unveiled to mortal sight![1]

Then the Unmanifest was made manifest in Krishna, including and unifying in Itself everything in the Universe in
all its splendour:

> Out of countless eyes beholding,
> Out of countless mouths commanding,
> Countless mystic forms enfolding
> In One Form: supremely standing,
> Countless radiant glories wearing,
> So He showed! If there should rise
> Suddenly within the skies
> Sunburst of a thousand suns
> Flooding earth with beams undreamed-of,
> Then might be that Holy One's
> Majesty and Radiance dreamed of!
> So did Pandu's son behold
> All this Universe enfold
> All its huge diversity
> Into One Vast Shape, and be
> Visible, and viewed, and blended
> In one Body—Subtle, Splendid,
> Nameless—the All-Comprehending
> God of gods, the Never-Ending
> Deity![2]

God so manifested can be attained, not by *karma*, works,
alone, but by *bhakti*—faithful and loving devotion to this
Personal God. Just as the Hebrew Prophets would have

---

[1] *Bhagavad-gita*, xi. 7–8 (p. 63).   [2] Ibid. xi. 10–11, 12–13 (pp. 63–4).

men substitute righteousness and the worship of the One
God for material sacrifice and formal obedience to the law,
so the *Gita* requires 'faith and love' in place of 'all the laws':

> Take My last word, My utmost meaning have!
> Precious thou art to Me; right well-beloved!
> Give Me thy heart! Devotion to Me give!
> Give sacrifice and reverence to Me!
> So shalt thou come to Me! Abandoning
> All duties, do thou fly to Me alone!
> Make Me thy single refuge! I will free
> Thy soul from all its sin! Be of good cheer![1]

Conversely, if man is to love and trust God, God likewise,
in His Personal aspect, loves man and desires that he should
be righteous, as the God of the Hebrews does. The man

> Who hateth nought
> Of all that lives, living himself benign,
> Compassionate, from arrogance exempt,
> Exempt from love of self, unchangeable
> By good or ill; patient, contented, firm
> In faith, mastering himself, true to his word,
> Seeking Me, heart and soul; vowed unto Me—
> That man I love! Who troubleth not his kind,
> And is not troubled by them; clear of wrath,
> Living too high for gladness, grief or fear,
> That man I love! Who dwelleth quiet-eyed,
> Stainless, serene, well-balanced, unperplexed,
> Working with Me, yet from all works detached,
> That man I love. Who, fixt in faith on Me,
> Dotes upon none, scorns none; rejoices not,
> And grieves not, letting good or evil hap
> Light when it will, and when it will depart,
> That man I love! Who, unto friend and foe
> Keeping an equal heart, with equal mind
> Bears shame and glory; with an equal peace
> Takes heat and cold, pleasure and pain; abides
> Quit of desires, hears praise or calumny
> In passionless restraint, unmoved by each;
> Linked by no ties to earth, steadfast in Me,
> That man I love! But most of all I love

---

[1] *Bhavagad-gita*, xviii. 64–6 (p. 109), altered (cf. E. J. Thomas, *The Song of the Lord*).

> Those happy ones to whom 'tis life to live
> In single fervid faith and love unseeing
> Drinking the blessed Amrit of My Being![1]

that is, His Eternal Life.

There are thus in Indian thought three stages on the way to the Divine: the *karma marga* or way of works—ritual worship and the performance of caste duties valued less for their 'fruits' than for the virtues they express; the *bhakti marga*, the way of trusting love for God manifested as a Person distinct from the worshipper; and the highest stage, so hard that only the few—the sage, the saint, those who have attained spiritual freedom—can attain it: the *jnana*, the conscious realization of Brahma, the mystical experience in which the human self, no longer separate, is lost and found in the Supreme Self. To the souls of men in every stage of development—to the wise and to the simple—God reveals Himself. To the Brahmin and the saint:

> Who serve—
> Worshipping Me the One, the Invisible,
> The Unrevealed, Unnamed, Unthinkable,
> Uttermost, All-Pervading, Highest, Sure—
> Who thus adore Me, mastering their sense,
> Of one set mind to all, glad in all good,
> These blessed souls come unto Me. Yet, hard
> The travail is for such as bend their minds
> To reach th' Unmanifest. That viewless path
> Shall scarce be trod by man bearing the flesh!

He therefore reveals Himself also to those who trust and love:

> But whereso any doeth all his deeds
> Renouncing self for Me, full of Me, fixt
> To serve only the Highest, night and day
> Musing on Me—him will I swiftly lift
> Forth from life's ocean of distress and death,
> Whose soul clings fast to Me. Cling thou to Me!
> Clasp me with heart and mind! So shalt thou dwell
> Surely with Me on high.

Below these, again, God manifests Himself to those still

[1] Ibid. xii. 13–20 (pp. 78–9).

treading the way of works, worshipping or merely working for Him:

> But if thy thought
> Droops from such height; if thou be'st weak to set
> Body and soul upon Me constantly,
> Despair not! give Me lower service! seek
> To reach me, worshipping with steadfast will;
> And, if thou canst not worship steadfastly,
> Work for Me, toil in works pleasing to Me!
> For he that laboureth right for love of Me
> Shall finally attain!

And last—most splendidly—God reveals Himself even to the failures:

> But, if in this
> Thy faint heart fails, bring Me thy failure! find
> Refuge in Me! Let fruits of labour go,
> Renouncing hope for Me, with lowliest heart,
> So shalt Thou come.[1]

Or, as He puts it, in words which combine the Hebrew ideal of righteousness with the Indian ideal of peace in the Eternal:

> If one of evil life turn in his thought
> Straightly to Me, count him among the good;
> He hath the high way chosen ; he shall grow
> Righteous ere long ; he shall attain that peace
> Which changes not.
> Ah! ye who into this ill world are come—
> Fleeting and false—fix fast your faith on Me![2]

The whole is summed up, in words that recall both the Hebrew and the Christian doctrine:

> I am alike for all! I know not hate,
> I know not favour. What is made is Mine!
> But them that worship Me with love, I love:
> They are in Me, and I in them![3]

I. 2

What a different world these ideas beget from that of the Chinese and Nordics, or even from that of the Semites and

[1] *Bhagavad-gita*, xii. 3–5, 6–8, 9–11 (pp. 77–8).
[2] Ibid. ix. 30–1, 33 (pp. 53–4)   [3] Ibid. ix. 29 (p. 53).

Catholics! For they look almost wholly inward: actions are interesting, not as they bring political freedom from anarchy and confusion, but as they bring spiritual freedom from ignorance and unreality; not as they draw men together, but as they draw the soul toward God. Clan administration and Parliaments—these smack largely of unreality; even Caliphs and Popes have too much truck with it. The soul of India is bent upon something vastly different: how shall I realize my true Self That is also the Universe?

With such views the Hindu ideal of character will not be ethical, but spiritual: not the man with filial piety, or respect for others, or even primarily righteousness, but he who escapes from *maya*—the unreal world of sense and mind—back into the Bliss of Brahma. The soul who thus forsakes the Way of Pursuit and turns back along the Way of Return is the *sadhu* or holy man: whether he be the *rishi*—the sage of old who in the forest first penetrated the mystic's secret; the *yogi* who 'concentrates' on the Supreme Spirit; the *mahatma* or 'great self'; the *sannyasin* who has 'renounced' all earthly attachments, all religious rites and ceremonies, but who loves all things, living according to the rule 'The world is my country; to do good my religion'; the *parivrajaka* or wandering teacher who issues from meditation that he may teach the world. Kalidasa the poet describes the supreme aim of life as 'owning the whole world while disowning oneself'.[1]

That is the ideal, which each in his degree tries to attain. The masses strive to perform their caste duties and take part in the worship of the temples. The higher spirits adore a Personal God. The devout Brahmin and the saint seek an increasing realization of the Spirit That is at once the soul of the thinker and the Universe Itself. Finally, after many deaths, the soul come home again will be able to say in the fullest sense: 'That art thou.' Such virtue is manifestly spiritual, not utilitarian: though it begins with duty to others, it does so that it may thereby come to trust and love God and finally to realize and enjoy the Godhead.

This spiritual ideal controls the Hindu conception of education. For the masses, to read and write is of small

[1] *Malavikagnimitra*, I. I.

account; men learn more by the spoken than by the written word. Especially is poetry the teacher of India, as it was of Greece; as painting has been of China and of Italy. The two great epics, the Great Poem of the Bharatas and the Career of Rama, give a magnificent ethical picture of manhood and womanhood. Krishna is here, not only as God, but as the model friend and counsellor—the ideal of manhood, as Rama is in the twin Epic. The tales are full, not only of valour, but of mercy and forgiveness. Yudishthira, setting out for Indra's Heaven, refuses to enter unless not only his wife and brother but his dog may enter too—an anticipation of the bodhisats of the Greater Buddhism. Here too are the ideal women of India. When the Lord of Death comes for the soul of her husband, Savitri, the Indian Alcestis, will not take No for an answer. 'Without him I am but dead, without him I do not even desire happiness.' Damayanti, faithful wife of an unworthy husband who gambles away his kingdom, refuses to follow his advice and return to her home. 'How can I leave thee alone in the wild forest? I would rather serve and care for thee, for there is no helper like a wife.' He forsakes her, and she weeps for grief and loneliness; 'but soon she thought of him more than of herself, and bewailed his sufferings'. He in turn 'praises the faith and forgiveness of women, since one whose husband had deserted her yet bore no malice, but sought him through all the world'. The recital of these Epics, and the performance of plays founded upon them, have through the ages formed a chief part of the education of the villagers of India. So has the singing of the lyrics that bloom from the *Vedanta*. Countless songs, sometimes of rare beauty, pass down the centuries on the lips of the people; only to-day are scholars awakening to the unwritten treasures preserved in the vernacular languages of India.

Indian art is also a great teacher. Indian temples are covered with crowded sculpture, Indian cave-halls with crowded frescoes; partly because the exuberance of Nature is reflected in the exuberance of art, partly because an exceptionally difficult religious philosophy is in more than usual need of the aid that art can give it—the eye helps the mind that is attuned to grasp the abstractions of thought. Nor is this art unworthy of its function; for whereas Greek art shows the gods as men—even if as superb men—Indian art, especially sculpture, shows them as gods.

Within these temples the ritual worship of the One God is adored under many Forms. Everywhere there are the emblems telling of creation, of destruction, of fresh creation. Pilgrimages to the temples and shrines are themselves education. Men hear, relate, act sacred things: the festival of Jagannatha, for instance, dramatizes the triumph of the Lord of the World. The education of the leaders of the community never ceases. The life of the three upper classes, like that of Plato's philosopher, is divided into four stages, alternating between action and contemplation, and leading up to the perfection of the soul. In the first or preparatory stage a man is a student—his unfolding nature is helped to develop mainly by transmitting to him something of the wisdom the world has already gained. Next, he is a householder—he must play an active part in promoting the welfare of society, including the raising and training of a family. When his work is done and his children have grown up, he becomes a recluse in the forest—meditating upon the Ultimate Truths in the light of his past experience. Finally, if his soul is great enough, he becomes a *parivrajaka*, a wandering saint, who issues forth into the world once more to impart the fruits of his meditation. Such a 'desireless man' —in whom all thought of self is quenched in the thought of the Self—combines the bliss of union with the Divine with practical power as a spiritual teacher.

Every kind of education involves an appropriate technique. The Family, the Public School, even the University, foster the social rather than the spiritual virtues. The Way of Return—the Way of Renunciation and Self-Realization —is best learnt from some saint who is already treading it: *guru* and *chela*—master and pupil—is the tradition of Indian education. Monasteries play a smaller part in Hinduism than in Buddhism or in Orthodoxy; the Hindu contemplative is generally either a hermit or a mendicant.

Performance must needs fall short of an ideal so lofty. India was not exempt from the misfortune that overtook Taoism, Judaism, Islam, and Christianity: the superstitions of a primitive people crept in to corrupt a pure worship. The Brahmins made terms with the aboriginal inhabitants, whence the horrors of the ritual of Kali, the debasing cult of snakes, the propitiation of the cholera goddess and so on. Eroticism degraded the heroic Krishna to the amorous lover of the milkmaids of Brindaban; the worship of the Saktis or female powers of creation degenerated into lustful orgies. The unity of the manifold in Brahma has been obscured as well as illustrated by the multitude of the gods.

Excited perhaps by the tropic luxuriance of the jungle, the Indian imagination lacks discipline, and is apt itself to become a jungle. Not so much indeed as the more practical peoples suppose: Indian history is less interested in events than in their spiritual meaning, Indian science less in facts than in their Cosmic significance. Nevertheless Macaulay is not altogether unjustified in criticizing Indian history for its kings thirty feet high, and Indian geography for its seas of treacle and butter. Indian thought, again, is too easily hospitable to inconsistencies. 'Did you ever hear of such a thing as ten subtracted from ten leaving ten? Still, this is what the Veda teaches us, and we believe it.'[1]

But it is in its imperfect conception of the social virtues and of social institutions that Hinduism is most sadly to seek. Lying is politeness; it is only the peoples whose interest is the solidarity of society who value highly the telling of truth. Nepotism is a duty to one's family, not a wrong to society at large. Even murder is not infrequent. The doctrine that misfortune is the result of sin in a previous life has led to the perpetuation of many abuses. Child marriage, purdah, suttee, have wronged the lives of women; the miserable lot of the Untouchables at one end of the caste system has been too often the counterpart of the arrogance of the Brahmins at the other. Some organization of course there has been; the villages have in many parts been governed as 'little republics' by panchayats, councils of elders. Ancient guilds promoted the quality of the crafts and the welfare of the craftsmen; an ever-increasing elaboration of the castes has provided by heredity for the continuance of a diversity of services, ennobled by the sanction of religion. But the

[1] Lord Ronaldshay, *The Heart of Aryavarta*, p. 190.

lack of an adequate central government has left India defenceless against the invader, and the peasant a prey to grinding poverty and often to the wildest anarchy. In the absence of constitutional experience, terrorism has sometimes been resorted to as an instrument of government. Nevertheless India, rightly resenting the permanent rule of a foreign Power, is now skilfully co-operating with the British in the difficult task of establishing a workable Government that shall unite her infinitely varied Provinces and States, restore Indian culture, and give her poverty-stricken people the livelihood they need. Characteristically she draws her inspiration from Mahatma Gandhi's principle of non-violence.

The tremendous ideal of Hinduism, though in its integrity for the philosophic or saintly few, has in a measure laid its hold upon the multitudes also. In India as elsewhere the people reverence their highest leaders; and though this reverence does not imply a perfect understanding, they do their best to follow them within the limits of their powers. Just as the Nordics admire physical science and great men of science, and the lesser lights imitate them in the laboratory and observatory; just as the Hebrews revered the Prophets, but lowered the Law of Righteousness to the level of a code of ritual, and the Kingdom of God to a material kingdom; so the people of India do their best to follow, even if from afar, the saints and sages of the Vedanta. The mass of the people are by no means idolaters: under the form of a material object they are really worshipping the One Spirit. The multiplicity of gods does not deny the Divine Unity, but emphasizes that That Unity embraces all things in their infinite variety. Everywhere the people are conscious of His Presence. The peasant, seated under the sacred fig-tree, will say: 'The Lord of all is in this tree; He is in the roots; He is in the leaves; He is everywhere in the world.'[1] Innumerable humble souls, incapable of the highest flights of thought, are nevertheless able to talk with interest and intelligence of the great philosophies. Many of the villages have their mystic or mystics, men or women. Notwith-

[1] Heard by Sir T. W. Holderness, *Peoples and Problems of India,* p. 114.

standing Communal clashes, there is often a deep feeling of
the oneness of the religion that underlies the diverse rites
and worship of Hindu and Muslim, a feeling that descends
directly from the teaching of Kabir and of the great poets
who followed him—whom the West hardly knows. No book
in India has so great an influence as the *Gita*, with its emphasis on the sacred duty of every man and the Omnipre-
sence of the Divine. The Prime Minister of a vast Province
will read a portion of it every morning to attune his mind
for the duties of the day. The great nobleman has his
Garden of Meditation, 'bathed in that atmosphere of mystic
Pantheism, in which the Indian delights to bask as he does
in the golden glory of his sunlit air'.[1] Texts from the
Upanishads are graven upon the walls; above a pool of cool
water stand many shrines. The Buddha is here, with his
code of love; and the *lingam* and the *yoni*, emblems of the
mystery of the creation, preservation, and destruction of the
Universe. The mystic symbol Om bids man to meditate
upon Brahma,[2] 'That from Whence these things are born;
That by Which when born, they live; That into Which
they enter at their death'.[3] India seeks God as no other
civilization has done.

I. 3

More than in any other civilization therefore there has
always been in India a struggle to attain the real definition
of the Supreme Good. Hence the Vedantist philosophy—
the monism of the Supreme Self—has had many rivals and
many revivals. The flight from experience involved in the
Indian ideal resulted in an effort to return to experience.
The Sankhya system accordingly maintained that the Universe does not consist of Brahma, but of Nature and a
plurality of selves—spirits or persons. Nothing, however,
proves more decisively the strength of the Indian ideal than
the relative failure of efforts to rest upon nothing but experience. The Yoga philosophy added God to the Sankhya
system. Yoga means 'concentration' on the Supreme Self;
and the Yogi discovered that he could, by mortification of

---

[1] *Heart of Aryavarta*, pp. 191–2.   [2] *Taittiriya Upanishad*, i. 8.
[3] Cf. ibid. iii. 6.

the senses, by rigidity of posture, by breathing and other exercises, attain an ecstatic vision of the Divine and certain abnormal powers. He freed himself from the fetters of the flesh to gain a clearer insight into the world of the spirit.

The Vedantist ideal has perpetually renewed itself throughout Indian history, as the Confucian ideal has renewed itself throughout Chinese history; there have been as many Neo-Vedantist as Neo-Confucian Renaissances. In particular, when Buddhism at length merged itself into its parent, Vedantism broke forth with an unparalleled splendour. Sankara, the greatest of Indian philosophers, defined the Vedanta in its most absolute form: the 'One without a second' embraced Reality in every shape and kind. Succeeding commentators admitted in addition to Soul the subordinate principle of matter: Ramanuja thus distinguished selves from the Self; Madhva, things, selves and the Self. The nineteenth century witnessed another Vedantist Renaissance under Ramakrishna the saint and Vivekananda the philosopher. To-day the poetry of Tagore and the syntheses of Radhakrishnan are making that Renaissance world-wide.

By its very nature indeed Vedantism is universal; for when God is everything, what faith can be without Him? Hence it has by no means confined itself to developments from within, but has given birth to new forms through marriage with influences from without. Under the influence of Islam Kabir and his followers originated the Panth movement that led to the religious and then to the religious-military culture of the Sikhs. Muslim Akbar reacted to Hinduism with toleration and synthesis. Under the influence of Christianity Ram Mohan Roy and Swami Dayanand Saraswati founded respectively the Brahma Samaj or Church of God and the Arya Samaj or Church of India. Both these movements develop two ideas that are implicit in the Pantheism of the Supreme Self—that underlying all religions is the one religion of the One God, and underlying all nations is the brotherhood of mankind.

It is the remarkable development through generation after generation of the spiritual ideal of the Vedanta that gives to Hindu civilization its highest claim to greatness.

II. 1

But the most far-reaching of the developments of Brahminism was Buddhism, as the most far-reaching of the developments of Judaism was Islam.

'That art thou.' But alas! human frailty sadly confesses to itself: 'That art thou not.' But if I am not That, how am I to become It?

The greatness of Gotama the Buddha was that, long before the *Gita* was written, he answered that problem: he changed 'That art thou' to 'That shalt thou become'. Men grow, he said, as the lotus grows: beginning in the mud and darkness of the senses, rising through the dim water by moral growth, flowering at last in the beauty of the spirit under the light of Truth. Still more pregnant, because more strenuous, is his metaphor of the Way: he showed the 'Highway of Becoming', that not merely the saint but all men might travel until they reach 'the height of the Immortal'.[1] Men proceed along this Way like a rolling wheel (a metaphor that was destroyed when later monks showed the wheel, not on a road, but in the air). If the longest list of Buddhist terms refers to enlightenment, the next longest refers to energy, effort, endeavour, striving—not to meditation. If a man cannot yet say 'I am the Self', he can at least say 'I will be guided by the Self', which thus becomes to man the Supreme Law. So for poor foolish, sensual, unkind man Dharma—already in Hinduism the guide of conduct—takes the place of Brahma; the Divine Spirit is conceived as the Divine Will. The Conscience That is in his own heart says to him 'Do this, not that', if he would proceed along the Way to the Immortal. The emphasis shifts from the Object to the subject: only as man struggles onward to the Light can he pass from the round of change from birth to death, and from death to birth into mystic peace of the Eternal.

Thus Gotama was to Hinduism what Muhammad was to Judaism and Luther to Catholicism. All three accepted the fundamental ideas of their inheritance, but sought to bring them within reach of human imperfection and need. All

---

[1] Mrs. Rhys Davids, *What is the Original Gospel of 'Buddhism'?*, c. 7.

three rejected a priestly class, and told of a direct relation between the soul of the layman and the Will of the Divine.

Evil presented itself to Gotama much as it had done to the sages of the Upanishads. What impressed him supremely was not what impressed the contemporary Hebrews, the sin that alienates man from God, but the evil that afflicts humanity as such, the impermanence of mortal man and of all things. The facts about him are not certain. It may be that the Gotama of history left his home, not to 'renounce' but to learn, making the 'grand tour' of a young nobleman who lived too far from Taxila to study at the University.[1] It may be too that the struggle with temptation is legendary: that he was then too advanced to need to struggle. Be that as it may, the tradition that has influenced half Asia, perhaps the gradual creation of his monks, is that of a young Prince, newly married, surrounded by the pleasures of the world, who was stirred to the depth of his soul as he looked on birth, disease, decay, a corpse. All material or 'compound' things were changing, impermanent, transitory; and suffering was the portion of all. To this day the Buddhist chants:

Sabbam dukkham, everywhere suffering,
Sabbam anattam, everywhere changing self,
Sabbam aniccam, everywhere changing things.

How to escape this never-ending round of woe?

At first Gotama essayed the traditional way. Leaving his home, his bride, his new-born babe, he made 'the Great Renunciation'. Then for some years he practised asceticism, and under the instruction of two Brahmins sought to realize his oneness with the Supreme Spirit. Finally, after a last struggle with the temptation to return to the life of worldly enjoyment, 'enlightenment' (*bodhi*) came to him under the fig-tree; he saw (so the ages have believed) the Noble Way by which man should for ever escape from sorrow, a Middle Way that was neither self-indulgence nor asceticism. Whoever formulated the eight stages of Gotama's own Way of Becoming—whether he or his monks—there can be no doubt of its insight and spiritual value.

The Way was a progress to perfection, moral and spiritual.

---

[1] Mrs. Rhys Davids.

Of the eight stages the first was a change of mind—'right views'. Men must begin by understanding two truths that were already fundamental to Hinduism. First, the things of space and time, the material world, are always changing, and not in them is to be found emancipation from suffering and rest for the soul of man. Next, 'the body is not the self, the mind is not the self': the implication is that the innermost self or soul, which uses body and mind—the fullness of man's being—intuitively apprehends the Fullness of Reality.[1] (The West, not understanding this, has supposed that Gotama taught that man has 'no soul'.) Besides these traditional Hindu views man must understand four further truths. First, suffering—that is the disease to be cured. Second, suffering is caused by *tanha* (craving), animal desires. Third, 'emancipation' from this craving is possible. This was his perpetual message: 'just as the great ocean has one taste only, the taste of salt, so have this doctrine and this discipline but one flavour only, the flavour of deliverance.'[2] Fourth, man can be delivered by following the Noble Eightfold Way.

The next four stages of the Path relate to the moral life. A man's intention must be right. He must intend the eradication of wrong and the growth of a right disposition in his own heart: deliverance from sensuality, stupidity, and ill-will—the three cardinal sins of Buddhism—and the attainment of love for others, including the will not to injure any living thing. This second stage is therefore the stage of self-discipline, the overcoming of *tanha* or animal passion, leading on to temperance—the condition on which the more positive virtues depend. Thus the first two stages of the Way consist in a recognition of evil and of the fact that it can be overcome, together with the intention to overcome it.

With these beginnings, speech must be right, and so must action; these are the third and fourth stages. 'Right speech' speaks for itself. The all-important thing about action is that it should be inspired by friendliness or love (*metta*) and joy. 'All the means that can be used as helps towards doing right are not worth the sixteenth part of the

---

[1] Mrs. Rhys Davids, *Outlines of Buddhism*, p. 46.
[2] *Vinaya*, i. 1. 239.

emancipation of the heart through love: for the radiance and glory of love towards living beings outshines all else as the moon outshines the stars, the sun the darkness of the rains, the morning star the night.'[1] There are four 'sublime conditions': love, sorrow at the sorrow of others, joy in the joy of others, equanimity in one's own joys and sorrows. Not only does this love extend to all men and women, regardless of caste, but to animals as well. No violence or injury may be done to any living creature. As in Plato's *Symposium*,[2] love is gradually to extend till it embraces the whole world. 'Our mind shall not waver. No evil speech will we utter. Tender and compassionate will we abide, loving in heart, void of malice within. We will be ever suffusing such a one with the rays of our loving thought. And with that feeling as a basis we will ever be suffusing the whole wide world with thought of love far-reaching, grown great beyond measure, void of anger or ill-will.'[3] An early Buddhist poet sings:

> As, recking nought of self, a mother's love
>   Enfolds and cherishes her only son,
> So measureless let thy compassion move
>   And compass living creatures every one;
> So soar and sink in chainless liberty,
> Free from ill-will, purged of all enmity!
>
> Toward the whole world, above, below, around,
>   A heart of love unstinted in thee be,
> At one with all, with no dividing bound;
>   Hold ever this in wakeful memory,
> Standing or walking, sitting or upcurl'd,
> This state of heart is best in all the world.[4]

The whole universe is to be pervaded with thoughts of love —with kindness, pity, sympathy, and equable feeling.

As men advance along the Way, their lives come in a measure to stand apart from those of their fellows. The fifth stage concerns the right means of livelihood. Here Gotama himself set up the ideal, not of asceticism, not even

---

[1] *Iti-vuttaka* (Logia or Sayings), pp. 19–21 (shortened).
[2] 210 (Jowett's translation).   [3] *Majjhima*, i. 129.
[4] *Metta Sutta* 8, *Sutta Nipata*, 148–50. Cf. Saunders, *Epochs in Buddhist History*, p. 22.

of poverty, but of frugal simplicity: he admits that he wore laymen's clothes and fed like laymen if it suited him. He resembles not a little the Little Brother of Assisi, who was so much in love with Lady Poverty that he gave away all he had, yet was so little of an ascetic that he ate meat in Lent. In the Way the monk is to have no home, to sleep in trees, to dress in rags, to take round his begging-bowl and beg a small meal. It is not the begging that signifies, but the bowl —the unwillingness to be a slave to creature comforts, the indifference to things that are superfluous.

So then, after entering the gateway of Right Views, four stages of the highway are concerned with positive social virtues and with the negative virtue that is their condition— the disciplining of the body and its passions. But plain living leads to high thinking; in the last three stages of the Way the pilgrim's eyes, no longer blinded by hatred or craving but strengthened by the love of all living things, will become open to the light, and so at last attain Reality.

The sixth stage therefore is Right Effort or Endeavour— the effort to explain logically, to philosophize. Of the three cardinal sins dullness is the worst: stupidity is the antithesis of enlightenment. This intellectual alertness will presently result in an effortless awareness of Truth, of Reality, at all times—the penultimate stage. Whatever the disciple is doing, going out or returning, standing or walking, speaking or being silent, eating or drinking, his mind will be clearly conscious of all that his act means—its transient character, its spiritual significance, the Permanence only of the Dharma. In this way he will see those fleeting appearances that men call Nature and persons *sub specie Eternitatis*. The last and highest stage is Samadhi (concentration), the mystic union of the soul with the Eternal.[1] It is the cool, calm joy of him whose soul reflects Reality: 'the Universe and all things in it are serenely reflected in his mind as the starry heavens are mirrored in the calm sea.'[2] It is probable that, like the religion he was reforming, he identified Reality with the Divine Spirit, Brahma; while he differed from that religion in laying stress rather upon the Dharma.

[1] For Gotama as a mystic see Sir S. Radhakrishnan, *Gautama the Buddha*.
[2] *Avatamsaka Sutra*.

He to whom the Self is dear,
Who longeth for the Great Self—he
Should homage to the Dhamma pay.[1]

Dharma is in fact Brahma in Its relation to the progress of the soul.

This last stage is thus virtually identical with the realization of the Supreme Reality which is the goal of Hinduism; the difference being that, whereas Hinduism concentrates on the Object or End to be attained—the Nature of the Reality and the explanation of its illusory appearances—Buddhism concentrates on the subject and the means—man and the Way by which he may be delivered from suffering and reach that End. Gotama did indeed speak of the goal as 'the height of the Immortal'; but as a practical reformer, a saviour of men, his whole effort was bent on improving man, that his eyes might be opened to the Light. Just as Confucius talked little about supernatural beings, as likely to interfere with the solution of his social problem, so Gotama refused to answer four questions: whether the Universe is Eternal, whether It is Infinite, whether life is the same as the body, whether the perfect man exists after death. In other words, starting from the same premises as the earlier sages, in his conclusions he was silent where they spoke—as to the Nature of the Godhead; and eloquent where they said little—as to the way man may reach the *attha*, the undefined aim or goal in which man realizes his immanent Divinity and attains 'the height of the Immortal'. This goal was speedily identified with arahatship, the state of him who is 'worthy' here and now. It would seem he accepted the traditional belief in Brahma and man's realization of Him, but felt that his own mission lay in pointing out that to imperfect man Brahma can be known only as Dharma, the Law of Love and Light.

Thus the Way led, on its negative side, to *nirvana*—the 'blowing-out' or extinction of those sins of sensuality, stupidity, and hate in which thirst or craving (*tanha*) takes form, and from which suffering springs; and on its positive and

[1] Quoted by Mrs. Rhys Davids, *What was the Original Gospel in 'Buddhism'?*, p. 46.

therefore more important side to arahatship—the worth of man's nature and its peace in the Truth. Arahatship means 'the highest we desire'; Gotama did not define perfection—man has to discover what it is.

But his power, like that of all great thinkers, lay not only in his doctrine, but in his conviction of its truth. Shortly before he died he said to the beloved disciple: 'It may be, Ananda, that in some of you the thought may arise, "The word of the master is ended, we have no teacher more." But it is not thus, Ananda, that you should regard it. The Truths and the Rules of the Order, which I have set forth and laid down for you all, let them, after I am gone, be the Teacher to you.' His last words were: 'Behold now, brethren, I exhort you, saying: "Decay is inherent in all component things! Work out your salvation with diligence!" '[1]

II. 2

Gotama's teaching went to the root of the social organization of the time. Hinduism had organized society in castes, higher and lower, and had justified this inequality as the result of the good or bad conduct of individuals in their previous lives. Gotama's conception of love induced him to abandon the caste system altogether, including the Brahmins and their priesthood. In place of caste gradations he substituted equal sodalities of men and women—the origin of the Sangha or Society—united in fellowship by following the Way, and particularly by the love enjoined in its fourth stage. Yet how soon a master's teaching is corrupted! As Hebrew Prophecy hardened into the Law, the knowledge of God into mere obedience, the apostolic following of Jesus into an Apostolic Succession, so these seekers after the goal narrowed in course of time into an order of monks, till the laymen stepped in to restore the Founder's comprehensiveness. Asoka, that great Emperor who was turned from successful dictatorship by contemplating the horrors of war, reasserted the religion of goodness and intelligence for all men and women. Thirty-five of his edicts remain graven on rock and pillar. 'Thus saith His Majesty:

[1] T. W. Rhys Davids and C. A. F. Rhys Davids, *Dialogues of the Buddha*, Part 2, vi. 1, 7.

Father and mother must be obeyed; respect for all living creatures must be firmly established; truth must be spoken. These are the virtues of the Law of Piety, which must be practised. The teacher must be reverenced by the pupil; the proper courtesy must be shown to relatives. This is the ancient nature of piety, this leads to length of days, and according to this men must act.'[1] Thus to Asoka, as to the Chinese and Nordics, moral virtue is the foundation of the State: filial piety, reverence for learning, courtesy, truth-speaking. Religion, though it produces much more than social solidarity, nevertheless produces that too. And what Asoka preached, he practised. Love led him to such practical measures as the digging of wells, the cultivation of medicinal herbs, the planting of shady trees by the roadsides, the appointment of officers to supervise charities. It led him (so men believed) to send missionaries far beyond his own domains to Ceylon and Burma, to the borderlands beneath the Himalaya, to the Greek Kingdoms of the West. 'If a man's fame can be measured by the number of hearts who revere his memory, by the number of lips who have mentioned, and still mention, him with honour, Asoka is more famous than Charlemagne or Caesar.'[2] 'Thus did the benign influence of the Dhamma begin to spread, and its significance as an international bond for the next thousand years cannot be estimated.'[3]

II. 3

The Buddha had said little as to the Nature of Reality, and already at the Council of Patna[4] opinions were divided as to the orthodox view. The Elders held that man cannot know Reality, or even that there is no Reality to know; and Gotama's reticence on the point hardened into agnosticism and even atheism. The ideal of man on earth was still arahatship, the state of the man who is 'worthy'. But arahatship was succeeded by *nirvana*, which to these thinkers means the end of birth and death. This School of Buddhism is called by its critics the Hinayana or Lesser Vehicle.

[1] Quoted Saunders, *Epochs*, p. 32.   [2] Koeppen.
[3] Saunders, *Epochs*, p. 31.
[4] Probably met between 237 and 227 B.C., the last years of the reign of Asoka (Vincent Smith, *Early History of India*, p. 169).

On the other hand, the exponents of the Mahayana or Larger Vehicle fill in the gap where Gotama is silent, not with atheism, but with various views of the Divine Reality and of man's relation to It. Arahatship left unsatisfied the longing of reason for God; to the Buddhist, therefore, the One Eternal Spirit manifested Himself either as Gotama the Eternal Buddha, or as a number of Buddhas, or as the all-but Buddhas called Bodhisats. As the *Iti-vuttaka* or Sayings put it, the Buddha 'mounted the empty throne of Brahma'[1] and became the 'God of all gods'.[2]

The ideal of the Bodhisat sprang from the overflowing love for one's neighbour that is so large a part of right action. All men are on their way to Buddhahood; and no one who is perfectly loving can be willing to enter into salvation while any other remains outside. Those who have come to the Way's end will therefore voluntarily stop short of Buddhahood, until they can bring all other living beings to the goal with themselves. The Bodhisats are therefore beings of infinite compassion, the saviours of men; the greatest can save men from Hell and assure their rebirth in Heaven. Heaven—the Paradise of Bliss—is the dwelling-place of the Buddhas and Bodhisatvas and of the souls they save.

In a classic passage in the 'Larger Book of the Paradise of Bliss'[3] Gotama the Buddha (here called Sakyamuni) tells a vast concourse of the monk Dharmakara, who vowed that he would become a Buddha, 'equal the unequalled, and be peer of the peerless'. But as he trod the Way to Buddhahood, he vowed 'the king of vows'. 'O Blessed One, if when I attain Buddhahood all Bodhisats living in these Buddhalands attain it not, as they hear my name and share my merit, may I not attain to that perfect enlightenment!' So he becomes Amitabha or Amitayu, the Buddha of Endless Light and Life, Whose Excellencies are inexhaustible, Whose Western Paradise lacks no beautiful and pleasant thing and is free from the hindrances that make the attainment of enlightenment so hard to the dwellers upon earth.

At the same time faith tended to take the place of merit

---

[1] *Iti-vuttaka* (Saunders, *Epochs*, p. 42).

[2] *Milinda Panha* (quoted ibid.).

[3] *Sukhavati Vyuha* (*c.* A.D. 100), Sacred Books of the East, xlix, part ii.

as the means of salvation. Gotama had demanded faith, not
in himself, but in his teachings; faith was, he said, 'the root
of Right Views'.[1] It was only as a concession to the laity that
he countenanced faith in himself at all, the monk was to have
faith in his teaching only. 'Whoso shall turn to me with faith
and love shall reach one of the heavenly worlds; and what-
soever monk shall conform himself to my Teaching, walking
in full faith in it, he shall attain to Full Awakening.'[2] Faith
in the Teacher has its reward, but it is a smaller reward than
that given to faith in his Teachings. But after Gotama's
death faith in the Teaching tended to pass more and more
into faith in the Teacher, as it did in the case of Jesus; thus
at the ordination ceremony faith was from early days expressed in what are called the Three Refuges (Jewels, as
they were afterwards called): 'I take refuge in the Buddha,
in the Dharma, and in the Sangha.' The smaller of the
Paradise Books lays down that man can be reborn into the
Paradise of Bliss simply by loving faith in the Buddha—just
as the *Gita* teaches that salvation is to be won by *bhakti* or
loving faith in Krishna.

The greatest of all the Mahayana books is the 'Lotus of
the True Law', the 'Wonderful Law'—the Universal Law
that grows out of the earthy blindness of *tanha* as the pure
and lovely flower of the Lotus grows from the muddy
darkness of the pool.[3] The central purpose of the book
is to show the Buddha as the incarnation of the Eternal,
and man's salvation as knowledge of Him—just as the
central purpose of two contemporary books, the *Gita* and
the Fourth Gospel, is to show the incarnation of the Eternal
in Krishna and in Jesus, and man's salvation as faith and
love towards Them. In the *Lotus* the Buddha, seated on the
Vulture Peak in the midst of the gathered hosts of Buddhas,
saints, and lesser beings of all ranks, down to the lowest
spirits in Hell, declares that there is only One Way (*Eka-
yana*) of salvation—namely, Buddha-knowledge. He, the
Leader of the world, appears to reveal it, so that all at
last shall be saved.[4] 'The triple world is My Domain, and

---

[1] *Udana*, p. 68, Rhys Davids, *Dialogues*, p. 187.   [2] *Majjhima Nikaya*.
[3] *Sad-dharma Pundarika*, Sacred Books of the East, xxi, translated by
H. Kern.   [4] Ibid. ii. 54 (p. 46).

all in it are My sons; they are in a house on fire, and I, set upon saving them, warn them of its evils. But they will not listen, because all of them are ignorant, and their hearts are attached to the pleasures of sense.'[1] But he does not treat all alike: with skilful Tact (*Upaya*)[2] His Infinite Compassion tempers His Teaching to the capacities of each. The simplest things are counted for righteousness; they are the beginning of the Way. 'If men build shrines in brick or clay—even if they pile up little heaps of dust in mountain or forest with devotion; if little children, as they play, make mounds of sand in honour of the Buddha—all these enter into enlightenment.'[3] Though the Way is always one and the same, there are three gates or stages of it—seeking for the goal, solitary meditation, and the full Buddhahood of those that, themselves enlightened, teach others and so become their saviours. 'Into this darkling world appears the Most Wise, the great Compassionate Physician, and like a skilled teacher shows forth the Wonderful Law by stages, revealing to the most advanced supreme Buddha-Enlightenment, to those of moderate attainments the middling enlightenment of the solitary Buddha, and to the disciple who is afraid of the mundane whirl a still lower enlightenment.'[4]

The Bodhisat who would set forth the teachings must first put on the Blessed One—as Paul urges the Christians of Rome to 'put on the Lord Jesus Christ'.[5] Any Bodhisat who in the last times shall set forth the Law shall do so 'after having entered the abode of the Tathagata, after having put on his robe and sat in his seat. What is the abode of the Tathagata? It is the abiding in love to all beings. What is the robe of the Tathagata? It is the delighting in sublime forbearance. What is the seat of the Tathagata? It is the grasping of the doctrine of the *sunya*'[6]—that is, the unreality of the world of sense, and the Mystery of the Ultimate Reality. Just as Krishna says 'Bring Me thy failures',[7] so

---

[1] *Sad-dharma Pundarika*, Sacred Books of the East, iii. 87–8 (p. 88). Kenneth Saunders, *Lotuses of the Mahayana*, pp. 27–8.   [2] Ibid., ii.

[3] Ibid. ii. 80–1; Kern, p. 50; *Lotuses*, p. 29.

[4] Ibid. v. 60–2; Kern, p. 138; *Lotuses*, p. 27.   [5] Romans xiii. 14.

[6] *Sad-dharma Pundarika*, x. 15; Kern, p. 222; *Lotuses*, p. 26.

[7] *Bhagavad-gita*, xii. 11 (Arnold, p. 78).

even the most insignificant, even the worst of living creatures
shall be saved. 'Buddhas ye shall all become. Rejoice and
be no longer doubting or uncertain.'[1] Here, as in the *Gita*,
is the doctrine of universal salvation.

Then comes the revelation of Gotama as the incarnation
of the Eternal. After a pause of many millions of years
Bodhisats issue in hosts from the earth, and innumerable
saints from many worlds—great multitudes whom no man
can number—disciples whom the Buddha has aroused to
perfect enlightenment, His spiritual sons. He is the Eternal
Lord and Father, the Supreme Spirit, like the Trimurti—
Creator, Ruler, and Destroyer of the Universe, Self-Existent
from all Eternity, the Judge at the last Judgment; yet He
has taken human form that He may work the salvation of
the world. 'From time beyond reckoning I have reached
enlightenment, and never ceased to teach the Law. I have
roused many Bodhisats and established them in Buddha-
knowledge. I have brought myriads to full ripeness. I have
shown the place where suffering is extinguished. I have
revealed to all my skill in educating.'[2]

In all our suffering, Heaven is around us; those whose
eyes are open see the Universe as Paradise, though souls in
sin imagine that it is burning.

'When creatures behold this world and imagine that it is burning,
even then My Buddha-field is teeming with gods and men. Manifold
are the pleasures that these enjoy—pleasure gardens and chariots in
the air; this field is embellished by hills of gems and by trees abounding
with blossoms and fruits. So is my field here, everlastingly. But others
fancy that it is burning; in their view this world is most terrific,
wretched, full of every woe. Yea, many millions of years they may
pass without mention of My Name, My Law or My Order (the Three
Refuges). That is the fruit of sinful deeds. But when mild and gentle
beings are born in this world of men, they immediately see Me revealing the Law, owing to their good works.'[3]

The last part of the *Lotus* indicates the consummation
and perpetuation of this revelation, and consists mainly of
accounts of the great Bodhisats. There stand men's helpers

---

[1] *Sad-dharma Pundarika*, ii. 99, 144; Kern, pp. 53, 59; Saunders, *Epochs*,
p. 64.   [2] Ibid. xv. 1–3; Kern, p. 307.
[3] Ibid. xv. 11–12, 14–16; Kern, pp. 308–9.

and saviours, foremost among them the two who usually accompany Sakyamuni, forming a Trinity: Manju-sri or Wisdom, 'the Prince Royal', and Avalokitesvara, Compassionate Love. This Bodhisat is 'the All-Sided One' who can appear either as the Lord of Mercy, condescending, like another Krishna, to men's trusting love; or as the Lady of Pity, to whom the sad heart of the East turns for consolation as the sad heart of the West turns to that other Lady of Sorrows, who likewise bears a child in her arms.

> O thou whose eyes are clear and kind,
> Whose loving eyes reveal love's mind,
> Lord of the lovely face and eyes,
> Like to the sun dost thou arise,
> Whose knowledge ever burneth bright,
> Who spreadest lustre in thy flight.
> Like rain divine that quenches fire
> Thy Law puts out our false desire,
> Rejoicing in compassion, lo!
> Our refuge, thou, from every foe.[1]

Then there was the Bodhisat that is to come, Maitreya or Maitri, whose name means Friend. Into this sorrowful world he, like another Messiah, was to bring a new era of enthusiasm. There, too, were Bhaisajyaraja, the Healing King, and many more. In the Greater Buddhism men saw above the sufferings of earth a host of mighty and merciful Beings through whose grace, accepted in love and faith, they might find escape from evil in this world and in a future Paradise of bliss.

But amid the increasing numbers of Buddhas and Bodhisats the need of the mind for Unity presently reasserted itself; and Buddhism sought for human perfection in *prajna* or intuitive wisdom—that immediate experience of the innermost self that Hinduism had found to be superior both to the perception of the senses and to the reasoning of the mind. On its philosophical side this 'perfection through intuitive wisdom' grappled again with the original Indian problem of the One Reality, now called Citta or Mind, underlying the half-real or wholly illusory appearances of the changing things of sense; and on its religious side sought

---

[1] *Sad-dharma Pundarika*, xxiv. 20–3; Kern, pp. 415–16; *Lotuses*, pp. 28–9.

for an explanation of the manifold Buddhas and Bodhisats
in the One Original Buddha (Adi-Buddha) Whence all the
rest proceed. The needs of reason had brought Buddhism
back to the Vedanta.

Thus the course of Indian thought had run full cycle.
Beginning with the supreme intuition 'That art thou' which
merged subject and Object, it had shown This Spirit manifested as a Personal God Whom men could love and trust,
or serve in daily duty. Meanwhile, starting afresh with the
ideal of progress to its goal, it had risen once more to the
idea of loving trust in a Divine Person, and finally returned
to intuitive knowledge of the Mind of the World.

II. 4

These developments of Buddhism have enabled it to conquer half Asia. If in the land of its birth its philosophy and
theology led it back to its parent Hinduism, it left behind
a gentleness towards man and beast that India has never
lost, and a criticism of caste that still bears life-giving fruit.
Ceylon, Burma, and Siam are still the home of the Lesser
Buddhism, where some men at least seek a dying out of their
desire for the things of this world that shall lead to a dying-
out of death or even of existence altogether. In the poverty
and disasters of China, and amid the miseries of Japanese
anarchy, Amitabha or 'Amida', with His saving Grace, was
destined to become the equal of Sakyamuni, the historic
Buddha himself; it was principally or wholly through loving
faith in Him, not through merit, that the members of the
Jodo or Pure Land Schools were enabled after death to reach
the Paradise of Bliss. The *Lotus* became the foundation book
of the more comprehensive systems of Buddhism, afterwards
developed in China in the monasteries of the Tien-Tai
Mountains, and in Japan in the Tendai School named after
them, as well as of that founded by Nichiren. The theologians of Nepal and Tibet developed the notion of the Original Buddha. In China and Japan Contemplative Buddhism
(Jnana or Dhyana becomes Chan or Zen) took firm root.
The Buddha was in the mind, transfiguring the world; and
he who could realize this knew eternal peace, no matter
what happened to the body. To-day in many lands millions

pray the prayer that looks forward to the Buddha That is to
come. 'May I meet Metteyya when he comes to lead multitudes to the haven of salvation. May I see the Lord of
Mercy and be wise in the Three Scriptures.'[1]

This teaching led to the education of the peoples of south-
eastern, eastern, and central Asia in the ideals of spiritual
progress, loving trust in the Divine Pity, consciousness of
the unity of all things in God. The Buddha has indeed
shown the skilfulness of the true Teacher—in the Buddha-
fields God fulfils Himself in many ways.

The ideal figures of Buddhism are the *arahat* who is
'worthy' and the *bodhisat* whose salvation involves the salvation of others. Buddhism began as a reform of Hinduism,
and Buddhist education does not differ fundamentally from
that of the parent religion. Here again is a splendid worship;
here again are pious pilgrimages. But whereas Hinduism
lays special stress on the learning of the *chela* from the *guru*
and on a life of solitary contemplation in the forest, the stress
of Buddhism has always been upon the monastic life and its
studies. From the first, Buddhists tended to be monks; and
at all times and places they have loved to build their monasteries upon the mountains. One of the greatest glories of
Buddhism, as of Islam and of Catholicism, has been its
monastery-Universities. Not Samarcand or Cordova, with
their mathematics, science, and philosophy, not Paris or
Oxford, with their medicine, law, and theology, have done
more for their own civilization or for mankind. At Taxila,
in the land where Kanishka summoned the first Council of
the Larger Buddhism, were developed the great ideals of the
Paradise Books and the *Lotus*. At Nalanda, near the Bamboo
Garden where the Buddha taught in the rains, a line of nine
Colleges facing pools of blue lotus and deep red kie-ni-
flowers housed the ten thousand monks whose reflections
begat the vast metaphysical treatises of Intuitive Wisdom.
From remote China, across demon-haunted Gobi and furious
Himalaya came the Wandering Scholar to drink of the
fountain of Truth and return with many a cupful. The
mountain-monasteries of the Tien-tai nursed a catholic
study, at once devotional and philosophic, of the Lotus and

[1] Attributed to Buddhaghosa.

the Intuitive Wisdom; those of Korea and Tibet contain
vast libraries that store the riches of long study and meditation. In Japan Buddhism has from the first civilized and
enlightened. It made Nara and Kioto the centre of a culture
whose loveliness has endured till to-day. In 1270 its monks
organized in a temple the first public library, containing all
the Chinese and Japanese books then in existence; and
temple schools have provided ethical and other education
for the sons not only of *samurai* but of merchants and craftsmen. Monks in their millions have studied the historical
Buddha, the Eternal Buddha, the Eternal Reality.

To this day the Buddhist monastery is the school of
south-east Asia where the need of merit and enlightenment
is impressed on the young heart. A new Buddhist movement, headed by Tai-hsu, adapts the Mahayana to the needs
of the new China, sending out bands of eager young gradu-
ates to preach 'the salvation of all living things'. Japan can
boast her great Buddhist scholars—Suzuki, Anesaki; the
Sanskrit texts are critically studied in her Universities. In
both civilizations the Pure Land School still glows with
eager faith in the Divine Love, the Meditation School calls
forth the living energy of the human mind.

In a society so minded reliance has been placed rather on
virtue than on organization—on the Law rather than on laws.
From Asoka onward kings have been devout supporters of
the Buddha. Kanishka summoned to the Punjab the Council
that sponsored the early Mahayana. Not a few Chinese
Emperors have been ardent Buddhists. Prince Shotuku, the
Asoka of Japan, introduced Buddhism to his country and so
gave it the faith to endure and the gentleness to assuage the
future ferocity of her fighting men. 'Without Buddhism
(he said in the new constitution he based upon it) there is
no way to turn men from wrong to right.' The Kings
of Burma and of Siam have been steadfast upholders of
Dharma.

The peoples have followed the kings. As elsewhere, there
has been among the masses a dilution of the ideals of the
leaders. The primitive animism of Burma has inserted its
tree and water spirits, the Bon animism of Tibet its devils
and tantric magic. The fierce ambitions of Japan have

turned its monks into soldiers, the laziness of human nature degraded its mendicants into parasites. Nevertheless, just because it brought the great goal of Hinduism within measurable reach of the multitude, as Gotama intended that it should, Buddhism has achieved a unique success. The Sangha and the monastery have been important instruments of rule, especially in Tibet; but, to a greater extent than the respect of the Nordics for their neighbours, and even than the family virtues of China, the 'merit' that Buddhism inculcates—self-discipline, loving gentleness, steady seeking after enlightenment—has dispensed with the need for laws and organization, and itself served as the foundation of society.

Hence the meek have inherited the earth: Buddhism extends from Ceylon to Japan, from Cambodia to the Volga. Like a great tree it has put forth many branches, to serve the needs of many peoples and many minds; and beneath their shelter live multitudes of men and women, singularly care-free and happy, for they follow the Law that leads to the Light.

III

Since the fall of Constantinople[1] the principal home of Orthodoxy on earth has been Holy Russia; and the land of Russia has had a great effect upon the Orthodox spirit. It is a land of sadness and of laughter; of icy winter, and of sudden spring; of forest and wolf, of lilac and nightingale. Just as the tropic heat, and especially the rainy season, of India have been favourable to contemplation, so the long dark cold of the northern winter, binding the earth with snow and frost that often make work impossible, has given the Russians leisure to contemplate; while spring and summer, covering the land with an enchanting loveliness, have wakened in them a wonderful love for the beauty of the world about them. Embracing all is vastness, mystery. As the highlander is moved by the sublimity of his mountains, but finds no beauty in the flats, so the Russian, cabined and confined among mountains, is moved by the sublimity of his plains. His sky-domed steppes reach to a horizon he can never find, his mysterious forests stretch impenetrably

[1] A.D. 1453.

to the unseen, the sands of his deserts know no bounds. The long darkness of the winter nights, the long sunlight of the summer days, impress on him the immensity of time. Infinity and eternity encompass him. 'In many ways (says Count Keyserling) the Russian soul is in tune with that of the old Indian; the fundamental relation to God and to Nature of both peoples is the same. The background of all Asiatics is that of concrete infinity, the infinity of space and time.'[1]

This vast world is a world of resurrection. The long darkness and cold of winter give place to a sudden Easter-burst of spring—the resurrection of all living things to a new life and light and love and rejoicing.[2] The peasant—for Russia, like India, is a land of peasants—goes forth to sow his seed in the furrow, looking for its resurrection in the harvest; he sows his body in 'that deeper furrow the grave', looking for a resurrection to Eternal Life.[3] The shining sky above him is the symbol of Heaven—in his early Epic Songs he speaks of 'the golden-domed tower where all is heavenly with sun and moon, stars innumerable and white dawns'.[4]

These first Epic Songs—composed by the people in the days of paganism and of St. Vladimir[5] and repeated and renewed on their lips for a thousand years—strike the two great notes of the Slav temperament: the sanity and the mysticism of the workers and dreamers of the fields. Already the three chief classes of historic Russia are portrayed: the knight, Dobrynya the dragon-slayer; the priest's son, the cunning Alyosha; and—greater than either—the simple peasant, represented by Mikula the Villager's Son, who afterwards became St. Nicholas, patron of agriculture, and by Ilya of Murom, the chief hero of the songs. The tales are full of sanity and strength. Often they end on a quiet note of peace. 'None of these forty heroes and one ever again roamed the open plain seeking adventures, or stained their white hands with blood. When young Kasyan Mikailovitch

---

[1] *The Travel-Diary of a Philosopher.*
[2] Cf. S. Aksakov, *Years of Childhood* (J. D. Duff), xvii.
[3] J. Dover Wilson in *War and Democracy*, v, p. 186.
[4] Isabel Florence Hapgood, *The Epic Songs of Russia*, p. 102.
[5] *c.* A.D. 956–1015.

came to his own land, he raised a Church to Mikola of Mozhaisk, and began to pray constantly to God, and to repent of his sins.'[1] There is a rough humour, breaking out in pithy proverbs like the favourite: 'Long is a woman's hair, but short her wit.' There is a great love of things—their richness, their brightness, their beauty, their romance—silk of Samarcand, scarlet ships, Saracen chain-armour, fine Arabian bronze 'more precious than gold'.[2]

At the same time the Slavs, like the forest sages and like Gotama, were aware of the transience of human life and of the things of this world: 'O age, old age, like a raven thou hast alighted on my turbulent head, and youth, thou youth, my lovely youth, thou hast flown away like a falcon over the open plain.'[3] This sense of the transience of the material seems to be at the bottom of their mysticism: not only does one thing symbolize another through some quality that is felt to be common to them both, but the visible world is significant of something more important and more real. When the Hero Svyatogor cannot lift the wallet of the Villager's Son, though he strains at it till the blood streams down his face, he is told the reason. 'The whole weight of the world lieth therein.'[4] No wonder that when Russia became Christian the Villager's Son was identified with Christ the Saviour of the World! While the Nordics saw the things of this world and little beyond, the spiritual eye of the Slavs saw the Unseen beneath the seen. Hence a mystical religion came easily to them. Unlike the Nordics, the Slavs are a naturally religious people.

These early Russians worshipped Nature gods—notably Perun the Thunderer—gods represented by wooden idols, though there were neither temples nor priests. A faith so primitive could not survive contact with the higher religions surrounding it—Judaism, Islam, Catholicism, Orthodoxy—any more than the primitive beliefs of the Arabs could survive contact with Zarathustrianism, Judaism, and Christianity. Vladimir 'the Fair Sun', Grand Duke of Kiev, determined to adopt a higher worship. He rejected Judaism on the ground that the Anger of God had scattered the Jews

---

[1] Hapgood, op. cit., p. 75. [2] Ibid., pp. ix–x.
[3] Ibid., p. xi. [4] Ibid., p. 12.

from their country; Islam because it forbade the drinking of
wine, 'the joy of the Russians'—among the Bulgarian Muslims on the Volga 'there is no gladness, only sorrow and a
great stench; their religion is not a good one'; Catholicism
because in Germany it enjoined fasting, and in Rome his
envoys saw 'no beauty' in the temples. But in Constantinople—Tsargrad, the 'city of Caesar'—they were present at
a service in St. Sophia—probably the Litany of St. John
Chrysostom—and reported: 'We no longer knew whether
we were on earth or in Heaven; we saw such beauty and
magnificence that we know not how to tell of it.' Then they
spoke of Christ the Incarnate Word, and of His Passion and
Death. Vladimir listened in awe and was baptized into the
Orthodox faith; his people, dragging Perun into the Dnieper, followed his example.[1] Their motives were characteristic of the Russians: they rejected what would discipline
their passions, and accepted what was lovely and mysterious.

III. 1

'Christ the Incarnate Word': that is the message of the
Fourth Gospel and of the open letter which forms its epi-
logue. As the Hindu prays daily:

> From the unreal lead me to the Real,
> From darkness lead me to Light,
> From death lead me to the Immortal,[2]

as the Buddhist turns to Amitabha, the Buddha of Endless
Life and Light, as Plato and Plotinus disclose the Reality
That gives Light like the Sun, so also the Fourth Gospel
reveals the Spirit of Truth or Reality Whose Life, Light,
Love, and Joy form the Divine Reason That irradiates the
world.

God, like Brahma, is at once Truth or Reality—'He is
the Real God'[3]—and Soul or Spirit, Who must be 'worshipped in spirit and in reality';[4] in a word, He is 'the Spirit
of Truth', Who shall 'lead men into all Truth'.[5] Further,

---

[1] *Chronicle of Nestor* (*c.* 1056–1114).

[2] *Brihad-aranyaka Upanishad*, i. 3. 28.

[3] Gospel 17. 3, Letter 5. 20 (Moffat's translation is largely used in what
follows).   [4] Gospel, 4. 24.   [5] Gospel, 16. 13.

'God is Love'.[1] The Orthodox sees, as the Hindu sees, that
such a Being can be known, not as He is in Himself, but
only under the form of a Person. The Hindu says '*Neti,
neti*', the writer of the Fourth Gospel: 'No man has ever seen
God, but God has been unfolded by the Divine One.'[2]

This Divine One is Jesus, the Logos or Reason Who is
the Origin of all things, as in the *Gita* Krishna, and in the
Lotus the Buddha, is the Divine One, the Origin of all
things. The writer affirms this in the Prologue of his Gospel.

> Reason existed in the very beginning,
> Reason was with God,
> Reason was Divine.
> Through Him all existence came into being.[3]

Life and Light came to lighten men's darkness and death:

> In Him Life lay,
> and this Life was the Light for men,
> but the darkness did not master It.[4]

'Reason became flesh and tarried among us; we have seen
His Glory, seen It to be full of Grace and Reality. Grace
and Reality are ours through Jesus Christ.'[5] The Source of
Life feeds man's spiritual hunger: is the 'bread of life',[6] Giver
of 'living water, welling up to eternal life'.[7] He brings the
paralytic back to health, raises the widow's son, and Lazarus
from the grave itself. 'I am the resurrection and the life.'[8] He
is the Light, enlightening those born blind. 'I have come
into this world to make the sightless see and to make the
seeing blind.'[9] Life and Light are the same. This is Eternal
Life, that they may know Thee, the only Real God, and
Him Whom thou hast sent, even Jesus Christ.'[10]

The Divine Reason is not only Life and Light, but also
Love and Joy; these too It brings to man. 'I will declare
Thy Name to them, that the love with which Thou hast loved
me may be in them and I in them.'[11] Knowledge and love
are concomitant. 'Every one who loves is born of God and
knows God; he who does not love does not know God, for

---

[1] Letter 4. 8.   [2] Gospel 1. 18.   [3] Ibid. 1. 1, 3.
[4] Ibid. 1. 4.   [5] Ibid. 1. 14, 17.   [6] Ibid. 6. 35.
[7] Ibid. 4. 11, 14. [8] Ibid. 11. 25.   [9] Ibid. 9. 39.
[10] Ibid. 17. 3.   [11] Ibid. 17. 26.

God is Love.'[1] 'He who says he is "in the light" and hates his brother is in darkness still. He who loves his brother remains in the light.'[2] And knowledge and love are joy. 'As the Father has loved Me, so I have loved you. As I have loved you, you are to love one another. I have told you this that My joy may be within you and your joy complete.'[3]

Thus like the *Vedanta* and Platonism, the Fourth Gospel shows a Universe in which Reality diminishes as it recedes from the Centre: from the Father, the Spirit of Truth, springs the Son, the Divine Reason, Who was with Him from the beginning, but is less than He. 'The Father is greater than I'.[4] Then come those who participate in the Life and Light, Love and Joy of the Divine Reason, the 'children of God'; and finally 'the world', 'the darkness', the 'children of the Devil',[5] who have as yet no share in It. Unlike the *Vedanta*, however, the Gospel does not think of men and things as illusory appearances whose Reality is God. It is not Pantheist; God, the Logos, God's children, the world are real beings. Yet through the first three the same Divine Life pulses. 'I and My Father are One',[6] says Jesus; 'I am the vine, you are the branches. He who remains in Me, as I in him, bears rich fruits.'[7] And He prays: 'As Thou, Father, art in me and I in Thee, so may they be in Us. I have given them the glory Thou gavest Me, that they may be one as We are One—I in them and Thou in Me—that they may be made perfectly one.'[8] There is no higher expression of the mystic unity.

God the Father communicating His Truth through the Divine Reason to men forms the very heart of the Orthodox idea of the Universe. The Light and Love and Joy that come from the Divine Life unite all living beings in the Church; they raise the individual spirit to living union with God. This view has been formulated by Khomiakov in his almost canonical essay 'The Church is One'.[9] His friend and follower, George Samarin, summarizes it in the words: 'The Church is a living organism of Truth and Love; or

---

[1] Letter 4. 7, 8 and note 18.   [2] Ibid. 2. 9. 10.
[3] Gospel 15. 9, 12, 11.   [4] Ibid. 14. 28.   [5] Letter 3. 10, Gospel 1. 5.
[6] Gospel 10. 30.   [7] Ibid. 15. 5.   [8] Ibid. 17. 21–3.
[9] *c.* 1850. W. J. Birkbeck, *English Church*, vol. 1, pp. 192–222.

rather, she is Truth and Love, as an organism.'[1] This organism is united (says Khomiakov) by two bonds, an outer, the sacraments, and an inner, faith, hope, and love—the gifts of the Holy Spirit. The outer is by far the less important. 'Many have been saved without having been made partakers of so much as one of the Sacraments of the Church (not even of Baptism), but no one is saved without partaking in the inward holiness of the Church, of her faith, hope and love.' As in the *Gita*, 'every good work which is done in faith and love and hope is suggested to man by the Spirit of God, and invokes the Unseen Grace of God'. This inner bond, then, is the essential; and the greatest of the three, here on earth, is love. For though faith and hope are also the gifts of the Spirit, both are incomplete; when made perfect in the life to come, faith 'will have become full inward knowledge and sight' (the intuitive knowledge of the innermost self is indicated) 'and hope will have become joy—for even on earth we know that the stronger it is, the more joyful it is. Love alone will preserve its name.'[2] Thus if reason be defined as knowledge, love, and joy, then faith, hope, and love are its embryo, the anticipation here on earth of the reason that will be made perfect hereafter. Reason, incomplete or complete, is the essential bond of society.

This conception of a Church whose unity springs from the faith, hope, and love that are the working of the Spirit of God within it involves three consequences, which the Russians sum up under the name of *sobornost*. *Sobor* means a Council; and *sobornost*, like bodhisatship, indicates that the way of salvation is collective, not individual only. The word has no exact English equivalent. It comprises the notions of catholicity—the inclusion of the whole; symphony—the harmonious union of diverse parts; universality—a turning of all towards the One: comprehensiveness, equality, unity.

First, the Church is as wide as the Universe.

'Those who are alive on earth, those who have finished their earthly course, the future generations who have not yet begun it, those who,

---

[1] Birkbeck, op. cit., p. xxx.
[2] Khomiakov, ibid., sec. 10, p. 222.

like the angels, were not created for a life on earth, are all united together in one Church, in One and the Same Grace of God. The rest of mankind, whether alien from the Church, or united to her by ties which God has not willed to reveal to her, she leaves to the judgment of the Great Day. Upon those who do not hear her appeal she pronounces no sentence.'[1]

Next, God's Truth is not declared by Pope or Patriarch or priest to the laity, but directly perceived by the soul of man and woman. The Church (says Khomiakov) does not 'require an external phantom of Christ (the Pope) such as the Romans believe in. The invisible Head of the Church had no need to bequeath to her an image of Himself in order to pronounce oracles, but has inspired the whole of her with His Love in order that she may have the Unchangeable Truth within herself.'[2] The historic reason for the difference no doubt is that, whereas the Nordics who came under the sway of Rome were by nature a this-worldly, not a religious, people, and so were disciplined by the Roman priesthood as unruly schoolboys are disciplined by their masters, the Slavs were naturally a religious people, and therefore the gulf separating the Roman clergy and laity never opened in the Orthodox Church. 'In the Eastern Church (wrote the Eastern Patriarchs to Pope Pius the Ninth) neither the Patriarchs nor the Councils have ever been able to introduce anything new, as the depository of the faith is with us the body of the whole Church, that is to say, the people itself.'[3] It is the Church as a whole, not the clergy or an assemblage of bishops, who can recognize a Council as Oecumenical. Hence, in the measure in which men receive the Truth they are equal: lay or clerical, simple or learned, humble or highly placed, white or coloured. One of the great glories of the Orthodox Church is the eminence of the laity in Theology and in Council. The ideal of the Orthodox Church, like that of the Hindu and the Buddhist, is mystical, intuitive: the soul must know God for itself, or it cannot know Him at all. Even the dogmas of the Nicene Creed—'the

---

[1] Ibid. sec. 1, p. 193 (slightly altered); sec. 2, p. 194.

[2] *L'Eglise Latine et le Protestantisme*, quoted Birkbeck, p. li.

[3] Declaration of the Eastern Patriarchs in reply to the Encyclical of Pius the Ninth to Christians of the East, 1848, Birkbeck, p. l.

Symbol', as the Russians significantly call their one Creed—must be rightly understood by each individual, or they are valueless.

Last, notwithstanding what seems to living men her division, the Church is One. Her unity follows of necessity from the Unity of God: for the Church is not a multitude of separate individuals, but the Grace of God living in rational creatures who willingly submit themselves to it. Herein lies the distinction between Orthodoxy and Protestantism; for in Protestantism it is the individual soul rather than the community of souls that seeks God. Rather Orthodoxy resembles bodhisatship: if Grace is for all, those who have found it cannot be content till all have found it. As Khomiakov puts it: 'No one is saved alone. He who is saved is saved in the Church, as a member of her, and in unity with all her other members. If any one believes, he is in the communion of faith; if he loves, he is in the communion of love; if he prays, he is in the communion of prayer. Wherefore no one can rest his hope on his own prayers.'[1] As the Abbot Dorotheos writes, in the little book which used to be placed in the hands of novices in Russian monasteries: 'If we imagine a circle of which the Centre is God and the radii are the souls of men, it will be evident that the approach towards the Centre will mean an ever increasing proximity between the radii.'[2] One cannot draw nearer to God without drawing nearer to man.

Thus it is in the Church—not as an earthly institution, but as a Cosmic community—that the soul finds its end—union with the Truth of God through light and love. Plato, the great forerunner of the thoughts of the Fourth Gospel and of the Eastern Church, spoke long ago of the end of man as 'likeness to God'. Carrying on his thought into Christian times, Athanasius said: 'God has become man that we might be made Divine'; and Gregory of Nyssa, one of the Four Fathers of the Eastern Church: 'God united Himself with our nature in order that our nature might be made Divine through union with God.'[3] The pseudo-Dionysius united both expressions: 'To be made Divine is to be made

---

[1] Birkbeck, sec. 9, p. 216.   [2] *Love of God and Man.*
[3] *Oratio Catechetica Magna,* c. 25.

like God, as far as may be, and to be made one with Him.'
Jesus himself did the same when he said to the sons of God:
'Be ye therefore perfect, even as your Father in Heaven is
perfect.' This union with the Divine, this participation in
the Divine Life, Orthodoxy calls Theosis.

To participate through knowledge and love in the Living
Truth of God is thus the ideal of Orthodoxy, as it is of the
Book which principally inspires it. The *Vedanta* (though it
allows no independent reality to Nature or man) has a similar
ideal. Like the *Vedanta*, too, the Orthodox conceives of this
life as a descent from and return to the Divine. If the
Brahmins speak of the Way of Pursuit and the Way of
Return, Origen, like his fellow-pupil Plotinus, sees salvation
as the retracing by the soul of the steps by which it has
descended from the Supreme Good to mix itself with matter.
All men (Origen held) have a pre-existence in God; there is
a premundane fall of each individual soul; the world of
matter is created and the fallen souls are clothed in flesh;
sin, evils, and demons dominate the earth. Then the Divine
Reason is incarnate, the Spirit is imparted. Ultimately the
soul of man will be liberated from its unnatural union with
the sensual (the liberation that the Hindus call *moksha*), and
all things will be restored to God.

Like the *Gita*, the Paradise Books, the *Lotus*, and Paul,
Origen thus holds the doctrine of universal salvation. Ortho-
doxy follows him, though with somewhat halting steps.
Man shall rise from the dead, Nature shall be transfigured.
This, to the Orthodox, is the meaning of the Eucharist:

'It is not only for the individual that the Lord's Supper has a central,
living, mystic meaning, but for the whole community, the whole
Church, yes, for all mankind. For here the Divine mingles with
the human, the terrestrial; here in the Eucharist praise and sacrifice are offered to the Lord for the whole world and by the whole
world ("Offering Thine to Thee from Thine, for all men and all
things"), and the whole Cosmos is hereby potentially ennobled and
sanctified in that the earthly elements of bread and wine become
the Glorified Body and Blood of the Son of God. That is why the
idea of all creation assembled in spirit round the Eucharistic altar so
constantly recurs in the old liturgies of the East. For through Him,
through His death and through the glorification of His Risen Body,

here mystically represented, creation partakes of the glory of the redemption.'[1]

Only to the spiritual has this sacrament meaning: 'The Holy to the holy ones!'[2]

III. 2

Such are the sublimities at the heart of Holy Russia. How far have her people been able to live up to them?

The ideal character is the holy man or woman, the saint; whether layman or monk, uncanonized or canonized, matters little. He or she may be the man or woman in the village recognized by the neighbours as living the life of Christ. He may be the monk in the monastery, the hermit in the forest or the mountain, the Teaching Elder who has communed in solitude with God and returned to communicate his knowledge to men. What makes the holy man is the knowledge of God's Truth. In *The Brothers Karamazov* Father Zossima tells his monks that they 'keep the image of Christ fair and undefiled in the purity of God's Truth';[3] that where two have been united in 'living love', in those two 'God's Truth has been fulfilled';[4] that 'in the worldly and all those who set themselves up above the people of God, God's image and His Truth has been distorted'.[5] Truth (*Pravda*) is the foundation-stone of the Russian's mind and heart; from it he builds the rest of his world. When he does wrong he will say: 'That is not in accordance with Truth'; when he feels great happiness, he knows that the Truth is shining upon him. And the Truth is to him first and foremost the Truth of God, and in particular of God made man in Jesus Christ, Whom he often calls the Sun of Truth.

This Truth of God the Orthodox Russian knows within himself: It is 'the Voice of the heart', in obedience to Which lies his peace and his joy. The medieval epics of Russia are full of passages showing the *kenosis* or humanity of Christ— His humility, His poverty, His obedience to this inner

---

[1] N. Arseniev, *Mysticism and the Eastern Church*, p. 58.
[2] Quoted ibid., p. 56.
[3] Dostoievsky, *The Brothers Karamazov*, p. 332.
[4] Ibid. p. 342.   [5] Ibid. p. 333.

Voice. Thus Orthodoxy, like Hinduism and Buddhism, knows that the Supreme Reality is directly revealed to the innermost self, to *prajna*—intuitive wisdom; the philosophy of the discursive intellect is only a preparation leading up to this, and one to which Russian minds have attended less than Indian.

With such an ideal the education of the Russian was inevitably directed to a knowledge, not of this world, but of the other. He could not as a rule read or write; but he knew more important things, the things of the spirit. As in India, great tales, great art, great music were his masters; his schools were worship, pilgrimage, contemplation.

But where India heard the Epics, Russia heard the Gospels—the Holy Four accompanied the Orthodox from the cradle to the grave. They told of the incarnation, life, teaching, passion, and resurrection of One greater than Krishna or Rama, Divine incarnations though they were. In place of the philosophies of India the Russians—young guardsmen, court ladies, girls, peasants—read the writings, largely mystical, of the Greek Fathers and of the Fathers of the Desert—in a collection called the Philokalia. The heroes of Indian Epic may be compared with the national heroes of Russia, saints one and all, whether Princes, soldiers, statesmen, monks, Teaching Elders: Vladimir, Alexander of the Neva, Peter of Moscow, Sergei, Seraphim. Apart from them Russia, like India, was little interested in history; it was not for the record of events she cared, but for their interpretation. Have the Bolsheviks desecrated St. Sergei's Monastery[1] and scattered his relics? His bones (say the peasants) have gone down deep into the earth, and will not again return to light till Russia is freed from atheism. Untrue to physical fact, but true to spiritual!

Art, too, taught the Russian as it taught the Indian. The very shape of the churches, round or equilateral with rounded domes, suggests to his mind the infinity of the world unseen. The chief symbol of the Orthodox Church is not, as in Catholicism, the Crucifix, but the holy picture, the ikon; and just as Indian sculpture shows gods that are not men but gods, so the ikon shows the forms, not of earth,

---

[1] The Troitsa (Trinity), about forty miles north of Moscow.

but of Heaven, visible, not to the earthly, but to the spiritual
eye. Russia was as full of singing as of nightingales, and the
music of the Church lifted her soul to Heaven.

In Divine worship the Orthodox enters into another and
a truer world. 'In God's Church', wrote St. Cyril of the
White Lake in the fifteenth century, 'stand in awe as if you
were standing in Heaven. Church is the earthly heaven,
when Christ's sacraments are celebrated.' The three great
Liturgies or Communion Services make it clear that before
the holy gifts of Christ's Body and Blood the Church on
earth mingles with the Church in Heaven, the seen world
with the unseen; but the Eastern Church does not attempt
a dogmatic interpretation of this mystery. She regards it as
a symbol of the final transfiguration of the whole world—
of all Nature and of all spirits—to the likeness of God.
Crowning the yearly services is Easter, the 'feast of feasts';
for Easter signifies that man, having suffered and died with
Christ, may rise again with Him to Life Eternal in God.
As one of the songs of the Eastern Church puts it:

'Let the Heavens rejoice in seemly way, and let the earth be glad;
let the whole world give praise, both the visible and the invisible:
Christ is risen, joy eternal! Now is all filled with light, the Heaven,
the earth and the underworld; let therefore all creation praise Christ's
resurrection which is its firm foundation! We give praise for the
slaying of death, the destruction of Hell, and the dawn of a new Life,
Life Eternal.'[1]

'The joy of the resurrection', says a lay theologian, 'is
the keynote of the Eastern Church's whole outlook upon
the world; joy in the risen living Lord, joy in His Life and
Glory, for His Life is also our life transfigured, eternal.'[2]

The Nordic is inclined to regard the Orthodox as super-
stitious. He sees him washing in a sacred spring to cleanse
himself from sin; kissing the relics of saints or holy ikons
to gain virtue; believing that miracles happen. Yet in all
these cases there is as a rule first and foremost a genuine
worship of God: the physical act or natural object is a
symbol that stimulates and aids worship, in the manner of a
sacrament. Nature is only an outward and visible sign,

[1] Quoted by Nicholas Arseniev, *Mysticism and the Eastern Church*, p. 17.
[2] Ibid., pp. 17, 42.

of which the inward and spiritual meaning is in the heart. No doubt there is an element of danger; as unless a clear distinction is drawn between the spiritual and the material, the mind may come to believe, first that virtue lies in the symbol instead of in the thing symbolized, and then that the thing symbolized has no reality. Thus, when the Bolsheviks desecrated the holy things and destroyed the Churches, the more ignorant Russians expected that God and His angels would descend and overwhelm the impious, and were disappointed when He failed to do so. Yet the belief was not wholly mistaken: God overcomes the impious, but in His Own Way, not in man's.

Pilgrimage played a great part in the education of the Russian people, as in that of Hindus and Buddhists. Almost every Russian went on pilgrimage, near or far, to church or monastery or other sacred place; some even so far as the Life-Giving Grave at Jerusalem, there to live with Christ, die with Christ, and rise with Christ during Holy Week and Easter. These pilgrims were among the great teachers of Russia. In the monastery refectory, the old peasant woman and the young guardsman would talk side by side in an equality of dignity. Wherever the poor man wandered he sought and received entertainment in the cottage of the peasant, returning his welcome by telling of his spiritual experiences and of the holy things he had seen. Some, like the *sannyasins* of India, were perpetual pilgrims, wanderers from monastery to monastery and from shrine to shrine— 'beggars in the name of Christ'.

But pilgrimage is of the soul as well as of the body—from the kingdom of this world to the Celestial City. As a Russian philosopher puts it:

'The Russian overcomes with great ease and lightness of spirit any kind of bourgeois ideas, abandons any regular way of life, any life conforming to rules and regulations. The type of the wanderer is so fine, so characteristic for Russia; the wanderer is the freest man upon earth. He walks upon earth, but his element is the air; he has not grown into the ground, he is not bound to it. The wanderer is free from "the world", and all the burden of the earth and of earthly life is limited for him by a wallet, carried on the back.'[1]

[1] N. Berdiaeff, *The Fate of Russia.*

This freedom of the spirit is akin to the poverty of Francis, the *moksha* of the Hindu.

'The greatness of the Russian people and its call to a higher life are centred in the type of the wanderer. The Russian type of the wanderer found its expression, not only in the life of the people, but also in the life of culture, in the life of the best part of its educated class. Here also we know wanderers with a free spirit, not tied to anything, eternal wanderers, seeking the Unknown City. The Russian soul is burning in a flaming quest for Truth, for Absolute, Divine Truth and for the salvation of the whole world and general resurrection to a new life. This soul is always grieving for the woe and sufferings of the people and of the whole world—and its pain knows no relief.'

But the greatest teacher of the Russian as of the Indian spirit was contemplation. Each village, more or less, would have its 'contemplative'—sometimes stock-still, like the yogi, for hours together. Men who were not monks—statesmen, soldiers, intellectuals—would for a time attach themselves to the monasteries, there to live the 'idiorrhythmic' life. Men in the heyday of youth often entered a monastery and gave themselves to a religious life: still more often, men who had passed the age for military service put away the cares of life that they might prepare themselves for death. This stress on contemplation prevented Orthodox monasteries from becoming, like those of Islam and Buddhism, monastic universities; it drove men to prayer more than to study, to mysticism rather than to philosophy. Those whose passion for God burnt brightest would become hermits in the forest or the mountain; and of these some, it might be after fifteen years of lonely prayer, would return as *startsi* or Teaching Elders to instruct the pilgrims who flocked to consult them, not only in the things of the other world, but of this world too. Nor was this life of contemplation a mere selfish escape from the world: men entered it 'to serve God and man', though the service was spiritual rather than utilitarian, the inspiring of sanctity rather than the social work of the slum. People felt that no one did so much for them as the hermit, for the holiness of his life of worship and prayer brought not only him but them nearer to God. St. Seraphim,[1] one of the greatest of hermits and Teaching Elders, used to say

[1] 1759–1833.

that if any one acquired 'peace of soul, thousands around
him would be saved'; and the same power to heal and bless
exists in saintly men and women to-day amid the horrors of
the Soviet concentration camps.

The perfect Russian life thus has in principle the same
four stages as that of the Brahmin and the Platonic philosopher. A man begins with learning from others in school
and university; he goes on to the active life of the householder, the citizen, and the conscript; then he passes to the
monastery or the wilderness, there, like the forest recluse, to
seek in contemplation a higher knowledge, not from book
or teacher, but from God in his own heart; and finally, like
the 'desireless' *parivrajaka* and the *bodhisat*, at one with
God's Truth and therefore with men, he returns as a Teaching Elder to the further service of mankind.

Thus the Russian people learned to look on this world as
the image of another and a truer; and this view was the
source at once of their weakness and of their strength. The
neglect of the things of this world led to a lack of discipline
that showed itself in many spheres: in violence, in ineffectiveness, in political ineptitude, in inexact thinking, in religious perversions; yet a constant realization of the other
world led to the consecration of the people and of their daily
life. Between the two extremes is to be found an agonized
repentance and a ready asceticism, but not the moral struggle
for daily self-discipline that is characteristic of Chinese and
Nordics.

Russians (it has been said) are 'volcanoes, extinct, quies-
cent or in eruption'.[1] The seventeenth-century Memoirs of
the Archpriest Avvakum are full of incredible violence.
'When his father was flogging me (the Archpriest) with the
knout, he tried to dissuade him, so that his father chased
him with a drawn sword.'[2] A youth will throw a book at a
man because he does not like his face; or wreck a car because
the owner wears a ring that offends him. Economic sharp
practice stirred the workers to pogroms. The class war bred
unparalleled massacres and cruelties.

---

[1] Stephen Graham, *With the Russian Pilgrims to Jerusalem*, p. 81.
[2] *The Life of the Archpriest Avvakum*, pp. 86–7.

The indiscipline of the Russians also explains their ineffectiveness. There is a fecklessness in the private lives of some of them, dramatized in Chekov's *Cherry Orchard*, that puts the Nordic to despair. Lack of interest in this world also explains their political incapacity: either they are indifferent to government, or they misunderstand it. The obligations of serfdom were unjustifiably continued for a century after the correlative obligations of the land-owning *barins* were removed.[1] A series of revolutionary Oppositions opposed the Imperial Government with impossible aims and impossible methods. The Decembrists wanted liberty, equality, and fraternity for Russia, without seeing how inapplicable at the time the first two were, or (as Father Zossima saw) how valueless unless interpreted in a moral sense.[2] The Nihilists[3] held that the only valid laws were the laws of Nature—those of morality, of the State, and of religion were consequently to be scrapped; and they sabotaged the reforms of Alexander the Liberator no less by abusing their new liberties than (like Bengali terrorists) by throwing bombs. The 'Cadets'[4] wanted a British Parliament without British apprenticeship or British conditions; and proposed for one session of the Duma a programme that Britain would have achieved in two centuries. The Bolsheviks twice failed to bring into being a Communism still more unsuited to the Russian genius.

Russians are clever and indefatigable talkers; but even here a neglect for the realities of this world induces in them an undisciplined passion for theories, whether these bear any relation to facts or not. Even in the field where the Russian spirit is most at home—religion—this indiscipline breaks out. The Khlysti or Flagellants believed that the Deity entered into a peasant, and that ever since Christ and His Mother and the twelve Apostles have been incarnate in every generation. Some of them—Rasputin among them —have encouraged promiscuous immorality on the ground that to be saved one must first sin. The horror of sin has given rise, in the Skoptsi or eunuchs, to self-mutilation, in the followers of one Philip—the Philippovtsi—even to self-

---

[1] Catherine the Great to 1861.   [2] *The Brothers Karamazov*, pp. 333, 336.
[3] *c.* 1860–90.   [4] 1906.

immolation: whole villages have burned themselves to death. The Doukhobors and the Molokani have refused to perform, not only military, but civil duties.

But if the Russian is violent in evil, he is equally violent in repentance. The liturgical prayers, the lives and teachings of the greatest saints, are full of the need for it. 'Wallowing in the depths of sin I cry unto the Unfathomable Depths of Thy Mercy.'[1] The peasants would lynch a horse-thief, and then grieve in an agony of repentance; a man will insult some one he dislikes, and then apologize with hearty shame. Dostoievsky has drawn the village contemplative, motionless, wondering whether he shall burn down his native village or make the pilgrimage to the Life-Giving Grave. Which will he do? He may do the one; he may do the other; he may do both. 'The incurable drunkard of the village picks himself up out of the mire one afternoon, renounces drinking, and starts off for Jerusalem. The avaricious old mouzhik, who has been hoarding for half a century, wakens up one morning, gives all his money to some one, and sets off begging his way to a far-off shrine.'[2] An old Russian song relates how a robber chief, Kudeyar, living a life of violence and debauchery in the forest, suddenly repents of his evil ways and enters a monastery 'to serve God and man'. Hence the Russian welcomes suffering, for it helps him in the struggle to overcome the enemy—to turn from the things of the flesh to the things of the spirit.

Holy Russia was not primarily a political State, but a religious community; the Russian would describe himself, not as Russian, but as Orthodox. The Nordic State contains the Church, the Orthodox Church contained the State. Like the Holy Roman Empire, the Orthodox State was conceived to exist to serve moral ends. It arose out of man's sin—his lust, his greed, his pride of power—the begetters of war and faction and the other distempers of this world; the State was there to correct these. Russians indeed temperamentally incline to minimize the duties of the State, or even to dispense with it altogether. Bakunin and Tolstoy were both anarchists, though one would have society ruled by the laws

---

[1] Quoted by Arseniev, *Mysticism*, p. 51.
[2] Stephen Graham, op. cit., p. 81.

of Nature, the other by the laws of God. And indeed the
villages of Russia, isolated for the most part over an immense area, have as a rule known little interference from
officials until the coming of the Bolsheviks. Some were for
many years undiscovered altogether.[1] And the people were
pleased, for, as in some Buddhist lands, politics and State
action interested them but little; religion had their heart.
The villages were ruled by Councils or Soviets, heads of
households, who regulated local matters and cared for little
beyond. The peasants would reject the decisions of Courts
of Law in favour of those of a private arbitrator, called in
by them to decide '*po Bojeski*—according to God'. They
thought he could decide more equitably, because he could
consider—as the law could not—all the circumstances of the
case. At the centre the people liked a strong Government.
The Tsar, the 'Little Father', was trusted to do justice; as
the people said: 'The Tsar is far away; when he knows, he
will set things right.' From time to time, for over two centuries,[2] the Tsars would summon Sobors or Councils of the
wisest of their people, whenever consultation on great
changes was desirable. These 'Beloved Men' were either
elected by groups of nobles, clergy, and merchants, or
nominated for their probity and authority by the Government. Peter the Great introduced into the Government the
democratic principle that service was everything, rank nothing. Thus the Government of Russia rested as naturally
on a basis of religion and personal morality, as that of
Britain on a basis of law and constitutional custom.

The State therefore as such meant very little to the
Russian. It was a means to an end; his chief care and joy was
to know and love God. There was a genuine consecration
of everyday life to God—a realization of His Presence in
every place and act. The land was one vast sanctuary.
Churches abounded, worshippers thronged the glorious services. Every room, every market, every public building,
every city gate, every railway station had its holy ikon of
Christ or Christ-bearer or saint, before which prayer was
made; each room became a Chapel and the whole land Holy
Russia. The calendar was full of meaning. The peasant,

---

[1] Stephen Graham, op. cit., pp. 63–4.   [2] 1550–1766.

singing a Te Deum, would turn his cattle out on St. George's
Day, and drive them home on St. Michael's. Religion consecrated the family. Birthdays celebrated, not the man, but
his saint. Marriage was the symbol of the union between
Christ and His Church. Death was the symbol of Christ's
death, the gateway of the resurrection to Eternal Life. Every
act was sacred. A Russian built his house beneath the Cross
of Christ; he entered to live in it with blessing and prayer.
When he started on a journey, he prayed before the station
ikon; were the journey long or dangerous, he would assemble
his family, servants, and friends in solemn worship. Holy
Russia had not a Church; she was a Church,[1] a part on earth
of the Church Universal.

III. 3

The defeat in 1812 of the military Dictator of Europe
liberated in Russia energies comparable with those of Athens
after the defeat of the Persians and of England after the
defeat of the Armada. The Germanization of the eighteenth
century was in large measure thrown off, and Russia found
herself anew; in a spring quickening the great steppe put
forth shining blooms of many kinds. The Slavophils redis-
covered the splendour of Slav civilization—its love of beauty,
its humanity, its mystical heights. Teaching Elders sprang
up in many monasteries, most notably at Optyna Pustin,
where Dostoievsky, by no means the only great thinker to
live the idiorrhythmic life there, painted from Father Am-
brosi, the greatest *staretz* of them all, the immortal picture
of Father Zossima. Theology and philosophy quickened in
the minds of laymen. Khomiakov, greatest of Russian
theologians, formulated and spiritualized the conception
of the Church. Soloviev, versed in the philosophy of the
East, developed a Theology that united Eastern and Western beliefs in a Universal Church and upheld the Christian
ideal of universal brotherhood; and a philosophy that laid
stress on the spirituality of all Being, absolute oneness,
and the evolution of the God-man. A lively movement for
reform manifested itself in the minds of the Bishops and other

[1] *The War and Democracy* (Macmillan & Co., 1914), p. 171.

high dignitaries of the Church;[1] after two hundred years[2] the Patriarchate was restored, and the Patriarch Tikhon exercised a profound influence arising, not from scholarship or statesmanship, but from the holiness and simplicity of his life and character. The music of Moussorgsky and of Tschaikovsky reflected the energy and the yearning of the Russian soul, the ballet of Diaghilev its love of an other-worldly splendour and beauty, reminiscent of the Epic songs. After a thousand years these songs were discovered and recorded, and re-awakened Russia put forth new songs from the lips of Pushkin.

But perhaps in this Renaissance the Russian soul found its most perfect expression in the novel, as the Italian had done in painting and the German in music. In the great novels the passing panorama of this world is minutely and vividly recorded, but always as interpenetrated with the spirituality of another, higher and more real. The buyer of '*dead souls*' is a fraudulent humbug—rubbing shoulders with an assortment of ignoble human beings; yet in the end all is changed—the virtue of a single man redeems a world. Tolstoy drew himself in Pierre, a sensual young soldier, who yet thinks: 'Life is everything, life is God. All is changing and moving, and that motion is God. And while there is life, there is the joy of the consciousness of the Godhead. To love life is to love God. The hardest and the most blessed thing is to love this life in one's sufferings, in un-deserved suffering.' Above all Dostoievsky reached the peak and the pit of the Russian soul. From the mystic heights of a transfigured world Father Zossima foresees the future awaiting Russia. 'They have science; but in science there is nothing but what is the object of sense.' They bid men 'multiply their desires; but soon they will drink blood instead of wine'. They 'succeed in accumulating a greater mass of objects, but the joy in the world grows less'. Drunken peasants, money-lenders, greedy merchants, fac-tory children—alas for them all! Nevertheless 'God will save Russia, as he has saved her many times. Salvation will come from the people, from their faith and from their meek-

[1] Nicholas Zernov, 'The Russian Episcopate and Church Reforms', *Church Quarterly Review*, April 1934.   [2] 1700–1917.

ness. Even the most corrupt of our rich will end by being ashamed of his riches before the poor, and the poor, seeing his humility, will respond joyfully and kindly to his honourable shame. God will save His people, for Russia is great in her humility.'

Such insight is possible only to those who are conscious of the Unseen in the midst of the seen. The followers of the Platonic Gospel are themselves Platonists. 'On earth we are as it were astray, and if it were not for the precious image of Christ before us, we should be undone and altogether lost. Much on earth is hidden from us, but to make up for that we have been given a precious mystic sense of our living bond with the other world, with the higher heavenly world, and the roots of our thoughts and feelings are not here, but in other worlds. That is why the philosophers say that we cannot comprehend the reality of things on earth.'[1] Sankara and Plato are similarly conscious of an intuitive or mystical vision that rises higher than philosophy. Zossima goes on: 'God took seeds from different worlds and sowed them on this earth, and His garden grew up and everything came up that could come up; but what grows lives and is alive only through the feeling of its contact with other mysterious worlds. Heaven lies hidden within all of us—here it lies hidden in me now, and if I will it, it will be revealed to me to-morrow and for all time.' Those whose eyes are holden (says the Buddha in the *Lotus*) see the world as burning; those who have Buddha-knowledge see it as Paradise.

When a man's eyes are thus opened he becomes, like Christ, at one with all living things. The Russian hermits, like the Desert Saints, are close at heart to the forest beasts, and many tales tell of the friendliness of the beasts to them. Like Christ the greatest Russian spirits feel themselves called to be saviours of others, bodhisats, as bearing a vicarious responsibility for the sins and sufferings of all men. 'When any one of us falls, he falls alone; but no one is saved alone.'[2] 'Make yourself responsible for all men's sins, for as soon as you sincerely make yourself responsible for everything and for all men, you will see at once that it is really so, and that

---

[1] *The Brothers Karamazov*, p. 341.
[2] Khomiakov, Birkbeck, p. 216.

you are to blame for every one and for all things.'[1] Hence,
as in the Gospel and in Shakespeare's last plays, the supreme
spirit of forgiveness. As the Grand Duchess Olga, daughter
of the Emperor Nicholas wrote, when the Imperial Family
were in the hands of the Bolsheviks, and the shadow of
impending death lay dark upon them:

> Give us strength, God of Justice,
> To forgive our brother's trespass,
> And with Thy meekness to bear
> The heavy, the bloody Cross.
>
> And on the threshold of the grave,
> Breathe on the lips of Thy servants
> The more than mortal strength
> To pray meekly for their enemies.[2]

'Love a man even in his sin,' says Father Zossima, 'for that
is the semblance of Divine Love, and is the highest love on
earth.'

From of old Russia has believed herself called to a Mes-
sianic mission. 'We preserve the image of Christ, and it
will shine forth like a precious diamond to the whole world.'[3]
Russia's meek monks 'keep the image of Christ fair and
undefiled in the purity of God's Truth', and when the day
and the hour comes, they 'will show it to the tottering creeds
of the world! That star will arise in the East.'[4]

'Russia is the most Christian country in the world,' wrote
an English observer in 1914, 'and her people are the most
Christlike.'[5] Illumined by the loftiest ideal, falling often,
deeply, terribly beneath it, Holy Russia has perhaps caught
a clearer glimpse than any other people of the life of the
Kingdom of Heaven. If her sun is clouded to-day, it has not
set. 'God will save Russia, for the peasant has God in his
heart.'[6]

---

[1] *The Brothers Karamazov.*
[2] Translated by Maurice Baring, *The Times*, January 18, 1926.
[3] *The Brothers Karamazov.*   [4] Ibid.
[5] Dover Wilson in *War and Democracy*, pp. 170–1.
[6] *The Brothers Karamazov.*

VI

THE PROPHETS OF THE KINGDOM

THUS each of the rational civilizations looks at some aspect of Reality which gives it its character and distinguishes it from the rest. Not indeed that there is a gulf between them; for all in lesser or greater degree have points of contact with others, and some indeed take a wide view of Reality. Chinese civilization, for instance, characterized by the this-worldly interests of Confucius, nevertheless produced also the view that the Universe emanates from the Tao, though that other-worldly view is less well understood and therefore less characteristic than the first. The moral-spiritual civilizations, again, look both towards the seen and towards the unseen world, and thereby gain a width of view denied to the civilizations that are predominantly moral or predominantly spiritual; they would be synoptic, but for the fact that they look at each in a somewhat limited way, their freedom of thought and action tending to be subjected too much to the authority of Law or dogma, the 'learned' or the priest, and their conception of the Divine Nature to restrict itself for the most part to a Personal God Who is the Moral Ruler of the earth. Buddhism again, that tree of many branches, ramifies in many directions, ethical and devotional, philosophic and mystical; but its ethics never took the form of a well-organized earthly society, and Buddhism therefore remains only less otherworldly than its parent.

None of these civilizations, therefore, however wide the vision of some of them, has succeeded in seeing Reality as a Whole. Yet there have not been wanting teachers to point out that reason cannot thus limit itself: reason requires by the law of its being, not a part, but a full, satisfaction, and this is to be found, not in any one aspect of Reality, but in the Whole. Nothing that is true can be inconsistent with anything else that is true, and all the parts or aspects of Reality must therefore be consistent with one another; in other words, Reality must be a Unity embracing all its parts, and reason is not fully developed until it contemplates them all and their relations with one another. Rational civilizations, like rational men, differ as they see different aspects of that Unity; they become united as they come to see all aspects, the Universe. As the Abbot Dorotheus says: The nearer men draw to God, the nearer they draw to one another.[1] As the Fourth Gospel says: The Truth shall sanctify men, that they may all be one.

If the great teachers of mankind—Confucius and Shakespeare, Isaiah and Paul, Sankara and the Buddha, have taught men to look upon this aspect or upon that, the greatest teachers of all would have them look upon every aspect, upon Reality in its entirety, Nature and man and God together. Such was Leonardo; such were Socrates and Plato; such above all was Jesus. In their view men were to be 'spectators of all time and all existence, ever longing after the whole of things both Divine and human';[2] they were to 'love God with heart and mind and soul and strength, and their neighbours as themselves'. These teachers were therefore the Prophets of a united humanity, the Kingdom of God that is to be.

I

Although the Athens of history falls far short of the ideal set up by its noblest spirits, it is nevertheless an example— and the sole example—of an attempt to synthetize good of every kind in a single State. There—for a few short years— her statesmen and philosophers tried to realize the Chinese and Nordic ideal of social harmony and personal freedom in a democracy, and to make this democracy the setting of the Indian and Russian ideal: her citizens were to love wisdom and beauty and so attain to Ultimate Truth. The view that Athens was secular-minded is apt to overlook, not only Socrates and Plato and Aristotle, but Aeschylus and Pheidias and Pericles.

How came it that Athens—there in the sphere of the both-worldly civilizations—lived so keenly and freely in this life and yet was so deeply concerned with the other? This tiny State, tucked into a pocket among lofty mountains, could

---

[1] *Love of God and Man*, Chapters 17–19, 21.
[2] *Republic*, vi, p. 486 (Jowett's translation).

not live, first without gathering its people within a city-wall for defence, and secondly without sea-faring; both processes broke down custom and highly individualized them. Then the victory over autocratic Persia and the 'unchanging laws of the Medes and Persians' liberated the little city-state from fear and gave scope for free institutions in which a love of beauty and wisdom could flourish. But why did she want them to flourish? It may be that, as a great Hellenist has suggested,[1] the agony of the earlier sea-migrations quickened the search for Unseen Reality, as the consciousness of change and death quickened it in the forest sages and the Buddha: 'they saw early the world that is behind the ordinary world of human strivings, more real and more intangible.' It is certain that the vanishing of Pericles' dream of a city of beauty and wisdom in the Peloponnesian War led Socrates and his friends to look for another Athens, that should stand upon deeper and surer foundations.

With these moral and spiritual ideals in combination the great Athenians sought to educate free and virile men of the world who should survey the whole Universe and love things human and Divine. Pericles tried first, there in the little city-state round the Acropolis: and when he failed, Socrates and Plato tried again, and, both failing and succeeding, founded that Republic that never was on land or sea, but is seldom far from the minds and hearts of men.

I. 1

The Athenians, like the Confucians, maintained that man is by nature good: like everything else, he has his *arete*—his special perfection or excellence or goodness—and this perfection is itself beauty. Their ethical ideal was therefore the kaloskagathos—the man whose excellence made him beautiful—beautiful in body and beautiful in mind. Such a man (they thought) would be temperate, courageous, just, sensible: virtues very like those expected by the Confucians. Moreover, excellence should not be allowed to go to sleep—left as a mere *dunamis* or possibility; it was an 'energy' that should be developed to the full. The colourful pages of Herodotus show this notion in operation: the

---

[1] Gilbert Murray, *The Rise of the Greek Epic*, p. 90; cf. p. 55.

Athenians travel, trade, fight, make friends, question, with a ceaseless curiosity and enjoyment.

But how should men be trained to this splendid ideal? Outwardly by athletics, thought the Greeks, with the Nordics; the training of the naked body, 'gymnastic', was one half of education. But Greek athletics laid special stress on beauty, not of the body only, but of the mind; athletic meetings were occasions for music and poetry and sacrifices to the gods—Pindar has brought out the full splendour of such festivals. That was the second half of Greek education —devotion to the Muses, 'music'. The Muses, 'the mindful ones', were the goddesses of song and of the liberal arts that were akin to song—epic, lyric and erotic poetry, tragedy and comedy, sacred hymns, choral song and dance, history and astronomy. 'Harmony', or music in the stricter sense, played a great part in Athenian education, as it did in Chinese (China had a Classic of Music, now unfortunately lost); the strains of the lyre and harp in the city 'and the shepherd's pipe in the country'[1] could discipline their passions, and stimulate their courage. As in India, the chief teachers were two great Epics; in words that were themselves virile or tender music, men listened to the tales of the prowess and the love of Achilles, the adventures and temperance of Odysseus—as the Chinese read in the old songs and histories of the virtues and vices of bygone rulers and peoples, and the Nordics formed themselves on the examples and warnings of the Bible and of the classics of Greece and Rome. Drama sprang from these Epics, as it sprang from the Indian Epics: a drama that dealt with sin and doubt, with temperance and the Divine government of the world. The visible arts were teachers too. If man had his *arete* and beauty, so had things; and the Athenians delighted to bring this out—not here and there, but everywhere. Accordingly Athens, like China, overflowed with beauty—from the great temples and statues that inspired a new view of religion, to the cups and pots of household use whose fragments went on to the rubbish heap. The very names were beautiful— Cleomenes, Famous Might, Aristonoe, Noble Mind; like the Chinese Lady Precious Stream and Little Summerdress.

[1] Plato, *Republic*, iii. 399.

These people were sociable, of the market-place and the palaestra; theirs was not an ideal that led into a forest or a cell. Athenian democracy wove public and private action into a single web. Every free citizen served as a judge, spoke and voted in the Assembly, fought when necessary as a soldier or a sailor, was liable to be chosen by lot as a member of the Council and of the administration of the City or of the outlying Districts. No other community has ever realized so completely that the development of individuality begins (though it is far from ending) in active good citizenship. Nor did this public service prevent a vivid and vigorous private life. Pericles, the statesman whose genius brought this great society to its highest pitch, summing up the Athenian ideal over the graves of those who had fallen in the Peloponnesian War (as Lincoln was to sum up the American ideal over the graves of those who had fallen in the Civil War) combines the harmony of Chinese and the freedom of Nordic civilization. The law (he said) secured equal justice for all, and all respected authority, even the unwritten law recognized only by public opinion[1] (a British trait). But this did not interfere with liberty, for each man did what he liked and allowed his neighbour to do as he liked, recognizing any special excellence or merit in rich and poor alike. Though they were a fighting people, they educated themselves, not for fighting, but for a free and full life—with games and sacrifices and other relaxations. They welcomed the foreigner as well as his goods. Their freedom turned them to the love of beauty and the love of wisdom. But both were to be pursued temperately—the one with economy and the other with manliness. 'We are lovers of the beautiful, yet simple in our tastes; we cultivate the mind, yet do not become soft.' Accordingly (he said) Athenians did not copy their neighbours, but were an example to them: Athens was 'the school of Hellas'.

Pericles' speech was the light of the sun; the Peloponnesian War was the shadow of the cave. Freedom to do what one liked was excellent, so long as what one liked was beauty and wisdom; but what if this liking were shallow-rooted, and a statesman like Pericles were followed by a

[1] Thucydides, ii. 35–46 (Jowett's translation).

demagogue like Cleon? Then faction and war took the place
of beauty and wisdom, and the Athenians could say to the
Melians: 'Right is only in question between equals in power.
The strong do what they can, and the weak suffer what they
must.'[1] That is the principle of the Materialist State. There
were not wanting Sophists to teach that it was correct; but
the results of this break down upon the finer spirits of the
day are to be seen in the tense anguish of Thucydides as he
chronicles the failure of the Periclean ideal, and in the
wistful scepticism of Euripides as he questions the Divine
government of the world.

I. 2

But the cataclysm of the Peloponnesian War led also to the
rebuilding of Athens, though this time as a Heavenly, not
an earthly city. Looking upon the ruin of hopes so fair, wise
men drew the lesson of her failure, and in their teaching
built the city with a deeper insight into the soul of man and
the nature of the Universe in which he lives.

The architects of this Republic were Socrates and his
philosophic family, Plato and Aristotle; centuries later the
New Platonists were to infuse much of the master's spirit into
the Roman and the Orthodox Church. Not that the first intention was philosophical only: it was also political. Athens was
decaying, but she had not yet perished; and Plato, no less than
Demosthenes, strove to restore her while yet there was time.
That is why his teaching took a political form. The city-state,
though divided by the factions of rich and poor and often at
war with its neighbours, could (he thought) by temperance
and wisdom become, not two cities, but one; and if he retained soldiers it was to guard the city, not to attack others.
Plato chastens Athens so fiercely because he loves her so
deeply. But there is nothing narrow in his love. When the
time comes, he is just as ready to help Syracuse as Aristotle
is to tutor the heir of Athens' greatest enemy. It is in form,
not in spirit, that Plato thus differs from Jesus, whose
historical environment was wholly different. Jesus lived at
a time when divisions had broken down, and a single
political system, newly organized by Augustus, extended

---

[1] Thucydides, v. 89.

over the Mediterranean world. It was natural therefore that he should give his message to the world, and that his object should be, not the direct reformation of the State, but its elevation through the elevation of the individual.

Doing as you liked (Socrates and his followers perceived) was all very well, but there must also be discipline and order; without these freedom degenerated into licence and chaos. Athens had fallen because, lacking discipline, her egoism was stronger than her altruism: she had misused her position as head of the Delian League, she had cynically attacked others during the War. The State must become moral, and therefore men must become moral; they must be educated accordingly. 'What is education?'[1] they asked. Taking the four traditional virtues, they answered that men must discipline their animal passions and so become temperate, while at the same time preserving their spirit and so remaining courageous. Thus, gentleness and manliness together, such as are found in the watch-dog or the gentle man, would give the State soldiers, the 'Guards', whom it could rely on to defend it. The study of the Muses and the disciplining of the body must therefore be renewed with fresh zeal. But, besides soldiers to defend the State, merchants and workers were needed to supply its material wants, and—above all—statesmen, and not demagogues, to lead it. And Plato found, just as the Hindus were finding, that justice consisted in each of these four classes or castes performing its own function or duty—its *sva-dharma*—in the State. Like the Catholic Church in the Middle Ages, he did not try to suppress men's acquisitive and fighting instincts, but to turn them into the right channels, and so make them, not destructive, but serviceable both to the soul and to the community. Only in so far as men are thus both temperate and just could they pursue their true end— wisdom and beauty. The Socratic way was therefore a middle way or mean, a 'nothing-too-much', a harmony between body and soul, flesh and reason.

But who were the true rulers, and how were they too to be educated? That was the crux of the problem, in Athens no less than in China. In a true State (he argued) the

[1] *Republic*, ii. 376.

leaders would be those who truly love wisdom or beauty—
'philosophers, lovers of wisdom'; and at this point Athens
made her greatest contribution to mankind. She showed that
the truly wise man not only makes society peaceful and
prosperous, but uses its peace and prosperity to explore and
enjoy the greatness and beauty of the Universe itself. To
train such men was the highest task of the State.

These 'lovers of wisdom' would be those who, freed by
temperance from the temptations of this world, could turn
their minds and hearts to the Loveliness and Reality of the
world that reason must think and the senses cannot know.
True love, said Socrates at Agathon's dinner-party, is a
thing that continually widens its range: beginning with the
beauty of the body it rises to the beauty of the mind, and
thence to the beauty of institutions and laws, the beauty
of the sciences, until finally it embraces the whole Ocean
of Beauty—the Universe itself.[1] That was the idea that
governed the education of these 'philosopher-kings'. After
the usual training of the body and study of the Muses for the
first twenty years of their lives, they were educated for
fifteen years in the co-ordination of the sciences and in
philosophy; then, at the age of thirty-five, they descended
for a further fifteen years into this visible world, this cave of
shadows, here to guide the State. From fifty onward they
were to live chiefly in the contemplation of the Supreme
Good, occasionally returning to politics.

'The time is now arrived at which they must raise the eye of the
soul to the Universal Light Which lightens all things, and behold the
Absolute Good; for that is the pattern according to which they are to
order the State and the lives of individuals, and the remainder of their
own lives also; making philosophy their chief pursuit, but, when their
turn comes, toiling also at politics and ruling for the public good, not
as though they were performing some heroic action, but simply as a
matter of duty; and when they have brought up in each generation
others like themselves and left them in their place to be governors of
the State, then they will depart to the Islands of the Blest and dwell
there.'[2]

Thus their career has virtually the same four stages as

---

[1] *Symposium*, 210.   [2] *Republic*, vii. 540.

that of the Brahmin and the *staretz*: education, action, contemplation, followed by the action of the statesman who can view the here-and-now in the light of the Eternal Good.

On this view the men who compose society differ according to the degree in which they apprehend Reality. There are four of these degrees.[1] At the bottom come those for whom neither nature nor education has done anything at all—the animal man who knows of nothing beyond material things, who sweats for his pleasures or his empires, but in either case is grasping only at shadows—shadows cast (no doubt) by reality, but themselves without reality at all; his state of mind is *eikasia*, the perception of shadows. Then come the three stages in which man's true, super-animal, rational personality gradually unfolds itself. At first men only understand that there *is* some explanation, physical and moral, of this world of the senses, and accept at second-hand the explanations offered by more developed minds: these people have 'faith' or conviction. Those who can understand these explanations for themselves have risen to 'understanding'—their logical and philosophical powers have got to work, and they conceive intelligible 'ideas'. But 'reason' in the full sense of the word—a man's soul or spirit, the fullness of his personality—is satisfied only when it is aware of the One Eternal Principle whence springs the excellence of the 'ideas' themselves: the Supreme and Final Excellence that Plato calls, if regarded as the Object of knowledge, 'the Idea of the Good',[2] if as the Object of love, 'the Ocean of Beauty'.[2] Thus, as in India, personality unfolds itself in three stages; and, as it does so, Reality reveals itself in three stages too. To Socrates and Plato, as to the Hindus, the world of changing material things—the world of becoming —is intelligible only on the assumption of this Unchanging or Eternal Being, 'the Universal Light That lightens all things, the Absolute Good', That gives meaning to all lesser good; to 'know oneself' is to know That Universal Supreme Principle, as to reach the innermost self is to know that it is Brahma—'That art thou'. This knowledge is an intuition, a mystical experience, a consciousness of the Godhead

---

[1] Ibid. vi. 511.   [2] Ibid. vi. 508.

within, a realization of oneness with the Universe; though What That Good, That Principle, That Godhead is words cannot tell—*neti, neti*. It can only be indicated in metaphors and myths.

The philosopher who rules the State and seeks to reach the Divine Reality and Beauty is (Plato says) 'a soul that is ever longing after the whole of things both Divine and human, the spectator of all time and all existence',[1] as well as the 'lover of the Ocean of Beauty'. He is 'synoptic'—he not only sees all things, but sees them together, in their relations one with another, and therefore as a unity. Such a one has attained 'likeness to God'—has become like Him 'holy, just, and wise',[2] and that, in the view of the wisest Athenians, is the true end of man.

These philosophers are, and can be, no authoritarian rulers. Their outlook, and consequently their actions, are poles apart from those of the materialist, the dictator; as the terms are here used, authority is inconsistent with philosophy. The just analogy is not between dictator and subject, but between saviour and saved; they would rescue their people from their egoisms and the faction and war these breed, and raise them through temperance to the love of wisdom and beauty. The philosopher-kings stood in the same relation to the Republic as the Confucian scholar-rulers to What-is-under-Heaven, the Buddha to the Buddha-lands, the Christ to Christendom: regenerators of the people by their example, bringers of the light to them that sit in darkness. And the peoples responded by acknowledging that relation, and found help, not from authoritarian rulers, but from men wiser and greater than themselves. Saint Bernard could sway all Christendom because men realized that he saw the mystic vision. The ideal of the Catholic Middle Ages was that Christ, by virtue of His Wisdom, ought to be King of men; that men, by virtue of their temperance, would be ready subjects of such a King. That was Plato's view of the matter in the *Republic*; and if in the Catholic world this relationship tended to degenerate into one of mere authority and subjection, that was but a caricature of the original, as the authoritarian view of the philo-

---

[1] *Republic*, vi. 486.   [2] *Theaetetus*, 176.

sopher-kings is a caricature of Plato's view. Nor surely was
Plato wrong: until the world comes under the sway of such
philosopher-kings, it will not be saved.

I. 3

Aristotle and Plotinus carry on Plato's thought. Aristotle's 'practical man' is he who practises the moral virtues
in society—virtues that are all instances of temperance, a
'mean' between two extremes; for Aristotle, too, would not
destroy men's appetites, but have them gratified in due
proportion to the rest of him. The more developed personality of the 'theoretical man' or thinker contemplates the
Universal Reality, and particularly Reality in its Highest
Form. God to Aristotle, as to the Hindus, is a Being with
Everlasting Life and Perfect Blessedness, engaged in never-
ending Self-Contemplation; the perfect Simplicity and Im-
mutability of Whose Nature brings Him the purest and
serenest Bliss.[1] The moral virtues cannot be ascribed to
Him, for they are dependent on material bodily terrestrial
conditions. He is the First of all substances, and Himself the Unmoved Mover, the necessary First Source of
movement; acting on the world as the Primary Object of
love, in Whom alone desire and reason are alike satisfied.
But it is only 'a Godlike kind of man' that can thus see God.

Plotinus, the 'New Plato', has the same idea of the soul
penetrating through its envelope of obscurity and illusion
till it reaches the Light of Reality; only with him it would
seem that Hindu influences have emphasized the unreality
of all that falls short of the One. Plotinus is a Pantheist: all
things, just in so far as they have Being, are Divine, and God
is All in all. From this 'One' issues Nous or Reason, at once
Thought and Being; thence the world-soul, and from that
individual souls, whose end is to return to the One whence
they came; and the way of return is that of all thinkers—
right action, contemplation, union with the Divine. The
first stage is that of the 'civic virtues', which lead to a 'purification' of the soul from the evils of sense. Then come the
'Divine virtues', contemplation of corporeal things in their
multiplicity and harmony and then of the 'ideas' of the world

[1] *Metaphysics*, l. 7. 9.

of Nous or Reason. But thought, a kind of motion, cannot attain the One: in the highest stage therefore the soul, in yogi-like silence and utter concentration, loses itself to find itself in ecstatic union with the Highest. In that moment of indescribable bliss it is bathed in the Light of Eternity, swallowed up in Divinity. Here once more is the *ananda* of the Hindu absorbed in the Bliss of Brahma.

What Buddhism has been to South and East Asia, Hellas has been to West Asia and Europe: the conqueror-saviour. Virgil and Horace re-created the temperance and beauty of her poetry. Virgil in turn profoundly influenced the Catholic Middle Ages, while Horace gave grace to eighteenth-century Europe. Greek science, especially medicine and mathematics, waxed in the Renaissance of Islam, which in turn passed them on to Salerno and Europe. The precepts of Plato taught the Greco-Roman Renaissance that the observation of Nature is impossible without mathematics. The philosophy of Aristotle was eagerly fastened on by the Muslim Renaissance, and further developed by its philosophers, from Persia to Spain: huge encyclopaedias were produced after his manner, and Avicenna and Averroës developed the loftiest reaches of his philosophy. The Islamic Renaissance handed on the Arabic text of Aristotle to the Catholic Renaissance, whose thinkers, translating it into Latin, compared it with the recently compiled Sentences of the Christian Fathers, and so unveiled the great vision of the later Scholasticism. Plato's philosophy influenced the Jew Philo, who in turn influenced the writer of the Fourth or Platonic Gospel, which has illuminated Orthodoxy. Augustine was a Neoplatonist immediately before he was a Christian, and Neoplatonism inspires his teaching. The Christian Neoplatonist 'Dionysius' so profoundly affected Catholic writers that his works, if lost, could almost be restored from the pages of Aquinas. Even greater has been his influence upon Orthodoxy. Neoplatonism also deeply affected the Sufis: the philosophy of the greatest of them, Jelal-ud-din Rumi, is virtually that of Plotinus.

Yet the ideals of the great Athenians required a still ampler statement. Athens had not abolished slavery, though an uneasy conscience tried to justify itself by the argument that some men are 'by nature slaves'.[1] If the philosophers were to be the saviours of the masses, insufficient attention was nevertheless bestowed by Plato on the education and training of the masses. If Plato's patriotism was not narrow, and his Guards were only for defence, he had nevertheless not envisaged a world-state where war should be impossible among men of good will. Socrates and Plato were the fore-runners of a philosopher-king whose 'good news' knew no such limitations.

II

At the moment when Augustus was pacifying the Roman Empire, one Jesus started to preach a profounder doctrine of the State, and, indeed, to declare that he himself was the Head of it. For this he was put to death while yet a young man. 'The Kingdom of Heaven', says the voice of Jesus from the Gospels and Oxyrhynchus, echoing that other voice from Athens, 'is within you; whoever shall know himself shall find it. Strive therefore to know yourselves, and ye shall be aware that ye are the sons of the Father, and ye shall know that ye are of the City of God, and that ye are the City'.[2] These words sum up his teaching. The Kingdom is within us; society will be what the men and women who compose it make it. They themselves are the City: the Kingdom of God is on earth. But more than that: if men 'know them-selves' they will be aware that they are both 'the sons of God' and 'of (or in) the City of God': when they reach a knowledge of their true or innermost selves they will find both that their nature is Divine, and that the Kingdom that is on earth is part of the Cosmic Kingdom of Heaven. Here then was a Kingdom that was a synthesis of all Good, a United King-dom of Heaven and earth. And its end was the blessedness of gods.

II. 1

In the first place, then, men must come to understand their own nature: humanism—the education of character—is the foundation of the State. Accordingly, the initial step is intellectual—metanoia, a change of mind. Change your

---

[1] Aristotle, *Politics*, i. 4.   [2] *Logia* (Grenfell and Hunt).

point of view—abandon your materialistic outlook for 'Right Views'—and the Kingdom of Heaven is at hand.

This change of mind will make it possible for a man to escape from his merely animal desires and to find his soul. 'If any one wishes to follow me, let him deny himself, take up his cross, and so follow me; for whoever wants to save his life will lose it, and whoever loses his life for my sake and the Gospel's will save it. What profit is it for a man to gain the whole world and to forfeit his soul? What could a man offer as an equivalent for his soul?' Not that Jesus, like an ascetic, looked on material things as evil in themselves; indeed, he scandalized the respectable people of the day by his enjoyment of them. They complained that he, the Son of Man, came eating and drinking, and men said: 'Here is a glutton and a drunkard, a friend of tax-gatherers and sinners.' As he said, he and his friends piped to them, and they did not dance. But he did say that material things were evil in so far as they hindered man from the vision of the Universe, that sonship which was their true life; his ideal was Plato's *sophrosune*, temperance.

> If your hand is a hindrance to you, cut it off;
> If your foot is a hindrance to you, cut it off;
> If your eye is a hindrance to you, tear it out.

Better to get into the Kingdom of God without material things, than to keep the material things and not get there. Here is no hard and fast rule, but a principle: there is a tremendous severity, combined with a tremendous freedom. *If* your body hinders you, the severest self-discipline; if it does not, the fullest enjoyment. 'Every one has to be consecrated by the fire of discipline.'[1]

When it comes to the particular forms which sin or materialism takes, he says least about the appetites of the body, more about the dangers of wealth. Not that wealth is bad—our Father knows that we have need of material things. But where a man's wealth prevents his entering the Kingdom of Heaven, the whole should be resigned. 'Go and sell all that thou hast, and thou shall have treasure in Heaven.' That rich young man must 'lose his life to save

---

[1] Mark ix. 49 (Moffat's translation is largely used).

it'. But far the severest and most frequent warnings are against the desire for fame and reputation, the self-centred longing to stand well in the eyes of others, because this can so easily take a hypocritical disguise of goodness, and so is the hardest sin to recognize and root out. One day walking along the road his followers quarrelled as to which of them was the greatest. Jesus told them: 'If any one wants to be first, he must be last of all and the servant of all.' On this account he denounced the good men of the day: 'Beware of the scribes! they like to walk about in long robes, to get saluted in the market-places, to secure the front seats in the synagogues and the best places at banquets; they prey upon the property of widows and offer long unreal prayers. All the heavier will their sentence be!'

The reason why these egoistic desires that have their origin in the body are bad is that they blind the eye of the soul—'hinder' men from the knowledge and love that are their true happiness. They make men 'dull of heart'; ignorance and stupidity, with the egoism from which they spring, are, in Jesus' view as in Gotama's, the fundamental sin.

> Ye have eyes, but ye see not,
> Ye have ears, but ye hear not,
> Lest ye see with your eyes, and understand with your heart,
> And be converted.

'Understand with your heart'—know things with the knowledge that is love.

This control of animal desire and of the stupidity it breeds liberates a man's spiritual energy. Like Gotama, and like Plato and Aristotle, he taught that the condition of progress is not Grace from without, but a grand energy from within —the energy of the Divine nature in the sons of God: an energy that reaches towards perfection, the fulfilment of a man's true nature or end. The lazy servant who does nothing with his opportunities is deprived of them and punished. The unjust steward, a criminal committing a serious fraud, is held up as an example to the lukewarm children of light for his energy in 'looking ahead'. The enterprising lad who left home (his Father let him go) to become a spendthrift and a debauchee, discovered that the way of materialism was a blind alley, and 'arose and came to his Father', now to be vigorous, not in a far country, but in his Father's house; hence the feast was made, not for the un-enterprising elder brother, but for the energetic prodigal. 'The Kingdom of Heaven suffereth violence, and the violent take it by storm.'

The true energy is an energy of knowledge and love, and therefore of enjoyment. But Jesus does not expect that man shall reach his goal at once; he asks the uttermost that each soul can give, but never more that it can give. Like other teachers he makes clear that progress from the beast to the God must be gradual, a path or way with steps and stages, not a sudden leap or bound. And his way is in essence the same as theirs—the way of Gotama and the *Gita*, Plato and Aristotle, Plotinus and Origen: faith, knowledge and love, union with the Divine. To the multitude he proclaims the need of 'faith', by which he means anticipated knowledge; and of works—ceremonial and ethical obedience to the Law of Moses and the law of Rome. He saw a man at work on the sabbath, and said: 'Man, if thou knowest what thou doest, blessed art thou; but if thou knowest not, thou art accurst and a transgressor of the Law.'[1] It is ill to break the law through wilfulness, well to break it through understanding. As spiritual power increases a man may rise from faith to knowledge and love, the very core of Jesus' teaching. When at the end of his career he was asked what was the chief of all the commandments, he replied: 'The Lord our God is one Lord, and you must love the Lord your God with your whole heart, with your whole soul, with your whole mind and with your whole strength'—with your whole being. The correspondence to the Hindu Way of Return is striking. Your whole strength—the way of works or *karma*; your whole mind and heart—the way of love or *bhakti*; your whole soul—*jnana*, the mystic union that is bliss or *ananda*. But Jesus also gave the lesser realities their full due. The second commandment was: 'You must love your neighbour as yourself'—other spirits are our other selves. The third commandment is implied in his lovely parables of the countryside, his joy in 'the lilies of the field' and in the

---

[1] *Logion* from Oxyrhynchus.

trees that 'put out their leaves when Summer is at hand', his regard for food and clothing. 'You must love Nature.' The highest stage of all is reached when the soul, the innermost self, thus embracing all Being, realizes that it is a 'son of God', of Divine Origin and therefore of Divine nature, and so can become 'perfect as its Father in Heaven is Perfect', reunited with Him in the Divine Life.

Perhaps it is not fanciful to see in the Way of the *makarios*, the man who has the blessedness of a god, some resemblance to the Eightfold Way—'Divinely blessed are those who feel poor in spirit, for theirs is the Kingdom of Heaven.' The only gateway into the Kingdom of Heaven is the humility of the man eager to learn; the man with the open mind who can say with Socrates that he 'knows nothing', who can start on the journey with what Gotama calls 'Right Views' and Jesus 'a change of mind'. Then comes the self-discipline that leads to temperance: those who weep, not over death but over evil, shall laugh, for they shall overcome it and be free from it; evil by its very nature cannot endure, it must turn its energies from objects that do not satisfy to those that do. The Buddhist Way puts the positive side of the case: in so far as a man is free from evil passions, he has Right Intentions or Desires. The next three stages correspond to what that Way calls Right Action, and relate to the right attitude towards man. The meek shall inherit the earth: their gentleness to all living things shall convert foes into friends. Those who hunger and thirst after righteousness shall be satisfied; righteousness will reign over an earth that meekness has united. The merciful shall obtain mercy: those who with the pitying love of the *bodhisat* bring the less fortunate to blessedness shall enter into blessedness themselves. After these moral or social virtues come the intellectual or spiritual virtues, the virtues pre-eminently of the contemplative, relating now, not to men, but to God. 'Divinely blessed are the pure in heart'—pure of evil of any kind—'for they shall see God.' In this stage, which corresponds to Right Endeavour, the mind whose sight is cleared can make a rational or philosophic effort to see or know God, though still as a separate Being. Then come the 'makers of peace': not merely peace without, but peace within—the peace of God that passeth all understanding, the peace to which Jesus referred when he said: 'My peace I give unto you.' Those who have this power are sons of God in the fullest sense, no longer separate from but sharing the Divine Life. Finally, such Divinely blessed souls, like Plato's wisdom-lovers, rise superior to any evil the material world and those who are entangled in it can inflict on them —persecution, denunciation, slander. These are not, like the poor in spirit, merely approaching the Kingdom of Heaven—they are in full possession of it, and their reward is rich. 'Rejoice and be exceeding glad': they are blessed with the blessedness of God.

II. 2

'Thy Kingdom come, Thy Will be done on earth as it is in Heaven.' This Kingdom of those who know and love is no vague dream, but something that already exists 'in Heaven', and is also coming into being 'on earth'. Just as in each individual it begins with a change of mind, a change of outlook, so in the world at large it 'cometh not with observation'. It is spiritual, not material; the entirely inconsistent forecast about Jesus 'coming in the clouds with great power and glory' clearly derives from the apocalyptic literature of the day, and though believed by Paul is disproved by history. This hidden coming is not a break with the past, but a development of it—Jesus is neither a reactionary nor a revolutionary, but a conservative progressive. 'I am not come to destroy, but to fulfil.'

This Kingdom is to contain every class and every nation. Not only gifted philosophers but simple people are to be brought in to the feast: 'the poor and maimed and blind and lame from the streets and lanes of the town', and even the rustics from 'the highways and hedges.' And the Kingdom is to be world-wide—in that far transcending Pericles' or Plato's ideal city-state. 'They shall come from the East and from the West and from the North and from the South and shall sit down in the Kingdom of God.' That is necessarily so; for it is the Kingdom of God, and God is One. Moreover, in order to enter this Kingdom it is not necessary to recognize Jesus himself as one's Master or to call oneself a

Christian: what is necessary is to do the Will of God. 'Not every one that saith unto me "Lord, Lord" shall enter into the Kingdom of Heaven, but he that doeth the Will of My Father which is in Heaven.' 'He that is not against us is for us.' Jesus knows of rich and poor, East and West, Christian and non-Christian, only to include all in his Kingdom.

Just because a spiritual Kingdom is all-embracing, it cannot restrict itself to any one type of custom, institution, or law. Rules would have anchored it to place and time, principles give it the freedom of eternity. Jesus shows the Buddha's Tact or Upaya: just as the saving Buddha, the solitary contemplative, the learner, even little children making a sand-heap in honour of the Buddha, are all following the One Way to Buddha-knowledge, so those who shape the laws and institutions that best meet the needs of their country or their age all belong to the Kingdom of God, provided they lead to the knowledge and love that constitute that Kingdom. Jesus lays down immutable spiritual principles; but he leaves their changing applications to the wit and energy of men. Even when he is asked to apply them he refuses to do so, as in the case of the division of an inheritance between two brothers.[1] He elucidates the principle that must govern all education—the perfecting of men for union with the Universe; but he leaves it to others to devise and found schools and Universities, pilgrimages and monastic orders, discipleships and hermitages. He lays down the principle that must govern all politics and all economics if they are to fulfil the purposes of society, moral and material: 'Seek ye first the Kingdom of God and His righteousness'; but he leaves it to lesser men to work out the forms in which righteousness is to take shape—the family and the clan, Parliaments and Commonwealths, capitalism and socialism. Meanwhile they are to live up to the law as they find it: to offer the gift that Moses commanded, to render unto Caesar the things that are Caesar's. He lays down the principles that govern the development of moral and spiritual life. The root of ethics is temperance: if hand or foot is a hindrance to you, cut it off, that the soul may

---

[1] Luke xii. 13.

enter into life. But he leaves men to frame their own codes
of conduct in matters relating to sex, drinking, smoking,
the use of money, freedom or obedience, and so on, as may
best suit time or place. The root of religion is to love God
with mind and soul. But he leaves men to shape their own
Theologies and creeds, to win their own mystical experiences.

Thus, like all the great teachers—Confucius and Pericles
and Plato—but with even more emphasis than they, Jesus
insists that what is essential to society is the character or
spirit or point of view of the men and women who compose
it, not the rules and practices and institutions in which these
embody themselves. 'My Kingdom is not of this world'—
not material, but spiritual. 'Up, India, and conquer the
world with your spirituality', exclaims Vivekananda; and
Gandhi would have her conquer by 'soul-force'. Two out-
standing events of Jesus' life reinforce this teaching. At the
beginning of his mission he is offered 'the kingdoms of the
world and the glory of them' (Galilee was covered with
roads along which in all directions travelled the pomp of
Empire[1]), and he refuses. At the end, standing under a
little temple where men worshipped Caesar,[2] he admits that
he is the Christ, the Anointed King; and then—to show
that the Kingdom of God, unlike Caesar's, is not of this
world, he marches deliberately on Jerusalem to drive the
materialists from the House of Prayer that they have made
'a den of robbers', to refuse like Socrates to save himself
from the law that condemned him as a rebel, to be mocked
as a king and to be executed as a criminal. In all this he was
no would-be petty potentate, but the spiritual King of a
spiritual Kingdom, a mystic with a mystic's power of bringing the impossible into being. 'The King of the Jews' was
the Suffering Servant Israel embodied in a man, the Supreme Bodhisat who should heal the nations, 'responsible
for the sins of all', the saviour of mankind. 'I, if I be lifted
up, will draw all men unto me.'

The prayer taught by Jesus puts the Kingdom in per-
spective, as his account of the *makarios* puts the growth of

---

[1] Sir George Adam Smith, *The Historical Geography of the Holy Land*,
pp. 425 ff.   [2] Ibid., pp. 476, 478.

the individual. He begins at the Highest. 'Our Father Which art in Heaven.' The approach of man to God is not individual, but collective, a *sobornost*—'*our* Father'. God is the Father of men, who are consequently His sons, sharing His Nature, made in His likeness. Yet He is not a man, but a Being far transcending man's finite spirit in a Heaven that transcends the world of space and time. The first essential of human society is that He should be reverenced, 'hallowed'—known and loved and realized.

But realization—union—cannot come at once; it is the end of a process. Just as the Indian soul came to perceive that, to unite itself with Brahma, it must first obey the Dharma, so Jesus says that the way to hallow God's Name is to obey His Will. Where the finite will is at one with God's, His Kingdom has come: it already exists in Heaven, and is now also to come on earth.

> Thy Kingdom come,
> Thy Will be done
>> On earth as it is in Heaven.

That is the practical ideal towards which men who desire the Kingdom must steer their course. But here and now there are immediate necessities. 'Give us this day our daily bread' —that which is 'added' to those who first seek the Kingdom of God and His Righteousness. 'Forgive us our sins as we forgive others, and lead us not into temptation.' Love, even in its highest form—forgiveness—is possible to those who resist the temptation of the animal passions—lust and greed and above all pride. The prayer depicts the mountain from its summit to its base.

II. 3

'Know yourselves, and ye shall be aware that ye are the sons of the Father, and ye shall know that ye are of the City of God.'[1] The fulfilment of man is consciousness of his Divine nature; the Kingdom that is to come on earth is part of the Universal Kingdom of Heaven.

'Know thyself'; 'That art thou'; in the innermost self will be found 'the Dweller in the innermost'; men are 'the sons of God'. As a man's sons are of the substance of his

---

[1] Oxyrhynchus, *Logia*.

body, so men are in their true nature, their spirit or reason, of the substance of the Divine Reason, and are therefore themselves Divine. Their end, as Plato said, is Godlikeness; it is Theosis, the mystical union with God—the consciousness of Him in their own hearts—that is natural to them. For a man to complete his personality is to realize his Divinity.

Nothing short of that is required. 'Be ye therefore perfect' —*teleioi*, reach your *telos* or end—'as your Father in Heaven is Perfect.' And to be perfect oneself, at one with God, is to be full of love for others. 'Be ye therefore merciful, as your Father in Heaven is Merciful.' The *arahat* is also the *bodhisat*: the perfect self is full of compassion for others. Thus Jesus' teaching, like Shakespeare's at the end of his life, is that man is Godlike, and therefore full of forgiveness. This Divinity, this perfection, is the 'fullness of life' that Jesus said he came to bring—so far is he from impoverishing or diminishing life!

In proportion then as men fulfil their end and become perfect, they know and are one with God. 'Divinely happy are the pure in heart, for they shall see God. Divinely happy are the peacemakers, for they shall be called the sons of God.' Jesus never attempts to define the Infinite, the Eternal, the Ineffable—*neti, neti*. But the Personal Aspect of God is fully recognized, and His Presence pervades the Gospel, as the physical loveliness of Helen pervades the *Iliad*, though so little is said of either. Whenever God is spoken of, it is with the utmost magnificence:

> Man shall not live by bread alone
>   but by every Word That cometh out of the Mouth of God.

'You must worship the Lord your God, and serve Him alone.'

But men as they are now are not Godlike; they are prodigals who lust and suffer in a far country. Is it not a mere dream that human nature can ever reach its end, Divine perfection? No; for this Divine man has already existed. Every great man is in his degree the proof of the Divinity of man, nay, every spark of goodness in the least of men: but there is one man who claimed to be, and who was, in the full sense at once the son of man and the son of God.

Confucius must needs seek back to the sage kings of old for the examples of his teaching; Jesus was himself the example of what he taught—the perfect, the merciful, the *makarios*, the son of God. When the coatings of piety are scraped from the Gospels, he can be seen striding through their pages like a god. What is his claim to be called Divine? Not birth from a Virgin: his mother in the flesh was with his family when they said that he was 'out of his mind', and he declared his mother in the spirit to be 'whoever does the Will of God'. Not the descent of the Spirit upon him at his baptism—to which he never refers. Not the working of miracles: he refused to give a sign. Not his death and resurrection; he said: 'I was delivered to death on behalf of sinners, that they might return to the Truth and sin no more; that they might inherit that glory of righteousness which is spiritual and imperishable in Heaven.'[1] Not a unique position as the only-begotten Son of the Father: all men are the sons of God and all share in some measure the Divine Reason that is the Only-begotten of God. But whereas the eyes of other men were shut, or only opening, his were wide open; in him the Divine Reason was realized in full. He 'knew himself', the God, the Father, within him. He therefore claimed to be in a unique sense *the* son of man, *the* son of God, man made perfect, man as he is in origin and nature, and is meant to be again—differing from other men, not in kind, but in degree. The Mahayana Buddhists see all men destined to Buddhahood; Jesus is the living pledge of what men, half-blind, half-dead, half-wraiths as they now are, are destined to become. He showed in his own person—and this is his significance—not only that God descends to man, but that man ascends to God. In him the son of man meets the Son of God, the flesh the Divine Reason, the descendant of the beast the substance of the Father; in him manhood is united with Godhead, and the Destiny of all lesser spirits is made manifest. The goal of man stands revealed: human life must realize its Divinity.

That is why he is also the Anointed Head of the Kingdom of God. The greatness of Jesus lay in his claim, not that he was God, but that all men are God—he and they alike are

---

[1] Second-century appendix to Mark, given in Codex W.

sons of God. But whereas their Divinity was potential, his was actual. 'I and my Father are One.'

This towering mystic saw the Universe as 'the City of God', and all men therefore as 'of the City of God'. God is in all living beings and in all Nature, and they in Him. 'Where two or three are gathered together in my name, there am I in the midst of them'; and 'wherever there is one alone, I am with him. Raise the stone, and there thou shalt find me; cleave the wood, and there am I.'[1] Jesus pointed to the commonest people—the hungry, the thirsty, the stranger, the poor, the sick, the prisoner—and said: 'In so far as you did it to one of these my brothers, even to the least, you did it to me.' He took the commonest things of Nature —bread and wine—and said of them: 'This is my body, this is my blood.' And when he identified others with himself, he also identified himself with God. 'Whoso receives one of these little ones in my name receives me, and whosoever receives me receives not me but Him Who sent me.' The same mystical identification occurs when he says: 'Whoever does the Will of God is my brother and sister and mother.'

Men in the this-worldly and the both-worldly civilizations are apt to think of Nature and men and God as three separate orders of Being, without connexion one with another. The Pantheists, on the other hand, perceiving this error, have gone to the other extreme, and deny to Nature and spirits any real existence at all. But Jesus sees Nature and spirits, neither in isolation, nor as illusions, but united with the Divine and so with one another: all things are part of the Whole, and the parts partake in their measure of the Reality of the Whole. Like the Orthodox mystic he sees that 'all is like an ocean, all is flowing and blending',[2] and the ocean is God; like Dante he sees 'the scattered leaves of all the Universe bound by Love in One Volume'.[3]

II. 4

The life and teaching of Jesus, like those of the Buddha and of Socrates, have dominated a great part of mankind.

---

[1] Oxyrhynchus, *Logion* 5.   [2] *The Brothers Karamazov*, p. 340.
[3] *Paradiso*, 33. 87.

They have especially influenced the Nordic, Catholic and Orthodox civilizations of Europe and the New World.

After the death of Jesus his followers felt a new Spirit descend upon them, inspiring them to carry his good news in all directions. It was easy to go East, for Matthew presided over the custom-house at Capernaum in 'Galilee of the Gentiles' on or near the great trade-routes to Persia, India, and China, and Jews promoted the silk trade between Alexandria, Antioch, and China. The Apocryphal Acts of St. Thomas show the Apostle at Andropolis—Purushapura or Peshawar, the City of the Person—in Greek India. It would seem that at this or at a later time Hinduism formulated its doctrine of the Trimurti, Mahayana Buddhism that of its Trinity; while the authors of three of the world's greatest books, the Fourth Gospel, the *Gita*, and the *Lotus*, teach the same doctrine of the Eternal made man, in works whose very construction is similar. It may be that the secret of these missions still lies hidden in the libraries of Mahayana monasteries. The doctrinal disputes of the fifth century sent more missionaries eastward. The Nestorians spread over Asia, and in the seventh century mingled with Confucians, Buddhists, Zarathustrians, Muslims, Manichaeans, and perhaps Jews at Chang-an, the Chinese capital. Perhaps the Mahayana doctrines of salvation by faith in a Personal God and of a Western Paradise may owe something to this encounter. In 1265 the Nestorians had twenty-five Provinces and over seventy dioceses; Marco Polo passed through many of them on his way to China, and found them in many parts of that country. For a thousand years they pervaded Asia, till the invasion of Timur swept them from existence. The Monophysites, less widely spread, still endure.

The mission to the North-West has left a brilliant record in the Letters of Paul and the Acts of the Apostles. Peter became the first Bishop of Rome, the capital of the Empire; his primacy is plain to every reader of the New Testament. Paul with the eye of a statesman laboured to plant churches in Provincial capitals—Antioch, Corinth, Ephesus. From these centres the religion of Jesus spread over the whole Roman Empire, now peaceful and well-roaded, for a time in competition with other faiths and philosophies: Caesar-worship and Stoicism, Gnosticism and Mithraism, Manichaeism and Neo-platonism. After Constantine had established Christianity as the victorious faith it took many pagan elements —as Bede said, 'with the gladness of a new solemnity'—till after four centuries the Quinisext Synod stayed the process.

Ireland was early converted to Christianity, and Irish missionaries carried the faith to Scotland, to North England, and to Germany. From Rome came the Benedictines, Augustine to Canterbury,[1] then Boniface (a Devon man) to Germany,[2] where their monasteries became beautiful islands of labour, learning, and worship. Charlemagne converted Germans, and the Teutonic Knights Prussians and other Slavs, at the sword's point; the Crusaders tried to do the same with the Saracens. Francis carried not the sword but the word to the Sultan and his Muslims. Cyril and Methodius converted the South-Eastern Slavs, St. Vladimir the Russians of the Dnieper. Christianity lost its greatest opportunity when Pope Gregory the Tenth refused the request of Kublai Khan to send a hundred teachers to teach the faith of Christ to China and his vast Empire.

With the Discoveries a new era opened. Dominican friars accompanied the Spanish conquerors. Francis Xavier and the Jesuits carried the Catholic message to India, China, and Japan, to Central, South, and North America, often living and dying with unsurpassable heroism. Protestant missions followed later: Carey led the way in India, Livingstone in Africa. Orthodoxy advanced over Siberia and crossed the sea to Japan.

The good news, as it travelled, has been adapted to the varying capacities of men. Paul presented it in a way that would be understood by the Roman Empire of his day—by Jews, lawyers, Stoics, the initiates of the Mysteries. The Roman Church, long a schoolmaster disciplining wanton Latins and violent Nordics, presented a God Whose Grace reaches mankind principally through sacraments administered by priests. The Northlands, breaking from this uncongenial conception, read in an open Bible of a Moral God

---

[1] A.D. 597.   [2] A.D. 680–754.

Who sanctions a moral society. The mystical Slavs read the good news as the resurrection and transfiguration of all things through mystical union with the Triune Godhead.

The Nestorians abandoned some of the rigour of Orthodox asceticism; the Jesuits, in opposition to the Dominicans, went far to present Catholicism in a Chinese and an Indian dress. To-day Asia and Africa, reading with fresh eyes, see a Gospel that is not coated with piety, and a Jesus who is not overlaid with Theology. A Godlike man walks the earth, to whom mankind may pay joyful allegiance.

While the good news as interpreted by Paul has been the chief teacher of the Catholic and Protestant Worlds, and as interpreted by the Fourth Gospel the chief teacher of Holy Russia, the Synoptic Gospels have hitherto remained largely an undiscovered book. Their amiability indeed was difficult to miss, though the more ferocious Christians—Crusaders, Cameronians—have often missed it. Their wisdom awaits discovery by Man's several wisdoms—moral, moral-spiritual and spiritual—to become the religion of the future that shall unite mankind. 'I if I be lifted up will draw all men unto me.'

III

In the teaching of Socrates and of Jesus the ideals of all the great civilizations are shown as aspects of a single ideal, and in them therefore can be seen the crowning principle of synthesis that may be expected to combine the different civilizations in a single civilization. Man's true welfare, they say, consists in knowing, loving, and enjoying and ultimately in uniting with Reality in all the three forms in which man knows it—Nature, spirits, and God.

But what of this principle itself? Does Nature really exist? Do spirits? Above all, does God? If so, what are they? And in what sense can man be said to know them? Through the experience of the senses? Through the needs of the mind or reason? Through revelation? Through an immediate inner experience? Unless Nature, spirits and God exist, and can be known and loved, the argument rests upon a quagmire.

Each of the great civilizations tends to answer these

questions after its kind. The materialist and the this-worldly civilizations, being principally concerned with things and men, base their answer upon the experience of the senses, as interpreted by science. This view of the Universe is in the ascendancy to-day: and many of those who hold it somewhat naïvely suppose themselves to be the sole prophets of Truth. History, however, shows such views to be provincial; they have arisen in western Europe within the last few centuries, and have only recently spread round the world. At least equally important is the doctrine (to-day neglected) of the agency of spiritual beings or monads in the inanimate and animate worlds. But the greatest place in the history of humanity is occupied by the belief that the Supreme, if not the Only, Reality in the Universe is God. The both-worldly civilizations, being concerned with His Authority and Rule in this world, think of men's knowledge of Him as in the main due to a revelation, within the limits of which reason must work. The other-worldly civilizations, though they may inherit revelations, nevertheless place their principal reliance on reason arguing freely and on the intuitions of an inner and truer self.

III. 1

Is Reality Nature? Yes, cries the animal man; what I can see, hear, touch, smell, know with the senses, is real, and there is nothing more. Everything is mechanical; man is a mechanical product of Nature, and God is a myth. That is the materialist or Communist philosophy; and, though the innate good sense of the Nordics rejects it, they are hard pressed to find defences for their faith in God. The theory that Nature is the one true object of knowledge, and that God and the souls of men are things one can merely 'value', involves the antithesis that truth has no value and that value has no truth. There seems indeed to be no room for God; He maintains a shadowy and precarious existence on the fringe of things, or vanishes altogether. Hence when Darwin knocked out the doctrine of the creation of man by God, the faith of the Nordics was rudely shaken; while modern astronomical theories of the immensity of the Universe are devastating to puny man—the distances of the nebulae and the notion of a receding Universe frighten him. Natural science centres its interests round the body, and in its eyes death awaits the body and dissolution the Universe.

Yet this fear is groundless, for the rational (as opposed to the natural) self knows that Nature would be nothing—or at most a tap-tap of isolated, meaningless sensations—without elements contributed, not by experience, but by mind. It is mind that unites together different sensations—of smell, colour, taste, and so on—into a single body or thing. It is mind which sorts out the chaos of 'things' and orders them in classes—genera and species—a step taken by primitive man. Mind again in primitive man and his successors has taken clashing sensations of colour or sound and the like, and by means of forms and gradations has harmonized them into beauty. Once more, the man of science takes the unintelligible changes in things and makes them intelligible by discovering in them laws of Nature. In all these operations mind is at work striving to discover some unity more satisfactory to itself than the unrelated and therefore chaotic and jarring elements given it by experience. In each of the four cases, experience offers the finite, the changing, the many, and mind discovers in them respectively the one thing, the one kind, the one beauty, the one law.

Clearly mind does not get this desire for unity out of experience; it is in the mind itself *a priori*—beforehand; and without these four *a priori* categories of the understanding or mind neither objects, classes, beauty, nor law could be revealed. Moreover, the only test the mind has or can have as to whether a statement about Nature is true or not, is whether it satisfies this need of the mind for unity: does a law unite two hitherto unrelated things? Then it is true, because it has subdued disorder by combining two discordant things into a single harmonious unit or whole. If mind is to be satisfied, the whole of Nature must be shown to be a unity; the unity of her diverse elements is the sole test of what is true, what is real, in Nature. So much is this the case that Parmenides declared that Nature is a sphere equally extended in every direction; he was thinking of the unity that reason requires, but forgetting the diversity that experience obtrudes. Modern men of science are trying to connect all the sciences and so to discover the one science at the root of them that may explain them all and the objects with which they deal.

The sciences are concerned only with finite objects within Nature. But when mind thinks of Nature itself, it must needs think of a unity that holds all finite objects in its clasp: a unity therefore that is infinite both in space and in time. For, if it were bounded, there would still be space beyond; if it were temporary, there would still be time beyond; and in either case Nature would cease to be the unity mind must think it to be. The notion of some modern scientists that space is bounded would seem only to mean that the finite objects which alone can interest science must always lie within a measurable distance of each other. It is clear therefore that in Nature mind is looking for a single thing that shall be unbounded or infinite, and unchanging or eternal: and that its aim both in art and in science, as well as in the embodying and classifying that are now largely or quite instinctive, is to press a little nearer to this ideal. That is the true meaning and interpretation of these four processes. All point to the infinite and eternal unity that the mind itself requires.

Nature, however, very stubbornly refuses to obey mind, and long holds out against her: everybody knows how difficult it is to classify, or to beautify, or to explain by scientific laws the raw material of Nature. This disorder and ugliness and lawlessness are the defects that experience presents. But Nature has another kind of defect altogether, that no one can ever hope to remedy while Nature remains Nature (for it is inherent in the very ideal of Nature that the mind has formed for itself), namely, that even if perfect it would not be the self-sufficient being that it seems to be. For to itself it is a nonentity, that only ceases to be a nonentity as soon as it is known by another kind of being, namely, a mind or spirit. A spirit is far from being a nonentity to itself. On the contrary, it has a consciousness both of itself and of other existences. Matter depends on mind, not mind on matter. Is then this second kind of being, the conscious mind or spirit of men or other living creatures, the Reality that reason is seeking?

III. 2

Some peoples indeed, very conscious of themselves as spirits, do think of Reality, not as Nature, but as a world of living spirits. Primitive man often does so, and so in large measure until recently did the Chinese; to the early Greeks 'man was the measure of all things', and their gods and other spirits—of mountain and stream, fury and wisdom—took the forms of men and women. Reason's ideal of living spirits—derived, like the ideal of Nature, not from experience, but *a priori*, from the need the mind itself has for Reality—is that they should know (or understand), love, and enjoy; this three-in-one (of which temperance is the condition) constitutes reason. But do men and other spirits conform to it? Alas! no; experience shows that in their egoism and folly they are often as far from the ideal of spirit as material things in their ugliness and disorder are from the ideal of Nature. As a rule they too obviously do not understand, hate instead of love, are unhappy instead of happy. Here again reason sets out to remedy, trying to replace this confusion of wickedness, ignorance, hate and suffering with its ideal of temperance, knowledge, love, and happiness—just as when dealing with Nature it tries to discover in the chaos of the finite, the transient and the many, the body, class, beauty, and law that do something to restore to Nature its ideal unity.

And yet, even if the ideal of spirit be reached, it is again imperfect; for, just as the ideal of Nature required something else to know it, so the ideal of spirit requires something else to know. If Nature is an object in want of a subject, spirits are subjects in want of an object. In each of these two forms of Being, even were its ideal to be reached, reason would be only half satisfied.

III. 3

Is then the Perfect Reality, for which reason is seeking in order to satisfy her inherent demand, neither Nature, nor living spirits, but a Third Kind of Being, God? Many of the poets, thinkers, and seers who have seen deepest, hold that this is so; hold it beyond a shadow of doubt, because this solution satisfies their reason and because they have had direct experience of This Being. But these philosophies and intuitions demand high powers of mind, denied to most men. Lesser men, therefore, impressed by the fact that, while Nature and embodied man are visible through the senses, God is not, have thought it reasonable that He should make a special revelation of Himself beyond any knowledge of Him which unaided reason might be able to attain; and have often taken the poems, the prophecies and the philosophies of other more inspired teachers and canonized them as Divine revelations. The Old Testament, the Quran, the Bible, the *Veda*, the *Tripitaka*—some of them works with very mixed contents—have each been infallibilized as the Word, not of man, but of God, unalterable and all-sufficient. Yet poets and prophets and seers have continued to speak, and their words, like those of less creative teachers, have crept into the canon under the shelter of some great name of old —Job or Daniel or David—or been added to it as Tradition or Creed or Sacred Book. Other great thinkers have tried to interpret revelation in accordance with reason, to rationalize dogma—*credo ut intelligam*: Erigena and Anselm, Sankara and Nagarjuna. Yet others, less clear-sighted, have, like Duns Scotus and William of Occam, tried with best intent to subordinate reason to revelation, and thereby discredited the revelation they sought to exalt; for reason, as history has shown, will not be put to silence and denied her demands. To-day revelations have to accept the competition of other revelations; and choice becomes imperative. It is necessary to compare, to accept this and reject that; again reason bobs up.

Reason, unsatisfied not only with its experience but even with its ideal both of Nature and of spirits, is in search of a Reality that shall be on the one hand Infinite and Eternal and therefore the One and the Whole (for the Unbounded and Unchanging can have nothing beyond It), and on the other That shall know, love, and enjoy Itself, thereby uniting the ideals of Nature and spirit while free from all their defects. Such a Perfect Reality is God. Accordingly reason, when it thinks only of its own needs and not of what its mundane experience thrusts upon it, conceives that God is the One and only Reality, and therefore that Nature and finite spirits can in comparison with God be only unreal. As Spinoza put it: 'It belongs to the very nature of the human mind to know God.'

In God, then, reason comes very near to her goal. Nature and spirits, irrational in their chaos and wickedness, semi-rational as incomplete ideals, find their meaning and completion in Perfect Being; in God, as reason conceives Him, these two fragments are put together. He is, as the Pantheists have discovered, the One, Infinite, Eternal Reality Which, entirely devoid of evil, knows and loves and enjoys Himself—*Sat-Cit-Ananda*, Being-Thought-Bliss. For man Nature and spirits form, as it were, the ladder by which He can be approached, the symbols in which He can be discerned. For it is obvious that the Infinite cannot be grasped in His Entirety, as He really is, by the finite. Only the Infinite can understand the Infinite, only God can understand Himself; so far the Hindu is right in declaring *Neti neti*, the Hebrew Prophet in saying that God's Thoughts are above man's thoughts as the heaven is above the earth. But in the ideal of Nature that art and science and the rest are seeking, man can detect, even though only as in a glass darkly, the Unity, Infinite and Eternal, That is God; in the ideal of man, though again as in a glass darkly, the Wisdom, Love, and Bliss That are the Conscious or Personal Aspect of God.

On the other hand, if God is intelligible to man through Nature and spirit, Nature and spirit are intelligible to him only as they find their final Meaning and Significance in God, the Perfect Ideal That unites their half-ideals and so completes them. The two lower objects are not independent, but completed and perfected in the Highest Object. The reason why 'it belongs to the very nature of the human mind to know God', is now plain: 'for unless we knew God we could know nothing else'. Had we no ideal of God, we should have none of Nature and none of spirits. Neither Nature nor spirits would then exist for man, for it is only through the presence of these ideals in itself that the mind recognizes body, beauty, class and law, wisdom, love and joy and their corresponding evils; without these ideals all experience would be meaningless, even if it could be said to exist, and the thinker's very mind would then itself be nothing.

In other words, the mind does not derive its ideal of Nature and its ideal of spirit from any outward experience, but *a priori* from the depth of itself; and it finds these in itself because there is in itself that Perfect and Complete Ideal which is God. The mind itself begets these incomplete ideals; and without their consummation in the Ideal of God neither they nor the mind which evolves them would exist.

In conceiving, however, of God as the Perfect Whole and All of Being, uniting the ideals both of Nature and of spirits, it has conceived of One to Whom nothing distinct from Himself can ever be added. The separate existence of the reasoning self is thus inconsistent with the God Whom it conceives. Accordingly, in a super-rational experience the self must lose its distinction from God and, dying to itself, become a Self That realizes that It is not distinct from Him, but His Very Self. 'All that He has, all that He is, He gives; all that we have, all that we are, He takes.' On this ultimate height of human experience—now no longer mundane but mystic—Subject and Object cease to be separated. Man has ceased to be man, and with an 'unknowing knowing', above reason's knowing, has become One with the Father: 'I and my Father are One.'[1]

Thus the arguments of philosophy bring the soul to the gateway of its highest experience, its fullness, its bliss, but they do not enter it; for in argument there is still separation. The approach to the Divine remains incomplete until the whole spirit of man is at one with the Divine Spirit in an inseparable union. Travelling upward, by an increasing realization of the significance of his *a priori* knowledge of Nature and of spirits, to the Divine reason within him, he at length becomes aware that he is himself Divine, a participant of the Divine Nature, a son of God. Now he can say with the Hindu: 'That art thou', and understand Socrates when he bids man 'know himself'. This can never be set forth in literal or scientific language, but only in poetic myths or images, as Plato and the mystics know. 'The Idea of the Good' cannot be described; the Infinite Godhead

[1] Evelyn Underhill, *Mysticism*, pp. 430, 437.

is an Impenetrable Darkness,[1] a Mystery Ineffable. 'He that speaks does not know, and he that knows does not speak.'

Embodied man cannot sustain for long his union with the Divine: 'not for this were my proper wings.'[2] Yet this Supreme Reality transfigures all who have once been united to It. The results of the union are twofold, inner and outer. It gives the soul a sense of joyousness and liberty that is full of laughter and music;[3] just as one feels one's own weal and woe (says Sankara), so the spirit feels the Bliss of God. It gives a victorious power in lighting and leading the world of men and things that only those can possess whose souls are united with the Divine. The blessed spirits (says Suso), dwelling within the Ocean of the Divine Love,

'are stripped of their personal initiative, and changed into another form, another glory, another power. What then is this other form, if it be not the Divine Nature and the Divine Being Whereinto they pour themselves, and Which pours Itself into them, and becomes one thing with them? And what is that other glory, if it be not to be illuminated and made shining in the Inaccessible Light? What is that other power, if it be not that, by means of his union with the Divine Personality, there is given to man a Divine strength and a Divine power, that he may accomplish all which pertains to his blessedness and omit all which is contrary thereto? And thus it is that a man comes forth from his selfhood.'[4]

More than that. The animal mind thinks that the soul can die, because the body dies. But the mind that realizes that its own existence involves the existence of the Eternal knows also that it can never die. To the mystic this argument becomes experience. At the moment of its union with the Godhead the soul realizes that, being one with the Eternal, it is itself eternal. This experience of the mystics is the final, certain and unshakable ground for man's knowledge of the indestructibility of the spirit. Man is eternal because he is Divine. 'A man (says Tauler) who really and truly enters the Abyss feels as though he had been here throughout Eternity, and as though he were one Therewith.'[5]

[1] Eckhart.   [2] Dante, *Paradiso*, 33. 139.
[3] E. Underhill, *Mysticism*, p. 437.   [4] *Book of Truth*, quoted ibid., p. 424–5.
[5] Sermon on St. John the Baptist (*The Inner Way*, pp. 97–9), quoted ibid., p. 339.
For the argument of this section, see K. J. Spalding, *Talks on Philosophy*.

VII

THE COMING OF THE KINGDOM

SUCH then is the progress hitherto made by the different civilizations of mankind, and such the goal of progress as defined by its greatest teachers. There remains the practical problem, how to get from half-way-house to journey's end—from the unrelated diversity of the present to the diversified unity of the future.

To-day the situation of mankind is critical. The Sovereign State has broken down, just as the Greek city-state once broke down; and with it has gone, now as then, the environment hitherto suited to man's spiritual development. But the situation has never before been equally critical, because the technical developments of science, far surpassing any control of Nature the world has ever known before, have brought face to face the social, and with them the spiritual, interests of the whole earth. Science now gives man opportunities, on the one hand for destruction, on the other for development, such as have never hitherto been dreamed of. In the hand of wickedness or folly it can wipe out civilization and reduce the world to chaos; in the hand of good will and good sense it can abolish poverty and lay the material foundation on which the free spirit can rear undreamed-of splendours. So that there can be seen to-day, perhaps more clearly than at any other time, the contrast between the materialist and the moral society, the one only capable of war, the other desirous only of peace. Contrast what is happening to-day with the kind of State that Isaiah envisaged in his prophecy and that Jesus envisaged in his Gospel—the lamb shall lie down with the lion, God's Will shall be done on earth as it is in Heaven.

All this has taken mankind suddenly and unawares, like an avalanche. A crisis has, for the first time in history, come upon the world at once. The nations are now like beasts herded together in a cage, and without a keeper. Roman civilization could go down without affecting Chinese civilization; a broad ocean once hid America from Europe. Now, because of the facilities of communication, mankind is in the same boat, and must either founder together, or pull round together: crash to World-Ruin, or climb to World-Renaissance.

The fundamental question is: which of these two forces will prove victorious? Will society in the main follow its materialist or its idealist leaders?

I

The good things of this world are strictly limited, whereas man's desires for them, unless controlled by moral desires, are (as Plato pointed out) unlimited, and likely to clash. If two men set their hearts on the same girl, they cannot both marry her; if two nations set their hearts on the same territory, they cannot both own it. Materialist desires—desires that are not controlled by reason, the knowledge and love of one's fellows—are incompatible, nor will men, classes or nations that are in the grip of them have anything to restrain them; they will pursue their own power and wealth at the expense of others with an egoism that they term 'sound' or even 'sacred'. This egoism will make them hate all those who oppose them, and incubate a like hatred in others. It will also make them both ignorant and foolish. They will not see the Universe as it really is. They will study Nature, not for herself or for the service of man, but for the making of armaments or for economic autarchy. Instead of caring for men, they will form 'alliances', 'axes', and 'fronts' with other nations, that will lead to crises and wars, and will endure only so long as the parties think they will serve their own selfish interests. If they believe in God at all, they will respect Him only as an Ally of the State in these ambitions. This ignorance will cause them to make foolish mistakes, for those who cannot see clearly size up a situation wrongly. The conceited nation, like the conceited man, thinks it can do all sorts of things that it cannot do; both are riding for a fall. As Antony puts it:

> 'When we in our viciousness grow hard,
> (O misery on't!) the wise gods seel our eyes;
> In our own filth drop our clear judgments; make us
> Adore our errors; laugh at's while we strut
> To our confusion.'[1]

[1] *Antony and Cleopatra*, III. xi, 111–15.

Thus the cardinal 'virtues' of the Materialist State, as of the materialist man, are the three cardinal vices of the Buddhist—egoism, hatred, and a stupidity that plumes itself on being wise. Evil divides mankind.

There is no law of human history—any more than of zoological history—that implies the necessity of uninterrupted progress, the inevitability of evolution: dissolution is a possibility as well as development. Species which have seemed the strongest have perished, while weaker species have persisted, and civilization itself, which has only had a history of a few thousand years, may, because of its complexity and the strength of its disintegrating forces, conceivably crumble into a society as rudimentary as that from which it arose. Were the materialists to be victorious, it seems likely that the end would be the destruction of the Sovereign States, the political units in which man now lives; and with this man would lose his vigour, as he did when the Greek city-states decayed. Dark ages of uncreative chaos would return.

It may be indeed the Plan and Purpose of Almighty Wisdom to lead man by suffering to a knowledge of Himself. Nevertheless men, lacking the Divine Wisdom, dare not take upon themselves the responsibility of deeming that mankind needs such agony, and of allowing it to come. Only when they have expended their fullest strength to promote understanding and brotherhood dare they say that war is sent of God to purify mankind of its materialism. Yet if war and the ruin of war should so come, they may accept it with tranquil minds, seeing the Reality behind the show, working in calm confidence for the Commonwealth that is to be. Men do not live by the deeds about them; they live by the dream that is in their hearts. Where there is no vision the people perish,[1] but old men shall dream dreams and young men shall see visions.[2] The Kingdom of Heaven is not only in the future: it is here in the midst of all anguish for the eyes that are open to see it.

Should war now overturn civilization, the chaos of the world will resemble that of the Roman Empire when Rome fell before the Goths. It was the agony of that age that

---

[1] Proverbs xxix. 18.   [2] Joel ii. 28.

showed Augustine the progress of mankind from the Empire of pagan Rome to the 'one Commonwealth of all Christian men'. It was out of this vision that there arose— through long centuries of suffering—the splendour of the Catholic Church and of Catholic civilization. If our world crashes, new Augustines will arise to point mankind to the one Commonwealth of all true men. Reason cannot rest in misery; sooner or later she must once again lift her heart and head.

II

But it by no means follows that civilization will succumb to war. Rather, it is likely that war will succumb to civilization. A beast will sometimes get the better of man; but man on the whole gets the better of the beast. So rational man— moral and spiritual man—will get the better of animal man, the Moral and Spiritual State of the Biological and Materialist State. Evil wins battles, but Good wins campaigns.

To-day, as in the past, it is becoming apparent that the feet of the Dictatorships are of clay. Although the forces of materialism are strident, their clamour is raised to drown the harmony they deprecate; for in the totalitarian States, as elsewhere, good will and good sense are decidedly stronger than the blind hatred towards other nations or other classes that the Dictators inculcate so strenuously. The Dictatorships at least keep social life in existence: Marxism is the chrysalis of a truth; the older nation-states preserve the principle of individual liberty. The victory of the party of reason may therefore be expected to lead to the revival of nationhood founded on its own Good, moral or spiritual, and consequently to the nations uniting rather than competing with each other; the end of this movement being a single organism of which the limbs are the several nations and faiths, each in health, and each therefore working with and for the whole.

But if civilization is to be saved, such a new spirit must be aroused in man as was, in course of time, aroused in the earlier civilizations. China after the Chou reforms disintegrated in the Spring and Autumn Period and that of the Warring States, tried Dictatorship and found it wanting, and discovered it could live a better family and clan life when What-Is-Under-Heaven was united by Confucian morality under the Son of Heaven. The Greek city-states broke down, and after wars of kings and generals learned to think and act as cities and tribes that owed allegiance to a peaceful World-Empire. Rome itself, after its fall before the Goths and dark ages of barbarism, renewed the life of country and city in 'one Commonwealth of all Christian men'. In the same way the safety of modern civilization need not be despaired of, if there be aroused in its peoples a sense at once of a national and a supernational allegiance.

If this is to come to pass there must arise leaders—speculative and practical—competent to conceive and to realize this notion of a Commonwealth of Nations, a 'City of Zeus'; and peoples ready to follow such shepherds, because they respect and trust them. If the realization of both these conditions seems at the moment very difficult, yet it is by no means unlikely. For it is when evil raises its head and is making men's hearts to faint that the saviours of men have commonly appeared; and it is when men faint that they are willing to renounce the desires that have misled them, and, putting on the spirit of temperance, to follow the teachings of these leaders.

Such leaders leading, and such people following, there may arise—there surely will arise—a culture more worthy of the name of civilization than any that has yet appeared. For this will be, though infinitely diverse, one civilization and not many; a civilization without barbarians or Gentiles or foreigners; a civilization in which that competition alone will be respected that serves, or at least does not injure, others; a civilization, consequently, in which the things of the spirit flourish and the things of the body are not disregarded; in short, a civilization which understands and respects and is guided by that greatest of all practical principles: 'Seek ye first the kingdom of God and His Righteousness, and all these things shall be added unto you.'

For this consummation two things are needed: a 'change of mind' in all States, but especially in those that deliberately make the power and wealth of the State their supreme end; and a synthesis of the different kinds of Good which the Moral, Moral-Spiritual, and Spiritual States contribute respectively to the welfare of humanity. At present the Materialist States mistake the nature of Reality; the Moral and Spiritual States see, some one aspect of it, some another. The time is therefore come for mankind to make a deliberate effort to release and realize the ideal set before it by its greatest teachers, Gotama, Socrates, and Jesus, and by reason itself: namely, to know and love and enjoy Reality as a Whole, and in seeking that Whole itself to become united.

This moral and spiritual ideal cannot be advanced without purging society of those materialist impulses and ignorances that split it asunder. Unlimited desires for limited things cannot be satisfied, and inevitably breed rivalries and conflicts. The result is misery for multitudes, and unstable joys for an ambitious few. On the other hand, Reality is unlimited, and the desire for it can always be satisfied; it is organic, and therefore all true Renaissance is organic too. The only principle, therefore, capable of securing the unified and organized life of mankind, as of a man, is reason—virtue with its three sides, regulative, intellectual, and emotional, and the satisfaction that it brings. In its first stage reason, overcoming the egoism, stupidity, and hate of the Materialist State and of the materialist man, with their miseries and evanescent pleasures, shows itself as the moral virtues— self-discipline, clear-sightedness, and respect for others, with the peace and plenty that are their fruits. The result is happiness. Then, as soon as temperance has been attained and animal desires no longer even tempt, the moral develop into the spiritual virtues—the wisdom and love that, springing from temperance, produce a spiritual culture, a world of men of genius, who appreciate things and living spirits, not merely as they affect daily life, but in and for themselves. This is the stage of philosophy and imagination. Knowledge, and therefore love, apprehend more and more sides of Reality, in any or all of its three fields; and therefore the soul that knows and loves becomes more and more diversified while it remains essentially one. Thus, reason is the unifier that both discovers and combines innumerable diversities, in societies and in individuals. Here the result is joy. Last stage of all, those who, far above temptation, are united with the Godhead by an 'intellectual love' see all things issuing from Him and returning to Him: as one, therefore, with Him, and so with one another. The crowning result has been attained: bliss, rapture, ecstasy, everlasting felicity, the blessedness of God Himself. 'Truth, as it develops Itself in men and so makes them Divine, shows Itself as a harmonious activity throughout the world, in such fashion that every individual must seek for his own expression of the Truth and harmonize this expression with every other expression of It.'[1] In so far as men attain Truth, they attain unity: when men are 'sanctified by the Truth', they will 'all be one'.[2]

While, therefore, evil divides, Good unites: knowledge and love are as binding as wars and greed are disruptive. There is no such incompatibility between the various contributions that the Moral and Spiritual States make to the Good of mankind, as there is between the competitive ambitions of the Materialist States. On the contrary, they supplement each other; for if Reality is one, every one of its parts must harmonize with all the others. If therefore different kinds of Good seem to conflict, it is because either pride makes us adore our errors, or the powers of our mind are as yet too weak to penetrate the facts. If pride is purged and the desire for Truth energetically cultivated, the severing error will presently vanish and the real harmony become manifest. 'Right desires' and the energy they awaken are the condition of all Renaissance, whether local or world-wide.

If, therefore, in the selfish pursuit of material things men inevitably draw apart, in drawing nearer to Truth, to Good, to Reality—they will (as the Abbot Dorotheus said) inevitably draw nearer to one another. The beauties and the laws of Nature, and the arts and sciences to which they give birth, know no frontiers, notwithstanding that each land or city may attend to its own special aspect of them. A knowledge of the character and civilizations of their neighbours gives men understanding and therefore respect and love for

---

[1] L. P. Karsavin, who writes, however, 'throughout the *Christian* world'. Quoted by an English Europasian, *Russia in Resurrection*, p. 248.

[2] Fourth Gospel, xvii. 19, 21.

one another, and they direct their policy accordingly. As they study the Divine Nature, they see that God is not a National Ally or the Patron of a favourite, but a Universal Father, the Infinite and Eternal Source of all created beings. Thus the ideals of the Moral, Moral-Spiritual and Spiritual States—the States themselves in so far as they are temperate—are all compatible one with another, indeed, the complements of one another; the diversities of education, social structure, and religion to which they have given rise cannot merely be reconciled, they complete each other. The *disjecta membra* are not really *disjecta*; to the eye that is open they will be seen as the different limbs and members of a single organism. Doubtless the huge task of synthesis will be the work of a host of men and women labouring through the centuries, the powers of their mind increased as their hearts are purged of evil. But already this ideal may stand before them: the pursuit of the Good as a Whole will unite men in a single Commonwealth, which will more and more tend to become a religious community. Indeed, it is necessary that it should stand before them; for, unless mankind knows where it wants to arrive, its course will be zig-zagging and uncertain.

Only when there is this inner organic unity of mind and aim will outward forms be organic too. Khomiakov distinguishes between the external unity of the Church manifested in the communion of sacraments, and the internal unity of spirit—the faith, hope, and charity that anticipate the knowledge, love, and joy that are reason; the outer bond can be dispensed with, the inner is essential.[1] Similarly, in the Renaissance of the world and of its several parts it is always the same inner bond that is essential; the outer bonds of organization and institution are of value only in so far as they spring from and express the moral and spiritual life of men and of the societies they form.

Part of the mind sees part of Reality, and the mind that is wholly developed sees Reality as a Whole. Similarly, every rational civilization sees part of Reality; a fully rational civilization would put the fragments together and see the

[1] In Birkbeck, *Russia and the English Church*, pp. 212, 222.

Whole. To bring about a Renaissance in the full sense, therefore, three things are needed: to resuscitate the Good that each civilization sees, to harmonize it with the Good of others, and finally to unite every kind of Good until reason made whole sees Reality as a Whole. Thus Renaissance is of three kinds, that pass into and imply one another: Neo-Renaissance, Xeno-Renaissance, and World-Renaissance. To these correspond respectively three kinds of pseudo-Renaissance: Archaism, Deracination and Externalism.

II. 1

First, then, this ideal, far from steam-rolling to a dead uniformity the very diverse moral and spiritual civilizations that have sprung out of primitive society, will on the contrary develop to the utmost the native genius of each, whether in the field of education, politics, or religion. The history both of East and West has many examples of Neo-Renaissances, spontaneous developments of the original civilization—Neo-Confucianism, Neo-Paulinism and its offspring Neo-Thomism, Neo-Vedantism, Neo-Buddhism, Neo-Platonism. All illustrate the vitality of the central idea that gives each civilization its distinctive character.

Not indeed that every return to the past is a true Renaissance: there may be a mere copying or imitation of the externals of a dead past that misses its essence, a pseudo-Renaissance that may be called Archaism. Or there may be a clinging to old forms long after the life has gone out of them, a sticking to tradition that is no longer organic but has become dead matter: in a word, Reaction. Archaism may hark back to primitive barbarism, as does the modern music that strikes kettles and drums, the modern sculpture that models as it were in soap. In the twentieth century the last Kaiser still thought of the government of Germany in feudal terms, the last Tsarina of the government of Russia in terms of absolute Autocracy. To-day the German Faith Movement revives the mythology of Odin and Thor. Even the Anglo-Catholic movement, though it seeks to draw inspiration from a noble civilization, has perhaps succeeded in capturing the externals of sacrament and the ritual of worship rather than the immense vision of God and the

Universe that sent the Clunyites to reform the world, produced the new Orders and the Friars, took shape in Scholasticism and gave birth to the Universities, and found beautiful expression in the Cathedrals and the Comedy. A retrospective mimicry can never be a substitute for original vitality.

It so chances that almost every great civilization has preserved very early books, all of which depict men of fundamentally the same character and outlook as those who have succeeded them through the ages. The Book of Songs and the Book of History already show the essential characteristics of the Chinese, the Germania and the Saga those of the Nordics. The early Hebrew songs and histories and the early poetry of the Arabs anticipate Israel and the Enlightenment, Roman history and Paul's letters Catholicism. The Vedas foreshadow India, the Epic Songs Russia, Homer Athens. The characteristics thus shown in the beginning revive again and again in new forms in response to the challenge of new circumstances. The effort of the Confucians to cope with the Legalists produced Hsun-Tze and the Neo-Confucians of the Han; contact with Taoism and Buddhism produced the Neo-Confucianism of Chu-Hsi and other Sung philosophers. The absolutism of the Stuarts produced the Neo-Parliamentarianism of Pym and Hampden, the absolutism of the Tories the Neo-Parliamentarianism of the Reform Act. As in the moral, so in the spiritual sphere. The fall of Rome stimulated the Neo-Paulinism of Augustine; the incoming of the Scythians the Neo-Buddhism of the Paradise Books; the withering of Buddhism the Neo-Vedantism of Sankara and later Commentators; the challenge of the West the Neo-Vedantism of Ramakrishna and Vivekananda.

Not all the wearing of time nor the inflowing of other civilizations can obliterate this native genius. Notwithstanding the influences that Buddhism, Hellenism, and Christianity have exerted in the past and that Europe is exerting to-day, every civilization is still tenacious of its original ideal. China still reverences the scholar and expects to find in him her leader; she still shows her traditional temperance, and believes in righteousness as the principle of government.

The Jews, in a Dispersion of two thousand years, maintain the Law unbroken by persecution; the Wahabis base themselves on the puritanism of the Prophet. The ideal of India is still the rishi, the yogi, the sadhu; Mahatma Gandhi, preaching the doctrine of non-violence and soul-force, rules her not as a statesman but as a saint.

Nor is it probable, judging from the past, that any changes of time and tide, however violent, will suffice to wash away the original characteristics. Western nationalism is not destroying, but modifying, Chinese civilization, as Buddhism modified it in the past. It is not destroying, but modifying, Turkish, Arabian, and Indian civilization, as Muslim or Greek civilization modified them in the past. The culture of Holy Russia retains its essentials, for all the coatings of red paint with which the Bolsheviks camouflage it. 'An unbelieving reformer will never do anything in Russia, even if he is sincere in heart and a genius. The people will meet the atheist and overcome him, and Russia will be one and Orthodox. For the peasant has God in his heart.'[1] To be true to itself, each civilization must first purify itself of the elements of selfishness and superstition that now defile it: of the deadness or deadliness of its education, of the injustices that canker its social life, of its international callousness or selfishness, of the irrationalities that pollute its religion.

> That man's the best Conservative
> Who lops the moulder'd branch away.

And when the mouldered branch is gone, the tree will of its own strength feel the stirring of new growth, and break into fresh leaf and life as spring comes round again. The West is indeed in little danger of forgetting its past; Britons and Americans, for instance, will not drop the free constitution that had its origin in far-off centuries, for all the charmings of current fashion. But the East, as the West floods over it, has a special duty to preserve and strengthen everything that is true in its own cultures. If it is good for the Nordics to resist the lures of Communism and Fascism, it is no less good for Eastern communities to build their political systems upon their own and not upon imported

[1] Dostoievsky, *The Brothers Karamazov*, p. 334.

institutions. Some of the experienced Sheikhs who govern
the tribes of Irak may be illiterate, but they come of governing stocks and command the esteem of their tribesmen; they
are likely to govern better than a Chamber of Deputies
where elections are 'made' by an educated urban intelligentsia. The Hinayana and the Mahayana monasteries of South-
East and East Asia, the asrams and hermitages of India,
have a great part to play in the revival of the life of religion
in their own and in other lands. The first duty of the civilizations of Asia is indeed to preserve and revive the great
ethical and religious philosophies to which they have given
birth, together with the literature and art in which these
have expressed themselves. As an outward and visible sign
of a restoration of pristine vigour and self-respect, the civilizations of the East may well begin their Neo-Renaissance by
abandoning the ugly and unsuitable clothes of the West for
their own lovely raiment.

II. 2

But things were created different that they may meet.
Not all fruits grow on one tree; a great deal of grafting can
profitably be done. If the staple food of the mind must be
home-grown, the banquet of life is made richer and more
varied by delicacies imported from abroad.

It by no means follows that all borrowing is profitable.
It profits only on condition that the native civilization is
retained as the stock on which the alien shoot is grafted; for,
if the original is neglected or despised, men are left without
a criterion of what is good or bad in itself, suitable or unsuitable to their own culture. They can no longer distinguish
between the essential and the unessential, and so, in their
passion for what is foreign, borrow indiscriminately and
without understanding. Just as Archaism is the false form
of Neo-Renaissance, so Deracination is the false form of
Xeno-Renaissance. When the native growth is uprooted,
weeds take its place.

The chief exponents of this type of pseudo-Renaissance
to-day are the Westernizing Intelligentsias of the East. Thus
the Chinese Intelligentsia have for a time been tempted to
abandon their Confucianism, the Japanese their Buddhism,

the Egyptian Islam, the Indian the Vedanta. The Russian Westernizers have since the death of Peter the Great more and more despised the religion that is the heart of Holy Russia, together with the theology, the arts, and the customs in which it has taken splendid shape.

Meanwhile—in an indiscriminate admiration of the West —the Intelligentsias have taken over institutions and ideas that never had anything to recommend them anywhere. The young African and the young Burmese scorn the marvellous forests and forest lore of their fathers to serve, black-coated and literate, on office stools in towns. The Intelligentsias have introduced Communism into China, military and economic nationalism into Japan, the Police State and State interference in Church government into Russia. The untutored savage of the past would barter gems for beads or bottles; the unenlightened intellectuals of to-day renounce the moral and spiritual treasures of the East for the worthless or mischievous baubles of the West.

Again, what is excellent in itself and admirably suited to the country in which it originates may be misinterpreted and misapplied by another. The reason is that its essence lies hidden in the back of the minds of its originators—merely to copy its externals is to parody and pervert it. An African chief with two hundred wives is converted to Christianity. That seems too many for a Christian convert; but this Christian, beaming, has lived up to his creed—he has already strangled a hundred and ninety-nine. More civilized peoples have been hardly less crude. The British Constitution has been more often admired than understood; for it is mainly the British character, and the Constitution can be transplanted only if the character can be transplanted too. Hence Parliamentary Government, while it has succeeded in Scandinavia, Holland, the British Dominions, and the United States, where it is a native growth rooted in character, has gone to pieces in Japan, Italy, Spain, and Russia. Spanish intellectuals dominating the Cortes of 1931 went so far and so fast as to confound and dumbfound the country. The Russian 'Cadets', steeped in book learning, knew everything about the British Parliamentary system except what was worth knowing. They legislated for an Empire the size of

a continent as though it were an island the size of Great
Britain; for peoples without political interest or political
experience as though they were adepts in politics; at a speed
that would put through in a session a legislative programme
that Great Britain would have spread over centuries. Russian Nihilists, stimulated by the publication of *The Origin of
Species*, regarded the laws of Nature as all-sufficient, and
accordingly scrapped the laws of the State, the laws of
morality, and the laws of religion. Divorced from understanding, science begot an illegitimate family of bombs,
immorality, and atheism.   Knowledge brought other things,
but not its own self—as with Milton's foolish reader, who

> 'Uncertain and unsettled still remains,
> Deep-versed in books and shallow in himself,
> Crude or intoxicate.'

It follows that a genuine Xeno-Renaissance must graft on
to the native civilization what is at once good in itself and
capable of assimilation. In these cases there is no mere copying or imitation, but a genuine absorption and a new creation. It may, indeed, be an open question whether the
borrowing is appropriate or not. Did Buddhism enrich Confucianism or corrupt it? Chang Che-tung had a genuine
Xeno-Renaissance in mind when he said that Chinese learning was moral and Western learning scientific or practical,
and wished to supplement the one with the other.[1] Persian
painting owes to China its fascinating dragons and wisps of
cloud, and the vigorous line and energetic movement of its
horses, horsemen, and battle scenes; yet it remains distinc-
tively Persian. Virgil and Horace did not merely copy
Greek poetry and Greek metres—they re-created them as
Roman poetry. The nations of Europe, powerfully influenced by Italian painting, nevertheless produced, not imitations, but genuine German, Flemish, Dutch, English,
French, and Spanish art. The Graeco-Roman Renaissance
was a genuine Renaissance, because each nation adapted it to
its own genius. Turguenev Russianized the forms of French
literature as truly as Horace Latinized the lyrical forms of
Greece. Pushkin transmuted the spirit of Byron, and Tolstoy

---

[1] Gascoigne Cecil, *Changing China*, p. 267.

that of George Eliot, as thoroughly as Shakespeare natural-
ized in England the histories of Plutarch and the tales of
Boccacio.

What is true of education and literature is true also of
politics. 'Indirect Rule' is not destroying the native life of
Africa and of the Dutch East Indies, but impregnating it
with the best elements in British, French, and Dutch self-
government. Chinese reconstruction and Indian *sva-raj*
have had the good sense to avail themselves of British
experience and advice. While the forms of the British Constitution do not always suit foreign digestions, its spirit
agrees with them well. 'Civil and religious liberty' enriched
the French Revolution, Social Reform the New Deal.

Above all, thought can fertilize thought. The influence
of Greece upon Israel kindled the Kabbala and Maimonides;
upon Islam, the Muslim Renaissance and Sufism. Aristotle, collated with the 'Sentences' of the Fathers and baptized into Christ, enriched the Catholic Renaissance with a
wider-ranging Scholasticism. The Greater Buddhism, assi-
milating Hinduism, looked, at Taxila toward the Personal
God, at Nalanda toward the Eternal Godhead, and produced
the *Lotus* and the Intuitive Perfection. Orthodoxy has
absorbed into itself much of the mystical truth that underlies
Pantheism and bodhisatship.

Hitherto, East and West have between them boxed the
compass of error, the East in an excessive zeal for Westernization, the West in an indifference to the treasures of the
East. The time has come to adjust the balance. If Neo-
Renaissance is the special task of the over-Westernized
civilizations of the East, Xeno-Renaissance is that of the
self-centred civilizations of the West. In particular, it is for
the Schools and Universities of Europe and America, especially for the Universities whose tradition is predominantly
humanistic, to study the wisdom of the East. The Nordic
and Latin civilizations depend largely for their excellence on
what they have learned from Palestine, Rome, and Greece.
This pasture is still as sweet as ever if freshly cropped. But
they have now chewed the cud so long that it is losing its
savour; and it is absurd that Western studies should be
restricted to these three familiar civilizations, when the

unfamiliar civilizations of China and Japan, of Arabia and Persia, of Hinduism, Buddhism, and Orthodoxy lie green before the hungry mind. From China they will learn that fellow-feeling begets righteousness, and that righteousness is the foundation of good government: a principle that will fundamentally affect both home and foreign policy—leading at home to the friendly feeling between classes from which spring the redress of grievances and social services, and abroad to the 'good neighbourliness' that assuages strife and draws the nations together. From India they will learn that man is in his true nature a *bodhisat*, a saviour who sees all living beings as his other selves; that work is a sacrament that opens the eyes to a Moral God, through Whom is at last revealed the Eternal Godhead That is Bliss Supreme.

II. 3

Neo-Renaissance and Xeno-Renaissance are the father and mother of World-Renaissance. During a long gestation it is already in being, presently to be born to the light of day.

World-Renaissance consists in the organic union of the diverse excellencies of all existing civilizations, both moral and spiritual, purged of the vices that now hold them apart. In other words, it is an effort of each civilization so to expand itself that it may see, love, and enjoy, not only (like the Moral States) Nature and man, not only (like the Spiritual States) man and God, but Nature, man and God: it is an effort of the reason of mankind as a whole to apprehend Reality as a whole. World-Renaissance may therefore be defined as the completion of Xeno-Renaissance. It will come about through the perfecting by each civilization of every good element in it—and not merely of that element of good which most distinguishes it. Xeno-Renaissance implies a less complete Neo-Renaissance, World-Renaissance the perfected Neo-Renaissance of every civilization.

Otherwise, as in the case of Neo-Renaissance and Xeno-Renaissance, a false Renaissance will occur that may be called Externalism. Externalism is a uniting that is superficial or syncretic only, not organic. World-Renaissance seeks to combine the compatible, syncretism to combine the incompatible. Indeed, all pseudo-Renaissance belongs to this genus: the error both of Archaism and of Deracination is that they seek something that is merely external to the real life of the civilization that gave them birth. In World-Renaissance this Externalism may take several forms. In States conscious of their political disunion and futility, in contrast with the unity and success achieved by most Nordic Powers, it may take the violent form of a totalitarianism imposed by a Leader and his Party, whose forcible regimentation of the people is reinforced by an education and propaganda that dope instead of developing the activities of the mind. Yet both Germans and Italians, as the pages of Tacitus and the history of Rome show, have a natural aptitude for self-government that the accidents of politics have temporarily suppressed, and that would be revealed in a World-Renaissance. All materialist policy, relying as it does on force and contemptuous as it is of reason, is as such alien from organic development, and therefore an extreme form of Externalism; despite an appearance of uniformity, it creates disunion everywhere—disorder abroad and discontent at home. In democracies Externalism may take the form of a reliance upon mere laws, institutions, or policy—this or that specific for political disunion or economic injustice—instead of upon the sense of political brotherhood and love of justice that alone can give life to institutions and policy. In the Churches again, conscious that other Churches possess gifts that they themselves lack, Externalism may take the form of ambiguous and therefore empty formulae for reunion, so resulting in a spurious union; though even merely verbal agreements, however unreal, are evidence of a desire of one community to draw nearer to another, and so have some reality of charity beneath an appearance of intellectual agreement.

Examples will best point the distinction between the organic and the syncretic, the reality of unity and its appearance.

Already there is much underlying unity beneath the outward diversities of the civilizations, though the ordinary man is generally as little aware of it as Monsieur Jourdain

was that he was talking prose. The Chinese study the Confucian Classics, the British the classics of Palestine, Greece,
and Rome. But few realize that these seemingly different
peoples are educated upon the same fundamental plan—the
study of the principles of right living, and their embodiment
in great men, in good government, in literature, and in the
arts. The Chinese are trained in the life of the large family,
the British in the life of the Public School and College. In
both cases, the strains and stresses of a common life discipline the character and teach men to respect each other. On
the other hand, the Soviet Universities where Chinese and
Indians are taught Communism, afford an example of syncretic education; for materialist principles cannot be welded
to moral or spiritual principles otherwise than superficially,
and the result (if any) is to produce abnormality and confusion in the minds of the unfortunate students.

So in the political field. The British and other Nordics
early learned to discover and redress the grievances of the
subject, to educate the people gradually for self-government,
and in the process to set Government parleying with people
and class parleying with class. These living moral activities
gradually took to themselves appropriate forms, which have
never ossified, but, like every healthy living organism, con-
tinuously adapt themselves to the changes of the day: the
election of representatives, Parliaments, Ministerial responsibility, Colonial self-government, Dominion status, Federal
Union and the like. It is the spirit of such government, not
its forms, that is essential. Parleying, for instance, is more
important than Parliament; where men are unwilling to
parley, no Parliament can succeed. Now the Chinese reconstruction of 1930 to 1937 had little of the appearance of
Parliamentary democracy, but much of the reality: the
redress of local grievances, the period of political tutelage,
the constant intercourse between Government and people
on the vital problems of the day—above all, the realization
that a 'new life' was the first essential of a new democracy.
On the other hand, the Weimar Constitution of 1919 had
all the appearance of democratic government—to please
the Allies something was taken from every existing democratic Constitution—universal suffrage, local and central

Parliaments, plebiscites and the like. But the essence or reality was absent—the redress of grievances, the gradual training of the people, a sovereign Government that more and more taught the different classes of its citizens to parley with itself and one another. It is not any superficial imitation, but the same moral spirit expressing itself in forms adapted to its environment, that can genuinely unite the people of a country or the peoples of the world.

Similarly, the chief or sheikh administering justice to his tribesmen is much nearer the spirit of the Council described by Tacitus, the original seed from which Parliamentary government grew, than the Parliaments longed for by westernized effendis in Bagdad or doctrinaire Liberals in London. Americans, again, do not superficially resemble the Chinese; but President Roosevelt has insisted, with all the strength and insight of a Confucius, on the fundamental need of ethics in social life, and the unreality of ethics that do not express themselves in social relations. On the other hand, Mussolini's Roman Empire, were he to realize it, would be the old Roman Empire only in name, its antithesis in reality. For the Empire founded by Augustus was based on the freedom and diversity of the cities and tribes within it; the Fascist Empire is totalitarian, an enemy to such freedom and diversity. Augustus's Empire was an Empire of light taxes and small armies, whose aim was to preserve 'the majesty of peace'; the Fascist Empire is an Empire of heavy taxes and large armies, whose aim is to disturb a peace-loving community. In sum, the old Roman Empire, supplanting wars, stood for freedom and peace; the new Roman Empire, supplanting peace, stands for regimentation and war. The spirit of Roman greatness lives in the League of Nations; the Fascists are the counterpart of the barbarians without. How right were the Confucians and Socrates to insist on the need for definition!

This organic or underlying unity is still more manifest when the religions of the world are critically examined. A similarity of spiritual outlook and experience has led both Catholics and Buddhists to the monastery and the friary or 'brotherhood', Hindus and Orthodox to the hermitage and the life of the wanderer. The greatest teachers, those who

have most widely and profoundly influenced mankind, the
Buddha, Socrates, the Christ, teach essentially the same
doctrine: the need of man to pass out of the animal or
materialist life in order that, set free by temperance, his
growing knowledge and love may more and more apprehend
and enjoy Reality in all its forms, Nature, living spirits and
God, until at last he becomes blissfully united with them.
Hence the spiritual civilizations all declare that religion is one
—the one religion of the One God. On the other hand, where
a fragment is taken from one philosophy or religion and
another fragment from another and all are syncretically
welded together, as in the Gnostic systems, or where beliefs
are accepted without conviction, as in the decree uniting the
Greek to the Roman Church drawn up at Florence in 1439,
there is no living organic unity, but only a superficial show
of unity.

Wherever there is Externalism, whether in the field of
culture, of politics, or of religion, there is no cementing of the
wall, but only a futile papering-over of the cracks; no living
blossoms on the tree of Truth, but only a nosegay tied together
with string and destined soon to wither away. The produce of syncretism is like a centaur or a mermaid—the
union of two beings in one shape that could not live zoo-
logically.

In all these cases the difference is between the life of the
spirit and the deadness of mere borrowing or copying. In
the first, action is derived from the spirit of the people; in
the second, it is not derived from the spirit of the people,
but only from an imitation of the actions of other people.
There is an analogy from language. The native language of
a people is an outward activity coming from an inward
spirit; it therefore expresses that spirit easily and spontaneously. A foreign language, on the other hand, does not
come from the spontaneous thinking of the people, and
therefore expresses their thoughts unidiomatically and ungrammatically. It fails in consequence to form a real social
bond, and therefore is soon seen to be useless for the purpose
which it was intended to fulfil. Men will always revert to
their native language, and advance only as they enrich their

own language: that is a process which is perfectly possible for man, in respect of human institutions and culture as in respect of human language.

If institutions are of no use unless they are the expression of a living spirit, conversely, the living spirit is sure to create the institutions it needs for self-expression. When the end to be attained is really alive in the spirit of the people, the means that are used will be like spontaneous speech. This is so, whether the aim be materialist or moral. For example, the League of Nations was largely the outcome and instrument of a false egoistic spirit, and its principle was to that extent not brotherhood, but expediency. A spirit of political brotherhood, on the other hand, would lead to a League of Nations from which egoism was absent—in other words, it would form its own speech, spontaneously and naturally. Just as the Nordic spirit has led to democratic institutions— in England, for example—so that democracy really depends upon the existence of a brotherly spirit among its members, so out of a European or a world-wide spirit of brotherhood would spontaneously arise the institutions that would express it. The League of Nations had to some extent that element in it, and therefore it may be pointed to as a likely expression of the feelings of brotherhood that are present even to-day among the peoples of the world. The idea behind the League of Nations might be likened to the rather stammering speech of a boy as he grows older and tries to understand the profounder speech of the people about him. That is a spontaneous development which is not by any means merely theoretical; within the dross of the League of Nations is the glint of gold. To that extent, then, it is an institution that shows like the promise of the future. It is already like seed lying in the ground; tended by good husbandmen it may develop into those harvests of political peace which will be the food of the nations.

The lives of men are indeed very much like their languages—difficult to lead, as their languages are difficult to speak. Yet what is more spontaneous in man than the power to learn so difficult a thing as his own language? How naturally the child with his simple grammar and vocabulary advances to acquire the culture and the language of his own people! Similarly, the nations now are in the condition of childhood. The language of their culture is still immature; but with the proper education it will steadily become more ample, more vigorous, and they will think and talk spontaneously, not like children, but like adults. In short, as nations they will attain something of the character of the geniuses, the great individuals, of each nation. The genius is the man who spontaneously develops a greater apprehension of the world and of the nature of man in it, and therefore speaks the language, as he thinks the thoughts, not of a child, but of a man.

Under a dispensation of peace, then, men's minds would be freed to develop the greater language of the spirit: they would be ready to listen to the teachers who speak the language of God. There would now spontaneously appear something akin to the Wandering Scholars and Teachers of Islam and of Catholicism. Man, anxious to tread another path than that he has hitherto trodden, would find helping hands to lead him along it. Art, literature, philosophy, all the activities of the spirit would develop.

In the ultimate distances of all he would see the great peak of human life; he would see God, and he would know that his path led to God; he would understand the words 'I am the Way, the Truth and the Life'. As he looked back upon the path along which he had come, he would know that in his former wanderings he was not in the Way; he had no true life. He would know that what he then called civilization was really only confusion of spirit and error of reason. And now his speech would become a song.

Fortunately, the speech of man has already advanced beyond the stammering stage. The several rational civilizations have each its own eloquence, and Neo-Renaissance will ensure that none shall have spoken in vain— that nothing valuable shall be lost, but rather preserved and purified and perfected, to play its full part in the future.

> China and Ind, Hellas and France,
> Each hath its own inheritance;

And each to Truth's rich market brings
Its bright divine imaginings,
In rival tribute to surprise
The world with native merchandise.[1]

Given this Neo-Renaissance, China will still maintain and develop her ancient harmony—the harmony of every man with himself, his kinsmen, the State, the Universe: and the Nordics the self-disciplined respect for others that results in the orderly freedom in which they enjoy and develop their love for Nature and man. More and more the watchword of the Hebrews will be Righteousness (the best of all antidotes to anti-Semitism), the Righteousness of God informing a righteous society; and of Islam the surrender of man's will to the Will of God. The Catholic will still worship the God of Grace Who saves man from sin and lifts him from the natural to the Supernatural. The soul of India will strive to say 'That art thou'—the Brahma, the Dharma, Whom Krishna and the Buddha incarnate. And the goal of the Orthodox will still be *sobornost* and Theosis—the transfiguration of all things and the resurrection of all men to Eternal Life in union with the Divine. The City of God is a City of many mansions.

There is a *sva-dharma*, a justice, a 'doing of one's business or duty', not only for individual men, not only for castes or classes, but for nations. Each nation has its special contribution to make, its own vision, whether of Nature or of society, of the individual soul or of God. 'Desert not your *dharma* for that of another,' says the Indian saw.

Yet every one of the great civilizations, even at its best, is incomplete, and would still be so even were it to attain its ideal; each has great tracts of Reality that it does not see, great gaps in its experience that have still to be filled up. Thus, while the this-worldly civilizations supplement each other—Chinese and Nordics may learn from each other how better to conduct the affairs of this world—both have still more to learn from the other-worldly civilizations. The *Vedanta* and Buddhism and Orthodoxy may reveal to them other worlds of which at present they hardly dream. Simi-

[1] Robert Bridges.

larly, India and Russia, learning from each other, need to go
to school with the this-worldly civilizations to learn how to
conquer poverty and to combine order with freedom.

It is because of this strong dissimilarity of ideals that
members of the moral and of the spiritual civilizations so
easily misjudge each other. The Englishman despises the
Indian for lying, the Indian despises the Englishman for
pursuing appearances—*maya*; for the ideal of the one is the
Truth-speaking that knits society together, and of the other
the Truth-seeking that restores the soul to the Godhead.

> O wad some power the giftie gie us
> To see ourselves as ithers see us!

By understanding the ideal of the other, each may learn his
own weakness and the other's strength.

Limited in its interest though each civilization may
be, none can ultimately be satisfied till it embraces Reality
as a Whole. A genuine approach becomes much easier
owing to the fact that already a reaching of every civilization beyond itself is manifest. Offshoots or branches spring
out from each trunk, which in the case of other civilizations form the trunk itself. This-worldly China produced
the other-worldly philosophy of the Tao, which served as
an approach to Buddhism; and Confucius himself, though
all his emphasis was upon the moral virtues, nevertheless divined the whole range of experience: 'The highest
class of men are those whose knowledge is intuitive; next
are those whose knowledge is acquired by study; after them
come those who are dull-witted yet strive to learn; while
those who are dull-witted and will make no effort to learn
are the lowest of the people'[1]—the materialists. The practical English produced in the fourteenth century, Richard
Rolle, Julian of Norwich, and other mystics, in the seventeenth century the Friends and such Puritans as Cromwell,
whose aim was that his nation should become 'a people of
God'. Cromwell, too, distinguished the same three stages as
the *Vedanta* when he wrote: 'the true knowledge is not
literal or speculative, but inward, transforming the mind to
it'; and to-day the Archbishop of Canterbury speaks in the

---

[1] L. Giles, *Sayings of Confucius*, p. 106.

spirit of the *Vedanta* when he says: 'God is both the Truth which is sought, and the Spirit which moves men to seek it.'[1]

German achievements in the realms of idealist philosophy, mysticism, and music show the capacity of the Nordics for things other than democracy; just as the capacity of most Nordics for self-government shows the latent capacity of the Germans. The both-worldly civilizations not only look, by definition, Janus-like at this world and at the other, but put forth feelers beyond their proper limits downward into this world and upward into the other. If Catholic countries have felt the stirrings of the French Revolution, Jewry, Islam, and Catholicism have produced their Kabbalists, their Sufis, the mystics of the Rhineland, France, and Spain. Indian mysticism has shown in caste, and Buddhism in the ethical stages of the Way, an interest in the affairs of this world; Indians often show, too, great ability in government and organization. Holy Russia had her village soviets, her Provincial Councils, the Assemblies of the Church and of the State. It is by developing its less characteristic interests that each civilization will be able to draw nearer to those that are unlike itself and so to become more complete.

All this is very important, because it introduces the possibility of an organic synthesis in every nation, that can thus avoid the false synthesis represented by wrong remedies and empty formulae; it shows too that the final synthesis is not wholly alien to any nation. This characteristic of the several civilizations is therefore full of promise. It also reinforces the connexion between Neo-Renaissance and Xeno-Renaissance. Let the Chinese only develop their own culture in all its branches and they will find themselves learning naturally from the Christian religion in so far as they are Mo-ists and from Hinduism in so far as they are Taoists—no less than from the Parliamentary democracy that is cognate to them in so far as they are a democracy. Similarly Hinduism and Orthodoxy will be able to learn, as they are learning, not only the spiritual things that each has to give the other, but the arts of government and economic development that belong to the this-worldly peoples, and are

[1] *London University Centenary Commemorative Volume*, p. 62.

needed to supplement their own rather rudimentary social structures. Thus all civilizations have natural affinities. They stretch out their arms to one another, and will not be satisfied till they embrace.

Each of these civilizations, though full of diversities, is held together either by a moral or by a spiritual principle, or by both; and it is by moral and spiritual principles, and by nothing else, that all can now in their manifold diversities be united together.

The Moral State is that in which man disciplines his animal or material lusts—his desire for self-indulgence, wealth, and power—and thereby liberates himself both from the clouded vision that makes him see a situation wrongly and blinds him to the Good, and from the jealousy or hatred of his fellows that characterizes and divides materialist society: for when passion is removed he can begin to see clearly, and when he sees his neighbour clearly he begins to like him—to feel a 'fellow-feeling' for him, to respect man as man. This feeling implies both sincerity or good faith, and a love of righteousness or justice, which in turn result in peace and prosperity, in place of the old poverty and war, and in the political and economic customs, laws, and institutions necessary to sustain them. Here is a happy world.

Human experience is at one upon this matter. Confucius pointed out that ceremonies, institutions, and laws are of no value unless the spirit that inspires them is a fellow-feeling for one's neighbour, and that this involves self-discipline and sagacity. Fellow-feeling (he said) includes righteousness and sincerity. These three moral virtues are also those of the Greeks, the Romans, and the Catholic Middle Ages —temperance, justice, and prudence; their fourth virtue, courage, is a form of temperance, as in China justice and sincerity are forms of fellow-feeling. Similarly Nordic society rests upon self-discipline, common sense, and respect for others. As regards the results of these virtues, Mo Ti said that when men love each other righteousness ensues, and the result of righteousness is a material or utilitarian prosperity. 'How can there be anything good that is not also useful?' Jesus said. 'Seek ye first the Kingdom of Heaven, and all these things shall be added unto you.'

Experience therefore confirms that these three virtues—the moral virtues—are the only possible basis for political brotherhood—the world-wide society of the future. They will exert themselves in the old ways—in the redress of grievances, in the steady political education of the people, in 'parleying' between class and class and nation and nation—in argument and persuasion, not in threats or force; in good feeling, not in bad faith. These moral activities will express themselves in appropriate customs, laws, institutions—living, growing, adapting themselves to changing circumstances. Parleyings will result in Parliaments, the need to cure economic injustices in economic 'Administrations', and the like. The Moral States are likely to draw together: in particular, the British Commonwealth and the United States, combining the greatest material resources with moral ideals and practices of government, have a special responsibility for political leadership. It may be that the need for co-operation will bring a habit of common consultation and action that will result in the rebirth of a World Political Council or League of Nations that shall keep the peace, and of a World Economic Organization to ensure a just distribution of the vast material resources of the earth. Or it may be that such a League may now be thought, like the American Confederacy or 'League of Friendship' that preceded Federation, to be inadequate to its aim; and that the Powers in which democracy is already in working order—the Scandinavian Kingdoms, the Netherlands, France, Switzerland, Great Britain, the United States, Canada, Australia, New Zealand, and South Africa—may, following the great American precedent, prefer a Federal Constitution that will, at the cost of an out-of-date and perilous sovereignty, secure beyond a peradventure the peace of the world, make possible a common foreign policy, and, with a common currency, open an immense area to the great prosperity springing from free trade.[1] On this nucleus of English-speaking and neighbouring democracies other Moral States are likely to crystallize: China to bring her age-old vision of righteousness in

---

[1] Cp. Clarence K. Streit, *Union Now.*

government at home and abroad, groups of the smaller
Powers their often more developed civilizations, India the
treasure of her spirituality; to be followed in due course by
the present dictatorships as soon as their rulers, like their
peoples, have come to themselves. In such a world peace
would be secure, and the lavish wealth of tropic lands and
seas, the fantastical riches that science can produce, and
the elimination of the waste of men and materials made
possible by a humane 'rationalization' of industry, would
accrue to the benefit and not to the injury of mankind.

The first thing therefore is to get the political situation
right; the root problem is political conversion. When the
spirit of brotherhood is alive in men, social discontent will
disappear in a system of peace and plenty. Nor is this at all
unlikely. The ordinary people of to-day are not a bad lot;
they have a feeling of brotherhood, though it has often no
means of expression. The political sore spreads over a great
part of the body politic, but it is not very deep. The process
of health, the feeling of human brotherhood, is growing
beneath this sore, and the very soreness of the body politic
is giving energy to the process. Those who live in the
healthier parts of this body politic—the democracies—are
becoming more conscious of the value of democracy than
ever before—witness President Roosevelt's Messages, and
the heroic tenacity of the Chinese before the aggressor. On
the other hand, those who live in the sorer parts of the body
politic are becoming more conscious of the soreness of
dictatorship, of the pains involved in a denial of human
brotherhood. The two processes together will make for the
health of the whole body through the understanding by all
that the only healthy life of a political kind is to be found
through human brotherhood, through respect of nation for
nation, class for class, creed for creed, and man for man.

But the process needs speeding. What purifying and
wholesome diet is to be given to the patient? How is the
moral reformation which alone can bring about political
reformation to be achieved?

First, the moral statesmen may emulate the materialist
statesmen. As Lenin, Mussolini, and Hitler have set going
currents of materialism through East and West, so Chiang

Kai-shek and Gandhi, Smuts and Roosevelt are voices that carry over immense countries or over the whole world.

But this is not enough: men must be trained, in character and understanding, to the work of shaping the new world of political and economic brotherhood between classes and between nations.

Education accordingly needs the quickening of a new vision and a new spirit. If men are to escape from their misfortunes into a better world-order, natural science must be studied, not for itself alone, but in its relations to society and to the Universe: the student and man of science has also social responsibilities and philosophic and religious responsibilities. So with humane studies. The principles of character, bad and good, need close attention, both in themselves and in the examples of bad, good, great, and Godlike men furnished by history and by literature; to know the best and greatest men, and to contrast them with others, will enlighten and inspire the young. The same principles need to be further studied as they inform the several civilizations, materialist, moral, and spiritual; so that men, instead of despising other nations, may understand, make allowances, admire, and love them. Above all, all education must culminate in a study of God—at this stage a Personal or Moral God, the God Who has 'shown man what is good' and requires of him that he shall 'do justly, and love mercy, and walk humbly with Him.'

If this is the end in view, the necessary means will take shape. The Universities of the world will co-operate to bring it about. Civilization, for instance, may be studied in three ways: in its men, in its books, in its arts. As Chinese pilgrims spread Buddhism over China, as Wandering Scholars fostered the Graeco-Muslim and the Catholic Renaissances, so interchange of staff and students between the Universities of country and country, of East and West, will do much to enlighten and unite humanity. A Library of the World, consisting of its greatest books translated into the principal languages, would help to familiarize each with the philosophies and the imaginations of all. Photographs, records, and other reproductions would make the masterpieces of the world in a measure the property of mankind.

The Union of Universities, the League of Learning, needed for co-operation of this kind would probably culminate in a World Council of Culture, such as the Committee of Intellectual Co-operation is perhaps destined to become.

Universities that so conceive their functions do more than teach, more than research: they stand as cities of light in a dark world. Pursuing the third and greatest of these ends, they will train their men and women, not as careerists, but as servants—servants of God and man; that these may go forth (as Confucian scholar-rulers and Clunyite monks went forth) determined to take in hand the sorry earth and convert it into a civilized society, a brotherhood in which men shall be self-disciplined, clear-sighted, respectful of their kind. They will go into every calling so inspired—agriculture, business, government, the professions; above all, using the means of education, not for propaganda, but for enlightenment, that the press, the radio, the films, travel, may become the University of the Peoples.

In a word, *the new studies will make the new men, the new men will make the new world.*

Out of the moral and social virtues there will naturally spring an efflorescence of virtues that are more than moral —that are spiritual. A sense of political brotherhood gives men freedom of speech, action, thought—to a large extent they can do as they like; and while this liberty without self-discipline degenerates into licence, it develops with it a more illustrious virtue than was seen before. The self-discipline that controlled man's selfishness now becomes temperance: the egoistic passions dead, an unimpeded energy lives in men. The clear-sightedness that has taken off the bandages of the animal nature becomes wisdom, as the eyes of the soul gaze upon the great vision of the Universe. The respect or fellow-feeling for man involved in political brotherhood becomes love for men, who are now linked in a more than political, in an individual or spiritual brotherhood. With these changes happiness deepens into joy. Thus the world passes on from political and moral virtue to spiritual virtue, and this takes form in art, literature, and other spiritual activities superior to the merely practical interests of daily life. And so men with their spirits purified make ready to turn to the Light Itself, to pass from the things that are caused to the Being That created them, through Whom alone they can be perfectly understood.

This is indeed the heart of the teaching of all the great Masters, and especially of those three who have had the widest and deepest influence over mankind. All teach that man's joy lies in temperance and in the knowledge and love of the Universe for which it frees the soul. The Buddha would have men rid themselves of the three cardinal sins of egoism, stupidity, and hate, that they may love all living things as themselves and finally attain the Divine 'height of the Immortal'. Socrates preached temperance that men might win to knowledge and love of the Good, and especially of the Supreme Good, the 'Idea of the Good', the 'Ocean of Beauty'. Jesus would have men cut off hand and pluck out eye if it offends them—if body hinders spirit—that they may love God with heart and mind and soul and strength— their whole being—and their neighbour as themselves. All, too, said that men must proceed by stages: along a Way, said the Buddha; from the shadow-world to faith, thence to reason, thence to the mystic's intuition, said Plato; from the faith and works of the multitude to knowledge and love and thence to a realization of the Divine sonship, said Jesus. Man the animal becomes man the God. Buddhism, Platonism, and Christianity, that between them have conquered Asia, Europe, and America, for all their outward differences are at heart one and the same.

No wonder, then, that the spiritual civilizations and those that are most akin to them tend to see that all religions are at root one religion, the revelation of One God. If all men are Brahma, only one religion is possible: every religion is a re-evolving of God out of man, the return of the soul to its Origin. The many contradictions are only apparent: the Truth adapts Itself to different circumstances and different natures, showing part of Itself to one and part to another. As Krishna says in the *Gita*: 'They also who, possessed of faith, worship other gods and make offering to them, verily make offering to Me, even though not in accordance with ancient rule.'[1]

[1] *Bhagavad-gita*, ix. 23.

In the *Lotus*—the book that did so much to carry Buddhism over East Asia—the Buddha says there is but One Way of Enlightenment that leads to the Buddha-knowledge that is the goal of all; yet with the 'skilful tact' of the great teacher he says also that it may be followed in diverse fashions according to men's characters and capacities. Kabir sang:

> Hari (Vishnu) is in the East, Allah is in the West. Look within your heart, for there you will find both Allah the Bountiful and Ram.
> All men and women are his living forms.

'As the rains run in many streams to one ocean, so worship flows in many forms to One God.'[1]

A Holy Man of Benares said after the World War:

'East and West are two archways through which the sun passes on his large orbit of wandering—but is there East and West to Him Who watches that fiery form dance from space to space? When I sit and meditate, gradually as I pass onward I raise my hand to the Ultimate Truth. Then I behold other hands coming from other parts of the world to rest upon the same shining Oneness. They, my brothers, are touching the same Truth as I. How can there be a conflict between them and me? Are we not God? I urge thee, my son, go back to the West and bring me my brothers. They are weeping in the dark who toil to build the road of God. Ask them to unite all peoples and all worlds. When thou hast found them, you will talk like men together, not like ants in terms of little rival hills, East and West. They will tell you that there is neither East nor West, but only the Spirit-seekers and the matter-mongers. The war is between these two.'[2]

The Sufis take the same view. All religions and revelations are the rays of a Single Sun. The Bab in Persia and Ahmad in the Punjab likewise declare that all religion is the manifestation of the Holy Spirit, uniting mankind in a brotherhood of peace and mutual service.

Orthodoxy, too, despite a certain Byzantine narrowness, cherishes the doctrine of *sobornost*: catholicity—the inclusion of all; symphony—the harmonious combination of different parts; universality—the turning of all to the One, and their drawing nearer to one another as they draw nearer to Him.

---

[1] Hindu saying.   [2] D. G. Mukerjee, *My Brother's Face*, p. 92.

So with the great Greek thinkers. Plato's philosopher is 'a soul that is ever longing after the whole of things both Divine and human, the spectator of all time and all existence';[1] a lover who, ever widening his range, at last embraces the 'Ocean of Beauty';[2] the end of man is 'likeness to God'.[3] Aristotle holds that reason is 'something Divine in man'.[4] Plato's view passes on through Philo to the Fourth Gospel, the New Platonists, 'Dionysius', and so to Orthodoxy, Catholicism, and Sufism.

Socrates and Plato are the forerunners of Jesus, who emphasized that reason is the inner bond of all synthesis—blessed are they who know and love God and man and Nature. Men are Divine, the sons of God, and are destined to form His Kingdom. That Kingdom will be world-wide; 'They shall come from the East and the West, and shall sit down in the Kingdom of Heaven.' It will not be made up of those who merely call him Lord. 'Not every one that saith unto me Lord, Lord, shall enter into the Kingdom of Heaven, but he that doeth the Will of my Father Which is in Heaven'—he who knows and loves. As with space so with time—he gathers all into the Kingdom: 'I am not come to destroy, but to fulfil.' To-day the so-called non-Christian peoples of the world, accepting the Christian Gospels and rejecting Christian Theology, are perceiving in Jesus the Universal Lord who can fashion the earth into the Kingdom of God. He belongs no more to the West than to the East, and his rule is a spiritual rule. 'I, if I be lifted up, will draw all men unto me.'

The moment is therefore coming to seek amid the multiplicity of religions the one religion of the One God that is revealed by reason, foreshadowed in the universal religions, and perfected in Jesus Christ; to realize the vision of Ram Mohan Roy, the union of Asia and Europe in which neither shall sacrifice its individuality, but both come together in a 'Church of Brahma' where all may worship the One God. The harvest is ripening but unreaped. Much has yet to be interpreted and developed before the 'one way' is made manifest in its various forms. Beneath the outward multi-

---

[1] *Republic*, vi. 486.   [2] *Symposium*, 210.
[3] *Theaetetus*, 167.   [4] *Ethics*, x.

plicity of religions beats the one religion that is the heart of all.

Different religions can be no more steam-rollered into uniformity than can different forms of education and different political forms. On the contrary, each has its contribution to make to religion's rich and many-sided unity. Outward diversity, inner unity will be the principle on which mankind will gradually realize that its many religions are in essence but one religion. Knowledge knows many things, love loves many things, because Reality has many sides—hence the diversity of religions, of civilizations. But Reality is also One, and just in so far as reason enlarges itself to know and love that One, just so far it attains unity, and the civilizations in which it expresses itself attain unity likewise.

In this one religion of the One God that all the spiritual religions already see as in a glass darkly, and of which the Buddha, Socrates, and the Christ have proclaimed the principle, all the true civilizations, Eastern and Western, so-called non-Christian and so-called Christian, will find place and fulfilment. Religion is to long for and love Nature: her beauty, with the Chinese, the Italians, the Greeks; her laws, with the Nordics; her infinity, with the Taoists. It is to 'long for things human', to 'love our neighbour as ourselves'. Confucianism is only a particular application or development of this principle; Nordic democracy is another, on the level of fellow-feeling and respect for men. The righteousness, self-surrender, and moral virtues of Judaism, Islam, and Catholicism are other applications; the loving gentleness of Buddhism is yet another. Above all, religion is 'to long for things Divine', to 'love God with heart and mind and soul and strength'—all our being. The Moral God—the God of Righteousness, Compassion, Grace—unfolds the side of the Divine Nature That loves living things and wills their welfare here and hereafter; the Eternal Infinite Being-Thought-Bliss is the Ultimate Godhead That soul can experience, but mind cannot know. Religion develops the idea of the Way, and to this too come many contributions. Hinduism conceives it as a *karma marga*, then a *bhakti marga*, leading to *jnana*: Buddhism as right living, then right thinking, leading to 'the height of the Immortal'. The Greek

Fathers and Orthodoxy declare the Way to lead up from good works to Divine contemplation and so to Theosis; Jesus himself would have men love God with their strength, with their heart and mind, with their soul. At the End of the Way the mystics, whether of East or West, hold all things together, for they see the connexion between them: they see that all spirits come forth from God and are therefore Divine, destined by their Divine nature to return to Him, to become Buddhas, to become Platos, to become Christs, sons re-united to the Father Whence they came.

The religious ideal, like the political ideal, will clothe itself in appropriate forms. A Sacred Book of the World, like that compiled by Keshub Chandra Sen for the Church of God, composed of the greatest passages from the greatest books, but claiming only the authority of reason, would unite together all lovers of the Truth. Those who worship may draw together in a common devotion, at first private, then public, using a World Book of Prayer and Meditation. All men may pray:

> From the unreal lead me to the Real,
> From darkness lead me to Light,
> From death lead me to the Immortal.

A World Calendar of Saints—Confucius, Eckhart, Isaiah, Leonardo, Sankara, Plato—may lead men to realize the amazing achievements of the spirit of man. A League of Religions may visibly unite all those who care for the things of the spirit against materialism; and such a League would greatly facilitate these and other common undertakings. This League would probably be focused in a World Council of Religions, as education in a World Council of Culture, and government in a League or Federation of Nations and an Economic World Council.

So, by slow but sure degrees, may the one religion reveal itself, and a secular society develop into a religious community—the City of God, the Kingdom of Heaven on earth. Then men will see that all life is religious—education, politics, and economics; the life of the good householder and good citizen will be lifted up till (as the *Gita* says) work becomes worship. Their aim will be to make every activity in life conform to the Will of God, so far as man has yet discovered It; to discover It still further by living both the active and the contemplative life. Such a community will be bound, not by any mere outward bond, not by any Book or Creed guaranteed by priests to be Divinely revealed, but by the higher revelation that belongs to this second stage—the inner bond of a temperate knowledge and love—the reason that is joy. And this knowledge, love, and joy will continually find expression in works of argument and imagination.

But the soul in its upward progress does not stop even at knowledge and love; it rises to that union with the Godhead and the Universe in which subject and Object are united. There is here a spiritual marriage between the soul and the Godhead, an 'intuitive reason' that is also an 'intellectual love of God', a 'knowledge above knowledge' that is the realization of the Divine. The soul has risen above joy to ecstasy, rapture, bliss.

In this final consummation 'the Spirit of God, that is, the Spirit of faith, hope and love, will reveal Himself in all His Fullness, and faith will then have become full inward knowledge and sight, love will still be love, and hope will have become joy.'[1] (Khomiakov's terminology may differ, but his meaning is the same.) Man 'unites his glance with the Worth Infinite'.[2] In the ecstasy of this union the soul is 'beside itself'.[3]

The Godhead realized in this union is perceived to be far more than the Moral God Who sanctions the activities of the moral man: to be the Eternal and Infinite Reality, Knowing and Loving Itself, Whose Self-Knowledge and Self-Love is Supreme Bliss.

O Light Eternal Who only in Thyself abidest,
Only Thyself dost understand, and to Thyself,
Self-understood, Self-understanding, turnest Love and Smiling![4]

The conception of the Hindu is the same: the Godhead is *Sat-Cit-Ānanda*, Being-Thought-Bliss, the Reality That is Conscious of Itself, and Whose Self-Consciousness is Ananda, the Supreme Delight.

[1] M. Khomiakov, 'The Church is One', in Birkbeck, *Russia and the English Church*, i, pp. 221–2, shortened.
[2] Dante, *Paradiso*, 33. 80–1.   [3] Plotinus.   [4] Ibid. 33. 124–6.

But an Eternal Being can be known only in part by a mind in time, an Infinite Being only in part by a finite mind. Hence to man the Godhead in His Fullness is a Mystery, a 'Nameless Nothing', a 'Hidden Darkness, unknown and never to be known', 'a Still Wilderness Where no one is at home'.[1] '*Neti, neti*—Not so, not so.'

Himself Uncreated, He is the Creator of all things, all things are of Him; Himself Unmoved, He is their Mover, all things long to return to Him. As soon as the soul is reunited with Him, it sees that, since all things are, like itself, of and from Him, they are in essence one with Him, and through Him one with one another. 'When I attain this blessedness of union '(says Eckhart), 'then all things are in me and in God, and where I am, there God is, and where God is, there I am.'[2] As Father Zossima puts it, for hearts that can truly love, 'all is like an ocean, all is flowing and blending.'[3] Tolstoy says of the peasant-soldier Karataev: 'His life, as he looked at it, had no meaning as a separate life, it had meaning only as a part of a Whole, of Which he was at all times conscious.'[4] Hence the mystic holds himself responsible for all men and all things. He is the *bodhisat* who realizes that all other beings are his other selves.

This unity extends not only to the animate but to the inanimate creation. The Taoist painters are conscious of the Tao in mountains and streams, birds and flowers; and Wordsworth has

> a sense sublime
> Of Something far more deeply interfused:
> A Motion and a Spirit, That impels
> All thinking things, all objects of all thought,
> And rolls through all things.

As Isaac Penington put it: 'All truth is shadow except the Last Truth. But all truth is substance in its own place, though it be but a shadow in another place. And the shadow is a true shadow, as the Substance is a True Substance.'[5]

---

[1] Rufus Jones, *Mystical Religion*, p. 226.
[2] Quoted ibid., p. 233.   [3] *Brothers Karamazov*, p. 340.
[4] *War and Peace*, p. 1225.
[5] Quoted Buchan, *Cromwell*, p. 68.

Dante says that when he looked into the Deep Light of the Godhead:

> Within Its Depths I saw ingather'd,
>   bound by Love in one volume,
>   the scatter'd leaves of all the Universe. . . .
> The Good That is the Object of the will
>   is Therein wholly gather'd, and outside It
>   is that defective that Therein is perfect.[1]

'Cleave the wood, and there ye shall find me,' Jesus said. 'Where two or three are gathered together in my name, there am I in the midst of them.'

The mystic alone can see the joy to which imperfection and suffering lead, and therefore he alone can understand them. 'I was a Hidden Treasure and I desired to be known; so I created the creatures in order that I might be known,' says a Tradition of Muhammad. 'I saw and knew' (says Boehme), 'how the fruitful bearing womb of Eternity brought forth. So that I did not only greatly wonder at it, but did also exceedingly rejoice.'

Even for the eye of man, evil exists for the betterment of good. Change and multiplicity brighten the face of Eternity and Unity, ignorance and hatred that of Wisdom and Love.

> Whom best I love, I cross; to make my gift
> The more delayed, delighted.[2]

This view rules out the possibility, not indeed of punishment, but of unending punishment—of a Hell whose gates are for ever shut on its prisoners. Moreover, if sin and suffering are present evils to men, they yet know that in God's Eternal Now the betterment of good by ill has not still to come, but is already present. 'Nothing new comes to Him from the future' (says Eckhart), 'for He dwells in the Now.'[3]

If God is the Source of the individual soul, God is also its End; if God is the Source of the entire creation, God is also its End. These are mystical certainties, truths that are the very essence of the Universe. The self falls from its Origin to tread the Way of Pursuit and Power, then rises

---

[1] *Paradiso*, 33. 85–7, 103–5.   [2] *Cymbeline*, v. iv.
[3] Sermon viii.

to climb the Way of Renunciation and Realization. 'I am the Father of the World; all men are my children; all are destined to Buddhahood,' says the Buddha in the *Lotus*.[1] There will be, says Origen, a 'final restoration of all things to God'. The mystics all know that reunion with their Source is the consummation of all things.

This account of the progress of mankind seems all to be contained in Plato's allegory of the cave. The prisoners chained are the materialists, at once egoistic and ignorant, the cause of the Athens of Plato's day, and the cause of the Europe and East Asia of our own day. This is the stage of shadows: its armaments and its empires, all its ambitions that lack righteousness and mercy, are only shadows. Then, as men overcome their egoism and see more clearly, they also attain political and moral virtue. They still belong to this world indeed, but they see that it contains more than shadows; there exist such things as Nature and fellow men. They do not yet understand; they have but faith, they do not yet know. But he who has attained so much insight, political and private, into the visible world is ready to advance into a world unknown to the ordinary man, a world not of sights and sounds and of the body, but one revealed to the super-sensuous eye of the spirit of reason, the spirit of active understanding. Such a man has passed into the world of light. Last, having become accustomed to that and exercised himself in it, he looks up to the Sun That is the Cause of light, and having become engrossed in That and Its Per-fections he sees with and in its Rays all that he had only half seen before.

These three stages (not counting the first or materialist) carry the mind as it develops gradually deeper and deeper into Nature, spirit, and God—into every side of Reality, the Whole Universe. In the shadow stage man is an egoist pursuing merely animal objects, and this makes him blind and foolish and unfriendly; this stage has there-fore its own way of representing spiritual objects. It views Nature for material ends—for luxury, for armaments and so on. The Dictator treats man as a means to the making of a

[1] Quoted Kenneth Saunders, *Epochs in Buddhist History*, p. 47.

great Materialist State. God is looked on as an instrument for the success of the egoistic policy that is being pursued.

So with the three following stages: each has its own development of the mind and its corresponding view of these three parts of experience. For instance, Nature is treated by the democratic man as a means to his existence as a free individual; man is treated with respect, because the passions are controlled and man's sight partly restored: God is regarded as the Power Who gives sanction and authority to that respect and to the self-control and conscience that accompany it.

The spiritual man on the other hand treats these objects fundamentally from the point of view of his own rational insight—the wisdom and love that spring from temperance. Each object is considered for its own sake, without any reference to the needs of man as a political or ethical being. He therefore sees Nature as an object to be understood, as something that exists in and for itself: he does not consider what its good may be for man and his life, but what the good of it is for his mind. Similarly with man. He does not consider man from the point of view of any political institution, or look at him historically, but asks, as in the case of Nature: 'What for my mind is man? How is it that he is a part of experience?' And similarly with regard to God. His interest is not set in motion by any inquiry as to the Attributes of God that are of interest to him here and now as a man, but rather by the inquiry what God is in Himself and for Himself. He asks, like St. Thomas in boyhood: 'What is God?'

Finally, the mystical man sees the Universe of the rational man in its Final Truth and Perfection; he sees well and finally what the rational man saw only obscurely. A new experience dawns upon the soul, and he, a 'desireless man', sees, not now with the eyes of human reason, but with the eyes of Divine reason, and with the heart of Divine love. He no longer asks therefore: 'What is God?'; he knows 'That art thou'. He now sees all things in God, and God in all things. Like Angela of Foligno, he 'sees all creatures filled with God', in a manner that beggars description.[1]

---

[1] Evelyn Underhill, *Mysticism*, p. 351.

III

'The Kingdom of God cometh not with observation'; as we passed from the moral to the spiritual, from the spiritual to the mystic, it has stolen upon us unawares. In that Kingdom the buried personality of humanity will have risen from the tomb, its soul shine forth from the muddy vesture of decay. The reason of mankind, released from the body's unruliness, no longer in darkness, will more and more reveal and enjoy the Divine Perfection of the Universe in all its parts.

'The Kingdom of Heaven is within you'—not in armaments, not in institutions, but in men and women. That is so already: the Kingdom comes in the individual heart before it comes visibly on earth. Man is by nature good, rational, nay Divine; and if his true personality now lies enveloped in the evil of the irrational animal nature, a pearl soiled by the mud, an eye that has fallen from light into illusion, it must yet repent, purge itself, return from a far country to its Father's home. The men in whom the Kingdom is are therefore the masters and not the slaves of the body and its ambitions, and so are able to grow in knowledge-love and enjoyment of Nature, of spirits, and of God, until finally, united with the Divine Universe, they attain to fullness of life, to completeness of personality—hold within their cup of being a draught of the Simplicity, the Tranquillity, the All-Embracing Love of the ocean-like Tao, know the reason within them as part of the Divine Reason, attain to 'likeness to God', the 'perfection' of the sons of God, and realize the Divinity of human nature. Many men and women with this knowledge and love, or with this mystical insight, have already trod the earth, are here in our midst to-day: Confucius, Shakespeare, Isaiah, Rumi, Sankara, Gotama, Socrates, Chuang-tze, Eckhart, Jesus. Great men, not necessarily famous men: the peasant Karataev, the monk Zossima, many a soul unregarded in time, magnificent in eternity.

Thus come to itself the soul, like the philosopher in Plato's noble vision, can rise victorious over every circumstance, however terrible to the animal nature. 'When

creatures behold this world and imagine that it is burning,
even then my Buddha-field is teeming with gods and men.
In their view this world is most terrific, wretched, full of
every woe; that is the fruit of sinful deeds. But when mild
and gentle beings are born in this world of men, they
immediately see Me revealing the Law, owing to their good
works.'[1] War, revolution, death may come, but they cannot
touch this Kingdom.

'Thy Kingdom come, thy will be done on earth as it is in
heaven.' In the second place, the Kingdom of God is the
ideal society that is to cover the earth. This is not indeed
metaphysically certain, as the end of the soul and the end of
creation are certain; for none knows what determines the
characters with which men are born into the world, and it is
conceivable that a preponderance of animal or mixed natures
might continue. Nevertheless the marvellous moral and
spiritual progress made by mankind in the last few thousand
years points in the opposite direction; and if and as progress
continues, true education will hasten its steps. The ideal
State is moral:

> All things in common Nature should produce,
> Without sweat or endeavour: treason, felony,
> Sword, pike, knife, gun, or need of any engine,
> Would I not have: but Nature should bring forth
> Of its own kind, all foison, all abundance,
> To feed my innocent people.[2]

Isaiah, though he retains this innocence, is more positive and
spiritual—the ideal State rests on a knowledge of God:

> The wolf shall dwell with the lamb,
> and the leopard shall lie down with the kid,
>   and a little child shall lead them.
> They shall not hurt nor destroy
>   in all my holy mountain:
> For the land shall be full of the knowledge of the Lord
>   as the waters cover the sea.

Zeno foresaw the City of Zeus, Augustine the City of God;
the Son of God foretold the Kingdom of God.

---

[1] *The Lotus of the True Law*, xv.   H. Kern, pp. 308–9, shortened.
[2] *Tempest*, ii. 1. 159–65.

Only as through a glass darkly can we foresee what this Kingdom will be like. Untainted by lust and the unfitness lust brings its men and women will be beautiful: 'how many goodly creatures are there here!'[1] There will be no greed, no avarice; but in a community of friends there is likely to be a community of goods, as in Plato's *Republic* or a happy family or an Oxford College: 'those who love have all things in common'. No longer will men be tempted to dominate over others; for their powers will be exerted, not to harm, but to serve them. And where righteousness is, the good things of this world will not be wanting: 'Seek ye first the Kingdom of God and His Righteousness, and all these things shall be added unto you.'

Temperance will have freed the wings of wisdom for her flight in the sun. It is sometimes thought that there would be little for great men to do, were there no disorder to curb or despair to fight; but the men of the future will have greater enterprises than the work of nursemaids keeping naughty children in order.

They will love Nature in all her aspects—her beauty, her law, the philosophers her infinity. They will be statesmen loving men in the mass, and poets and painters loving them individually.

They will love God as the mystics love Him, more and more realizing their union with Him. To this Kingdom the several civilizations will each have brought its tribute: the freedom of moral men in a moral society, a community obedient to a Divine Ruler, the realization in the Godhead of the Godlike soul. The Kingdom of Heaven on earth will have both its political or moral and its religious or spiritual aspects.

These men and women will know that the Kingdom of God is also Cosmic or Universal: our Father is 'in Heaven', His Will is done 'in Heaven'. Here there is a metaphysical certainty; for it is the Very Nature of the All-Powerful Love That reason must needs think, to bring all things to eternal blessedness. In this Cosmic Kingdom the souls of men will penetrate ever more deeply, reverently, and blissfully into

---

[1] *Tempest*, v. i.

the Infinite Mystery That contains and explains the Universe. Here life will have reached the 'Hymn of Joy', the struggle and sacrifice of earth have ended in Sanctus, Sanctus, Sanctus. Here all will be transfigured *sub specie Eternitatis*, all be seen in the 'glory which suffereth not itself to be surpassed by longing'.[1]

In this 'restoration of all things to God'[2] the Prodigal returns home to the Father and the feast: creation 'glorifies God and enjoys Him for ever'.[3] 'The Godhead is Bliss. Out of Bliss these creatures spring, by Bliss they live after their birth, and into Bliss they return when they depart hence.'[4] 'All comes from Him, all lives by Him, all ends in Him. What a fathomless wealth lies in the Wisdom and Knowledge of God! How inscrutable His Judgment! How mysterious His methods! Glory to Him for ever, Amen!'[5]

From the heights of the future men and women will look down into the depths, and behold the past with wide-eyed astonishment. They will be amazed when they see men pursuing baubles for beauty—the shadow-wealth of the things that perish, the little dust of a great empire. 'How' (they will say) 'could men prefer fortune to friendship, the love of gold to the love of God! Why did class suffer class to famish amid abundance, and nation prey upon nation like beasts in a jungle or pike in a pond!' How tawdry will look great armaments beside great music! how hollow the dictators beside the mystics! 'Unnatural' (they will exclaim) 'for man to sell his birthright for a mess of pottage'; themselves as incapable of such follies as great orators of speaking ungrammatically!

But mankind (they will see) found a chart of the ocean, a sign-post by the way: following its true principle, it set its face toward its true goal. True teachers and leaders arose, and the peoples followed: great statesmen, from Confucius to Lincoln, pointing out man's duty to man; Newtons and Shakespeares and Leonardos, revealing the wonders of Nature and of men and of God; forest sages and Rhine-

---

[1] Dante, *Paradiso*.   [2] Origen.
[3] Presbyterian Shorter Catechism.   [4] *Taittiriya Upanishad*, iii. 6.
[5] Paul, Romans xi. 33–6 (Moffat's translation).

landers to tell that man and God are One, in time and in eternity. Already the peoples of East and West showed distinct signs of civilization; and though far greater ages were to come, ages when the peoples had put off their brutishness and become wise and loving and gay, the great men and women of these early ages were yet the mirror in which those who looked could see reflected the civilization of the future. In this mood of meditation men will remember, too, that mankind had been on the earth almost a million years before civilization began to flower; that in the short space of four thousand years the unfolding of its flower-cluster was remarkable; another four thousand years and what progress could not reason make in enlightening and unifying the world! They will bethink them that mankind will yet have millions of years to live upon earth, in joyous and never-ending exploration of things finite and Infinite, Natural, Human, and Divine.

The men of the Kingdom of the future will thus be able to note the stages of man's advance: the insane raving, then the stammering speech, the clear talk, then the great song. In the Buddha's image they will see society, as they will see the soul, beginning in the darkness of the mind, growing up through the twilight of the water, expanding like the bloom of the Lotus under the light of the Sun. They will see the story of mankind, like the story of the soul, as a Divine Comedy in three Acts: the animal beginnings, the moral and spiritual development, the return of the creature to its Father and its bliss.

Date Due